In Praise of Radiant Beings

A volume in
Current Perspectives on Confucianism, Taoism, Buddhism, and Education
Hongyu Wang, Jing Lin, Heesoon Bai, and Xin Li, *Series Editors*

In Praise of Radiant Beings

A Retrospective Path Through Education, Buddhism and Ecology

David W. Jardine
University of Calgary (Retired)

INFORMATION AGE PUBLISHING, INC.
Charlotte, NC • www.infoagepub.com

Library of Congress Cataloging-in-Publication Data

A CIP record for this book is available from the Library of Congress
http://www.loc.gov

ISBN: 978-1-68123-604-9 (Paperback)
978-1-68123-605-6 (Hardcover)
978-1-68123-606-3 (ebook)

Printed in the United States of America

Contents

Introduction

"It Only Makes it Better"

The Privilege of Youth

> When [the work] was hardest, it would often feel the most joyful. The only way to approach something that's really hard has got to be with joy, because if you don't approach it with joy, it's just a machine and it'll grind you up. The lesson I took from that is that doing something joyfully doesn't make it any easier. It only makes it better. (Colbert, 2015)

Having retired on July 1, 2015 from my position in the Faculty of Education at the University of Calgary made the opportunity to put together this collection of work both timely and a strange gift. It is an odd experience to not only assemble but also re-read and write about work done over a span of 25 years. It is humbling, humiliating at times, and a bit disburdening as well. Retrospect is a fascinating act, because, of course, it is not simply reporting on what happened but also actively making it have happened that way. Things turn out to be precedents or accidents or successes or failures only in light of what comes of them, and despite the best or worst of intentions.

My work has been in schools, with teachers and student teachers, and graduate students in education, and in the presence of curriculum—the knowledge entrusted to teachers and students in schools. My studies of and practice in hermeneutics, Buddhism, and ecological dispositions is how I have made my way in doing this work, thinking it through, and reading and

In Praise of Radiant Beings, pages xi–xxx

writing about it. This book is dedicated to teachers and students who find themselves caught in the confines of schooling, and to those newly arriving to the work of interpretive scholarship. I hope it proves useful.

My take on the relationships between education and Buddhism is a peculiar one with many side trails, failures, and breakthroughs. Buddhism is something that lured my attention decades ago, and for ignoble reasons. I was age 16 going on 17 in the summer of 1967 (Jardine, 2012). "That is the privilege of youth, to seek everywhere the new and novel possibilities" (Gadamer 1986, p. 59). Enough said, for now, about that lovely privilege and the advantages I took of it. But that lure kept coming around.

I took an undergraduate degree in philosophy and comparative religious studies, and then an MA in philosophy where I studied Edmund Husserl's phenomenology with Gary Madison (see Jardine, 2016), who brought Hans-Georg Gadamer to McMaster University (Hamilton, Ontario, Canada) during my time there (Jardine, 1976, 2015d). Dr. Madison had done his PhD with Paul Ricouer at the University of Paris on the work of Maurice Merelau-Ponty. Then, I was on to my own PhD at the University of Toronto's Ontario Institute for Studies in Education, with Dieter Misgeld who did his work first with Gadamer, and then a second PhD with Jurgen Habermas.

Meanwhile, my interest in Buddhism just simmered on the side of Doctoral work on Jean Piaget's genetic epistemology (Jardine, 1984, 1987, 1992a, 2005, 2005a, 2008a, 2012f).

All this is to say only that a sense of lineages, of being a very small part of threads already alive and at work in the world rooted in me early (see Jardine, 2012; 2016), and provided a certain pleasure and a certain comfort and, frankly, an odd sort of built-in nostalgia or reminiscence of melody lines. It was no coincidence that The Beatles spoke, in 1967, of "twenty-years ago today" and that that folding over of time and memory stuck, and sticks, here, now, doing a "retrospective."

Scholarship, study—these matters of education in a broad sense—were and have continued to be refuges and reliable, tough, demanding, companions. And there is something about lineages in the atmosphere of Buddhism, of recalling teachers and their gifts and failings. There is something, too, of traditions of thought and etymologies of language in hermeneutics, and something, too, of ancestry and the long living memory of places, as well as felt folds of sustainability and the impermanence of relations, in an ecological body-disposition. I have found, over the years, that this can be akin to the work of classrooms when they come alive, that, for example, when we study animals and their habitats, whole ancestries of work, of voices and ideas and images, stand up alongside us, both as an open-space for our own work, challenging it, summoning it, shaping it, strengthening it, but sometimes blocking our way and needing to be called to account, here, now, in this classroom. "Why do we have to know this?" should not be demeaned by trivial versions of "relevance," like turning mathematics into buying pickles at a store or having Jane leave a train station. It should be a question posed to the lineage that handed us this task of coming to know. It should, with this example, be a way to pay attention to *today's* meetings of 21st United Nations "council of the parties"—COP21—in Paris (the naming of which provides an opening into why democracy, its attempted exportation to Iraq, and the rise of ISIS, provides rich and fertile and treacherously difficult grounds for thinking both inside and outside of a Social studies classroom). As these simple references show, this "calling to account," this "relevance" is not a permanent state. These particular events have already trickled from memory. This "hermeneutic situation" is more akin to Hannah Arendt's image of how "natality" (1969, p. 174) lies at the heart of education, as the reason why things must be always "set right anew" (p. 192). Impermanence is part of the heart of education itself.

But here's an upending twist that I will leave to readers to unravel. I have found—and this book, in various ways, illustrates this finding—that this question of "Why do we have to know this?" tends to come up only when what we are enjoined to know has become boring, flat, mechanical, 'just-for-the-test', lifeless, unrevealing, distant, abstract, and so on. When a classroom, instead, can hit upon the sparking beauty of Pythagorean proportionalities, or the real live-wire of questions about democracy in a Social Studies class, or the water shortages of California lately read through the lamentations of Jane Yolen's *Letting Swift River Go* (& Cooney, 1998), then, often, the question of why we have to know this gets overwhelmed by deeply aesthetic and experiential questions like "What *is* this?" "Where *are* we?" and the more hidden and nebulous experience of being shaped, right now, right here, in seeing this photo of the plastic gyre in the Pacific Ocean, and knowing without saying so that things are now different. I am now different. *Now*, in the presence of such enlivening, the questions that get posed to the lineage are not veiled accusations about a burden it has imposed, but pleas for wisdom, for comfort, for help—tell us what you've seen, help us understand what is happening to us. Explain why you haven't acted, why the latest environmental agreements are optional. The complex pedagogy of this upending is what I have discovered lurking in Buddhism, in hermeneutics, and in ecological thinking.

During my PhD, I was hired as a substitute teacher in the day care system in Toronto, Ontario—a relief from the blank page in front of me. I was rather bad at it, but I could last a day or two in the fray of very young children, guitar in hand. Because of this job and a PhD on Jean Piaget, I ended up with a job running part of the Laboratory Preschool at the University of Guelph, and teaching undergraduate courses on Early Childhood Curriculum. Here is where my still-nebulous, never-quite-disappearing interest in Buddhism began to slowly, slowly re-emerge. It was in relation to the matters being taught and explored with and by children, what we set out in front of them. What I seemed surrounded by in the language and imagination of much of educational talk was a certain thinness regarding the abundant inheritances of the world entrusted to teachers and students in schools. Many in education seemed enthusiastic "about children," but not necessarily about the worlds in which they encountered them. I recall those plots of sod and forest ground dug up and trays, with butter knives to parse the soil, count, sort, identify, smell, and pencils and weed guide books and worms, yes worms, nothing better for 4–5 year olds. Or me. Spell bounding.

If my own experience of the world is thin and joyless, it is only thinness and joylessness that I have to offer in teaching, in learning.

The World is Not Scarce but Abundant

> Listening to and watching French Immersion Grade One children couple together found words and posting them for all to see—and then up goes this accidental couplet, *neige/noir*, "black snow," and how we all gasped a bit at the beckoning incomprehensibility of it: the feel of a world approaching, of aggregate intelligence, of language living instead of dead, of winter darkness, and of the warm presence of us huddled together over this classroom happenstance. So momentary, but just because of this, the true weal of words is felt approaching and whooshing overhead.
>
> We duck and giggle. In brief. *Neige noir.* I must remember this. This isn't a big deal, this. It's a small one. (Jardine, 2015a, p. xvi)

Imagine: beautiful books, beautiful geometries, the mix of paints that always ended up grey-brown from repeatedly cross-dunked brushes, the pungency of mosses brought in with magnifying glasses, or abandoned wasps nest explicated with careful cuts and splayed out to see, and the giggly eruptions had by all when tearing them apart with great patience and accuracy. Look, this, see, smell that, what a color, and all that radiantly caught, however briefly, in smiles and puzzled brows on teachers' and students' faces alike. Crawling inside the belly of a beautiful book, leaning in towards each other in this most ancient of acts:

> "Story," the Old Man Said, looking beyond the cave to the dragon's tracks. "Story is our wall against the dark." He told the tale: the landing, the first death, the second. They heard the rush of wind, the terrible voice, a scream, then another. Beyond the wall, the dragon waited but could not get in. (Yolen 1998, from the back cover)

Amidst all the tears at parents leaving them behind, or the frustrations of tiredness and impatience (theirs and certainly mine) or too many other bodies crowding around, there were these refuges of sorts of experiences that provided reliable relief from the fray: "leisure and opportunity," as I would later read in the work of the profound Buddhist scholar Tsong-kha-pa (2000, pp. 117–128). Open spaces, "free spaces" (Gadamer, 1986, p. 59) somehow. Room to breathe for an ex-asthmatic.

Once they are broken open, explorations of the world's fabrics, its great ecologies, allow each child and each teacher to emerge as themselves, fully in the presence each of their own failings and abilities—patience, love, curiosity, creativity, meticulousness, a way with words or paint or a cuddled affection or wordless wonder. That is to say, *this fabric is more abundant, more forgiving and generous and difficult than any one of our lives alone can measure,* so, in exploring these things, in studying thus in the presence and grace of each other, I can be relieved of some narrow confine of my "self" by working it *out,* not simply working *on it.* This is why it feels spacious even when that fabric binds and pulls at my attention. *Just look* at this painting by Dale Auger. Just think for a minute about the monsters in these books (Jardine, 1994c) or about Coyote's ventures (Clifford, Friesen, & Jardine, 2008), or dropping perpendiculars and bisecting angles (Friesen & Jardine, 2009) or the ways of bears or birds or cats or stars, or sorrow, or "black snow" (Jardine, 2015a), living and non-living (Jardine, 2008a), thunderclaps (Friesen, Jardine, & Gladstone, 2010), war (Jardine, 2012) and old shoes (Jardine, LaGrange, & Everest, 1998). Writing. Reading. Listening. Speaking. Viewing. The Great Language Arts.

This is the insight that scrawls across Buddhism, hermeneutics and ecology, and that provides a way to read the often-calcified life of classroom. *The world is not scarce and thin but abundant* (Jardine, Clifford & Friesen, 2006), and my own way through it is not much to go on by itself, because my own life is very often scarce and thin and needs to leisure in abundance outside these confines. I don't want to "tell my story" (as became *de rigueur* for a while in educational thinking). I want to be *relieved of it* by going to a place (*ecos-, topos-/ topica-*) where I can meet others who can read me back to myself from beyond my own failings and limits and delusions, beyond the story I've presumed.

I recall an undergraduate elementary school curriculum class on campus, when I offhandedly mentioned The Group of Seven and one student said that he'd never heard of it. So I'll tell you a secret. My hidden and (luckily) unvoiced immediate response was a sort of "oh-my-god" "kids these days" scorn—an old, inherited affliction of mine that still needs more burning off. This gave way, I'm relieved to say, to an onrush of a strange, dual affection, both for the lovely prospects of experience in store for this student (I was *almost* jealous), and for the lovely prospects of experience that constitutes this lovely locale, this lovely, variegated, beautiful, topography just waiting. And, actually, there is a third thing here. Because of this student's arrival and unanticipated admission, I had opened up and handed back to me my own longstanding affection for The Group of Seven, as if, somehow, for the first time. Puppy love! Again, no sense hiding this: *this* is one reason I love teaching, because it asks for love from me, for students and their lot, but a love of the world as well. For me, this is pedagogy in its moment of being itself. And it is also something about scholarship, too, study and its opening effects.

This is also what all that stuff about "conversation" means in hermeneutics and why there is a hint in it of a Buddhist understanding of the interdependent emptiness of our selves, and therefore the abundant interlacing of our common lot:

> This belongs to the nature of a fruitful conversation. When we do not listen with such clear good will that the other recognizes in you his view of what he means, then we are merely sophists. (Gadamer, 2007f, p. 416)

The difficult conversation that is at the heart of education itself is not a matter of exchanging opinions but a great and joyous and repeated humiliation of my failing in the face of the full measure of the world and then trying, all over again, to get to my feet in the concert and comfort of others in the same fix. This is why my route in lacing together Buddhism, ecology, hermeneutics and education is via curriculum via our common, contested courses through the teeming and sometimes fraught spaciousness of the world.

Not Plain Clean Gifts

> What comes through the hole (*porta*) has its source beyond the wall and cannot easily be detached from the gap (*chaos*) of its entry. Opportunities are not plain, clean gifts; they trail dark and chaotic attachments to their unknown backgrounds, luring us further. One insight leads to another; one invention suggests another variation. More and more seems to press through

> the hole, and more and more we find ourselves drawn out into a chaos of possibilities. (Hillman, 2013, p. 94)

But this very word "scholarship" needs rescue, because it seems so heavy and burdensome. Its root is in Latin, *schola*, meaning "leisure." It also entails "a holding back, a keeping clear" (On-Line Etymological Dictionary)—again, Tsong-kha-pa's "leisure and opportunity," with opportunity summoning the Latin *porta*, "gate"—with Hermes as the god of passages "between," of gates and doors and portals. Scholarship as the cultivation of an experience of inhabited spaciousness and ease and readiness for experience, such that that new appearance of a Rose-Breasted Grosbeak in the bush outside the bedroom window can be as thrilling, as overwhelming of my self, as it deserves. First one I've seen hereabouts in 30 years. This fall, 2015, full of more orange than usual in the Aspens' turnings, but these are not plain, clean gifts. There might be portents of global warming, perhaps, wrapped up in that thrill, of the oil reasons for new war and economic chaos in Alberta these past months and years. All this arrives in halos, radiant, with potatoes to dig up and retired memory curled up near fires.

Joy, however fleeting, must be sought in the work of facing what is unavoidably a deep wound:

> Here, mythology shows Hermes knowing the ruse and deception that opens the way until the constellation shifts. Hermes here is like Eros, whose father was Poros, "resourcefulness," "way-finder." ... Situations require this opportunistic knowing about where the openings are and when the time needs voice. In an encounter, the lacuna, the weak place ... gives the opportunity. Perception of opportunities requires a sensitivity given through one's own wounds. Here, weakness provides the kind of hermetic, secret perception critical for adaptation to situations.... The weak place serves to open us to what is in the air. We feel through our pores which way the wind blows. We turn with the wind; trimmers. An opportunity requires a sense which reveals the *daimon* of a situation. The *daimon* of a place in antiquity supposedly revealed what the place was good for, its special quality and dangers. The *daimon* was thought to be a *familiaris* of the place. To know a situation, one needs to sense what lurks in it." (Hillman, 2013, pp. 101–102)

You'll be running into many animal familiars in the chapters that follow, ecological lurks of lessons that need learning, messages, teachers that arrive just in time. Oh, and, don't worry too much about these Hillman passages. I still don't completely "get" them, but that's why I remember them, save them and repeat them to myself, here, again. Given the proper attention, their draw increases. I first read them over 20 years ago and I still love them more than I understand them. They are like old wives tales of black cat familiars on witches' brooms. And there's some lingering link between the suffering spoken of in Buddhism, the *pathei mathos* ("learning through suffering") from Aeschylus that is cited by Hans-Georg Gadamer (1989, p. 356) as central to a hermeneutic understanding of coming to know, and its echoes in Hillman's words about wounds, about a sensitivity to what's in the air. Buddhism, hermeneutics and ecology all suggest that such sensitivity can and must be cultivated. It is the work of teaching and learning. Scholarship, here, entails becoming more open to what arrives and what that fresh is asking of me, of us, of our work, of schooling and students and the like.

Taking on the State of the Object

> The other children knew what Kole needed. They knew that he was only beginning to learn to read. They knew he had a hard time making friends. They knew he needed their love, so that's what the children did: They loved him. They didn't try to "fix" him, or rush to teach him how to read. They were patient. They simply read to him. And inadvertently, these children helped Kole learn to read, by nurturing in him a love of books, by spending time cuddled in close reading to him, loving him into a reader. (Molnar, 2014, p, 93)

In a way, that has ever-since remained a weird analogue to the detailed work of scholarship at its best, working with young children (and with teachers and students in schools, with graduate students wanting to study education) pushed me, again and again (and again just now starting up a new year's ventures), to the limits of my own confined experience of my own countenance. My "self" was challenged to become more expansive in perfect parallel to allowing the confines of the topics we explored, the stories we read, the paints mixed and blocks stacked and tipped over, to explode their own confines and reveal rich, rigorous, recursive, ongoing relations and dependent co-arisings (see Doll, 1993):

Understand "meditation" as it is explained in Dharmamitra's *Clear Words Commentary* (*Prasphuta-pada*):

> "Meditating" is making the mind take on the state or condition of the object of meditation. (Tsong-kha-pa, 2000, p. 111)

To the extent that the objects of the work of teachers and students in schools are expansive, abundant and interdependent nests of relations, to the extent that we can let go of the contrivances of permanence and fixity regarding "the curriculum" and the topics we teach (to the extent, therefore, that they can become spacious topographies, ecological places rather than isolated bits and pieces), to that extent, by meditating on these objects, I myself am beckoned to take on this state regarding my own fears and foibles and protective bounded-ness, regarding my experience of my very self itself.

"Take this feeling of letting go as your refuge" (Chah, 1987, n.p.) sounds fearsome at first, but it hides a joy and a relief, an *experience.* Again, via hermeneutics and the work of James Hillman, I link it to *aesthesis* and to giddy breath uncontained by the strictures of schooling. By the way and by no coincidence, I had asthma as a child, till age 12, when puberty scared it off and The Beatles arrived and high school started all within a year.

As my work developed, this focus on the ecology of things and their relations became legible as nothing more or less that an old phenomenological adage: *mensuratio ad rem,* Edmund Husserl's (1970) *Zu den Sachen selbst* "to the things themselves," (see Gadamer, 1984, p. 318), filtered up through hermeneutics into a task that perennially and repeatedly faces us when we want to know what is happening to us, our lives, our world, our breath and bearing. "All understanding involves a momentary loss of self" (Gadamer, 1977, p. 51) but at once this involves the slow, sometimes arduous and painful (re)-gaining of a sense of my self more spacious than first thought. This gaining is "a task that is never entirely finished" (Gadamer, 1989, p. 301) and it must be always taken up again in the face of the circumstances that draw us away into distractions and duties. But not just this. Against sheer phenomenology, the immediacies of "my experience" is in fact full of deceptions, encodings, repressions, hidden histories of all shapes and sizes that end in *the appearance of immediacy.* Our "immediate experience" is, in fact, profoundly mediated, entangled, inherited, distorted (deliberately or otherwise), suppressed, embodying of forgotten panics or defeats or victories, lost hopes and desires, lost cultural threads and remnants.

This is why one of the at-first most unfathomable passages in Hans-Georg Gadamer's *Truth and Method* (1989, pp. 60–64) is where he details how, in German, the very idea of talking about "my experiences" (*Erlebnisse*)—that seemingly most innocent, most immediate and obvious and commonplace of things—entered into usage only in 1870 in Germany, where it was coined and codified in order to give a name to the proper object of the "human sciences" (pp. 64–70). And this is why, following and elaborating on the work of Paul Ricouer, Gadamer (1984) and others speak of the "hermeneutics of suspicion" regarding what *appears* immediate, and given, and beyond doubt, even (and in education, perhaps especially) the recourse to the apparent immediacies of "experience" (*Erlebnis*) itself. The hermeneutic tradition branches and proliferates at this juncture, and great and variegated lineages of suspicious work become a source of insight and hesitation.

Thus, an affinity, again, so well voiced by David Loy in his brilliant essay, "Indra's Postmodern Net" (1993, p. 481):

> Until recently, Western philosophy was largely a search for the one within the many, the Same that grounds Difference. Our century has seen the end of this project: not its realization but its abandonment. Perhaps the most dramatic refutation has come from psychology, in Freud's demonstration that our ego-consciousness is not Cartesian and autonomous but irretrievably split, buffeted by psychic forces it cannot control because it is a function of them. Others have questioned our supposedly self-sufficient self-consciousness by emphasizing the differences inherent within language. The Swiss linguist Saussure taught that meaning is a function not of any straightforward correspondence between signifier and signified, but of a complex set of phonetic and conceptual differences. Later the French critic Roland Barthes pointed out that each text is a tissue of quotations: not a line of words releasing the single "theological" meaning of an author-god but a multidimensional space where a variety of writings blend and/or clash. Today Jacques Derrida argues that the meaning of such a multidimensional space can never be completely fulfilled, for the continual circulation of signifiers denies meaning any fixed foundation or conclusion. Hence texts never attain self-presence, and that includes the text that constitutes me. What would happen if these claims about textuality were extrapolated into claims about the whole universe? (Loy, 1993, p. 481)

That extrapolation is what one finds in Buddhist thought and practices. It is found, too, in ecological thinking when it escapes the confines of "environmental education" and ripens into an understanding of all of the educational enterprise:

> There is one further aspect of Hermes that may be worth noting, namely his impudence. He once played a trick on the most venerated Greek deity, Apollo, inciting him to great rage. Modern students of hermeneutics should be mindful that their interpretations could lead them into trouble with the "authorities." (Smith, 1999c, p. 27)

The Good Qualities of Sandalwood

My untangling of the world has and still runs far ahead of my untangling of my self. Far ahead, enough to feel slightly off-kilter even pretending to put this book together. I feel a bit like a character described by Tsong-kha-pa (2000, p. 74):

> Those who achieve their own livelihood by praising or explaining the good qualities of the trainings, while not striving diligently to practice them, are not suitable to be teachers. That sort of meaningless praise is only words. It is similar to when someone who diligently seeks sandalwood asks one who makes a living by explaining the good qualities of sandalwood, "Do you have any sandalwood?" and that person replies, "No."

I do recognize and remember its smell, however, and can sense when it's nearby and can more reliably point ahead on the path others might take than I can tread that way myself. Such is my lot.

This book is not at all about Buddhism and education, but about a *very specific thread of Buddhist lineage* that has *very specific demands and characteristics.* My relationship to Buddhism stayed as mere flirtation and hesitation until I came upon lineages of it that were amenable to my circumstances as someone interested in curriculum theory, in ecological and eco-pedagogical thought, in what the hell is going on in schools, in the dances of language at the edges of things, and in the refuges of philosophy and the purposeless joys of scholarship into the interweaving delves of the world.

Nothing is good medicine in itself. It was simply the medicine I needed, and even then, I didn't swallow it whole or follow the doctor's orders obediently.

A Word about Tsong-Kha-pa

A word, then, about Tsong-kha-pa (1357–1419 CE) and the Buddhist lineages he embodies. I cannot for the life of me recall what it was that lead me originally to purchase Tsong-kha-pa's three volume *The Great Treatise on the Stages of the Path to Enlightenment* (2000, 2002, 2004) in 2006 and then to read it cover to cover every year since, every underlining in a new color, marginalia now on top of marginalia, comments on comments. Tsong-kha-pa composed this text (finished in 1406) as a commentary on Atisha's (982–1054) *Lamp for the Path to Enlightenment* (trans. 1997) ("in Sanskrit *Bodhipathapradipam.* In Tibetan this is *Byang chub lam gyi sgron ma*" [Sonam, 1997, p. 23]). Atisha's text is itself an attempt to draw together what had become two disparate streams of Buddhism: "the method side of the Buddha's instruction . . . comes down to us through Maitreya; the wisdom side . . . comes to us through Manjus[h]ri" (Sopa, 2004, p. 12). And each of these two figures has their own descendants who revived and kept alive these sides of the Buddha's instructions: "Nagarjuna [second century C.E.] re-established the [wisdom] teachings of emptiness by way of Manjusri, while Asanga [fourth to fifth century C.E.] reestablished the method teachings by way of

Maitreya" (p. 13). The arc of explication set out by *The Great Treatise on the Stages of the Path to Enlightenment* has been commented upon and reiterated down through a long lineage, many of whose proponents have and will be cited herein (Lobsang, 2006, Pabongkha, 2006, Patrul, 1998, Pelzang, 2004, Sopa, 2002, 2005, 2008, 2016, Yangsi 2003).

Here is an example of how this worked as medicine. Having worked for three decades in a Faculty of Education, the antagonism between theory and practice, between studying and "doing," is near and dear to my heart and always a reliable source of heartbreak, much heat and little light. So Tsong-kha-pa's work fell into this heartbreak with great clarity. Here, he is citing Kamalasila's (circa 740–795 CE) *Stages of Meditation*:

> What you meditate on with wisdom arisen from meditation [practice] [the lineage of Maitreya down through Asanga] is just that which you know with the wisdom that has arisen from study and reflection [the lineage of Manjushri down through Nagarjuna]. You don't meditate on something else. (Tsong-kha-pa, 2000, p. 52)

Hence a wonderfully apt image of what happens in practicum placements in schools and in on-campus university courses when this goes astray:

> It is like showing a horse a racecourse before you race. Once you have shown it you then race there. It would be ridiculous to show the horse one racecourse and then race on another. Similarly, why would you determine one thing by means of study and reflection, and then, when you go to practice, practice something else? (p. 52)

This site of repeated embattlement was only one of the ways in which Tong-kha-pa's work was able to be illuminating and answerable to things that often fell outside of its own immediate orbit of concern. It illuminated, in 1406 CE, both the woeful and dull-minded failings of much University scholarship in education that has lost track of the life it is *about* while it was, at the same time, illuminating of how often classroom practice can be, frankly, profoundly "anti-intellectual" (Callahan, 1964, p. 8). Of course, if "intellectual" means having lost touch with the life of one's object of study, well, "anti-" certainly makes sense. Tsong-kha-pa confirmed for me a contention that is also deeply buried in hermeneutics, that these are dependently co-arising sufferings and that something of a hermeneutic phenomenology whose "object" of concern is precisely life-as-lived provides a lineage of scholarship that seeks and bears proximity to the lives of teachers and students in schools, the life of curriculum as lived, and so on.

So, I feel both queasy and confident about "using" Tsong-kha-pa's (and others') work in this way—queasy because I have inevitably distorted this lineage for my own purposes, but confident because I have tried to make this Buddhist lineage answerable to real and relevant and important circumstances—teachers, students, schools, curriculum, and how to find our way with joy and compassion in this often-afflicted midst.

The particular allure of what finally caught my attention about Buddhism and allowed it to start taking deep and serious root, is best and most simply described by Ajhan Chah from his lovely book *Being Dharma: The Essence of the Buddha's Teaching* (2001). He describes how the vital stream of meditative mindfulness and stillness and practice that is key to Buddhist ways is, by itself, not enough:

> There are two kinds of peacefulness. One is the peace that comes through *Samadhi*. The other is the peace that comes through Wisdom [*Vipassana*]. The mind that is peaceful through *Samadhi* is still deluded. Such peace is dependent on the mind being separated from phenomena. When it's not experiencing any contact or activity, there is calm, and consequently you get attached to the happiness that comes with that calm state. But as soon as there is impingement through the senses, the mind gives in right away. It gets to be afraid of phenomena [and, as we'll see in what follows, then retracts inward and secures its "self" all over again]. (p. 91)
>
> . . .
>
> The peace that comes from wisdom is distinctive, because when the mind withdraws from tranquility [and moves back out into the mess of the world], the presence of wisdom makes it unafraid. With such energy, you become fearless. Now you know phenomena as they are and are no longer afraid.

Buddhism (in this line and lineage) is not a way to simply calm down and retreat and become passive and unaffected by the life world. It is not passivism, retreat, or withdrawal or indifference. It is, instead, a way to avoid becoming caught up in the fray of the world by stilling oneself (*Samadhi*) and *then*, "you need study" (Tsong-kha-pa, 2000, p. 61) *that very world.* When one ceases, however momentarily, from being caught in the fray of the world (the hermeneutics of suspicion), one can, with composure, turn *towards* that world and begin to unravel what is at work *in that very fray.* One can study what its realities are, what its delusions and concealments and attachments entail, its lures, afflictions, and breakthroughs without simply being caught in them (see Tsong-kha-pa, 2000, pp. 45–128). One can, in other words, do interpretive research of the life-world, the world as lived.

In such interpretive work, what has been given up is precisely what Buddhism asks us to give up: a belief in or pursuit of some solid foundation (some substance, some permanent, self-existent thing) for this roiling living. Studying and practice do not have the goal of being done with once some fixity has been secured: "exactly because we give up a special idea of foundation in principle, we become... closer to the real givenness, and we are more aware of the reciprocity between our conceptual efforts and the concrete in life experience" (Gadamer, 1984, p. 323). Studying concrete life experiences that are full of layers of remembering and forgetting, concealing and unconcealing—all this is a hint that this lineage is always and already linked to questions of pedagogy and its well-being, detailed descriptions on how to rely on a good teacher (Tsong-kha-pa, 2000, pp. 69–91) that, in the (translated) language of Tibet in 1406 CE, are just arcane and odd enough to rattle the moribund cages of contemporary educational discourse.

Not incidentally, Nishitani Keiji (1900–1990, and cited throughout the following chapters), as well as his teacher, Nishida Kitaro (1870–1945), were both greatly influenced by Martin Heidegger's (1889–1976) later meditations (see Nishitani, 1982; Nishitani studied with Heidegger from 1937–39). For example, see his "A dialogue on language between a Japanese and an inquirer" (1971a) in which he directly references Shuzo Kuki (1888–1941), another student of Kitaro's who "died too early" (p. 1). Kuki studied phenomenology with Edmund Husserl in Freiburg and then went on to study with Heidegger in Marburg and gave lectures at Kyoto University on Heidegger's work in 1939. Let me add in passing that, in finding these threads for this introduction, I've just happened upon Michael F. Marra's (n.d.) "A Dialogue on Language between a Japanese and an Inquirer: Kuki Shūzō's Version" which is casting me back over these matters all over again. Such is the joyous suffering of scholarship.

If It Actually Exists, It Must be Possible

Here is where Buddhism, ecology, hermeneutics and pedagogy converge with great energy: "Do not devote yourself just to piling up words in great numbers without engaging in practice" (Tsong-kha-pa, 2000, p. 61). Thinking, words, study, can most assuredly pull us away into architectures of ideas and theories and abstractions that have clean lines and alluring facades but that are not experientially liveable spaces. Education, as much as any living practice, has suffered from the imposition of this or that great idea, new contrivance or rubric or procedure. Education knows firsthand that models have had the tendency to be anorexic, too thin to live and to unable to gain sustenance from the living fabrics of the world, and the shapes of good practice. "What should be adopted and what should be cast aside

[?]. The purpose of knowing [these things] through study is to do them" (Tsong-kha-pa, 2000, p. 61).

Thus, too, something is outlined here regarding the very purpose of writing and scholarship itself:

> Shantideva in his *Engaging in the Bodhisattva Deeds* and *Compendium of Trainings* states "I compose this in order to condition my own mind." (Tsong-kha-pa, 2000, p. 111)

> The more you practice these things, the more accustomed your mind will become to them, and the easier it will be to practice what you had initially found difficult to learn. You will have visions of the Buddha day and night. (pp. 185–186)

An important point, here, however, is that such visions are not extra-terrestrial or exotic. Anything but. It is simply the thrilling arrival of that Rose-Breasted Grosbeak and my ability to be there when it happens, and nothing more than that. "What happens to us over and above our wanting and doing" (Gadamer, 1989, p. xxviii) is hard to glimpse when we're caught in the constantly distracting emergencies of our own wanting and doing, or the racing hallways of schools and always-upcoming something or other. There is nothing otherworldly about studying these circumstances and our lot in them. A joy hides there. I've seen it and been a small part of it in many real classrooms with real teachers and real students and real, everyday demands. If I may, from Chapter 14:

> Up against the too often pronounced exhaustion and desperation and despair of "this sort of thing is not possible in my school/with my sort of students/in this part of town/at this grade level/with this school administration/in this school board/in this subject area/with these parents/under these economic conditions," and so, on and on, we offer an old and pointed response of our late colleague, teacher and friend, Patricia Clifford: "if it actually exists, it *must* be possible."

It exists. It is possible. But it is often quite obscured, quite hidden, and this quite often by how we might approach this open, joyous, difficult space.

Hitherto Concealed

This is why I want to cite in full two passages whose affinity is, in retrospect, a root of this whole collection. First, from the translator's introduction to *Introduction to the Middle Way: Chandrakirti's [c. 7th Century CE]*

Madhyamakavatara *with Commentary by Jamgon Mipham [1846–1912]* (Blankelder & Fleetcher, 2002, p. 9, italics mine):

> "To hold that the world is eternal" the Buddha declared, " . . . is the jungle of theorizing, the wilderness of theorizing, the tangle of theorizing, the bondage and the shackles of theorizing, attended by illness, distress, perturbation and fever." It is important to assimilate this passage in its entirety. It points to a reality that transcends ordinary thought but is nevertheless still knowable. To say that it is possible to know something that is beyond thought carries the important, indeed astonishing implication, that *there is in the mind a dimension that in the vast majority of living beings is wholly concealed, the existence of which is not even suspected.*

And then from Hans-Georg Gadamer's [1900–2002], *Truth and Method* (1989, pp. 99–100, italics mine):

> We will have to hold firmly to the standpoint of finiteness. [This] does not mean that [the human subjectivity] is radically temporal, so that it can no longer be considered as everlasting or eternal but is understandable only in relation to its own time and future. If this were its meaning, it would not be a critique and an overcoming of subjectivism, but an "existentialist" radicalization of it. The . . . question involved here . . . is directed precisely at this subjectivism itself. The latter is driven to its furthest point only in order to question it. In disclosing time as the ground hidden from [subjective] self-understanding it . . . opens itself *to a hitherto concealed experience that transcends thinking from the position of subjectivity.*

I'll have cause to cite these passages again in full in what follows. It is one way of becoming accustomed to them, re-reading them in different emergent circumstances. The light of each circumstance casts new shadows, makes hidden folds differently illuminated.

What slowly emerges (I hope) in what follows is *an experience* often concealed in the spellbinding clamors of everyday life or in the buzzing clarities of theorizing. It is an experience that is too often marginalized, privatized or subjectivized when it does raise its head (see Gadamer, 1989, pp. 42–100) or deemed a sort of mystical and Romantic or Orientalist obfuscation of the way things "really are" in the "real world" of schools and economics and markets and war and other hard facts. From the Latin *facere,* "to make." This world of schooling is not "the real world." It is just how the world has thus far happened to turn out, and the causes and conditions of such turning can be understood, unraveled, and we can unravel ourselves from this turning and, in small, sometimes quite meager and temporary ways (given the largeness of the looming of things), take a breath.

This experience is immediate and intimate, but it takes repeated practice and hard study to release and realize this immediacy, and even then it is not released once and for all and it is easily and understandably frightened off. As the exigencies of every life rise up, so, too, rises up the tendency to retrench, harden and once again conceal. This "un-concealing" (one etymological flourish of the hermeneutic concept of "truth" as *aletheia* [see Moules, 2015]) can be, therefore, frustrating at first. It can seem like deliberate obfuscation or weird otherworldliness. But, with practice, the path will clear, the ears pop:

> Why did he tell us to practice and find out for ourselves? Some people really worry about this. "If the Buddha really knew," they say, "he would have told us. Why should he keep anything hidden?" This sort of thinking is wrong. We can't see the truth in that way. We must practice, we must cultivate, in order to see. (Chah, 2005, p. 111)

And, rest assured, as with any practice worthy of our while (see Chapter 17), days will pass and amnesia and somnolence and distraction will rise up, and the exhausting acceleration of the world will make panic seem normal—"it'll grind you up." But when you return to the joyful practice, *it will be right where you left it,* patiently having waited for your return.

The essays in this book explore both how to come to experience the world this way and provide ways to decode the sirens that call us away from this rich, difficult, and abundant experience. We should have no illusion, however. To the extent that it induces a questioning of the somnolence of contemporary schooling (coupled as this sleepiness is with a weird form of hyper-vigilance), it proves Gadamer's adage, that "understanding is an adventure and, like any other adventure, it always involves some risk" (Gadamer, 1983, pp. 109–110). Understanding is never a "plain, clean gift." It is not always good and happy news, finding out about the fix we are in. All three lineages of Buddhism, ecology and hermeneutics are thus inherently pedagogical, inherently in a position of teaching and encouraging a type of learning consonant with this generative, lived experience of a living world of relations, ancestries, suffering, and dependently co-arising causes and conditions. All three, each in their own way, encourage practice, patience, stillness, whiling, and study and do this against a background that has let go of delusional hopes and desires for fixity, immortality and finality. This letting go is a heartbreaking, joyous refuge (Jardine, 2012d). The good news, here, is that we are all in the same fix, and our deliberate and studied commiseration makes our suffering sufferable, joyous.

This joy doesn't make it any easier. It only makes it better.

One Last Indulgence for Now

I must beg one last indulgence from readers (you've been very patient so far). What follows is an emergent path of thinking and one characteristic of interpretive work that is also a characteristic of meditative practice, is returning to an object, an example, a passage, a citation, and idea, and episode, and working it through all over again in light of new events, new relations and circumstances. What follows is not a path of concepts decided upon and then fixed beyond arising circumstances, and thus left behind when a new chapter ensues. There is no "been there, done that" about this sort of work, this sort of research and study. It is, instead and deliberately, a path of recurrence, of reading and re-reading. I was able to teach that *Truth and Method* course 25 times because the circumstances that called it to account always shifted enough to cast it back into the life and vibrancy of this year's gathering (see Jardine, 2015). I can't tell you how many times I said, "Oh, *now* I get it!" only to say it all over again and again.

Every teacher starting a new year in September knows something about this ability to "see with fresh eyes" (Gadamer, 1989, p. 16), an ability that weaves together remembering and forgetting, taking hold and letting go and sometimes repeating as if for the first time. So there will be passages in the chapters that follow that are, on the face of it, simply repetitions. I hope they can be read, too, as the re-appearances of what will slowly become familiar names and faces and images, called to account again for why we might remember them and re-gain their acquaintance:

> It is somewhat difficult to establish, but once you are used to it, it will be like meeting an old acquaintance. (Kongtrul, 2002, p. 67)

> It's like making a path through the forest. At first it's rough going, with a lot of obstructions, but returning to it again and again, we clear the way. After a while the ground becomes firm and smooth from being walked on repeatedly. Then we have a good path for walking in the forest. (Chah, 2005, p. 83)

This collection, then, is also a handbook for a type of research that is having every-increasing success in the academy—"interpretive research," for lack of a more elegant term. In this book, I will demonstrate how the lineages of Buddhism, hermeneutics and ecology give us ways *to practice the craft of teaching and learning in the classroom* as well as ways *to study and articulate that practice.* My own personal relief came when I realized how these two things—practice and study—are somehow the same thing, the same gesture, attention and work.

In all of this, it's not only a matter of tough work needing to be approached with joy. Tough work can give rise to it. It has, with always varying and fleeting success, tempered my tendency to speed up and skitter, distracted, which, it seems some days, the whole world wants from me at every turn. Study can bring lightness, radiance, right in the midst of the heave of things and the skittery "Look at that! Look at that!" false promises that only leave me spent and out of breathe altogether. So this little insight that I've gleaned about writing, about meditation, about many things, that I should not do them "when I feel like it." "Feeling like it" is the *outcome* of doing them, not just the elusive cause.

So there it is. I hope some will find these writings to be useful. I hope they can provide the odd joyous reminder, the odd wee refuge, companionship and commiseration, even when the going gets tough, which it surely will, all over again.

Perhaps, especially then.

A Note on What Follows and Acknowledgements of Sources

The chapters in this book are organized chronologically over a span of 25 years, with the addition of some previously unpublished pieces. Added to each chapter is a newly written *Preamble* designed to elucidate some of the often hidden or latent relations to Buddhist thought and to provide readers with a sort of retrospective reading of a career of work and the slow emergence of ideas over that path and its windings.

Finally, a rather strange and difficult note, really. Regarding Buddhism, I don't *believe* it, nor do I believe *in it.* "The Buddha was saying 'wake up!' not 'I am the Buddha and you must believe in me'" (Sumedho, 2010, p. 64). What Buddhism has provided me is a way to think, a way to pay attention to and parse my way through my own experience, my own raising (including my philosophical background in hermeneutics and my interest in matters ecological), one that has provided, in mostly small but sometimes profound and life-changing ways, a sort of relief for myself and sometimes, when it works, those I teach. And this, again, is not because of how I might talk and think about Buddhism, but about how it allows me to talk about, for example, multiplying by fractions with a Grade Five student-teacher whose got stuck on what to do, how to proceed, or how it allows me, instructs me, to love proximity to a young child trying to pronounce an unfamiliar name, to draw towards the tellings and to work them through, again and again, learning patience by being patient, again, again. This sort of, shall

I say, distanced-proximal relationship to Buddhism is perhaps the weird freedom that is provided anyone not raised in a certain cultural or spiritual practice—that the life one is living comes first, and those practices are summoned up to give answer to that living.

Brace yourself. It's like this: "Cultivate love for those who have gathered" (Tsong-kha-pa, 2000, p. 64). And this: "to know the world, we have to love it" (Berry & Moyers, 2013), we have learn to love where we have gathered, to care for it as a gesture of caring for ourselves. Ecology. Buddhism. Hermeneutics. Education.

PREAMBLE 1

"We Twist Fibre on Fibre"

Joy,
Landlocked in bodies that don't keep—
—Newsom, 2006

Summer 1989. I was asked by Dr. Antoinette Oberg to teach a graduate course in the Faculty of Education at the University of Victoria. Many students that summer took a course from me in the morning and one from Ted Aoki (2005) in the afternoon. Several times both Ted and I were separately asked if we consulted about our classes and planned some sort of mutual venture over the two courses. We did not. Instead, both of us were, in a fashion, concerned in similar ways with similar circumstances, similar lived realities. In talking about curriculum, both of us went to the same place by quite different paths. Ted and I giggled more than once over the weird lot of those students that summer.

My own work had been centered on the nature of analogical language and how it provided a way to explode the harsh, Rationalistic understanding of identity and difference handed down by Western philosophy (see

In Praise of Radiant Beings, pages 1–7

Jardine & Morgan, 1987, 1987a). Instead of this alternative, my work focussed around a passage from Ludwig Wittgenstein's *Philosophical Investigations* (1968, p. 33), fragments of which will appear and re-appear in these collected essays:

> As in spinning a thread, we twist fibre on fibre. And the strength of the thread does not reside in the fact that some one fibre runs through its whole length, but in the overlapping of many fibres. Don't say, "There *must* be something common" but *look and see* whether there is anything common to all. For if you look at them you will not see something that is common to *all*, but similarities, relationships, and a whole series of them at that. To repeat: don't think but look! We see a complicated network of similarities, overlapping and criss-crossing: sometimes overall similarities, sometimes similarities of detail. I can think of no better expression to characterize these similarities than "family resemblances." (*Familienahnlichkeiten*)

If we step away from the stringent options of identity and difference and attend, along with Wittgenstein, to how we *live with such matters*, the alternative is more forgiving, flexible, variegated, and murky than either: kinship, relatedness, similarity, likeness, of-a-kind-ness. Much of my work prior to 1989 and thereafter involved exploring these matters within this confine and in light of an admiration for and critique of Jean Piaget's genetic epistemology (Jardine, 1984, 1987, 1988, 1992a, 2005, 2005a). Note how the invocation of "kinds " "kinships" and "family resemblance" already summons up something about pedagogy. German: *Kinder*, "children." And "kindness" defined as "natural affection" (Online Etymological Dictionary, hereafter OED).

Then, in that summer of 1989, I went to the University of Victoria bookstore and bought and read for the first time *The Sun My Heart* (1988) and *The Miracle of Mindfulness* (1986) by Thich Nhat Hanh, as well as *The Unsettling of America* by Wendell Berry (1986). The combined effect of reading these texts was a euphoric mixture of something brand new and some ancient breath I'd already taken. I had flirted on and off with Buddhism since my undergraduate degree in Religious Studies at McMaster University in Hamilton, Ontario (1970–1974), and these texts contained new-old echoes of matters ecological, matters of place and settling down, of interrelatedness, of breath, and learning the ways of that place.

Curriculum topics as living topographies, perhaps.

Fields of relations.

Since moving to the foothills of the Rocky Mountains in 1986, I'd experienced this first hand through leaving the place I'd been raised, that I had been raised *somewhere.* What these texts provided me was clusters of images, ideas, shapes and forms of language, all of which lived outside of the established confines of the language and thinking of educational theory and practice. But, more than this, they provided me and still provide me a way to see something of the living character of pedagogy itself, a way that much "educational research" and the strangulated language that is its orbit failed to provide. A breath of fresh air.

It is no coincidence for the life of my work and the paths it has taken that I live on an acreage far enough outside of Calgary, Alberta to watch bears walk by, to have the silence of deer companions, and to have dogs killed, now and then, by cougars:

> My dog Daniel just brought down the other deer leg from Cougar Ridge. He stood and waited again, just up at the skirt of the forest, facing the house. There's a pedagogy, here, but it is hard to tell who is the teacher and who is the student: the leg? The ridge? The dog? Domestication? Herd animals? Settlement? That bloody death and all its fears and chases and falling to gravity? Or perhaps the deaths of two of my other dears at the very same cougar locale a few years back? Or the feeling of being already likewise pursued and those Buddhists who say that the only way to outrun what is coming is to stop running. Another old story: when you are chased by the Lord of Death and you trip and fall and your body scatters into blood and bone and air and earth and water, *who will the Lord of Death pursue*? Who was the Lord of Death pursuing before that trip and fall? Or during that buzzer-driven race to cover the curriculum too often conceived in panic and regret? Who? That old thing we read that Gary Snyder (1990, p. 175) cites from Dong-Shan, a 9th century Chan/Zen Master: "One time when the Master was washing his bowls, he saw two birds contending over a frog. A monk who also saw this asked, 'Why does it come to that?' The Master replied, 'It's only for your benefit.'" This leg, its blood, Daniel's waiting, is for our benefit, as are the little panics that schooling arouses without warning or recourse. But then we're left with the task of understanding, a path now not quite laid out, almost ready to be taken. Step. (Seidel & Jardine, in press a)

My work at the University of Calgary was, at least at first, in curriculum in Early Childhood Education, and my dissertation was a phenomenological/hermeneutic critique of the work of the genetic epistemologist Jean Piaget. I was also involved in practicum supervision and visited countless classrooms from Grades 1 to 3. What exploded was a vivid experience of the kinship threads of the world that were *already at work* in the lives of teachers, of students, and of the knowledge entrusted to them—in the books they read, the practices of printing and the angularities of triangles, the institutional constrictions they suffered, the joys of the great and ever-abundant materiality of the world and the cusps of its venture and exploration and lateral obediences to the fabric of things. A profound intimacy and immediacy of lived experience, woven and re-woven, glimpsed but often simply ignored or marginalized, understandably, but to terrible effect, in favour of the day to day work of getting along. As shall be cited again later, not only are we "always open onto the horizons of others but also, more important, [we] are *always already everywhere inhabited* by the Other in the context of the fully real." (Smith, 2006, p. xxiv). Back, then, both to Wendell Berry's habitable work and to the idea of "inter-being" from Thich Nhat Hanh (2003) (this being his translation of the Sanskrit *pratitya-samutpada*, more commonly translated as dependent co-arising. See below).

These events lead to an explosion of the shapes of writing I then began to seek out—interweaving threads, textile, *textus* and thus a call to not just write about different things, but *to write differently*. The very grammar of scholarly prose and its attendant methodological fetishes seemed to hold in place precisely some of the assumptions of identity and difference from which I wanted to slip away. Even the fabric of the text on the page seemed open to question and affectionate exploration. From *Speaking With a Boneless Tongue* (Jardine, 1992):

> Relations of Kind. Full of the kinships that bind our lives to each other and to the life of the Earth. Full of "analogical integrities" (Berry, 1989, p. 138)
>
> Articulations of: "that anciently perceived likeness between all creatures and the earth of which they are made" (Berry, 1983, p. 76). (Jardine, 1992, p. 183)
>
> . . .
>
> Analogical ("this is like that" integrities are not representationally obedient to some "higher" concept that they fall under. They are obedient laterally, to each other—(*ab audire* to listen, to give heed, to be attuned. Words and things "belong together" in relations of kind, in relations of breath and bone. Our freedom, here, is not licentiousness but the "give and flexibility" (Norris-Clarke, 1976, p. 188) the "open-texture" (Wittgenstein, 1968, p. 112) of kinds.
>
> [Expressions of affinities:
>
>> Understanding is the expression of the affinity of the one who understands to the one whom he understands and to that which he understands. (Gadamer, 1983, p. 48)]
>
> The song and words and breath of the poet are linked. The Earth is part of us and apart from us. Speech, well versed, resonates with the anciently perceived likeness between all creatures and the Earth of which they are made.
>
> Ecology is a type of writing-on-the-edge:

> "The true poem is walking that edge between what can be said and that which cannot be said. That's the real razor's edge." (Snyder, 1980, p. 21)
>
> (Jardine, 1992, p. 187–188)

The chapter that follows is a meditation on all the well-intended talk of "curriculum integration" in Early Childhood Education. That talk seemed to ignore "the integrity of the place that already houses us" (Jardine, 1992, p. 257). This dependently co-arising place seemed hidden by our circumstances, desires and pedagogical inheritances. Curriculum integration was repeatedly talked about as something we must *do*, thus concealing our lived circumstances by our wanting and doing—an old ecological portend of disaster. The following chapter is a first effort at gathering my wits around the arrival of these newly old ways of speaking, imagining, and thinking. To paraphrase David G. Smith cited above, this Earth that we are coming to know via various curriculum threads is *always already integrated.* The exact stake we have, therefore, in disintegration into separate curriculum areas, separate grade levels must be uttered and understood and treated with great delicacy. After all, for example, infesting probability or grammar with Grade Level Expectations is like introducing an exotic species into an environment that then becomes simply and easily overrun.

There is a specifically pedagogical thread here worth making explicit. Kinship relations cannot resolve themselves into a matter of identity and difference that would somehow solve this relation, as if it were a problem. We are kin and the ambiguity and shifting nature of such mutual kindness is not an error that needs to be resolved, but a living circumstance which we must come to live with well—and which must therefore be always re-won:

> This, then, is a kind of progress—not the progress proper to research but rather a progress that always must be renewed in the effort of our living. (Gadamer, 2007a, p. 244).

In this surrounding, the language of context, of circumstance, of relation, boded well, because, after all, in the orbit of pedagogy, "it depends" *does not mean, "anything goes."* It means a vigilant sensitivity to my dependents and, also and at the same time, to my own dependency on those who have come before and to the Earth we inhabit. Teaching and learning become thinkable as intergenerational acts (Friesen, Clifford, & Jardine, 2008). Knowledge becomes thinkable as an inheritance to which we bear a responsibility for its well-being and ours in its sway. Echoing here also is my reliance on the early work of David G. Smith, especially his two articles "Children and the Gods of War" (1999a) and "Brighter than a Thousand Suns: Facing

Pedagogy in the Nuclear Shadow" (1999b). His images of "not a problem to be solved" and children being "part of us but also apart from us" (1999b, p. 138–139) became and remain clarions for my own work, and you'll notice these images arising over and over again in what follows.

As far as Buddhist thought goes, I'll offer only this for now. Central to all that follows is an interrupted understanding of how things, ideas, images, and selves *exist.* These things are *not* self-contained identities that exist independently of anything and everything else. They *are,* instead, dependently co-arising, coming and going "gatherings" such that "in" the "nature" of each element is reflected all the other elements that support and sustain its being what it is. Simply put, if you are learning about Pythagorean calculations, nearby are Cartesian co-ordinates, square numbers, tri-angularity, the geometry of circles, and, too, adding, subtracting, multiplying, counting, proportionality and images of beauty and properness, even Aristotle's proper proportionality and the Thomist reflections on the proportionality of analogical relationships. Even Pythagoras' secret cult is nearby and its affinity to the sometimes seemingly "closed shop" world of those who deeply "get" mathematics. Pythagorean calculation *is* all of these things, because without any of these kin, it cannot be what it is. It "is" a field of relations, a surrounding of sustaining ideas, lineages, formulae, faces, places, names, applications, limitations and the like. Trying to replace this array of relations with the bare bones of the Pythagorean theorem is an act of violation. Those bare bones are one way, one path, in and through this array, not a stand in or replacement for it. As shall be cited and re-cited below, "only in the multifariousness of voices does [it] exist" (Gadamer 1989, p. 284).

And the same is true of all the rich topics (ecologically put, "topographies, places"), for example, of a stone, of a tree, of the poetry of Don Domanski (2002, p. 245): "At the center of a stone or at the axis of a tree there's the silence of a world turning." Those Pine Siskins show up in the right places (see Jardine, 2013), which is why the ecological portends that shake our minds and bodies when they *don't* show up right, is such a deep and difficult matter to tolerate. Those oil spills; that belch of smoke, rattles our very flesh.

Without practice, you may not notice these things, but might simply experience a silent nervousness, an unexplained, low-level panic. With practice (as suggested by Buddhism, hermeneutics and ecological thinking) comes, slowly, the ability to suffer such sufferings, study them, open them up and open ourselves to these rattling dependencies.

Just to note in passing (and readers might especially experience this in the passages in Chapter 1 from Keiji Nishitani), that there is an at-first rather tortuous *grammar to these matters* that challenges the grammar of Western thinking and language and its subject/object/predication relations. It challenges the practices of reading and writing and research. At first, it sounds complex and tangled, but it is pushing up against the limits of a language/grammar that is premised on identity and difference. It is not a deliberate form of obfuscation or mystification. It is not at all "otherworldly." Not at all, even though it will feel that way at first. It is (often tortuously, in the Tibetan tradition) rigorous, deliberate and clear. You do have to get used to it, however. It is not just a matter of writing about different things but also, in line with the *mensuration ad rem*, writing differently, in ways called for by the things themselves.

So these two Buddhist terms will appear and re-appear or be simply hinted at as we proceed:

- In Sanskrit, *pratitya-samutpada*, various translated as dependent co-arising, cosmic interpenetration, inter-being (and parallel, I will be suggesting, to ecological images of dependence and place, Wittgensteinian images of kinship and family resemblance, and hermeneutic articulations of the lived-horizons that surrounded each thing, word, idea, gesture or self) and;
- In Sanskrit, *shunya*, variously translated as emptiness, lacking self-existence, lack of self-presence, not being contained or finished or fixed within itself, not being reified into a self-identical, definable object that exists somehow independently of anything else, not, therefore, being a "substance" in the Aristotelian and Cartesian sense (more on this later).

So thus: to be empty (of self-existence, of a closed off, separate and "hardened identity" [Huntington, 2003, p. 266]) is to be full (of relations, of kin, of dependencies [dependent co-arising]). Emptiness, here, suggests radiance and abundance (see Jardine, Clifford & Friesen, 2006). It suggests that this "hitherto concealed experience" (Gadamer 1989, p. 100) involves an experience of *ek-stasis*, of breaking out beyond the confines of my self and the hardened stasis of identity. And it is not, then, a matter of a resorting to difference, because difference is born as the twin of identity. Giving up the self-existence of the one is giving up the other in the same gesture. Much more on this later.

1

"To Dwell With a Boundless Heart"

On the Integrated Curriculum and the Recovery of the Earth (1990)

> I like to walk alone on country paths, rice plants and wild grasses on both sides, putting each foot down on the earth in mindfulness, knowing that I walk on the wondrous earth. In such moments existence is miraculous and mysterious. People usually consider walking on water or in thin air a miracle. But I think the real miracle is to walk on earth. Every day we are engaged in a miracle which we don't even recognize: a blue sky, white clouds, green leaves, the black, curious eyes of a child; all is a miracle. (Hanh, 1986, p. 12)

I began teaching my undergraduate early childhood education class this year by handing my students a blank piece of paper and instructing them to write down as many possible ways the paper could be used to demonstrate, illustrate, or teach features of the various curriculum areas. Their ideas began as expected, with possibilities such as writing on it, painting or drawing on it, reading from it, folding it and making shapes, questions of where paper comes from, how it is made and used, and so on. But in the midst of this exercise came a striking advent for this class. Once they moved to questions of how the paper was made, one student suggested that you could talk about trees and still remain "linked up" with the paper, still remain "on topic." Once this shift of focus occurred, what began was a giddy onrush of

In Praise of Radiant Beings, pages 9–16

sun and soil and water and logging and chainsaws and gasoline and refineries. Because of this serendipitous turn of attention, suddenly and unexpectedly, everything came to be co-present with the paper. Everything seemed to nestle around it. Some topics seemed close to the paper, others distant, at the ends of long and tenuous tendrils of interconnection. Some connections were obvious and immediate, some connections were stretched, but nothing was absent altogether.

One striking feature of this class was that we seemed to go beyond a mere mental exercise to glimpsing something about the world and our experience of the world, a previously unnoticed interconnectedness of things hidden beneath the surface assumptions of difference and separateness that are so commonplace and that guide much curricular thinking.

> With the interdependence of all things or "interbeing", cause and effect are no longer perceived as linear, but as a net, not a two-dimensional one, but a system of countless nets interwoven in all directions in a multidimensional space. (Hanh, 1988, p. 64)

> All things in the world are linked together, one way or the other. Not a single thing comes into being without some relationship to every other thing. (Nishitani, 1982, p. 149)

> Even the very tiniest thing, to the extent that it "is," displays in its act of being the whole web of circuminsessional interpenetration that links all things together. (p. 150)

As we proceeded with reflections on this exercise, we realized that any object could have been used for this demonstration; *any* object could have been "drawn into the center" in a way that all other things organize themselves around this center. With any object, everything else seems to come forward but no special object in this implication has a privileged status as *the* center.

> The universe is a dynamic fabric of interdependent events in which none is the fundamental entity. (Hanh, 1988, p. 70)

While a piece of blank paper lends itself to curricular matters that are proximal to it (e.g., writing, drawing, questions of how it is made), pulling out this piece of paper tugs at the whole fabric of things, without exception. Paradoxically put, then, every object is a unique center around which all others can be gathered, and, at the same time, that very object rests on the periphery of all others, proximal to some, distant to others.

> To say *that a thing is not itself* means that, while continuing to be itself, it is in the home-ground of everything else. Figuratively speaking, its roots reach across into the ground of all other things and help to hold them up and keep them standing. It serves as a constitutive element of their being so that they can be what they are, and thus provides an ingredient of their being. *That a thing is itself* means that all other things, while continuing to be themselves, are in the home-ground of that thing, that precisely when a thing is on its own home-ground, everything else is there too, that the roots of everything spread across into its home-ground. This way that everything has being on the home-ground of everything else, without ceasing to be on its own home ground, means that the being of each thing is held up, kept standing, and made to be what it is by means of the being of all other things, or, put the other way around, that each thing holds up the being of every other thing, keeps it standing, and makes what it is. (Nishitani, 1982, p. 149)

No singular center will resolve this paradox, that a thing is, so to speak, not itself (i.e., it *is* only in relation to all other things and therefore summons up all those things that it seemingly is not in order to be itself) while being itself. If it were not for trees and sun and sky and water, there would be no paper, and to fully understand what this piece of paper *is* in an integral way requires bringing forth this paradoxical, interweaving indebtedness. It *is* the sun and the sky, not just some separate thing that just happens to be related to sun and sky. Without this happenstance, *there is no paper.*

The name for this paradoxical, interweaving indebtedness is the Earth.

From here, the class moved on to a discussion of the question of the nature and assumption of an integrated curriculum and the appropriateness of such a curriculum for early childhood education.

The Recovery of the Earth

The notion of the *integrated curriculum* is becoming common currency in early childhood education in Canada, and the articulation of this concept across grades K–6 is beginning in some circles. What seems to be missing in many current formulations of this notion is any deep sense of the difference it makes in our lives and the lives of children. Is it simply a new slogan that will become exhausted and empty, as have so many others in the consumptive flurry in education for the newest and the latest; or, does it speak of something new, something vital and generative, in the field of education? I believe that it is potentially the latter.

But this potential is difficult to assess and address. The exercise my students did in the class was a momentarily enjoyable one, but it is also one whose giddy insight is difficult to sustain. My students did report that they glimpsed something about the notion of integration in the curriculum, but it was almost impossible to sustain this glimpse and cash it out as something practicable. It was difficult to lie out in front of us as a set of propositions or formulae, not because of the complexity of the task or its arduous nature, but because what we were glimpsing was precisely not an object for our perusal or an objective set of relationships that we can set before us. Rather, we were glimpsing the way in which the Earth is our abode, our dwelling, and how our lives as teachers are an integral part of this dwelling. We live and think *in* this web of relations, not just *about* it. Our thinking itself is like sun and sky.

The notion of an integrated curriculum became a painful one for some students as they began to confront the fossilized residues and assumptions of their own schooling and, more pointedly, as they began practice teaching in situations of profound disintegration. The seemingly innocent and playful exercise we conducted did not make matters easier or clearer, nor did it make questions of applicability simpler and more straightforward. It made things worse. Underlying this difficulty are questions regarding images of our lives and the lives of our children that both sustain and ground the notion of the integrated curriculum. Something archaic and delicate and difficult needs to be recovered for the integrated curriculum to have any deep sense.

> The unnoticeable law of the earth preserves the earth in the sufficiency of the emerging and perishing of all things in the allotted sphere of the possible which everything follows, and yet nothing knows. The birch tree never oversteps its possibility. It is [human] will which . . . drives the earth beyond the . . . sphere of its possibility into such things which are no longer a possibility and are thus the impossible. It is one thing to just use the earth, another to receive the blessing of the earth and to become at home in the law of this reception in order to shepherd the mystery and watch over the inviolability of the possible. (Heidegger, 1987, p. 109)

If we begin to unearth the notion of the integrated curriculum, it begins to disrupt our deeply held beliefs and images of understanding, self-understanding, and mutual understanding, pointing to a sense of interrelatedness, interdependency, or interconnectedness that is belied by our analytic, definitional, and frequently disintegrative approaches to educational phenomena. It also belies the desire to finalize, control, master, and foreclose on vital curricular issues. It puts into question desires we may have, as educational theorists and practitioners, to get the curriculum "right," "straightened out," once and for all, for such desires require a basically disintegrative, analytic act aimed at rendering education a closed question, aimed at rendering human life lifelessly objective under the glare of knowledge-as-stasis.

Integration leads to glimpses of a truly lived curriculum, a true *curriculum vitae,* one that exudes the generativity, movement, liveliness, and difficulty that lies at the heart of living our lives, as educators, in the presence of new life in our midst (Smith, 1999a, p. 138-9), in the presence of children. A truly integrated curriculum involves the ambiguous and difficult ways in which our lives are intertwined with children—the irresolvable paradox of children "being part of us but also apart from us" (p. 175)—and the ways in which our lives together with children are interwoven with the life of the Earth. It is *this integer, this* whole, *this* integrity that the integrated curriculum voices.

Near the roots of the notion of the integrated curriculum is a strikingly simple image of education: "The essence of education is natality, the fact that human beings are *born* into the world" (Arendt, 1969, p. 174). Therefore:

> To preserve the world against the mortality of its creators and inhabitants, it must be constantly set right anew. The problem is simply to educate in such a way that setting right remains actually possible, even though it can, of course, never be assured. (p. 192)

Education, in this image, has to do with our fundamental orientation to natality and, therefore, our fundamental orientation and openness to the future. Although education often means the ceaseless proliferation of longer and longer lists, guides, schedules, and agenda, at its heart, it cannot be caught in the *stasis* that such a tendency requires and desires in the end. Rather, education is *ek-static,* a movement beyond what already is, a reaching out to the new life around us in a way that keeps open the possibility "that the people of this precious Earth . . . may live" (Fox, 1983, p. 9).

The integrated curriculum is, at its roots, more than a matter of the interrelations between curriculum areas or subject matters. It is an ecological and spiritual matter, involving images of our place and the place of our children on "this precious Earth." It requires a deep reflection on our desires to disintegrate children's curricular experiences in the name of manageability, ease of instructional design or territorial notions of the separateness and uniqueness of subject-matter specializations. As such, ignoring the ecological and spiritual consequences and character of the integrated curriculum plunges education into a peculiar paradox, an impossibility. We are able to diligently pursue ways to teach the mathematics, science, social studies, and language arts curricula without ever considering whether such diligence, such curricula, and such teaching work in concert with the continued existence of an Earth on which such knowledge may be brought forth. *Educare*—"bringing forth"—can too easily be understood, so to speak, "from the neck up," as if it just happened in the head, as if it were just a matter of effective teaching and affected learning, requiring no real place, no real space to occur. Such a strangulated approach to education forgets that it is not accumulated curricular knowledge that we most deeply offer our children in educating them. It is not their epistemic excellence or their mastery of requisite skills or their grade-point average, but literally their ability to live, their ability to be on an Earth that will sustain their lives.

If we begin to take the roots of the integrated curriculum seriously and begin to heed what it requires of us as educators, we must educate and we must understand the curriculum in ways that will sustain the possibility that all our efforts, and all the efforts of our children, and all these matters of so much concern in educational theory and practice will not be made suddenly trivial. A thorough grounding in mathematics is of little use if that knowledge is understood in such a way that there is no longer any real ground that is safe to walk. Mathematics must become earthen. We cannot sensibly aspire to well bound and defined and circumscribed images of knowledge and of being educated if those images belie the existence of the actual breath required to pronounce that aspiration.

attend, to be attuned.

Concluding Remarks I: "To Dwell With a Boundless Heart"

> It is as if young people ask for, above all else, not only a genuine responsiveness from their elders, but also a certain direct authenticity, a sense of that deep human resonance so easily suppressed under the smooth human-relations jargon teachers typically learn in college. Young people want to know whether, under the cool and calm of efficient teaching and excellent time-on-task ratios, life Itself has a chance, or whether the surface is all there is. (Smith, 1999a, p. 139)

The title of this paper voices how we might understand ourselves, not as an exception to this interweaving indebtedness and interrelatedness to the Earth, but as an instance of it. To dwell with a boundless heart is to understand "the self in its original countenance" (Nishitani, 1982, p. 91) as delicately interwoven in this earthly fabric in which we found woven all things, including the children we teach. We can draw boundaries around ourselves (and it is often appropriate to do so), but we cannot give ourselves boundaries without believing in the impossible—that our lives can go on, that we can be, without an ongoing conversation with "this precious Earth," one that includes our knowledge of it, but also includes our breathing of it.

> The self is here at the home-ground of all things. It is itself a home-ground where everything becomes manifest as what it is, where all things are assembled together into a "world" This must be a standpoint where one sees one's own self in all things, in living things, in hills and rivers, towns and hamlets, tiles and stones, and loves these things "as oneself." (Nishitani, 1982, pp. 280–281)

In a sense, then, this interrelatedness of things underlying the integrated curriculum requires seeing every action as an action on behalf of all, everything speaking on behalf of all things. Thus, when we think and talk about a topic in a classroom, we need to remember that *everything* is the home ground of all things, everything is full of relations. This concluding remark ends with a vignette.

Following a recent heavy oil spill off the coast of Washington State, my six-year-old son and I were watching the C.B.C. news. We saw film footage of an oil-covered duck struggling up on to a beach on the west coast of Vancouver Island. With each panicked lunge, its wing tips remained adhered to the slickened beach. Pictures of dead water fowl being shoveled up and put into green garbage bags followed.

We have all seen these scenes before, perhaps all too often. I have often felt rage or sadness, or I have simply turned the damn thing off. But when my son turned to me and asked me to help him understand what he was seeing, I felt something new. I felt humiliated.

Even though it is all too easy to over-romanticize and anthropomorphize this point, I suddenly felt my own humanness as rooted in the same soil as this creature, my own "humus-ness." In trying to understand this event and trying to help my son understand, I felt as if our understanding, our conversation, had to be brought down to Earth, humiliated in the proper sense. My son and I had to face our own indebtedness to this creature, to this oil, to this water, to this sand, to these scenes, to the power of these broadcast images, linking us to the production of this power, to its use, to the demands for it, to our demands for powering fuels, and then back to this oil, to this water, to this sand, to these scenes.

Watching and attempting to face these images, to make sense of them, produced the need for the very fuel that was now killing this creature. It was as if it was undergoing the pain on our behalf. To tell my son of oil tankers and accidents and cleanup efforts no longer seemed like the whole truth. The story seemed like a disintegrated curriculum-guide version of the truth, where the pain and indebtedness are laid out anonymously before us to either peruse or ignore at our leisure. I had to try to tell him (to tell *myself*) that we cannot "turn the damn thing off" by just switching off power to the television set. Not facing these images, turning them off, does not dispel our debt.

This realization became all the more difficult when my son and I watched a movie later that day, and a particular speech, in another context, in another place and time, hit too close to home, making the early scenes of ducks and oil and death, the earlier thoughts of indebtedness and humiliation, even more unforgettable:

> I am asking you to fight—to fight against their anger, not to provoke it. We will not strike a blow, but we will receive them and through our pain we will make them see their injustice. It will hurt, but we cannot lose. They may torture me, break my bones, even kill me. But eventually, even in my death, they will see their injustice and they will stop. (Gandhi, 1982)

Clearly, in quoting this speech of Mahatma Gandhi, I am guilty of a sort of gross anthropomorphism, but evoking the roots of the integrated curriculum as an ecological and spiritual matter requires a deeper, different response than those I have become accustomed to as an educational theorist. It requires a language of implication, of debt, of interrelation, a language that does not allow indifference; that does not allow us to "turn the damn thing off." Perhaps, the language that allows us to call this unfortunate incident of the suffering of slick birds some kind of discrete matter in the business of education—perhaps, that is the truly anthropocentric language, believing as it does, that the boundaries it draws it actually gives.

Nearing the finishing of this paper, news of the Valdez oil spill in Alaska.

Concluding Remarks II: This Piece of Paper

It is all too easy to be swept up in the happy interrelations of sun and sky and clouds and rain that nestle in this piece of paper. This piece of paper, this very one that I am writing on, this very one that you are now reading, may be the one the bleaching of which produced the dioxin that may have already given Eric, my six-year-old son, cancer.

Overstatement? Yes, perhaps; but only perhaps. As a colleague once said to me, we will be responsible to our children for the questions we do not ask. Failing to voice our real indebtedness to this precious Earth—our "original countenance"—may involve abandoning our children—my child—to an all too certain future.

PREAMBLE 2

"Don't Say 'There **Must** *Be . . . '"*

> Ignorance mistakenly superimposes upon things an essence that they do not have. It is constituted so as to block perception of their nature. It is a concealer. (Tsong-kha-pa, 2002, p. 208)

> Don't say, "There *must* be something common," but *look and see* whether there is anything common to all. (Wittgenstein, 1968, p. 33)

> No inclination is more dangerous to "seeing" . . . than to think too much, and from these reflections in thought to create supposed self-evident principles [which then] implicitly determine and unjustifiably limit the direction of investigation. (Husserl, 1970a, p. 50)

"To the things themselves" was Edmund Husserl's call in his phenomenology, intent as it is on explicating the life world, the world as lived (Husserl, 1970, 1970a) and this is why there is something of phenomenology lurking under all this—our lived experience is often obscured by a theorizing impetus, a speculative one, and ideological one, or one born of affliction, will, anger, ignorance, fear, or desire. The great task is to cleave to this experience and not be distracted or frightened by its countenance into rendering it into something more docile and safe and secure than it *is*. John Caputo (1987, p. 2) put this succinctly: "restoring life to its original difficulty" and not "betraying it with metaphysics."

In Praise of Radiant Beings, pages 17–22

But here is one of two twists—to re-phrase Husserl's words cited above, here is nothing more dangerous to "seeing" than *not thinking enough* and naively believing that what is experienced "immediately" and what is considered to "go without saying," to be "obvious," is not hiding long-standing presumptions that have shaped and sometimes distorted, or occluded that immediacy. "To the things themselves" is a constant and repeated task, not a given. "The great problem is precisely to understand what is here so 'obvious'" (Husserl, 1970b, p. 187). "Deeper analyses of these 'obvious' matters—all this leads to difficult investigations" (p. 169).

Here, too, is the other great twist from phenomenology to hermeneutics, because, despite his pleas for cleaving to "the thing itself," at the heart of Husserl's work is an exogenous desire to *render* lived experience and reify it into its *essential* structures, purging it of its accidents, its occasions, its outliers. His phenomenology is an "*eidetic phenomenology*" (Gadamer, 1989, p. 254):

> We cannot see how the "Heraclitean flux" of constituting life can be treated descriptively in its individual facticity. No [one] can hold fast to anything in this elusively flowing life. But [such] full concrete facticity can be grasped as belonging to its essence, and it is determinable only *through* its essence. The life-world does have, in all its relative features, a general structure. We can attend to it in its generality and, with sufficient care, fix it once and for all in a way equally accessible to all. (Husserl, 1970b, pp. 177–178)

You can clearly sense, here, the old warring options of identity (essence, generality, general structure) and difference (facticity, flux, elusive flowing). In the face of the uprising of insight into our lived circumstances, Husserl reeled and spun back into old Western-philosophical ways—grasping for essences and things that are permanent and fixed:

> Can the world and human existence in it truthfully have a meaning if... history has nothing more to teach us than all the shapes of the spiritual world, all the conditions of life, ideals, norms upon which man relies, form and dissolve themselves like fleeting waves, that it always was and ever will be so, that again and again reason must turn into nonsense, and well-being into misery? Can we console ourselves with that? Can we live in this world, where historical occurrence is nothing but an unending concatenation of illusory progress and bitter disappointment? (Husserl, 1970b, p. 7)

In light of the emerging work of his students, Martin Heidegger and Hans-Georg Gadamer, all Husserl can envisage is "succumbing to skepticism, irrationalism and mysticism" (Husserl, 1970b, p. 3) and phenomenology, without essence, falling into ruin, a scattering of differences, dissolving waves, illusion, bitterness, disappointment. Husserl cannot console himself with anything but something fixed once and for all.

In contrast to Husserl's eidetic renderings, it is *precisely* a fleeting, finite, worldly consolation that is at the heart of hermeneutics, because it does not see the alternative to fixed essences as simply a cascading, chaotic concatenation but, as per Wittgenstein's suggestion, a living fabric, a net of interdependent relations that have a way to them (Sanskrit, *Dharma*), a way that can be studied and untangled and rewoven, participated in, questioned, and transformed into new solidarities. The on-going wheeling of things (Sanskrit: *Samsara*) can be studied and understood without resorting to reifying essentialization, and such a slowly, painfully cultivated understanding of our living circumstances can provide a certain relief, a certain joy. Our relations can, shall we say, console us:

> Lacking in self-essence resembles social and historical constitution, understands individual things as constituted by their relations to other things and especially to groups, families, species, and kinds. Emptiness resists the autonomy of the individual [which now appears] uniquely European American. (Ross, D., 1999, pp. 213–214)

I can attest first hand to the hostility of some involved in phenomenological pedagogy when such suggestions about not pursuing essences are made—"you think anything goes" was the sad, and repeated, condescending refrain.

There are two things going on here. First, hermeneutics suggests that things are concealed in the seeming phenomenological immediacies of lived-experience. The immediate surface sheen of experience must be *interpreted*, not just described, and this itself is a profoundly risky, multi-layered task. Just because experience appears immediate, unmediated, does not mean that such experiences are not full to the brim of occlusions, silences, hidden histories of gender and power and culture and happenstance. They must be decoded, untangled, as we must also untangle how our very selves are implicated in these tangles, defined by them, silenced, fooled.

Second, we can face the venture of the world and come to know our way around without the understandable but concealing efforts of essentializing and fixing. We can learn to live with that venture by venturing it, practicing it, studying it, unmasking its concealments, interpreting it, decoding it, and not simply be drawn into that wheeling or away from it into delusional permanences. It is not an "experience" as per Husserl's phenomenology (German *Erlebenisse*) but is, rather, an "experience" (German *Erfahrung*, from *Fahren*, to journey, yielding *Vorfahren*, those who have ventured "before" [German *Vor-*], thus hinting at a hermeneutic interest in ancestors and tradition, analogous to a Buddhist veneration of lineages and lines of thought and practice). The goal of hermeneutic work is not to produce fixed essences, but to unfix them and get them back in to the living fabric that is our lot, into the vulnerabilities of our circumstances. The careful study requisite of hermeneutic work was called, by a well-known phenomenologist, nothing but "mind-f%&*ing." The speaker, here, shall remain nameless. I'll only note in passing that, in the tradition of Tibetan Buddhism embodied in Tsong-kha-pa, he very specifically equates how reification/essentialization is both the cause and the effect of hostility. It is war consciousness (see Jardine, 2012a). Much more on this below.

Experience is not something one "has" to be described, but rather something "undergone" or, shall we say, "suffered." Our whole life is precisely such undergoing, and in education, learning that is worthwhile is had precisely through such venturing. Thus Gadamer's (1989, p. 356) invocation of Aeschylus: *pathei mathos,* learning through suffering (see Jardine, Gilham & McCaffrey, 2015). We can become practiced and we can console ourselves with this as a refuge of commiseration and compassion. Studying the living circumstances of schooling can be "the path and the goal" (Seidel & Jardine, in press a). Much more on this as we proceed.

The phrase used in Hans-Georg Gadamer's *Truth and Method* (1989, p. 38) to pinpoint this locale of suffering is "the fecundity of the individual case," and how our knowledge of our circumstances always involves the susceptibility of our rules, laws, essences, themes, patterns, generalization, kinds, kinships, and other soft or harsh reifications, to being *called into question,* opened up, summoned to account by the on-going arrival of things. Kinships and kind expect this: the arrival of my son years ago turned me into a father and my father into a grandfather. His arrival rattled back over what seemed fixed and unfixed it, thus saving its life. The arrival of the next case belies the hitherto reification of the rule and asks it to understand itself as open to the difference the next case will make. This, of course, is a profoundly pedagogical point, that the next child's lingering over the pronunciation of a word is not simply one more example of something already fully understood, but, instead, the waking up of the life of the breath over texts. It *is* pronunciation, not just another example of it that falls under already understood and fixed rubrics and rules. Instead of such fixed rules, we have an ongoing fabric (Latin *textus*) being woven and re-woven, a text of which I am not the sole author. This undergone experience does not solely issue from "me." It transcends thinking from the position of subjectivity.

As for Buddhism, here is another central idea to its lineages: four noble truths. It is easy to simply list these, but a lifetime's work to live up to understanding their import:

1. The truth of suffering
2. The truth of the origin of suffering
3. The truth of the cessation of suffering
4. The truth of the path towards such cessation.

At the root of all this is ignorance of emptiness (i.e., an ignorance regarding dependent co-arising, ignorance that seeks permanence, stability, finality, fixity, essence), and therefore the relentless, panicky, manic, and afflicted grasping for something permanent that follows and causes suffering to spin and spin.

The reason it takes a lifetime to understand the import of such things and why I still hesitate in even talking about these matters, is not simply because of how "deep" are these truths and what they demand of me and my life. It is because *my life keeps coming*, keeps arriving, and new cases, new afflictions or incidents keep asking for understanding and thus keep bumping up against what seemed to be solved or resolved, what seemed to be fulfilled. I can tout it in theory with great aplomb and then lose it with the next moment's anger or regret (see Chapter 16), or the next moment's misplaced confidence. This vulnerability, this suffering, is part of the "original difficulty" (Caputo, 1987, p. 2) of human life. *It is not an error*, and, therefore, it *is* an error to marshal and guard myself against its occurrence.

This suffering has a familiar face. It is precisely the lot of the teacher and the student. Each September is precisely such an arrival, and no matter how much one prepares oneself, something of what is just about to occur is out of my hands. Part of the "path" of the Fourth Noble Truth is cultivating this readiness for a certain un-readiness, and the repeated and steadying practice this involves, of not giving ourselves over to the urge to fix this.

In other words, the First Noble Truth does not cease to have its alerting function as the other truths are realized. It is Noble, not accidental, and it thus persists in myriad masks of arrival, again, again. However, when a gravely ill young child arrived in Carli Molnar's class (Molnar, 2014; see also Seidel & Jardine, in press), precisely what that First Noble Truth means, and precisely how it summons questioning, action, sorrow, resolve, waiting, patience, worry, revivification, and so on, shows that that first truth is always revealing its fecundity because of the fecundity of the cases that arrive at its doorstep.

This is a profound pedagogical point. The way is not one of eradication of suffering that comes from the continued arrival of the world, but the eradication of that suffering that arises when we panic at the prospect and have not readied ourselves well.

2

"The Fecundity of the Individual Case"

Considerations of the Pedagogic Heart of Interpretive Work (1992)

A former studentteacher phoned me in a panic late one August, excited that she had been offered a job in an Early Childhood Education classroom starting the next week and, of course, apprehensive about all that might entail. She phoned, I suspect, as much for reassurance as for advice. Eight weeks later, well into the school year, she phoned again and recounted the experience of going to her new school just days before the children were to arrive.

The principal was not available when she arrived, and she was instructed by the school secretary that her room was "down there, Room 10." She had walked down the hallway to what was to be "her room" and paused. The door was shut and she spoke of this shut door being "imposing," "as if something was going on in there already" that of which she was not yet part of, something to which she did not yet "belong." As she told it, she knew that when she opened that door, somehow, "everything would be different," things would be, in her words "turned around." She sensed that,

In Praise of Radiant Beings, pages 23–42

once she "stepped in," she would be finally "crossing over" from student to teacher: "once I entered the room, I knew that would be *it*."

We have all had experiences similar to this. In some sense, and to some degree, we all understand what she is talking about. Her tale is familiar, familial, something with which we already have deep, unvoiced kinship (Wittgenstein 1968, p. 36). In the face of this undeniable sense of kinship and understanding, what is the task of educational inquiry with respect to such an incident? How are we to do justice to this particular episode that happened to a particular teacher at a particular time and place, while at once respecting the undeniable kinship we experience in hearing this teacher's tale?

This chapter explores how the interpretive disciplines understand and address the powerful "fecundity" (Gadamer, 1989, p. 38) of such incidents. Understood interpretively, such incidents can have a generative and re-enlivening effect on the interweaving texts and textures of human life in which we are all embedded. Bringing out these living interweavings in their full, ambiguous, multivocal character is the task of interpretation. There is thus an intimate connection between interpretation (concerned as it is with the generativity of meaning that comes with the eruption of the new in the midst of the already familiar) and pedagogy (concerned as it is with the regeneration of understanding in the young who live here with us in the midst of an already familiar world) (Arendt, 1969).

It is not simply that pedagogy can be one of the themes of interpretive inquiry. Rather, interpretation is pedagogic at its very heart.

The first section of this paper is a playful consideration of unvoiced philosophical assumptions underlying those forms of educational inquiry which begin with methodical acts of severance in order to ensure "objectivity" in what they might have to say about such an incident. The next section shows how this incident could be read interpretively, bringing out the difference in the underlying assumptions of such an interpretive reading. The concluding section of this paper attempts to weave together more explicitly the threads that bind together interpretive research and pedagogy.

The "Isolated Incident" as the Substance of Inquiry

"A substance is that which requires nothing except itself in order to exist" (Descartes, 1955, p. 275) This is a longstanding definition, cited here from Descartes (seventeenth century) but winding its way back into the work of Thomas Aquinas (thirteenth century) and from there, back into Aristotelian metaphysics (third century B.C.E.). I cite it here because for much work in educational inquiry, the fundamental given (the root of the notion of "data" as "that which is given or granted") in inquiry is not that original, ambiguously alluring familiarity that first strikes us when we hear this teacher's tale. Rather, what is strictly given is the "isolated incident."

The literal text produced by this particular teacher at this particular time in this particular situation—this, severed from all its abundant allure, is "that which requires nothing except itself in order to exist." This is the substance of (some forms of) inquiry. Such abundant allure is henceforth understood to be *subjective.*

Therefore, before we can begin such an inquiry, we must make this incident into something portioned off from anything else except itself. We must begin by systematic acts of severance aimed at retrieving the given ("the isolated incident") out of the amorphous web of interweaving meanings in which it was originally embedded and in whose abundant embrace it first appeared. We must sever any interconnections that are already at work before the methods of our inquiry are enacted. We must (ideally, at least) put out of play any understanding of or connection to this instance that we may have as inquirers. We must suspend any spontaneous familiarity or sense of kinship that it evokes in us, any sort of aesthetic appeal or experiential reminder. We must also put out of play any interconnections we see or suspect between this instance and any other meanings or tales or stories or narratives.

These two acts of severance—this instance from us and our lived familiarity with it, and this instance from other instances—will allow it to become a selfidentical substance, something that stands "without us" and without reference to any other incident. Thus severed, it no longer signifies or signals anything beyond itself. It becomes, as far as we know thus far, "an isolated incident," just itself and nothing more. These systematic severances have acted on the assumption (implicit in empiricism) that all that is given is the empirical instance. Therefore, any interconnections or evocations have been *imposed upon it* and these impositions must be put out of play before we can retrieve the integral instance itself. Our isolation of the instance, then, is done against the backdrop of the belief that it is "in fact" isolated. In this way, our methodical severances are not understood as violations of alreadyexisting, real, and vital interconnections. Rather, these severances involve systematically reversing those violating interconnections that have despoiled the actually isolated incident. We have retrieved the integrity of the instance by retrieving the isolated, individual (i.e., not further divisible) case.

This is a fascinating process to which we subject both the instance and ourselves. It is akin to a sort of purification ritual (Bordo, 1988, pp. 78–82) that both we and the instance must undergo. Regarding the instance itself, ambiguous linkages and telltale signs and marks of potentially violating interconnectedness are systematically eliminated, producing of a sort of virginal, untouched instance. And regarding ourselves, we can no longer approach this instance with the moist and fleshy familiarity with which we began. We must now simply "behold" it with what Alfred North Whitehead named the "celibacy of the intellect" (cited in Fox, 1983, p. 23). We must remain strictly within the parameters of the methods of severance we have enacted, for any other interconnection would despoil or defile the instance we have so carefully and methodically isolated and purified. Our connection to this instance thus becomes gutted. We understand it "from the neck up," uprooted from the dark and original familiarities and kinships which have been put out of play. And, correlatively, the instance itself loses its ambiguous allure and is rendered fully present. Along with the assumption that all that is given is the isolated instance, we find a correlative assumption: the given is equated with the clear and distinct. Any signs of ambiguity in what is given (in "the data") indicate that we have not yet rid the given of its impurities or not yet controlled for the possible interpenetrations of dependent and independent variables. The isolated instance, if properly isolated, is what it is and therefore can contain no ambiguity. Ambiguity or any other sign of a lack of clarity and distinctness is understood to be nothing more than a problem that needs to be fixed through further purifications and severances. An ambiguity in the data is thus simply the occasion to subdivide the problem and conduct a further study. The given, therefore, is univocal, clear, and distinct. Any entrails of meaning that might have wandered from it off into dark corners or that may have dug deep into our lives and drawn us into unanticipated, illicit interplays have been cut off.

A more direct and familiar way of putting this process is that, through these severances of the original familiarity in which we were immersed and which drew us in in the first place, we render this instance into an object and, correlatively, render ourselves into a "knowing subject" which has this object, not as something to which we belong and have a kinship or relation, but as something standing over against us. The instanceasobject now no longer fits into a complex fabric of interrelations in which I belong with it, but rather "stands out," isolated from what surrounds it. It becomes "obtrusive, importunate, and demanding of our attention" (Weinsheimer, 1987, p. 5).

From this original severance thus begins a long series of correlative movements between this instance and myself as inquirer. "Subject and object precipitate out simultaneously. Yet, even while separate, they remain interdependent, because the breakdown in the world [i.e., the tearing of the instance out of the fabric of familiarity in which it originally lived] corresponds to a breakdown in understanding" (Weinsheimer, 1987, p. 5). Once divested of the original, intimate knowing, I can no longer claim to understand this now severed object. That original allure never did know *the object.* It was just subjective.

In this way, "both subject and object are derivative and secondary, in that both precipitate out of the more primordial unity of being at home in the world" (p. 5), a "being at home" bespoken by the fact that I somehow "already understood" what this teacher said before the specific work of rendering it an object of research even began. This precipitated subject and precipitated object "are [both] determined negatively: the knowing subject [now severed from our original senses of familiarity] no longer understands and the object [now severed from its living context] no longer fits" (p. 5). Now "real research" can finally begin.

These fundamental acts of severance and the convoluted sequence of correlative purification transformations in both the object of inquiry and the inquirer give inquiry a peculiar and deliberate anonymity and rootlessness. Once we become severed from the abiding senses of kinship and familiarity and embodied allure that this instance evokes (once it becomes an "object" and I become a "knowing subject"), we are left with clear, univocal, given surfaces both regarding the instance and regarding ourselves. It is transformed into what objectively presents itself to us (i.e., univocal "key terms," or coded words, that can be accurately mapped and charted) and we are transformed into deployable methods that themselves have a clear and univocal character (Weinsheimer, 1987, p. 6). Once these instances of our lives become uprooted from their fitting place in the world and once we become uprooted from our familiarity with the world, inquiry into such (now "objective") instances becomes enamored of frequency and reoccurrence.

The only significance we can glean from these rootless surface readings of the incidents of our lives are from quantities and enumerable surface repetitions. When, for example, we hear a beginning teacher talk about the anxieties of opening the classroom door for the first time and entering in, speaking and writing of the resonant meaning of such an event is foregone in favor of an inquiry into whether a significant number of "respondents" will cite the same experiences, use the same words and concepts, speak in the same terms in their reports. Because we have actively and intentionally reduced this instance to an isolated incident, it becomes essential to collect more and more incidents in order to raise this first incident out of its isolation. Any interesting turn of events: we raise things out of their isolation through our knowing. We did not *create* isolation through our methodology. Because we have actively and intentionally restricted ourselves to that knowledge produced methodically, it becomes illegitimate to engage these instances in ways other than simply collecting them. This first instance becomes significant (that is to say, it points to something beyond itself) only insofar as it can now be shown to reoccur in a (mathematically) significant number of other equally actively isolated incidents. Significance thus becomes intimately linked with frequency. More pointedly put, significance becomes mathematized. This instance links up with others only under the watchful eye of this most celibate of disciplines.

The interest of such a mathematization of significance is not to better understand this instance and its meaning as a feature of human life, but to be better able to control, predict, and manipulate its future reoccurrences (Habermas, 1972). Above, we mentioned that, following upon the methodical severances of our familiarity with the world, there is a correlative negative determination of both object (which now no longer fits) and subject (which now no longer understands):

> The cognitive remedies for these twin defects are likewise correlative. The object is disassembled, the rules of its functioning are ascertained, and then it is reconstructed according to those rules; so, also, knowledge is analyzed, its rules are determined, and finally it is redeployed as method. The purpose of both remedies is to prevent unanticipated future breakdowns by means of breaking down even further the flawed entity and then synthesizing it artificially. Thus Gadamer speaks of "the ideal of knowledge familiar from natural science, whereby we understand a process only when we can bring it about artificially" (1989, p. 336). (Weinsheimer, 1987, p. 6)

Once these "cognitive remedies" are enacted, we can (within mathematically prescribed limits) predict the reoccurrence of such incidents and therefore we will no longer be "taken aback" by such reoccurrence. Such incidents will not allure us again and catch us off guard, with all the disorienting and disturbing consequences that such allure can have. These remedies (recall, produced of the original precipitation of "subject" and "object") prevent the possibility of understanding being provoked by something unwittingly and without methodical anticipation. Thus, "objectification" protects us from dangerous unanticipated turns that the world may take (this is precisely the strength of such work). It rules out of its considerations unanticipated ("uncontrolledfor") interchanges with the world.

Of course, the methodical attainment of such objectivity does not altogether prevent playful, riskladen, unanticipated interchanges. They will still occur. However, their occurrence is divested of any claim of or access to truth. Truth and method become identified. It is precisely this identification that the interpretive disciplines work against. Certainly, the methods of quantitative research can help us better understand this incident and their assertions can make a claim to truth. The interpretive disciplines suggest, however, that there is a "truth" to be had, an understanding to be reached, in the provocative, unmethodical incidents of our lives, a truth which is despoiled and thus left out of consideration by the methodical severances requisite of empirical work.

There is some truth, therefore, in abundance.

An Interpretive Reading of the Instances of Our Lives

> The term "initiation" in the most general sense denotes a body of rites and oral teachings whose purpose is to produce a radical modification of the person to be initiated. Initiation is equivalent to an ontological mutation of the existential condition. The novice emerges from his ordeal a totally different being: he has become *another.* (Eliade, 1975, p. 112)

"I knew when I walked through that door, I would be the teacher. Everything would be different." Perhaps this teacher's words can be read as a retelling of ancient and power-laden narratives of initiation and transformation, "insiders" and "outsiders," thresholds and boundaries, of being turned around in those moments when everything becomes different, of risking selfunderstanding and selfdefinition by moving into a new sphere, of repetition and renewal, of the turns and interplays of responsibility and irresponsibility, of the turns from childhood to adulthood.

Interpretive research begins with a different sense of the given. Rather than beginning with an ideal of clarity, distinctness, and methodological controllability and then rendering the given into the image of this ideal, it begins in the place where we actually start in being granted or given this incident in the first place. It begins (and remains) with the evocative, living familiarity that this tale evokes. The task of interpretation is to bring out this evocative given in all its tangled ambiguity, to follow its evocations and the entrails of sense and significance that are wound up with it. Interpretive research, too, suggests that these striking incidents make a claim on us and open up and reveal something to us about our lives together and what it is that is going on, often unvoiced, in the ever-so commonplace and day-to-day act of becoming a teacher. In this sense, our unanticipated, unmethodical being in the world—this happenstance phone call from a former student and her tale of walking down a hallway and standing by a closed door—can, quite literally in certain instances, make a claim to some sort of truth. Teachers like this story of this student-teacher because it "rings true" to the lives they have lead. That is, they find it all too familiar, now, as new children burst in on them once again. September.

When this teacher phoned me, her words evoked in me a sense of something already familiar that I did not fully understand, but somehow undeniably "knew." I felt suddenly implicated by her words, as if she spoke about something in which I was somehow already involved and which I somehow already understood but had forgotten or not explicitly noticed.

Interpretive inquiry thus begins by being "struck" by something, being "taken" with it—in this particular case, the unanticipated eruption of longfamiliar threads of significance and meaning in the midst of a wholly new situation. "Understanding begins . . . when something addresses us" (Gadamer, 1989, p. 299). This striking incident called for (Heidegger, 1968) understanding. For all its incidentalness, it aroused and generated a new and fresh understanding of something already understood. We got a glimpse of how very strange the familiar act of becoming a teacher is, how ancient and abundant. It opened up something that seemed "over and done with."

It is at this juncture that the true fecundity of the individual cases comes into play.

This teacher's story is not an isolated instance to which the concept of "initiation" is to be applied, as if "initiation" were already understood, already fixed and closed and definitively defined, and this instance were simply a replica or a copy of it. Rather, what this teacher's story speaks of *is* initiation—it belongs to initiation and therefore adds itself to what initiation can now be understood to be. But saying that this instance is initiation requires understanding "is" in the manner of *analogia entis*: in the manner of "analogical being." Its being initiation does not mean that it is identical in all respects to some pregiven and preunderstood fixed set of concepts (this would make the instance superfluous to this alreadyestablished meaning). But neither is this instance simply "nothing except itself," simply different than initiation. Rather, the instance is, so to speak, the generative offspring or "kin" of initiation. It bears a "family resemblance," (Wittgenstein, 1968) to initiation, interweaving with it in ambiguous ways that are not mathematizable into univocal terms that could be simply counted and recounted. For with this teacher's tale, it is not perfectly clear whether we have an unambiguous reoccurrence of some phenomenon, for this tale is not identical to any other instance of initiation (but neither is it simply different). What we have, rather, is exactly what we thought we had: something vaguely familiar, vaguely recognizable, something that bears a "family resemblance" that warrants further investigation.

Thus, the relation between the instance and that to which it seems to bear a "family resemblance" is always in a type of suspense. Interpretive inquiry does not wish to literally and univocally say what this instance finally is. Rather, it wishes to playfully explore what understandings this instance makes possible. There is not a question, then, of whether this instance "really is" an instance of initiation, but whether it is possible to understand it this way and what happens to us if we allow such an understanding. It justifies this approach by harkening back to the fact that it does not take up this instance as an "object" with certain given characteristics. It takes up, rather, as something which evokes and opens up an alreadyfamiliar way of belonging in the world, a possible way of being (i.e., "being an initiate"). This instance must be taken up as a "text" which must be read and reread for the possibilities of understanding that it evokes. Interpretation involves "making the object and all its possibilities fluid." (Gadamer, 1989, p. 367) That is to say, interpretation "make[s] the novel [this particular incident] seem familiar by relating it to prior knowledge, [and] make[s] the familiar [what we have already understood "initiation" to mean] seem strange by viewing it from a new perspective" (Gick & Holyoak, 1983, pp. 1–2). Thus, interpretive work doesn't simply read the instance into a pre-given, closed, and already understood "past," but, with the help of the instance, makes what has been said of initiation in the past readable again by reopening it to new, generative instances. The abundant ancestries of intitiation into teaching become real again, readable again, true again. To the extent that interpretation makes things readable, it is intimately linked up with a sense of literacy.

This particular instance, then, can be understood as bearing forward the phenomenon of initiation, reinvigorating it and thus transforming it, making it fruitful, making it a forbearer, not an "isolated incident." Initiation thus needs the instance to become and remain generative. Put the other way around, without living instances, initiation would no longer be a living feature of our lives; it would no longer be something that concerns us, that provokes us, that entices us. Initiation would no longer be an ongoing, vibrant narrative or story of which our lives and our experiences are an intimate part and to which we belong. It would simply be a lifeless concept or the name of some object which "stands apart" from the life we live, couched in some textbook, an object of indifference.

It is in this sense that the instance is fecund: it keeps the story (of initiation) going, a keeping going which adds to the story and which thereby changes what we will come to understand the already past chapters to have meant. What we have with interpretation is a process akin to having children. The birth of my son transformed me into being a father, and my father into being a grandfather. Paradoxically then, my son regenerated what I have come to understand the course of my life to have already been. He constitutes not simply the addition of one new, isolated element in a chain of events. He constitutes the necessity to rethink the whole chain and each event in it. Thus, we can legitimately speak of the "fecundity of the individual case" insofar as it is allowed to wind its regenerative tendrils out into the "old growth" from which it has erupted—insofar, that is, as we do not begin our work by severing precisely these regenerative tendrils of sense.

We end up, here, with one of the most telling features of interpretive work. Initiation is not a given whose features can be simply listed and to which instances can be simply compared. Rather, the relation between initiation and the instance is an interpretive one. The new instance transforms what initiation is, and initiation helps articulate what the instance means. The instance is thus irreplaceable in its particularity, because that very particularity can have a generative, transformative effect that cannot be and does not need to be "duplicated" because interpretive work allows us and requires us to experience it as duplicitous in the first place. It is this resistance of the particular to simple, helpless subsuming (under "themes" and the like) that helps interpretive inquiry from simply being a reiteration of conservative, traditional understandings. Those shared and contested understandings in which we live are called to account by this instance, made to "speak," change, accommodate, and, so to speak, "learn" through this encounter.

If an instance is simply duplicated in all respects over multiple cases, the duplicates add nothing new to our understanding of what initiation is. They will simply confirm its reoccurrence. More simply put, a quantitative study may provide us with irrefutable assurance that the phenomenon of "initiation" is reported to be widespread among beginning teachers (a valuable piece of information in and of itself). But it can accomplish this without opening up and contesting our understanding of what initiation is and what it means as, a feature of human life in general and of the practice of teaching in particular. It is this—adding to our understanding of our lives—that is of interest to interpretive inquiry.

We have to be careful here. This "adding to the understanding of our lives" is not a matter of establishing once and for all what certain objective features of human experience are and are not. We cannot fully know once and for all what "initiation" is because, so to speak, it *is not* yet. As something which forms a living part of our shared and contested human experience, we don't fully know what initiation is because we don't yet know what will become of it. And we don't know this because it is still coming. To the extent that we do not know what is to be made of initiation in the future—how it might appear and how those appearances might transform our understanding of what it means to be an initiate—our interpretive relation to this particular instance cannot be oriented towards having some "last word" about it as if it were an "object" that is simply present, that simply stands there before us to be univocally named. "It would be a poor hermeneuticist who thought he could have, or had to have, the last word" (Gadamer, 1989, p. 579).

A "good" interpretation, then, is not definitive and final, but is one that keeps open the possibility and the responsibility of returning, for the very next instance might demand of us that we understand anew. Interpretation doesn't keep the possibility of returning open in order to be fair or in order that everyone can have their own interpretation, but because of the nature of the matters at hand—the living human inheritance *is* open. This is deeply pedagogical: the next student teacher will return to the origin of the world and take it up again, here, now, in this way, with this face and flesh. This openness and susceptibility to interpretation—this vague familiarity which could have gone so many ways—is the nature of *data* in interpretive work. It is what is given. What is given is that things are still arriving. What is given is that the given contains, of necessity, an absence, a future.

This is one of the reasons that the language of interpretive inquiry (the language, one might say, of this book) can be, for some, so unfailingly annoying, for it purposely struggles against the tendency of language towards literalism and univocal declarations regarding what is and is not the case. Its language tends, therefore, to be more "playful" and seemingly less serious than other forms of inquiry. It is here that interpretive work can easily fall into puerile excess and narrative and emotional and poetic overload.

Despite its playful appearance, there are serious consequences at issue in the nature of interpretive work and its choice as a "research methodology," especially, I suggest, in education. Failing to keep open the possibility of returning to understand anew is at once demanding of initiation that it no longer be open to the possibility of fecund new instances. It becomes a frankly boring "theme" in a dissertation or in a research study. It renders the abundance of the human inheritance into a manageable and controllable array of fixed (or at least *fixable*) objects that need nothing except themselves and their numerable (quantifiable) "relations" in order to exist. It is equivalent to believing that the new, the young, have nothing to add, nothing to offer, no real work to do. It is equivalent to believing that the human story can go on without renewal and regeneration. It is, in effect, a desire for the death of the child.

We need to ask here the inevitable question: How do I know that this reading I have given this instance is reliable? Hermeneutically conceived, the reading of this instance is "reliable" if the instance begins to become open and lively and vibrant and memorable. That is, as a living part of the human inheritance, a reliable interpretation is one that reads this instance as part of the living human inheritance; that reads it, that is, for its living kinships, its possible bloodlines and family resemblances. How do I know that this is what I'm doing when I'm sitting here, trying to write and think about this event? How do I know I'm not just delusional, spooked by Descartes demons or black biles?

Well, I don't know all by myself or in advance of the reading and the writing itself. I cannot separate out in advance which features of my reading reveal nothing more than idiosyncrasies of my individual experiences and which features reveal something more—not the teacher's text "in itself," but the binding arcs of meaning in which I, that teacher, and the text belong together—something about the world of teaching, this living thread of the human inheritance. I'm not interested in this instance "in itself," but insofar as I am a teacher and a student of teaching itself. This is the part of the human inheritance in the midst of which this instance struck me in the first place, and that part of that inheritance out into which this interpretation proceeds. It is not an "absolute" interpretation. I cannot separate out in advance and by some pre-given method how the work of Mircea Eliade I read as an undergraduate student as an undergraduate in religious studies at McMaster University, or Johan Huizinga's texts on play, or my own life experiences, will end up having a bearing on my reading of this instance. "This separation must take place in the process of understanding itself" (Gadamer, 1989, p. 296). I can only find out about the revelations and distortions that my life brings to the images haunting that phone call from a student teacher by *working such matters out.* And I have to work these matters out *in public*—in writing, in talking to colleagues, and therefore in letting the distortions of my subjectivity work themselves out into a territory that can comfort. Coming to understand what is true of teaching in the appeal of this instance, what is generous and possible, is only after the fact.

Interpretation thus becomes a movement of shaping and making something of this instance and its human topographies. I have to let my preunderstandings and prejudices and presumptions fully engage this text; I must let them be brought fully into play and therefore risk that they might be changed, embarrassed, even humiliated, in confronting what this teacher's text has to say (Gadamer, 1989, p.299). I cannot have access to the blind spots all by myself and via an anonymous methodology.

Put more sharply and positively, for interpretation to engage, the text and I must be allowed to "play." And in such play, an unavoidable paradox of interpretive work comes to light. The fact that I happened to have read and remembered Mircea Eliade's work on initiation, the fact that I happened to have been called by this teacher and to have been struck by what she saidall of these "happenstances" made possible the interpretation that will then ensue (Weinsheimer, 1987, pp. 7–8). The interpretation is thus unavoidably linked to me. It is not something produced by a method that anyone could wield. However—and here is the paradox—what the interpretation is henceforth *about* is not me and my past experiences, but that *of which* I have had certain (however limited and skewed) experiences: initiation. In hearing from this student teacher, I am granted the occasion to work through those limitations all over again, hopefully then setting right or renewed what I brought with me to this event. Even though interpretive work is not possible without a living connection to its topic, it is *the topic*, not *the fact of a living connection* that is the center of interpretive work.

The same can be said of the reader of an interpretive study. If the reader has no living connection to or experience of something like the phenomenon of initiation, the study will be rather meaningless, for it will not address something to which the reader bears any "family resemblance." Again, this is not a matter of readers sharing in some univocal "universal(s)" or "themes" or "old chestnuts" regarding human experience. It is a matter of kinship, and kinships are not housed under universals.

Producing a "reliable" interpretive reading of this instance—"reliable" now meaning one in which those reading the interpretation find the exploration of the topic/topography of teaching find some insight and comfort and thoughtfulness about their lives—requires living with this instance for a period of time in order to learn its ways: turning it over and over, telling and retelling it, finding traces of it over and over again in what you read, seeing the nod of heads and faint smiles when it is used as an example in a class, scouring the references colleagues suggest, searching my own livedexperience for analogues of experience, asking friends if they have experienced anything like this before, testing and retesting different ways of speaking and writing about it to see if these different ways help engage and address possible readers of the work to follow. There is, as mentioned above, a creative movement of shaping and forming something in accordance with the ancient arts of writing (in particular, but, as we have all witnessed, this centrality of writing is being overwhelmed). It takes time to dwell with such an incident and allow the slow emergence of the rich contexts of familiarity in which it fits. I can learn the ways of this instance only by taking the time to experience where it "goes," and thereby seeing to what territories and terrains it belongs. This instance is thus not static but rather "leads" somewhere. Time is needed, blind alleys and lots of discarded work is unavoidable, but this time, this temporality, in an important sense, belongs to the instance itself. In spite of my deadlines and desires, very often insight and articulation "takes its own sweet time." Only over this unmethodical course of time does the full fecundity of the individual case come forward. They need to be worried over, mulled, meditated upon, thought about, forgotten and remembered. As a monk once said, you know something is beautiful if, because of your attention and devotion to it, it begins to glow.

And, some might say unfortunately, "there is no art or technique of happening onto things. There is no method of stumbling" (Weinsheimer, 1987, p. 7). This incident, which gave rise to so much, just happened. For a reliable reading to occur, then, it would never be enough to simply say what I think it means and leave it at that. But neither is it enough to simply turn it back to the "respondent" and ask what she intended it to mean, or whether she intended to mean something about "initiation" or "responsibility" or "becoming an adult" and the like, as if calling out to the author might save us the task of interpreting the text. The author's (respondent's) reading of her own story is not the lynchpin of hermeneutic work (as it might be for some forms of "teacher narrative" now gaining ascendancy in educational inquiry), as if the topic at hand is the subjectivity of the one traversing the topic. Rather, "we are moving in a dimension of meaning that is intelligible in itself and as such offers no reason for going back to the subjectivity of the author" (Gadamer, 1989, p. 292). The living, generative, abundant and even contradictory meaning(s) of the text are at the center, and the game of interpretation is afoot *for us all* in the face of this or any other text. This is the most profound message of interpretive work, whatever its topic: we find ourselves here, engaged in this world of teaching trying to make something of the experiences that happen to us, talking to each other, finding, one hopes, some solace and meaning in such conversations:

> Language is by itself the game of interpretation that we all are engaged in every day. In this game nobody is above and before all the others; everybody is at the center, [everybody] is "it" in this game ["The center is everywhere" (Nishitani 1982, p. 146)]. Thus it is always his turn to be interpreting. This process of interpretation takes place whenever we "understand." (Gadamer, 1977, p. 32)

Interestingly enough, this does not mean that the connection to the author is severed. That student teacher of mine hasn't disappeared in her uniqueness and individuality. It means, rather, that, in the face of this abundant trace line in the world—this "text" she produced—the author is one of us and not in some elite, "authoritative" position. Certainly, the author is in an elite position regarding the experiences she underwent, just as each of us is authoritative regarding what we think and experience and feel. However, once erupted into a text, none of us holds some authoritative sway over what those experiences and thought might mean, here, in this *world* of teaching. In fact, in this particular case, this new teacher was relieved to discover that her experiences were not just "hers," not just, as she put it "inside my head." She was relieved to find that what she was going through meant something to those with whom she spoke. The expression of her experience into a text thus relieved her of the burden of isolation. She discovered that her experience linked up with longstanding characteristics of human experience and articulation. She discovered that this experience had a character and vitality over and above the fact that she had undergone this experience and the fact that it had been powerful for her. This discovery, as mentioned above, puts a peculiar spin on the notion of "literacy." Decoding, counting, and recounting the surface signs (of texts, of experiences) is not especially adequate to becoming experienced in the world, knowledgeable in its ways. Rather, as we unearth the signs of life crackling underneath the surfaces, "we... become more literate [and] we may become less literal, [less] stuck in the case without a vision of its soul" (Hillman 1983, p. 28). Simply "telling my story" can unintentionally breed a type of literalism/illiteracy by disallowing "a vision of its soul." Such a "vision" would help liberate my story from being just mine (which bears a frightening resemblance to the severances and isolations requisite of objectivity). This is why language plays such a predominant role in interpretive work, for, by its very nature, it serves to raise up the instances of our lives out of the burden of their specificity (Gadamer, 1989; Smith, 1999). It allows us to escape "the compulsive fascination with one's own case history" (Hillman, 1983, p. 7). It makes it possible to see what one is going through as intimately wound up in human life as a whole, a generative "process that is continually internalizing and externalizing, gaining insight and losing it, deliteralizing and reliteralizing" (Hillman, 1983, p. 27). It thus allows us to read our individual lives as fully participant in the shared and contested, generative work of humanity as a whole. Thus, in interpretive work, the author's reading is but one voice among many, perhaps an especially unmindful and unattentive one, perhaps the very one best suited to read this text well. Sorting out this eventuality, as with so much of interpretive work, "depends." Interpretively understanding this teacher's text, then, is not a matter of unearthing her experiences, but of "clarifying this miracle of understanding, which is not a mysterious communion of souls, but sharing in a common meaning" (Gadamer, 1989, p. 292). "What emerges," in opening up a conversation with this instance "is neither mine nor yours" (p. 331) but is that "in which" we dwell together—the contours of that original familiarity and kinship that made this instance so telling in the first place.

"Understanding is the expression of the affinity of the one who understands to the one whom he understands and to that which he understands" (Gadamer, 1983, p. 48). None of us necessarily knows all by ourselves the full contours of the story each of us is living out, and none of us knows, except in the grimmest of ways, how it will turn out. This is why dialogue and conversation figure so predominantly in interpretive work, as contrasted with the "monologue" of scientific discourse (Habermas, 1972), suitable as such a monologue is to the univocal character of "isolated incidents" and the correlative univocity of the methods deployed by a "knowing subject." We know full well that we are not done with this topic, that we could have proceeded differently, that, had this former student-teacher's words been a different case, it may have required little more than consolation and encouragement, and that the meaningfulness of the conversational text of encouragement has its own ways and means of unfolding. We know something we've always known: this *Spiel* about initiation and about how to do hermeneutics is not for everyone, not a "good" interpretation in some universal sense. It won't last and is not everywhere welcome and not does not (*can*not, by the very nature of the matters at hand) preclude different interpretations from others and in the future. It is, once again, a *living* text, a fecund case.

One problem in doing interpretive work should be clear by now: knowing when to stop in the spinning out of implications of meaning. There are widespread possibilities embedded in this incident and there is no surefire method for guaranteeing that you haven't gone too far and stretched the incident out of all proportion. For example, when we begin to picture this incident as a retelling of the tale of initiation and then couple it with an innocent comment that I have heard from several principals regarding studentteachers and beginning teachers, sparks begin to fly: "I like having studentteachers in my school because the profession constantly needs new blood." The connection of "blood" with the rite of the initiation of the new ones into the profession (which literally means "those who take to vows," yet another feature of initiation rituals) becomes even more telling when we recall that rites of passage and initiation tend to take place in the spring—the time of Easter (itself a sacrificial blood ritual involving the opening of barriers and allowing the ones outside to come in), of graduation, as well as the time when interviews are often done by school boards seeking "new blood." At the tail end of this sequence, we may have gotten rather "carried away," but the implications are not meaningless. In spite of the fact that they can easily become too "wild," they are not altogether "unfitting." The "analogical kinships" of meaning still seem to pertain. The "family resemblances" persist despite being somewhat strained.

The problem of interpretive research, then, is one of withholding the interpretive impulse and developing a sense of proportion and, for me, housing this in the discipline of writing. Again, this is not a method that can be handed over (it is almost impossible to answer a question like "How do you do hermeneutics?"), but is a practice. It is a practice in a strong sense precisely because the incident under consideration and the concrete context of speaking about it (with this beginning teacher in the midst of her anxiety, in casual conversation with a friend, as a topic in a class, as a subject for an academic paper, etc.) will have something to say about what a "good" sense of proportion might be in this case or that. One cannot say, therefore, in general and ahead of time, what the practice of interpretation is like, as if it were a set of rules that needed to be simply applied to an incident independent of the contribution that incident might have regarding what needs to be said (Smith 1999). This point, again, bespeaks "the fecundity of the individual case" in the pursuit of understanding.

Concluding Remarks: On Interpretation, Pedagogy, and Hermes as Trickster and Thief

> Hermes is cunning, and occasionally violent: a trickster, a robber. So it is not surprising that he is also the patron of interpreters. (Kermode 1979, 1)

> When Hermes is at work one feels that one's story has been stolen and turned into something else. The [person] tells his tale, and suddenly its plot has been transformed. He resists, as one would try to stop a thief: "this is not what I meant at all, not at all." But too late. Hermes has caught the tale, turned its feet around, made black into white, given it wings. And the tale is gone from the upper world historical nexus in which it had begun and been subverted into an underground meaning. (Hillman 1982, p. 31)

> There is one further aspect of Hermes that may be worth noting, namely his impudence. He once played a trick on the most venerated Greek deity, Apollo, inciting him to great rage. Modern students of hermeneutics should be mindful that their interpretations could lead them into trouble with the authorities. (Smith, 1999c, p. 27)

It is admittedly rather frightening and disorienting to discover that the incidental story we might tell can have implications of sense that we did not anticipate and cannot fully control. We all know, and have all suffered in our own ways, how this has often meant that others have spoken in our stead and "for our own good" and how, so often as well, someone else might be able to read my own experiences back to me in ways I could have never imagined and that have saved my life.

To say that Hermes is a trickster and a thief is not to say that the one doing the interpretation is Hermes and the teacher I spoke with is the sole victim of the theft of meaning and the subsequent transformations of understanding that ensue. Rather, the playful tricks and turns happened to me as much as to her. It is not as if I could, in the inquiry I pursued, say anything I wanted or do anything I wished. I, too, was "subject" to Hermes's seeming whims, having things collapse without warning, gaining insights at the worst of times and losing them before I could catch them, muttering quite often while writing or rereading what I thought was so clear "'this is not what I meant at all, not at all.' But too late."

Pursuing interpretive inquiry is a potentially painful process, because it is not produced of a method which (ideally) will keep everything under control by severing all the tendrils of sense that can pull you in so many different, often incompatible ways. There is a risk involved in such work, a risk of "selfloss" (Gadamer, 1977, p. 51) and the recovery of a sense of oneself that is different (and not necessarily "better" or easier to live with) than the one with which we begin such inquiries. Its risk is increasing susceptibility to the world, not increasing managerial control.

There is a straightforward sense in which interpretive work is pedagogic: it is concerned with the regenerative and enlivening relationship between the young and the old. It will not abandon the new to some empirical isolation, but will always try to find its kinship there. It is therefore disruptive of fossilized sedimentations of sense, desiring to open them up and allow "the new" to erupt and thus allowing the old and already established and familiar to regenerate and renew itself and find its life again. It is oriented, thus, to "furtherance" (Gadamer, 1989, p. xxiv)—that is, reading what seem like deadened and deadening certainties for their liveliness, their life, their ongoing-ness.

But there is a different sense in which interpretive inquiry is pedagogic. The process of interpretation is not the simple accumulation of new objective information. It is, rather, the transformation of selfunderstanding. Living with this instance and following its ways and engaging my own life and the lives of others in an attempt to understand it has changed who I am and what I understand myself to be. New possibilities of selfunderstanding have opened up; old ones have been renewed and transformed and rejected. Some other matters have fallen from memory and into a darkness whose measure is hard to know. This is what understanding is like as a human endeavor. We try things, we fail, we succeed; things last for a time, become new again or fade, fit here and not there, will suffice now but maybe not later. What I understand myself, my work and the lives of my students to be have changed, for better or worse. And, of course, all these understandings cannot now be trumpeted as final, not because of a failure to "research" enough or write enough, but *because of the nature of the matters at hand.* The world *is* interpretable. It continues to arise and fall.

These will have to work themselves out over the course of my life and the lives of those I engage. Moreover, writing of this incident is not a matter of passing on information to a reader, but of evoking or educing a different selfunderstanding in the reader. The goal of interpretive work is not to pass on objective information to readers, but to evoke in readers a sense of the odd abundance in which we live and which we have inherited. Following the entrails of sense that this incident regenerated means, in however small a way, understanding who we are differently, more deeply, more richly. Unlike some work in educational inquiry which begins with a "knowing subject" that is fully in possession of itself ("itself' being defined as the methods it can deploy), interpretive work inevitably begins with a living subject in a living dialogue with the life that surrounds us. "To reach an understanding is not merely a matter of putting oneself forward and successfully asserting one's own point of view, but being transformed into a communion in which we do not remain what we were" (Gadamer, 1989, p. 379). In such a case, interpretive work is profoundly pedagogic, for:

> In the last analysis, all understanding is selfunderstanding, but not in the sense of a preliminary selfpossession or of one finally and definitively achieved. For selfunderstanding only realizes itself in the understanding of a subject matter and does not have the character of a free selfrealization. The self that we are does not possess itself; one could say that it "happens." (Gadamer, 1977, p. 55)

Afterword

One more playful turn. "Understanding is an adventure and, like any other adventure, it always involves some risk" (Gadamer, 1983, pp. 109–110). Involvement in interpretive inquiry runs the risk of getting quite lost in the flurries of sense that make up our lives. It faces, too, the dangerous insight that, so to speak, "getting somewhere" in understanding one's life is never finished—understanding "always must be renewed in the effort of our living" (pp. 110–111) and this need for renewal is not an accident that we can fix, but a situation that we must learn to live with well.

In the end, the notion of "initiation" is of especial interest to hermeneutics. Hermes, as mentioned above, was a trickster and a thief. He was also a messenger, a "gobetween." Initiation has to do with the rites of passage and with transformations in how we understand ourselves, and this is precisely the interest of hermeneutics. Hermes is identified with borders, with boundaries and with keeping open the gates between one realm and another: "to hear the messages in whatever is said. This is the hermeneutic ear that listens—through, a consciousness of the borders, as Hermes was worshipped at borders. Every wall and every weave presents its opening.

"Everything is porous" (Hillman, 2013, p. 96).

PREAMBLE 3

"The Deeply Experiential Ecology of 'Just This'"

> A friend of my son came to visit recently [now over 25 years ago], and I told him about the huge pond in our neighbour's field. The spring runoff had created a slough about eight feet deep. After discussing that it would be over his head if he fell in, over my son's head, and even over *my* head, he asked, "If a hundred year old man fell in it, would it be over *his* head too?"
>
> I answered, "yes, it's *that* deep."
>
> I told this tale to a mathematics curriculum colleague at the University of Calgary and got the response: "Isn't it cute when children get things mixed up?" (Jardine, 1992, p. 306)

> In walking down the stairs, the two year-old child's life is already pacing out mathematics in the rhythms of his steps, in the cadences of his breath, and in the recurring patterns of his mother's laughter (Jardine, 1994, p. 118)

> Resistance to "unambiguous designation" (Gadamer, 1989, p. 434) is precisely a sign of the resilience and life of a living system. (Jardine, 1994, p. 112)

These passages hark back to the streams of analogical and metaphorical language that have an unbounded character, but that form firm and flexible fabrics of dependent co-arising, empty of self-existence, but full, at

In Praise of Radiant Beings, pages 43–46

once, of relations—ancestral and inherited, at work in our time in visible and invisible ways, and also, of course, yet to be what they will become. This is true of the curriculum as inherited by schools. In schools, it is not as if things we are entrusted to teach and learn are fixed and given and then we simply have to abide the arrival of children not yet versed in such fixities. Instead, such arrivals open up what seems to have been closed, enliven what seemed dead and finished, helps us remember what is forgotten underneath the surface: "whether life itself has a chance or whether the surface is all there is." (Smith, 1999a, p. 139). Such characteristics—opening what seemed closed, enlivening what seemed deadened and passed, remembering what has been forgotten—are the characteristics of hermeneutic truth conceived as *aletheia* (Moules, 2015, Jardine, 2012e, p. 122).

Again, this sounds arcane, but it is manifest in those often pitiful worksheets we give children in schools, where "addition questions" are written in ways that no sane mathematician would every write them, such as "5 + 3 = __." A sensible mathematician would always do this: "5 + 3 = X" (see Jardine with Friesen, 1997). Leaving out the "X" turns "5 + 3 =" into a *question to be answered* rather than an equation whose equitability means that nothing *needs to be done*, but a whole array of things now *can be done*. The absence of "X" also makes everything immobile and shuts down all the roiling possibilities that swirl around "5 + 3 = X" (e.g., 5 = X – 3, one of an infinity of possibilities clustering around "5 + 3 = X" and holding it safe and secure in an environment of kin and kind). Putting "5 = X – 3" alongside "5 + 3 = X" releases it (and that which it is now alongside) from its sense of bound and enclosure. Each, shall we say, frees the other from its apparent fixity and self-enclosed, because each, shall we say, *is* that other. And, of course:

> If someone were to draw a sharp boundary I could not acknowledge it as the one that I too always wanted to draw, or had drawn in my mind. For I did not want to draw one at all. His concept can then be said to be not *the same* as mine, but akin to it. The kinship is just as undeniable as the difference. (Wittgenstein, 1968, p. 36)

Thus:

> We *can* draw a boundary for [any idea, image, thing, concept, self]: "but I can also use [them] so that the extension of the concept is *not* closed by a frontier" (Wittgenstein, 1968, pp. 32–33) I can *draw* boundaries or frontiers in such matters, but I cannot *give* such matters a boundary. (Jardine, 1992, pp. 292–293)

A whole stream of my later work explores how, when we are forgetful of this "draw but cannot give," such setting up of frontiers as if we can give them constitutes, in effect, pedagogy as an act of war [see Jardine, 2004, 2005a, 2008, Jardine & Naqvi, 2008, Jardine, Naqvi, Jardine & Zaidi, 2010, Jardine, 2012f), a "rage for order" (Jardine, 1992a).

Believing that we can give boundaries—believing, therefore, that things *have* boundaries and therefore *are* separately self-existent—is another way of describing a central thought in Buddhist philosophy and practice: reification. Of course, a fish is a fish, but if you reach into the aquarium and pull it out and point and say, "this is a fish," something of it *being* water (not just being "in" water) is manifest. We can and should and must make these distinctions between fishes and water, and such distinctions are sensible, practical, and understandable. However, *when we forget what we have done* and become attached to the *outcomes* of our doings, trouble arises, suffering ensues, because our doings have been concealed and the "nature" of things (as dependently co-arising) becomes confused with an outcome of our reifying, boundary setting actions.

As an aside, for back-reference to the idea of acts of war, see Samuel Huntington's "hardened identity" (2003 p. 266) as an *outcome* of hostility/fear leading to bounded-ness/safety and the protection of what is now bounded leading to increased hostility, leading to every increasingly vigilant and hostile bounded-ness, leading to an increase in the sense of threat, leading to increased vigilance, now blameable on those others who are "out of bounds." Parallel this with the same wheel in Tsong-kha-pa's [2000, p. 210] insistence on linking reification with hostility, both as its cause and its effect, and the subsequent attachment to such bounded-ness that forgets (the "Lethe"-inverse of *aletheia*) what it has done in reifying, clings to what it has bounded, leading to hostility, suffering and increased surveillance, and so on.

I suppose this isn't much of an aside at all. Reification conceals a truth about things, about our inter-being. This is why, in the chapter that follows, I asked my student-teachers about those imagined worksheets we found, each one showing "5 + 3 = 8." Given the worksheet and its design and its purpose, "8" is "the right answer," and that is not in dispute. "8" also unintentionally conceals the multifarious sufferings of its arrival, where, often, each child's path is different than the others, but yet still akin. "8" does not arrive as the solution to this kinship, because this kinship doesn't need solving. And it is too easy to imagine, in schools, all the hostility and heat that arises over getting it right which blinds, forgets, deadens, covers up, the myriad of that getting, that dependent co-arising.

"The right answer" conceals. And to the extent that it does, those student teachers are doomed to skate the panic-inducing surface of, so to speak, getting-it-rightness. When I pointed out that myriad to them, it was both profoundly obvious, but also vertiginous, because the firmness of "8" began to slip and slide out into fields of relations and overlapping paths of venture. It *feels* like chaos at first simply because of how accustomed we have become to reification, but there is nothing chaotic here. It is, instead, a myriad of living relations in a living field. It takes practice to transform what is at first vertigo into an often-pleasurable experience of spaciousness and interrelatedness.

The myriad ways in which "8" may have arrived, thus, is a gathering of kin, of ever-new relations, a gathering that does not conceal but opens:

> Those very mundane topics listed so dully in the curriculum guide thus undergo an "increase in being" Gadamer (1989, p. 40), if we treat them properly. If we treat them properly, as living features of a convivial world, nothing is quite yet what it will be. Those topics undergo such an increase because they "are not" yet fully themselves because they *are* open to a future that has yet to arrive where they will be taken up anew, beyond our wanting and doing. "A" is thus never quite equal to itself [because its self *is* all of its relations, including the unanticipated arrivals of next year's Grade Two class exploring addition]. This defines their *living character.* (Jardine, 2012e, p. 112).

And each new arrival, every sentient being, including those unforeseen, becomes exquisite, irreplaceable in this myriad, far beyond only human sentience, all the way to "the lure that pulls flowerheads to face the sun"(see Jardine 2006a, p. 270, Pinar 2006). Not one arrival is just "one more of the same," because even if that new arrival is fully and utterly recognizable, there it is again, portending recurrence, memory, and revivification of what seemed done. Each arrival makes "the same" different than it might have been without this stubborn particular, because "the same" *is* the fabric of relatedness. Grace, indeed.

Again, there is great vertigo experienced when such matters open up, and you have to get used to it, you have to practice. Otherwise, it can lead to panic. Panic can lead to feeling unsafe, to entrenchment and bounded-ness, reification. Thus, to recite a passage from the Introduction: "The more you practice these things, the more accustomed your mind will become to them, and the easier it will be to practice what you had initially found difficult to learn." (Tsong-kha-pa, 2000, pp. 185–186).

My own composure is thus at issue here. More on this below.

3

"The Stubborn Particulars of Grace" (1995)

Prelude

Canadian poet Bronwen Wallace entitled her third collection of poems *The Stubborn Particulars of Grace* (1987). Reference to this title comes up in a poem called "Particulars" which is full of the meticulous details of memory and reverie ("those Sundays at my grandmother's table") and which shows the way that our lives are always lived right here, in the face of these stubborn particulars. Wallace's work gains its deep resonances, its sense of wholeness, not through nebulous talk of grand things, but because it consistently "argue[s] the stubborn argument of the particular, right now, in the midst of things, *this* and *this*" (p. 111).

This stubborn argument of the particular is reminiscent of a fragment of William Carlos Williams' (1991, p. 224) "Spring and All" (written in 1923):

> So much depends upon the red wheel barrow glazed with rain water beside the white chickens.

Here, an ordinarily insignificant object is portrayed with such spacious clarity that the insight becomes unavoidable: somehow, *everything* depends

---

In Praise of Radiant Beings, pages 47–57

upon this red wheelbarrow. Somehow, from out a mindfulness to "*this* and *this*," the particular object, in its very particularity, becomes like a sacred place where the whole Earth comes to nestle in relations of deep interdependency.

This is one of the secrets of ecological mindfulness. To understand what is right in front of us in an ecologically sane, integrated way is to somehow see this particular thing *in place*, located in a patterned nest of interdependencies without which it would not be what it is. Differently put, "understanding 'the whole'" involves paying attention to *this* "in its wholeness." This rootedness in the particular is what helps prevent ecology from becoming woozy and amorphous—a disembodied idea that misses the particularities in the flit of *this* ruby-crowned kinglet pair in the lower pine branches and how this movement is so fitting here, in the coming arch of spring in the Rocky Mountain foothills.

Math Facts on a Teddy Bear's Tummy

During practicum supervision in Grade 1 classroom over the past year, I witnessed again a common sight. The children are in the middle of a "bear theme." In order to integrate with this theme and in order to make the work "more fun for the kids" (as one teacher put it), mathematics addition facts are printed on the stomach of a cut out line drawing of a teddy bear.

Such "activities"—where the mathematics questions are answered and the bears are colored in and posted on the wall of the classroom—are certainly carried out with the best of intentions. Blaming teachers for engaging their children in such trite activities in the name of "curriculum integration" belies the fact that we are *all* "witnessing the inevitable outcome of a logic [of fragmentation, severance and dis-integration] that is already centuries old and that is being played out in our own lifetime" (Berman, 1983, p. 23). More strongly put, we are all, however unwittingly, *living out this logic.* Teachers, children, administrators, University academics—we have all, in our own ways, been victimized by the uprootedness and "unsettling" (Berry, 1986) caused by this logic. Such classroom activities should therefore not be taken up as occasions for blame, but as interpretive opportunities that give us all ways to address how we might make our pedagogical conduct more integrated and whole.

What we see occurring with these math facts on a teddy bear's tummy is what could be called an "urban sprawl" version of integration. To integrate one subject area with another, one begins with the clear, unambiguous, univocal, literal surfaces features of a particular activity (for example,

"5 + 3 = __" as a so-called "math fact") and moves laterally, adding more and more (clear, unambiguous, univocal, literal surface feature) activities from different subject areas. We can hear in teacher's talk such as "I wanted to make the math stuff more fun for the children by linking it up to things they were already doing" the understandable desire to rescue "5 + 3 = __" from its flatness and isolation. Understood and presented merely as a "math fact," it is rather severe, so we find ways to remedy this malady by "dressing it up" through combining it with cut out line drawings of bears (which the children supposedly find cute and interesting).

The problem, however, is that such integration (if one could call it that) works precisely because it operates with the thinnest veneer of each area. Curricular integration becomes akin to formulations of post-modernism which so well describe the mood of so many elementary schools: a hyperactive play of surfaces juxtaposed at the whim of "the subject" (whether teacher or child), juxtaposable with facile ease precisely because we are dealing with uprooted surfaces which offer no real resistance and demand no real work. Integration in such a post-modern milieu becomes formulated as little more than surface co-presence or co-occurrence, bereft of any fleshy, experiential immediacy.

If we begin with a surface understanding of "5 + 3 = __" our efforts at integration can easily fall prey to the bizarre cultural-capitalist equation of the achievement of wholeness with the consumptive accumulation of "more." One makes "5 + 3 = __" (or any other curricular fragment) "whole," not by sticking with it, deepening it, opening up its "necessities and mysteries" (Berry, 1983, p. vii) but by adding more and more activities to it—surrounding and crowding it with other equally isolated, unopened particulars but, we might say, never "housing" it. In this way, to re-formulate Wendell Berry's (1986, p. 26) critique of the motto of the Sierra Club, our interest in "math facts" become *scenic*, something to "do," like, say, "doing" the Grand Canyon. Mathematics becomes akin to a tourist attraction, something to look at but never enter into, open up and learn to live with well. And we, in turn, become akin to curricular tourists, ready to be momentarily entertained and amused. However, since we just see the thin, tarted-up, presentable surface of things, we, along with our children, become equally subject to boredom, frustration and eventual violence. Given what is presented to us, it is little wonder that our attention is fleeting.

There is an odd logic at work here. Since, as a math fact, "5 + 3 = __" affords only the briefest consideration, what we begin to witness is the attempt to attain integration, not simply through the *accumulation of thin co-present surfaces*, but through the *acceleration of such accumulation*. One need think only of the typical tempo of early elementary school classrooms. What appears on the surface as vigor and enthusiasm is also readable as a type of hysteria and panic. Given that "5 + 3 = __" is understood to be an isolated curricular fragment (i.e., it is "un-whole"), there is no time to deepen it and dwell on it, to slow it down and open it up, because there is simply so much else to get done and so little time. As Wendell Berry suggests, for this way of being in the world of the classroom, "time is always running out" (1983, p. 76). As such, we can witness in so many classrooms (and, in fact, in so much of contemporary life) an ever-accelerating "onslaught" (Arendt, 1969) of ever-new activities and the odd equation of some sort of fulfillment with becoming caught up in such frenetic consumption. Many teachers and children are thereby condemned to constantly striving to "keep up" and to taking on the *failure* to keep up as a personal/pathological problem involving lack of effort or lack of will. Talk of slowing things down, dwelling over something and deepening our experience of it begins to sound vaguely quaint and antiquated.

An urban sprawl version of curriculum integration thus becomes convoluted with both a metaphysical and an eschatological belief. First, it is premised on the metaphysical belief that each curricular fragment (e.g., "5 + 3 = __") is what it is independently of everything else, independently of any sustaining relations. In this view, wholeness cannot be a matter of meditating on how "the whole" of our course might be refracted through *this* fragment or *this,* since it is precisely such refraction that is *denied* by this metaphysical assumption of severance and fragmentation. Second, and following from this metaphysical assumption, an urban sprawl version of curriculum integration suggests that wholeness and integrity is always yet-to-arrive. Education thus gets caught up in a type of eschatological anticipation—"an occult yearning for the future" (Berry, 1986) when integrity and health and wholeness might finally be achieved through the final accumulation of all the "pieces of the picture."

Reflections on a Class in Early Childhood Education: Placing "5 + 3 = 8" Back Into All Its Relations

In a recent Early Childhood Education "methods" course, we considered the following examples of Grade One children's "math facts" work:

1. 5 + 3 = 8
2. 5 + 3 = 8
3. 5 + 3 = 8

It was proposed that we had found these three samples in the files of three different children who have just entered our classroom. The following questions were posed: What do we now know about these children, these samples? What do they mean? What do they show? As expected, the answer, for the most part, was "very little." One student ventured, "These children know how to add."

Through a combination of considerations of Jean Piaget's notion of operations (1952), working ourselves with manipulative materials, and especially, frequent visits to a wonderful Grades 1–4 multiage classroom, what slowly became visible underneath the surface-presentation of "these children know how to add" was a roiling nest of multiple operations, multiple voices: "threads interweaving and crisscrossing" (Wittgenstein, 1968, p. 32). Rather than reading each "5 + 3 = 8" pathologically, as an isolated fact, we slowly became able to read each as a sign pointing beyond its isolation to a whole world of implicate relations.

One child holds five and counts on. A second counts them all out, showing us not only his own ways of working in mathematics, but showing us also that the child who can hold five is holding not just a "math fact" but a crystallized and stabilized nest of operations that this second child still needs to concretely re-embody and re-enact. Differently put, "5" is itself a doing full of under worlds of relations and connections and threads (for example, the accomplishment and stability of 1-1 correspondence and ordinal numerical sequences, the infinite implicate iterations of relations of "4 + 1," "3 + 2," "12–7," the square root of 25 and so on) *some of which* this child who holds five understands, some not, but all of which surrounds and houses and makes understandable and locatable his work, his efforts and his experiences. This child's work lives in these implicate relations and is deeply meaningful and sustainable only *within* them (and this in spite of the fact that some of these relations are, from the point of view of the child's own experiences, "beyond him" at this juncture: this is a profound and difficult ecological point—our lives and actions are sustained in part by what is beyond us, beyond what we know, experience or construct). Another child "just knows the answer" but cannot articulate the operations she performs. Another gets caught up in such articulations and takes on the task of filling out all the permutations of operations embedded in the question at hand, verging, for a moment, near calculus and the formulation of functionally defined sets.

What occurred here was a wonderful but also rather disorienting phenomenon for many student teachers in this class. They began to see that being stuck in the present tense with the three surface samples and then rushing to accumulate more and more in order to understand "the whole child," (or in order to "cover the whole curriculum") was somehow potentially misguided and unhealthy, for it skitters over the deeply experiential "ecology" of *just this*. "Underneath" the surface of each stubborn particular was an almost overwhelming richness, diversity—hitherto unnoticed communities of relations. But more than this, once opened up, we could begin to see how each stubborn particular—*this* child's work and *this* child's work—becomes reflected and refracted through all the other stubborn particulars, giving all the others shape and place and sense. Differently put, once *this* "5 + 3 = 8" becomes interpretable, it is no longer an isolated given which simply is what it is independently of everything else, like the unread work samples found in the children's files. It becomes "readable" as a multivocal sign that portends a whole nest of sustaining relations that are always already wholly at work and without which this stubborn particular would not be what it is. Each stubborn particular thus becomes placed within a nest of possibilities that house and sustain it. It becomes, in this deeply ecological sense, whole, through the slow, meticulous, disciplined working out of its relations.

Here we have a wonderful inversion of the metaphysical assumption of the urban sprawl version of curriculum integration. Each curricular fragment is what it is only in relation to the "whole," a whole now readable in and through the stubborn particulars of our lives.

It is important to add that this does not mean that every child should be relentlessly inundated with relations, possibilities and articulations at every turn. This would simply turn our interpretive efforts into another version of urban sprawl that acts irrespective of where we are and what particular relations are at work "*here* and *here*." This is the profound sense in which the particular is "stubborn": there is no way that we can replace the exquisiteness of this particular (child's work, for example). *This* work—*this* "5 + 3 = 8"—occurs at an irreplaceable intersection between the world of mathematics, this child's life and breath and attention and experience, the life and relations of the classroom, the hopes and actions and experience of the teacher, the working out of our curriculum and our culture in and through the institutions of schooling, and so on. Differently put, *this* work—the delicacies of this child's slow counting out of "5"—is the "center" of "the whole" of these relations. It is, in its own way, "a sacred place where the whole of the Earth comes to rest in relations of deep interdependency."

However (and this cannot be overemphasized, given our culture's tendency to inflate "child-centredness" to ecologically disastrous proportions) this work is, at the very same time, peripheral to (yet still housing of) the work of this next child and this. This stubborn paradox is at the core of curriculum integration. On the one hand, "the universe is a fabric of interdependent events in which *none* is the fundamental entity" (Hanh, 1986, p. 70): curriculum integration is not child-centered or teacher-centered or subject-matter centered, but rather gives up the fundamentalism that underwrites such centration in favor of a *world* of relations. And yet, at the same time:

> *The centre is [also] everywhere.* Each and every thing becomes the centre of all things and, in that sense, becomes an absolute centre. This is the absolute uniqueness of things, their [stubborn] reality. (Nishitani, 1982, p. 146)

The arrival of each new child in one's class, the arrival of each new piece of work is thus potentially fecund. Each stubborn particular carries the potential of re-opening and thus re-vitalizing what I have heretofore understood the whole web of delicacies surrounding "5 + 3 = __" to mean. This particular child always counts by twos and seems stuck there in a loop. She disassembles "5" and "3," re-sorts them and adds them two by two by two by two by setting out pairs of small wooden blocks in rows in front of her. This child brings a uniqueness and individuality and irreplaceability to this activity. But her actions are not just that. Her work cannot simply be accumulatively added the "the whole" of what we have heretofore understood "5 + 3 = 8" to mean. Rather, because of her work, that whole now "waver[s] and tremble[s]" (Caputo, 1987 p. 7). This fecund new case refracts and cascades through each particular relation that we took to be a given, giving each one a renewed and transformed sense of its relations and place in the whole. Without the arrival of such fecund new cases, and the portend of transformation and renewal that they bring, mathematics would become simply a given set of memorizable (but not especially memorable) facts and rules and would lose its sense of potency and possibility. It would thus lose its integrity as a *living* system.

What we have come upon here is a discipline of mathematics which is both open and closed, which has its own patterns and structures and operations, its own arrays of possibilities and potentialities, but which somehow is renewed and made whole by the arrival of the young. If we pay attention to the stubborn particularity of this "5 + 3 = 8," this arrival need not be caught up in an onslaught of accumulation and acceleration. Our attention to this "5 + 3 = 8" is slowed and held in place by the wisdoms and disciplines and sustaining relations of this "place" called mathematics. Conceived as a living system (one hopes that this is a warrantable image for our curriculum), mathematics not a fixed *state* (whether already achieved or yet-to-arrive). It is, so to speak, a *way* which must be taken up to be a living whole. There is, thus, a way to mathematics. Learning its ways means entering into these ways, making these ways give up their secrets: making these ways telling again, making them more generous and open and connected to the lives we are living out. Understanding mathematics thus becomes a type of ecological intimacy which always already contains images of children and the passing on of the wisdoms of the world to the young. Consider this passage as describing the "world of mathematics" and all it sustaining interdependencies:

> Some people are beginning to try to understand where they are, and what it would mean to live carefully and wisely and delicately in a place, in such a way that you can live there adequately and comfortably. Also, your children and grandchildren and generations a thousand years in the future would still be able to live there. That's living in terms of the whole. (Snyder, 1980, p. 86)

Living in terms of the whole requires somehow making the world of mathematics *liveable.* As such, it is not enough to simply delve into its indigenous operations and patterns; nor is it enough to simply abandon children to their own devices and, so to speak, let them have their way with mathematics and not teach the difficult lessons of how to pay attention to where they are and what mysteries this place offers.

It is here that we encounter a paradox: making the world of mathematics liveable requires going beyond mathematics itself in to the deep, patterned relations of the world which house and sustain the possibility of pursuing mathematics at all: patterns of experience and breath and bone and blood. It is in this deeper, fleshier discipline of repeated patterns of operations and structures and doings, mathematics becomes integrated. It becomes whole.

Interpretive Descent and The Mathematicity of the World

The patterned doings of mathematics are themselves not simply isolated facts. Rather, we find in the patterns and structures of mathematics "an anciently perceived likeness between all creatures and the earth of which they are made" (Berry, 1983, p. 76). Consider how the following passages describe the patterned doings of the human body (pulse, breath), the patterns of our Earthly lives (daily and seasonal cycles and rhythms) and the structure of language itself. Consider how these passages show that each of these refracts through all the others:

> The rhythm of a song or a poem rises, no doubt, in reference to the pulse and breath of the poet. But that is too specialized an accounting; it rises also in reference to daily and seasonal—and surely even longer—rhythms in the life of the poet and in the life that surrounds him. The rhythm of a poem

> resonates with these larger rhythms that surround it; it fills its environment with sympathetic vibrations. Rhyme, which is a function of rhythm, may suggest this sort of resonance; it marks the coincidences of smaller structures with larger ones, as when the day, the month and the year all end at the same moment. Song, then, is a force opposed to specialty and isolation. It is the testimony of the singer's inescapable relation to the earth, to the human community, and also to tradition. (Berry, 1983, p. 93)

Or, even more mysterious:

> Rhyme leads one no doubt to hear in language a very ancient cosmology. Rhyme is not only an echo from word to word. Arrangement for arrangement, the order of language evokes and mimes a cosmic order. In realizing itself, rhyme is tuned in to [this cosmology]. Rhyme and meter are praise. An indirect theology. (Meschonnic, 1988, p. 93)

Given this, we can see how curriculum integration cannot involve concertedly adding on language alongside mathematics or vice versa. Rather, it requires delving into the mathematicity of language itself—its patterns and structures and rhythms and tones and operations and grammars. And, once we crack the literalist surface of mathematics that might render it an isolated discipline, a cascade of implications ensues: the rhythm of mathematics, mathematicity of language, the language of music and rhythm, the music/patterns/rhythms of the world and, in the end, the profound mathematicity of the shifts and flutters in a bear's gait as it breaks from a walk into a run. Differently put, deep in the underworlds of "5 + 3 = __" we find a strong and sustainable integration of mathematics into a "bear theme." Or, better, we find the integration of bears and "5 + 3 = __" into a "whole" which embraces them both, each in their own way and refracts each through the other—structure, pattern, rhythm, operation.

This is an exhilarating movement—a type of meditational and imaginal descent into the crawling underworld of the particularities of our lives. Every thing—even just this red wheelbarrow, or that child's holding five tight in her fist for fear of losing it—abounds with connections, dependencies, relations. Every thing, every word, every curricular fragment is a potential opening in to "the whole"—"this and this" (Wallace 1987, p. 111). More strongly put, only through a deliberate and disciplined attention to the "stubborn particulars" is "the whole" anything more than simply a floating, and, in the end, unsustainable idea.

However, there is also a fearsomeness attached to the realization that the world is not a flat, clean, literal surface and that our sanity and wholeness/health cannot be had by skittering across such surfaces, however safe and secure such surfaces might appear at first glance. There is a fearsomeness attached to the realization that the world is *interpretable,* alive with implications and complicities that are always already at work in the intimacies of our everyday experiences, and that we cannot always control and predict what relations we might stumble on in the dark, no matter how well-laid our (lesson) plans might be.

But none of this goes quite far enough. The mathematicity in the gait of a bear as it breaks from a walk into a run is, in the end, a topic which still simply "floats." We could just as easily have mapped out the parabolic curve of its shoulders or counted its toes or graphed its offspring or lifespan in relation to other animals. The sort of interpretive descent that curriculum integration requires of us is far more fearsome and more experientially immediate than this allows.

In dwelling upon the mathematical changes in the gait of a bear as it moves from a walk to a run, I cannot avoid coming to reflect on my own living involvement in such Earthly rhythms, an "anciently perceived likeness" (Berry, 1983, p. 76) that embraces us both and makes the life of each complicit in the other. In walking up this hill and feeling the fluttering mathematical patterns of breath and pulse and steps, I come to better understand this creature and its mathematical being *in place,* housed by flesh and humus, housed by a mysterious immediacy. And, in understanding this creature in this way, I come to understand myself and my own living involvement in the ecological conditions under which this creature lives and which I live with it, pulling hard at this same air as it curves up the steep valley sides. It is the fleshy mysteries of my own life and my own wholeness and integrity that this bear and its steps pace out. And, it is mathematics—the very mathematics which I now teach my child—which has underwritten technological images of severance, fragmentation, commodification, and mastery that have ravaged this place, this bear's life and thereby mine along with it. To teach mathematics in an integrated way, therefore, requires more than simply dwelling in its indigenous intricacies and patterns. I must help children (and myself) place mathematics back in to the embrace of the Earth (in to the embrace of its kin, like the symmetries of these pine branches). Such embrace will help make it more generous and forgiving and liveable than it has become in the severities of our curriculum guides and the severities and violences of our unsustainable beliefs in its dominion as a "Father Tongue" (Le Guin, 1987) which silences all others.

It will help make it (and ourselves, and our children, and this bear, which paces out a life beyond our dominion) whole.

Concluding Remarks

It is impossible to divorce the question of what we do from the question of where we are—or, rather, where we think we are. That no sane creature befouls its own nest is accepted as generally true. What we conceive to be our nest, and where we think it is, are therefore questions of the greatest importance. (Berry, 1986, p. 51)

Just as it is my own wholeness and integrity that this bear and its steps pace out, so too it is my own wholeness and integrity that is foretold in whatever actions I do here, with these children in the classroom. In another Grade One classroom, children are completing subtraction equations on a white sheet of paper. When they are done, the rectangles, each with one equation, are cut out, curled up, pasted on Santa's beard and posted for parents to see during the Christmas Concert and classroom visits that surround it.

If we meditate for a moment on this activity, there is a sense in which it is, frankly put, insane. This is not to say that some children might not enjoy it. It is it to say that fostering such enjoyment abandons children to a flickering, hallucinatory vision of the Earth, of mathematics, of the events surrounding Christmas that is, in the end, an ecological and spiritual disaster that no amount of acceleration and accumulation can outrun. Such activities suggest that we no longer know where we are. Such activities, too, are disturbingly suggestive of where we might *think* we are.

In this chapter, I have been suggesting that curriculum integration requires a concerted, thoughtful resistance to such skittering hallucinations. To prevent the woozy visions often associated with such matters, curriculum integration and the wholeness it portends must not sidestep a disciplined, mindful attention to the "stubborn particulars of grace." But there is another suggestion here: these examples of math facts on a Teddy Bear's tummy and Christmas subtraction equations bear witness to a terrible logic that many teachers and children are suffering on our behalf. This is one of the agonies of ecological mindfulness: my own life is implicated in these very examples—"*this* and *this*"—as is my son's. This difficult knowledge, more than anything, is at the heart of curriculum integration and the ecologies of experiential education.

PREAMBLE 4

"Kids Running From Place to Place"

> Two ways of watching the second-hand of a clock. One may be paralyzed [or panicked] by the sense of time passing, mesmerized by the loss of all those moments which cannot be stopped from passing away; or one may be liberated by the realization that the second-hand is going around *now.* There is nothing mystical about this, just the simple fact that it is always now. The *now* does not change (it is always now) but flows (that now never ceases to transform). Such [transformation] is smoother than we are accustomed to, more the continuous flowing that Dōgen refers to, for the mind does not try to fixate itself by jumping from one perch to another, staccato-fashion, always trying to fixate itself. (Loy, 1999, pp. 47–48)

> You may try to sustain your meditation by jumping to this and that object of meditation. Though you may do this, you will not be able to take up your object of meditation with this method. (Tsong-kha-pa, 2000, p. 99)

"The fecundity of the individual case" was my first blush with understanding the deeply temporal character of ideas, images, things, concepts, selves and that this temporality did not mean the flickering on and off of one isolated moment after the next. It means that ideas (et al.) *are* continuously emergent and re-emergent in their very being themselves at all. They are not just in contemporaneous fields of relations. That field that they *are* is also temporal. They are not just "in time," but rather *are* temporal.

In Praise of Radiant Beings, pages 59–62

Not only do ideas (et al.) have a past. That past is turning out to be different than we might have imagined in the past. They are flowing gatherings, sometimes roiled and contested, sometimes unnoticed. They are, to recall Ludwig Wittgenstein's images, more like family gatherings, with all the contention and love that might entail.

This provides a way and, frankly, an excuse to still attention. To think back to Chapter 3, if all that was accomplished with the production of "5 + 3 = 8" was this isolated effort marked correct on a worksheet, this might cause a teacher to not still attention but rush ahead to get something more accomplished. If we experience it as a gathering, we're invited to gather what's going on in that gathering, and thus learning far "more" than one isolated thing, *because the thing itself* (the field in which "5 + 3 = 8" properly belongs in order to properly be itself) *is not isolated and singular.*

Put more familiarly, I go back and back again to triangles inscribed in circles and wonder, more and more, over Pythagoras' insight (see Friesen & Jardine, 2009), and these returnings are not exactly one after the other but rather accrue in the topic, the topography itself. In such meditative, slowing returns, time no longer stutters and hops along from one isolated fragment to the next:

> One is absorbed in it. It is more like a tarrying that waits and preserves in such a way that the [work being meditated upon] is allowed to come forth. To tarry is not to lose time. Being in the mode of tarrying is like an intensive back-and-forth. One "is completely there in it." It is not like running through a stretch of space until the finish line. It is like a growing fascination that hangs on and even hangs on through temporary disruptions [when I return to considering Pythagoras, the having-gathered remains to a certain degree, right where I left it] because the harmony with the whole grows and demands our agreement. We know this with special clarity in listening to music. (Gadamer, 2007b, p. 211)

This is a common experience often concealed under the day to day rushing of things, and one can hear in this translation of Gadamer's words the powerful almost tortuous struggle with (and sometimes seemingly *against*) language that comes from trying to express its shapes and contours. That is why, as with the practice demanded by Buddhism, "the nature of hermeneutical reflection requires a constant return to the praxis of hermeneutic experience" (2007b, p. 196). It is important, in reading this, to try to summon up how this experience has manifest itself in the reader's experience. It's there, I suggest, and a nearness to it can be encouraged. We just rarely speak of it. In the rushing of the world, it seem almost unreal, but this is just a story we've told ourselves. I hearken back to first reading Wendell Berry and Thich Nhat Hanh, as described in Preamble 1. The moribund story of educational theory and practice can be re-told, and such re-telling can provide a certain relief (as well as, of course, new senses of obligation and work to be done). Of course, this new telling should not now be believed to be "the real story," because that simply re-locates, instead of uproots, reification (see Loy, 2010).

So, all this is akin to Martin Heidegger's work *Being and Time* (1962) and its explorations of how, under the surface of idle talk (pp. 221–213), and the flattening and numbing distractions of the standard story that "one" ("they" [p. 149ff.]) believe, being *is* time and can be experienced thus—abundant, on-going, rich, diverse, impermanent, finite, gathering, summoning, and then, of course, scattering all over again in the face of day to day distractions and duties, and having to be re-won.

Having first read *Being and Time* in 1971, it took me over 20 years for this insight to properly begin rooting (see Chapter 2 originally written in 1992), that a thing is properly itself when it is not yet fully and finally itself. It is, one can say, "neither finished nor unfinished" (Liddell, in press) such that all the rush to get finished, all the worry over being unfinished, falls away. "Our stories are never finished, and therefore never unfinished. If reality itself is always incomplete, each moment ["now"] becomes complete in itself, lacking nothing" (Loy, 2010, p. 40). I would also direct readers to Ruth Ozeki's lovely novel *A Tale for the Time Being* (2013), which elaborates in touching ways a tale started by Dōgen (2007).

Cultivating and practicing this sense of gathering time can belie the panic that is endemic in many schools, of fleeting rushes of time being eaten up and lost. Study provides a form of this composure. I have witnessed this in so many classrooms, where time itself shifts when good work, work worth our while, is being done. This is not a matter of slowing down over bits and pieces any more that the "slow food" movement is about cooking fast food slowly. It is a terribly difficult matter of sidestepping that very fragmenting reification that sets in motion this wheel of acceleration in the first place.

I'll have a lot more to say about time in Chapters 13 and 17. For now, just this: if we fragment and isolate the living topics entrusted to teachers and students in schools, each now-bounded, now reified "piece" loses all its relations, and therefore doesn't warrant much consideration or lingering over it. This leads, then, to getting on to the next thing as soon as possible. Thus, under the presumptive desires for permanence and fixity, the mood of such arrivals tends to be one of panic and skittering and, as we can all witness every day, unbridled acceleration and the discourses of "More" and

"Never Enough." And, as many teachers and students now suffer, such accelerated consumption and hyperactivity come to rule the day, along with, of course, increasingly hysterical regimes of surveillance bent on keeping track of all this rush.

It is not even "kids running from place to place," (a phrase used in the upcoming chapter) because *there are no places* of stillness that require whiling once reification and its terrible consort, fragmentation, has run its course. This is why this is, among so many other things, an *ecological disaster.* All is hostility and attachment and exhaustion consuming one bit after the other and never having enough.

The sharp edge of the following chapter is about "environmental education" and how it has become marginalized into a sub-division of science education. I claim that education itself might be experienced as deeply environmental no matter what curriculum area is being considered.

4

"Under the Tough Old Stars"

Meditations on Pedagogical Hyperactivity and the Mood of Environmental Education (1996)

"Environmental Education"

The term "environmental education" can give us pause to consider how ecological awareness, ecological attunement, might be more than simply a particular topic among others in the classroom. It might help us glimpse how it is that *education itself*, in its attention to all the disciplines that make up schooling, can be conceived as deeply ecological in character and mood.

Ecology can provide us with images that help us re-conceive the traditions and disciplines of education as themselves deeply ecological communities of relations, full of long, convoluted histories, full of life and lives, traditions and wisdoms that require our "continuity of attention and devotion" (Berry, 1986, p. 34) if they are to remain generous, sustainable and true, if they are to remain livable. For example, mathematics can become conceived as a rich, imaginative place, full of topographies and histories and tales to tell, full of relations of kin and kind, full of deep patterns and powers. Mathematics might become conceived as itself a deeply interconnected, Earthly phenomenon, linked to patterns of breath and bone,

In Praise of Radiant Beings, pages 63–69

bearing kinships to patterns of language and song, linked, too, to symmetries etched in stone, to the spiral doings of leaves and to the sun downarching towards *sol stasis* and return.

Ecology can also provide images of what it would mean to talk of the classroom as a real, living community, full of traces of the old and the young, the new and the established and the often difficult conversations between them. Classrooms, too, can become full of a commitment to working out and working through those wisdoms and disciplines and traditions and tales, shared and contested, that have been handed down to us all. It can be a place full, in a deeply ecological sense, of "real work" (Snyder, 1980; Clifford & Friesen, 1993).

Ecological Mindfulness: Education Is Environmental

> ...the connections, the dependencies, remain. To damage the Earth is to damage your children. (Berry, 1986, p. 106)

> Ecological awareness always and already involves the presence of our children. Ecology thus always already involves images of pedagogy and the teaching and learning of the tales that need to be told for all of us to live well. As with pedagogy, ecology is always already intergenerational. (Friesen, Clifford & Jardine, 2008)

In this way, we can conceive of disciplines such as poetry, or negative and positive integers, or the histories of this land, as large, generous places, full of relations in which we might learn to live well, adding our work to these places, our memories and voices, our arguments and alternatives and differences. We can now ask of education itself that it help to develop:

> the sense of "nativeness," of belonging to the place. Some people are beginning to try to understand where they are, and what it would mean to live carefully and wisely, delicately in a place, in such a way that you can live there adequately and comfortably. Also, your children and grandchildren and generations a thousand years in the future will still be able to live there. That's thinking as though you were a native. Thinking in terms of the whole fabric of living and life. (Snyder, 1980, p. 86)

Understood in this Earthy, intergenerational way, education (and not just "environmental education" as a sub-branch, most often, of science education) has the opportunity, perhaps the obligation, to slow down the pace of attention, to broaden out its own work into the long-standing patterns and places we inhabit and which inhabit us.

It has the opportunity, perhaps the obligation, to take on a mood not unlike ecological mindfulness.

Manic Pace

> Manic pace is cultivated as a virtue in elementary schools. Teachers getting kids to run from place to place, activity to activity. All noise and no *sounds.* Quiet is undervalued as only the quiet of straight rows—*made to be* quiet by somebody, not *being* quiet. (Patricia Clifford, [then] a teacher at Ernest Morrow Junior High School, Calgary, Alberta)

It is fascinating to consider how, in these ecological desperate days, just as ecology is heralding the need for a continuity of attention and devotion, our schools are, in so many cases, full of attention deficits (itself a wonderfully co-opted marketing term along with its dark twin, "paying attention"). This is coupled with a sort of hyperactivity that precludes the slowing of pace and the broadening of attention to relations and interdependencies that love and devotion to a place require of us.

This all-too-apt image—"kids running from place to place, activity to activity"—is clearly not a phenomenon that appears simply in elementary schools. Rather, it is endemic to what is now widely described as postmodern culture in North America: an onslaught of frenetic, disconnected, fragmented images and free-floating meanings, a twirling free play of signs and signifiers and surfaces, none of which requires or deserves care or attention, none of which has a strong or vital link to any other fragment. In this flickering place, nothing *pertains* and therefore, of course, we can do whatever we desire. We make all the patterns or connections and they can, at our beck and call, always be undone and redone, as we like. Loosed, here, is an image of the human subject as isolated from any deep obligation or complicity or relation to anything. Loosed here, too, is the portent of ecological disaster.

Think, for example of television channel surfing, or, more recently, "surfing the net."

If the surface is all there is, then surfing is all that is required.

I can always, as one Grade Seven student put it, "switch" if things get demanding or bog down or become no longer amusing or stimulating.

And, of course, as with surfing, if one loses momentum, if one hesitates for a moment, you're sunk. Consider this horrible image:

> the subject of postmodernity is best understood as the ideal-type channel-hopping MTV viewer who flips through different images at such speed that she/he is unable to chain the signifiers together into a meaningful narrative, he/she merely enjoys the multiphrenic intensities and sensations of the surface of the images. (Usher & Edwards, 1994, p. 11)

And, in light of such a subject, the corpus of the world and the traditions we are living out become "part of the emporium of styles to be promiscuously dipped into. It becomes yet another experience to be sampled—neither intrinsically better nor worse" (pp. 11–12).

In this milieu, meaning and significance and connection get reduced to glinting surface stimulation. And since stimulation is inherently always momentary, new stimulation is always needed—new "activities" are always underway. And so we have a common feature of many schools—a relentless rush from activity to activity, all in the name of "keeping the children's interest."

Once this occurs, it is little wonder that panic sets in. And it is little wonder that Wendell Berry (1986) suggests that it is precisely this sort of unsettled panic that makes us excellent consumers of ever more and more activities.

Just as ecology has been suggesting, we find ourselves in schools helplessly feeding the voracious activity beast, finding ourselves sometimes taken by the exhilarating rush of it all, and finding ourselves unwittingly equating the ends of education with being able, in deft post-modern fashion, to manipulate surfaces to one's own ends and to live consumptively.

Ecological Healing

Perhaps the "ADD kids" in our classrooms can be understood to be like canaries in a mine shaft—warnings, portents, heralds, like the monstrous, transgressive child often is (Jardine, 1994a; Clifford & Friesen, 2008; Clifford, Friesen & Jardine, 2008), that airs have thinned and sustaining relations have been broken and need healing. Perhaps they are signs that education needs to become a form of ecological healing (Clifford & Friesen, 1994)—mending "all my relations."

A mending done through the recovery, through our teaching, of the generous wisdoms and patterns of the world.

This is the juncture where education can become environmental in a deep sense. It can be the place where we might slow the attention and broaden our relations to the Earth.

Consider, for example, the deep pleasures to be had in the mathematical symmetries and geometric curves of just this yellow leaf corkscrewing down from a late fall Cottonwood, and how it heralds the arc of seasons and the movements of planets and suns, and the bodily desires for shelter, and how many have stood here like this, stock-still, trying to read the deep patterns and dignities and eloquences of this place:

> I think probably the rhythm I'm drawing on most now is the whole of the landscape of the Sierra Nevada, to feel it all moving underneath. There is the periodicity of ridge, gorge, ridge, gorge, ridge, gorge at the spur ridge and the tributary gorges that make an interlacing network of, oh, 115-million-year-old geological formation rhythms. I'm trying to feel through that more than anything else right now. All the way down it some Tertiary gravels which contain a lot of gold from the Pliocene. Geological rhythms. I don't know how well you can to do that in poetry. Well, like this for example. Have you ever tried singing a range of mountains? (Snyder, 1980, p. 4)

Consider this reminder that the desire to utter this place up into the eloquences of language and rhyme is itself ecological work, the work of a place, and the work of the breath:

> The rhythm of a song or a poem rises, no doubt, in reference to the pulse and breath of the poet. But that is too specialized an accounting; it rises also in reference to daily and seasonal—and surely even longer—rhythms in the life of the poet and in the life that surrounds him. The rhythm of a poem resonates with these larger rhythms that surround it; it fills its environment with sympathetic vibrations. Rhyme, which is a function of rhythm, may suggest this sort of resonance; it marks the coincidences of smaller structures with larger ones, as when the day, the month, and the year all end at the same moment. Song, then, is a force opposed to specialty and to isolation. It is the testimony of the singer's inescapable relation to the earth, to the human community, and also to tradition. (Berry, 1983, p. 17)

Consider that perhaps our rhyming utterance of this leaf-fall "leads one to hear an ancient cosmology" (Meschonnic, 1988, p. 93) that is folded into language and breath itself.

. . . so that just this leaf opens countless tales, each one of which is about all the others, each one of which holds and deepens and quiets and places all the others.

. . . the pace of attention slows and broadens and becomes more stable, less frantic. We don't need to speed ahead, to keep up, to crowd and cram the classroom with activity after activity. We can slow and settle and return.

. . . so that just this leaf becomes the portal or opening in to a Great Council of All Beings gathering in interweaving relations and suddenly, it sits still, settled, and the whole of things starts to corkscrew around its stillness.

And then, just in time, Coyote [see Clifford, Friesen & Jardine, 2008] shows up, ready to tweak the nose of such ecological self-seriousness, watching the selfsame:

> beautiful little gold coloured Cottonwood leaves floating down to the ground, and they go this . . . this . . . this . . . this . . . this, this this this and he just watches those for the longest time. Then he goes up and he asks those leaves "Now how do you do that? That's so pretty the way you come down." And they say, "Well there's nothing to it, you just get up in a tree, and then you fall off." So he climbs up the Cottonwood tree and launches himself off, but he doesn't go all pretty like that, he just goes bonk and kills himself." (Snyder, 1977, pp. 70–71)

But, as we know, "Coyote never dies, he gets killed plenty of times, and then he goes right on travelling" (p. 71), teaching a little lesson on the way, that these patterns of leaves falling are their own, and remember where you are and who you are, and it's getting cold and enough writing and it's time to get the wind kicked up to hot breath walking again.

We Cannot Do to Children What We Have Not Already Done to Ourselves

Just as with much of our lives, many classrooms are full of cheap, trivial, laminate-thin hyper-stimulants meant to titillate, amuse or seduce us into wanting more. Just as with so many of us, many schools are full of teachers ravaged by the skittering activity that has become their daily work. Education, environmentally understood, requires that we refuse to participate in this ecological disaster. It requires that we find work to do, for ourselves and our children, that bears some dignity and Earthly discipline—good stories, large fields of thought, "big ideas" (Clifford & Friesen, 1993) that need children to re-think them, that are *that* generous and true.

As always with ecological work, the work begins at home. There is no one left over here to demonize. It is always first *my own* attention and devotion to the world and its ways that is at issue, my own ability and willingness to pursue experiences that deepen as they proceed, and to refuse, when I can, as I can, experience-as-[hyper]activity, experience-as-distraction.

The problem, however, is that healing the flittering of attention that underwrites much of our lives cannot be had quickly or painlessly or finally. Remaining alert, remaining open to new experiences is always a task to be taken up again, from here, with these children, this year, with these wisdoms of the world. We cannot do to children what we have not already done to ourselves (Clifford & Friesen, 1994). We cannot deepen their wisdom of and attention to the Earth and its ways until we have first taken on the work of this wisdom and attention ourselves.

PREAMBLE 5

"So, Here We Are"

Saints asleep in the Great Bear, the Great Bear asleep in the North Mountain.
—Domanski, 2013, p. 9)

So, here we are.
—Sopa, 2004, p. 1)

Just had a bear amble by last week, first one in a few years. Sentient being, this bear, one of innumerable beings that the Bodhisattva's vow vows to save from suffering. That vow says that I vow to save *all* beings, end *all* desires, master *all* Dharmas (teachings), and attain something unattainable:

> Sentient beings are numberless; I vow to save them.
> Desires are inexhaustible; I vow to put an end to them.
> The Dharmas are boundless; I vow to master them.
> The Buddha way is unattainable; I vow to attain it. (Hanh, n.d.)

Why take such a vow if the prospects of holding to it are so treacherously unlikely? Just that. *Precisely because of the expansive overwhelming-ness of that*

In Praise of Radiant Beings, pages 71–73

prospect, "I" get(s) overwhelmed and sat back here, me and Ursula, just for a moment, glancing at each other from afar, stopping for a moment in each other's tracks.

And then, 5:00 AM this morning, Orion in the chill, with word of a Great Blood Moon eclipse tonight.

All beings are your ancestors, including sentient beings, but here is where I veer a bit both towards and away from Buddhism. *All beings,* including the echoes of water off a rock face on the other side of the river, are my ancestors, co-determining of our co-arising. My interest in Buddhism and in ecological thinking thus dovetailed with my discovery, in 1992, of James Hillman's (2006) astounding article "Anima Mundi: Returning the Soul to the World" (originally published in 1982):

> All things show faces, the world not only a coded signature to be read for meaning, but a physiognomy to be faced. As expressive forms, things speak; they show the shape they are in. They announce themselves, bear witness to their presence: "Look, here we are." They regard us beyond how we may regard them, our perspectives, what we intend with them, and how we dispose of them. (Hillman 2006a, p. 337)

So that bear ambles by, and the tomatoes, September 27, 2015, are whistling in the greenhouse, facing this way for just a glance. I vow to smell them when I go by, and to know this scent, and to let my memory of it bleed out when it comes time to eat them after all this nurture. I vow to let my trivial hunger be of one suffering with the snap of it off the vine:

> I promise to cut the carrot,
> When I'm cutting the carrot. (Molnar, 2014a)

Hah! Sound so silly, eh? But "it's not so simple to do what you're doing" (Dorrie 2007) without threat or distraction, with love, patience, perseverance and so on. So it is, too, with all the topics, all the topographies of the Earth that we come to learn. To save them from suffering the suffering of isolation and fragmentation is to interpret them, that is, release them (and ourselves) into the suffering that must be faced once the boundaries have been breached, out into their porous, impermanent arising and to stay with them as they pass, and not turn away or retract into hostile enclosure. To save them from suffering is to save them from the suffering of false reification and enclosure. It is to bring them back, bring myself back, to what makes their life, my life, possible. This is why we learn to read:

> To read a place means you are able to dwell within it, to inhabit it, to gather from it the knowledge that makes life there possible, as well as intelligible and meaningful. (Chambers 2012, p. 187)

This learning, of course, entails its own suffering. But this suffering is now true and not the byproduct of fear, sorrow, exhaustion, distraction. It brings refuge:

> Taking the bodhisattva vow implies that instead of holding our own individual territory and defending it tooth and nail, we become open to the world that we are living in. (Trungpa 2006, n.p.)

Hey bear!

5

All Beings Are Your Ancestors

A Bear Sutra on Ecology, Buddhism, and Pedagogy (1997)

Transforming according to circumstances, meet all beings as your ancestors.
—Hongzhi, 1991, p. 43

First

Just spotted a year old black bear crossing HWY. 66 @ McLean Creek, heading north.

From a distance, struggling at first to resolve its colour and lowness and lopey canter into dog or cat likenesses as it stretched up to the side of the road and across and suddenly slowed into distinctive roundhumpness... bear!

Stopped and watched him amble up the shalysteep creekedge. Wet. Greenglistening. Breath arriving plumey in the damp and cold after days of heat waves... been 33 degrees C. and more for four days running in the foothills of the Rockies west of Calgary. Here, roaming in the edge between prairie and forest, between flatlands and hills and mountains—here, when summers break, they tend to break deeply.

In Praise of Radiant Beings, pages 75–78

Cold rain. Cold.

It is so thrilling to not be accustomed to this sort of experience, to have it still be so *pleasurable.* Bear. His presence almost unbelievable, making this whole place waver and tremble, making my assumptions and presumptions and thoughts and tales of experiences in this place suddenly wonderfully irrelevant and so much easier to write because of such irrelevance.

Bear's making this whole place show its fragility and momentariness and serendipities.

Bear's making my own fragility and momentariness shows.

That is what is most shocking. This unforseeable happenstance of bear's arrival and my own happiness are oddly linked. This "hap" (Weinsheimer, 1987, pp. 7–8) hovering at the heart of the world.

> My own life as serendipitous, despite my earnest plans. Giddy sensation, this.
>
> Like little bellybreath tingles on downarcing childgiggle swingsets.
>
> Felt in the *tanden* (Sekida, 1976, pp. 18–19, 66–67) in Walking Meditation. (Hanh, 1995)

Breath's gutty basement. Nearby, the lowest Chakra tingles with an upspine burst to whitesparkle brilliance just overhead and out in front of the forehead.

In moments like this, something flutters *open.* Shifting fields of relations bloom. Wind stirs nothing. Not just my alertness and sudden attention, but the odd sensation of knowing that these trees, this creek, this bear, are all *already* alert to me in ways proper to each and despite my attention. Something flutters *open,* beyond this centered self.

With the presence of this ambly bear, the whole of things arrives, fluttered open.

Next

All Beings are your Ancestors. The feary sight of him, teaching me, reminding me of forgotten shared ancestries, forgotten shared relations to Earth and Air and Fire and Water.

That strange little lesson having to be learned again: that he has been here all along, cleaving this shared ancestry, cleaving this shared Earth of ours, making and forming my life beyond my "wanting and doing," (Gadamer, 1989, p. xxviii), beyond my wakefulness and beyond my remembering.

It is not so much that this bear is an "other" (Shepard, 1996), but that it is a *relative*, which is most deeply transformative and alarming to my ecological somnolence and forgetfulness. It is not just that I might come awake and start to remember these deep, Earthy relations.

It is also that, even if I don't, they all still bear witness to my life.

Relations. Who would have thought? Coming across *one of us* that I had forgotten.

Coming, therefore, across myself *as also one of us*. Such a funny thing to be surprised about again. In the face of this Great Alert Being, I, again, become one of us!

Great Alert Being, this bear. Great Teacher. His and my meaty bodies both of the same "flesh of the [Earth]" (Abram, 1996, pp. 66–67 [see Abram & Jardine, 2000 for a later conversation]), rapt in silent conversations (Abram, 1996, p. 49).

Where, my god, have I been? And what have I been saying, betraying of myself and my distraction?

Then

This bear ambles in the middle of all its Earthly relations to wind and sky and rain and berries and roadsides and the eons of beings that helped hone that creek edge to just those small pebbly falls under the weight of his paws:

> Even the very tiniest thing, to the extent that it "is," displays in its act of being the whole web of circuminsessional interpenetration that links all things together. (Nishitani, 1982, p. 150)

The whole Earth conspires to make just these simple events just exactly like this:

> "Within each dust mote is vast abundance." (Hongzhi, 1991, p. 14)

This is the odd butterfly effect (Glieck, 1987, p. 17) fluttering in the stomach.

This, too, is the profound co-implication of all beings that is part of ecological mindfulness—that each being is implicated in the whole of things and, if we are able to experience it from the belly, from each being a deep relatedness to all beings can be unfolded, can be understood, can be felt, can be adored, can be praised in prayerful grace, a giving thanks (Snyder, 1990, pp. 175–185). Lovely intermingling of thinking and thanksgiving (Heidegger, 1968).

So the thrill of seeing this bear is, in part, the exhilarating rush felt in seeing it explode outwards, emptying itself into all its relations, and then retracting to just that black bear, now an exquisite still-spot ambling at the center of all things. And more!

> *The center is everywhere.* Each and every thing becomes the center of all things and, in that sense, becomes an absolute center. This is the absolute uniqueness of things, their reality. (Nishitani, 1982, p. 146)

Like breath exhaled outwards and then drawn in deep draughts. This inwardness and outwardness of emptiness (Sanskrit: *sunya*; Japanese: *ku*)—each thing *is* its relatedness to all things, reflecting each in each in Indra's Netted Jewels and yet each thing is always just itself, irreplaceable. Smells of the forests of mid-August and the sweetness of late summer wild flowers. Winey bloomy blush. Intoxicating.

All Beings are your Ancestors.

So

Hey, bear!

If we are to meet all beings as our ancestors, we must also meet all those very same beings as our descendants. This odd, fluid, difficult, shifting edge point between the ancestors and the descendants is where our humanity lives.

This is "the empty field" (Hongzhi, 1991) that opens and embraces.

It is also the lifespot of teaching and learning and transmission and transformation.

There are many Great Teachers.

All praise to bear and his subtle gift.

Bragg Creek, Alberta, August 8–10, 1997

PREAMBLE 6

"Subjectivity is a Distorting Mirror"

> By climbing up into his head and shutting out every voice but his own, "Civilized Man" has gone deaf. He hears only his own words making up the world. He can't hear the animals. They have nothing to say. (Le Guin, 1987, p. 11)

> All we can do is try to speak it, try to say it, try to save it. Look, we say, this land is where your mother lived and where your daughter will live. This is your sister's country. You lived there as a child, boy or girl, you lived there. Have you forgotten? All the children are wild. You lived in the wild country. (Le Guin, 1989, p. 47)

"Where . . . have I been?" (from Chapter 5). Indoors, hearing my own words making up a world. This isn't just a matter of getting out doors. I can't emphasize enough how long it takes me, out gathering wood for the winter, to actually *be there* out of the chittering orbit-absorption of self-narration. Being there takes a while. It is, however, a practice you can become practiced in. Sort of like this: in studying the ways of birds, or the inscription of a right-angled triangle inside a circle, or working on an essay whose topic is elusive, and so on."

> One is absorbed in it. It is more like a tarrying that waits and perserveres in such a way that the [work being meditated upon, the performance being watched, the topic being studied, the birds being observed or heard, the

In Praise of Radiant Beings, pages 79–82

> friendship that grows] is allowed to come forth [Heidegger and Gadamer sometimes use the phrase "comes to presence"]. To tarry is not to lose time. Being in the mode of tarrying is like an intensive back-and-forth. One "is completely there in it." It is not like running through a stretch of space until the finish line. It is like a growing fascination that hangs on and even hangs on through temporary disruptions [when I return to considering Pythagoras, the having-gathered remains to a certain degree, right where I left it] because the harmony with the whole grows [*Gebilde*]. (Gadamer, 2007b, p. 211)

This sort of meditative remaining with the object of meditation, this gathering, requires, then, of me, a certain level of "cultivation" (*Bildung*), but what is thus cultivated is not exactly my "self" but my ability to forego how my self persistently tries to foreground itself. It is a sort of "getting over myself" by giving myself over to detailing how things are (Dharma) with, say, that species of bird, or this unseasonal warmth of clothes on the line, January 28, 2016—both a pleasure and a slightly nightmarish portent. Of course. Buddhism, ecology, hermeneutics: these are all lineages regarding how to come to understanding and intimately experience what is happening to us. Pedagogy.

Hence, this little chapter on going birding with some old friends who were experienced in such things. It was not simply that they had great stores of "amassed verified knowledge" (Gadamer, 1989, p. xxi) ("Do not devote yourself just to piling up words in great numbers without engaging in practice" [Tsong-kha-pa, 2000, p. 59]). They were, and wanted to be, and were learning how to be *experienced*, practiced in being there and learning what it takes from the place itself. Hence this hitherto concealed matter of living in the wild of things, becoming practiced in hearing the animals or the Raven Call echo off the hill to the West, practiced in the smells of aspen leaves whirly gigging downwards. Practiced, daresay, in the topographies of place value, in the wilds even of mathematics, or grammar and punctuation:

> The truth of [hermeneutic] experience always implies an orientation to new experience. "Being experienced" does not consist in the fact that someone already knows everything and knows better than anyone else. Rather, the experienced person proves to be, on the contrary, someone who . . . because of the many experiences he has had and the knowledge he has drawn from them, is particularly well equipped to have new experiences and to learn from them. Experience has its proper fulfillment not in definitive [amassed] knowledge but in the openness to experience that is made possible by experience itself. (Gadamer, 1989, p. 355)

Read this again:

> Taking the bodhisattva vow implies that instead of holding our own individual territory and defending it tooth and nail, we become open to the world that we are living in. (Trungpa, 2006, n.p.)

"Everything is teaching us" (Chah. n.d.). This is about pedagogy at its heart:

> To use the hermeneutic adage, the world has become open to interpretation [to *exactly* the extent that I am open to the interpretability of the world]. And here is the great, seemingly paradoxical situation: "keeping ourselves open" and "keeping the world open" (Eliade, 1968, p. 139) are the same thing. As we become experienced, having cleaved with affection and made ourselves "roomier," the world's roominess can be experienced. (Jardine, Bastock, George, & Martin, 2008, p. 53)

One last thing that loops back to those "stubborn particulars" of Chapter 3, or that one specific oil-slicked bird from Chapter 1, or those different bears in Preamble 5 and Chapter 5. When my companions saw that it was *that* pair of nesting birds, I'm now reminded, years later, of this, harkening back to "the fecundity of the individual case":

> The individual case on which judgment works is never simply a case; it is not exhausted by being a particular example of a universal law or concept. Judging the case involves not merely applying the universal principle according to which it is judged, but co-determining, supplementing, and correcting that principle. It is truly an achievement of indemonstrable tact to hit the target and to discipline the application of the universal. Such a thesis admittedly sounds strange to our ears. (Gadamer, 1989, pp. 39–40)

This student in a crowded class, *that* suffering, *those* breakthroughs into spaciousness, an occasioned call for more patience than I might be able to manage—these are the locales of practice. And this is not simply a matter of that worn-out ecological adage of "think globally, act locally."

I must learn to think locally of what *this* demands of all my global dreaming. Buddhist meditative practice is not an abstract set of rules ("Dha[r]ma is not an ideal" [Sumedho 2010, pp. 83–96]) but a demand whose moist intimacy is mine alone. So, here, just on the verge of a chapter about birding, I'm thinking of schools and teacher and their woes and how it arises over and over and over again:

> As one becomes more confident in this practice, the subtleties start to come up. One becomes kind of world-weary. You go through a stage where you just look at this world and think it's crazy! "I'm living in a madhouse! Society is nuts!" And you think "No! Not this again! Don't they ever learn? Do we

> have to go through this again?" If you attach to world-weariness, you attach to just another thing. (Sumedho, 2010, p. 95)

Even though Buddhism describes practices for all, I myself must face what I must face because of my own circumstances. I myself must practice. "This experience is always to be acquired and from it no one can be exempt" (Gadamer, 1989, p. 356). It is "not something that anyone can be spared" (Gadamer, 1989, p. 356):

> What a man has to learn through suffering is not this or that particular thing, but insight into the limitations of humanity. Thus [this hitherto concealed] experience is the experience of human finitude. (p. 357)

No one can suffer this coming to know on my behalf. "You are the one who has to do this; nobody can do it for you" (Sumedho, 2010, p. 81). Like this: it is my own, personal, subjective task to overcome the concealing and "distortions" (Sumedho 2010, p. 63) that my own, personal, subjective life has wrought. It is my task to get over myself, and this over and over again.

"Subjectivity is a distorting mirror" (Gadamer, 1989, p. 276). Funny advice, then: "Don't take your life personally" (Sumedho, 2010).

How in god's name do you do *that,* then? Easy. I settle down and let myself look a while. Look, there's a Red-Winged Blackbird coming down the cliff-face, and that despite all my distractions and woes and world-weariness:

> It is where we can rest, where we can be, so we don't have to make it, hold it, or keep depending on conditions to allow it to exist. We realize that it is "the way it is" all the time whether conditions are pleasant or horrible. This is the refuge. (Sumedho, 2010, p. 47)

"To acknowledge what is" (Gadamer, 1989, p. 357). So, consider this. I go birding with old friends in part to be there and to be in a place where practice is joyous and easy and adorable.

The hope always is that, with such (comparatively) easy and safe practice, when I then come upon events in schools where the "No! Not this again!" rears up, where "acknowledging what is" tempts me to panic and withdraw and distort, or to become threatened and hostile and blaming, maybe, just maybe, that Red-Winged Blackbird's descent will be the teacher I need right then, right here, right now.

Maybe.

6

Birding Lessons and the Teachings of Cicadas (1998)

I went birding last summer with some old friends through the Southern Ontario summer forests where I was raised, crackling full of song-birds and head-high ferns and steamy heat. It was, as always, a great relief to return to this place from the clear airs of Alberta where I have lived for 11 years—academic, Faculty of Education, curriculum courses, practicum supervision in the often stuffy, unearthly confines of some elementary schools.

As with every time I return here, it was once again a surprise to find how familiar it was, and to find how deeply I experience my new home in the foothills of the Rocky Mountains through these deeply buried bodily templates of my raising. It is as if I bear a sort of hidden ecological memory of the sensuous spells (Abram, 1996) of the place on Earth into which I was born. How things smell, the racket of leaves turning on their stems, how my breath pulls this humid air, how birds songs combine, the familiar directions of sudden thundery winds, the rising insect drills of cicada tree buzzes that I remember so intimately, so immediately, that when they sound, it

In Praise of Radiant Beings, pages 83–88

feels as if this place itself has remembered what I have forgotten, as if my own memory, my own raising, some of my own life, is stored up in these trees for safe keeping.

Cicadas become archaic storytellers telling me, like all good storytellers, of the life I'd forgotten I'd lived, of deep, fleshy, familial relations that worm their ways out of my belly and breath into these soils, these smells, this air.

And I'm left shocked that they know so much, that they remember so well, and that they can be so perfectly articulate.

I became enamored, during our walk, with listening to my friends' conversations about the different birds that they had been spotting. They spoke of their previous ventures here, of what had been gathered and lost, of moments of surprise and relief, of expectation and frustration. Their conversations were full of a type of discipline, attention and rich interpretive joy, a pleasure taken in a way of knowing that cultivated and deepened our being just here, in this marsh, up beside these hot, late-afternoon sun-yellowy limestone cliffs.

Up-draughts had pulled a hawk high up above our heads. We spotted a red-winged blackbird circling him, pestering, diving.

Sudden blackbird disappearance.

Hawk remained, over a hundred feet overhead, backlit shadowy wing penumbras making it hard to accurately spot.

Where had that blackbird gone?

"There. Coming down the cliff face."

Sudden distinctive complaint around our heads. He had spotted us as worse and more proximate dangers to this marsh than the hawk that'd been chased far enough away for comfort.

My friends' conversations were, in an ecologically important sense, *of a kind* with the abundance of bird songs and flights that surrounded us—careful, measured, like speaking to like, up out of the hot and heady, mosquitoed air. And, standing alongside them there, sometimes silent, certainly unpracticed in this art, involved a type of learning that I had once known but, like cicadas, long-since forgotten.

I had forgotten the pleasure to be had in simply standing in the presence of people who are practiced in what they know and listening, feeling, watching them work.

I had forgotten the learning to be had from standing alongside and imitating, practicing, repeating, refining the bodily gestures of knowing.

I had forgotten how they could show me things, not just *about this place*, but also about how you might carry yourself, what might become of you, when you know this place well.

Part of such carrying, such bearing, is to realize how the creatures of this place can become like great teachers (see Chapter 5) with great patience. Such a realization makes it possible to be at a certain ease with what you know. It is no longer necessary to contain or hoard or become overly consumptive in knowing. One can take confidence and comfort in the fact that this place itself will patiently hold some of the remembrances required: like the cicadas, patiently repeating the calls to attention required to know well of this place and its ways.

So we stood together in the bodily presence of this place. Listening, watching, waiting for knowing to be formed through happenstance arrivals and chance noticings. Seeking out expectant, near-secret places that they knew from having been here before, often evoking slow words of fondness, remembrance and familiarity—intimate little tales of other times. Repeating to each other, with low and measured tones, what is seen or suspected. Reciting tales from well-thumbed-through books that showed their age and importance. Belly-laughing over the wonderful, silly, sometimes near-perfect verbal descriptions of bird songs: "a liquid gurgling *konk-la-ree* or *o-ka-lay*" for Peterson's (1980, p. 252) version of the red-winged blackbird.

Then settling, slowing, returning, listening and looking anew. Meticulousness: "at the edge, below the canopy of the oak, there, no, left, there, yes!"

These are, in part, great fading arts of taxonomic attention, and the deep childly pleasures to be had in sorting and gathering and collecting (Shepard, 1996). There is something about such gathering that is deeply personal, deeply formative, deeply pedagogical. As I slowly gathered something of this place, it became clear that I was also somehow "gathering myself." And as I gathered something of the compositions of this place, I, too, had to become composed in and by such gathering. And, with the help of cicadas, I did not simply remember this place. Of necessity, I remembered, too, something of what has become of me.

A birding lesson: I *become* someone through what I know.

This little lesson may be the great gift that environmental education can offer to education as a whole. Coming to know, whatever the discipline, whatever the topic or topography, is never just a matter of learning the ways of a place but learning about how to carry oneself in such a way that the ways of this place might show themselves. Education, perhaps, involves the invitation of children into such living ways.

This idea of a knowledge of the "ways" (Berry, 1983; [Sanskrit: *Dharma*]) of things and the immediacy, patience, repetition, persistence and intimacy—the "attention and devotion" (Berry, 1986, p. 34)—that such knowledge requires, is ecologically, pedagogically, and spiritually vital. It suggests that knowledge of the ways of red-winged blackbirds is not found nestled in the detailed and careful descriptions of birding guides. Rather, such knowledge lives in the living, ongoing work of coming to a place, learning its ways and living with the unforeseeable consequence that you inevitably become someone in such efforts, someone full of tales to tell, tales of intimacy, full of proper names, particular ventures, bodily memories that are entangled in and indebted to the very flesh of the Earth they want to tell.

It was clear that my friends loved what they had come to know and what such knowing had required them to become. They took great pleasure in working (Berry, 1989), in showing, in listening, in responding to the simplest, most obvious of questions. There is a telling, disturbing, ecopedagogical (Jardine, 1991, 1993, 1994b, 1995, 2000, 2010) insight buried here. Because a knowledge of the ways of a place is, of necessity, a knowledge webbed into the living character of a place and webbed into the life of the one who bears such knowledge, such knowledge is inevitably fragile, participating in the mortality and passing of the places it knows. A knowledge of ways, then, must, of necessity, include the passing on of what is known as an essential, not accidental part of its knowing. It is always and already deeply pedagogical, concerned, not only with the living character of places, but with what is required of us if that living and our living there is to go on.

Another birding lesson: if this place is fouled by the (seeming) inevitabilities of "progress," the cost of that progress is always going to be part of my life that is lost.

Some days, it makes perfect sense to say that all knowledge, like all life, is suffering, undergoing, learning to bear and forbear. Because of this fearsome mortality that is part of a knowledge of ways, we are obliged, in such knowledge, to cultivate a good, rich, earthy understanding of *enough.* We are obliged, too, to then suffering again the certain knowledge that in our schools, in our lives, in our hallucinations of progress and all the little panics these induce there never seems to be enough.

Sometimes, in bearing such knowing, I feel my age. I feel my own passing.

At one point we stood on a raised wooden platform in the middle of a marsh just as the sun was setting, and the vocal interplays of red-winged blackbirds' songs, the curves of their flights and the patterning of both of these around nests cupped in the yellow-and-black-garden-spidery bulrushes—audible but invisible sites bubbling full of the pink, wet warbling smallness of chicks—were clearly, in their own way, acts of spotting *us.*

"Ways" bespeaks a thread of kindred-ness with what one knows, a sense of deep relatedness and intimate, fleshy obligation. But it betrays another little birding lesson: that we are their relations as much as they are ours; that we are thus caught in whatever regard this place places on us:

> The whole ensemble of sentient life cannot be deployed except from the site of a being which is itself visible, audible, sensible. The visible world and the eye share a common flesh; the flesh is their common being and belonging together. (Caputo, 1993, p. 201)

Or, if you like, a more drastic mosquito lesson about living relations: "flesh is . . . a reversible, just insofar as what eats is always edible, what is carnivorous is always carnality" (p. 200). So, just as these mosquitos eat up my sweet, sweaty blood skinslicked under the lures of CO2 that drew them near, I get their lives in return, gobbled up into liquid gurgling *konk-la-rees.* This is the meaty, trembly level of mutuality and interdependence that crawls beneath all our tall tales of relations. This common flesh is the fearsome limit of our narrativity.

In a knowledge of ways, I do not simply know. I am also *known.* These cicadas and I turn around each other, each forming the other in kind, "both sensible and sensitive, reversible aspects of a common animate element" (Abram, 1996, p. 66). Even more unsettling than this, *as* we know this place, so are we known by it (Palmer, 1989). That is, the character of our knowing and how gracefully and generously we carry what we know reflects on our character.

One final birding lesson for now. Catching a glimpse of a blue heron pair over past the edge of the marsh, tucked up under the willowy overhangs.

Shore edge log long deep bluey sunset shadow fingers.

Sudden rush of a type of recognition almost too intimate to bear, an event of birding never quite lodged in any birding guides:

> "It's *that* pair!"

What a strange and incommensurate piece of knowledge. How profoundly, how deeply, how wonderfully *useless* it is, knowing that it is *them,* seemingly calling for names more intimate, more proper than "heron," descriptions richer and more giddy than "Voice: deep harsh croaks: *frahnk, frahnk, frahnk* (Peterson, 1980, p. 100)." Such knowing doesn't lead anywhere. It is, by itself, already always full, already always enough.

Perhaps this irreplaceable, unavoidable intimacy is why our tales of the Earth always seem to include proper names ("obligations require proper names" [Caputo, 1993, p. 201]), always seem to be full of love and heart, always seem to require narrations of particular times and places, particular faces, particular winds, always seem to invite facing and listening and remembering.

PREAMBLE 7

"Remembering This, You Will Weep"

> Develop the following ideas with respect to your teachers. I have wandered for a long time through cyclic existence, and they search for me; I have been asleep, having been obscured by delusion for a long time, and they wake me up; they pull me out of the depths of the ocean of existence; I have entered a bad path, and they reveal the good path to me; they release me from being bound in the prison of existence; I have been worn out by illness for a long time, and they are my doctors; they are the rain clouds that put out my blazing fire of attachment. (Tsong-kha-pa, 2000, p. 83)

Buddhist literature is certainly rife with the idea of finding a teacher, finding the right teacher. The right teacher is not simply a property of that person, but a property of a relationship that is given rise to by teacher and student alike. Rightness, then, is about what a student needs (and not just what they *think* they need). But also, rightness is about what the teacher needs as well, and not just what they *think* they need, what they had planned, what they hoped. When it works, each saves the other from themselves.

Students ask something of their teachers and vice versa, and they can drag each other down or up, in or out. I met David G. Smith in the summer of 1986 after 18 months of unemployment, and, well, we hit it off. We still call each other brother in the now 30-year wake of that meeting.

In Praise of Radiant Beings, pages 89–91

It was and remains like this:

At first your speech
Captivates listeners' minds
Then if they give it thought
It clears away attachment and delusion. (Tsong-kha-pa, 2000, p. 183)

I was still stuck, in May 1986, in a sort of fake relationship to education, having backed into the profession by trial and error. It was meeting David and, as any who've heard us both speak, "emulating" (Tsong-kha-pa, 2000, p. 72) him that made my work possible. Later that summer, I got a job in the Faculty of Education at the University of Calgary, and I just retired on July 2, 2015.

It was David's unwavering insistence that made and still makes it possible for me to remember this at every turn and during every dark night: "*everything* is teaching us" (Chah, n.d., italics mine), even that dark. "Where you are is a place to practice" (Tsong-kha-pa, 2004, p. 191) *not* somewhere else. It was David's relentless example of asking after the pedagogy of events and words and circumstances that broke open, for me, the often droning monologues of schooling and then sent me back to schools a bit more alert, a bit more "open to the world that we are living in" (Trungpa, 2006, n.p.).

This is why Buddhism insists that good teachers are "pleased by practice" (Tsong-kha-pa, 2000, p. 179), that they have "abandoned dispiritedness" (p. 71), and "abide in the lineage" (p. 70) and not only this. Good teachers not only encourage practice. They practice. They encourage "joyous perseverance" (Tsong-kha-pa, 2004, pp. 182–207) and they themselves persevere. Teachers draw us, as their students, into the lineages. So here is what David helped me consider more carefully. By his example of careful reading, he helped me read this passage properly: "Using only joyous perseverance, you will end up exhausted. If you practice with the aid of wisdom, you will achieve the great goal" (Tsong-kha-pa, 2002, p. 62). When I read it, this admonishment was meant for me, and for my often-infantile enthusiasm. And it was one that, once I was able to understand it well enough, I could pass along to my own students. Study, and let study settle your sheer enthusiasm. It doesn't spoil it. It tempers it, makes it strong and robust and resilient. Study is a "bridle set with sharp nails . . . fit for the difficult-to-rein horse of the straying mind" (Tsong-kha-pa, 2000, p. 71). And again, "do not make study and practice into separate things. Rather, the very thing that you practice must be exactly what you study and reflect upon" (Tsong-kha-pa, 2004, p. 221).

One last thing for now. Teachers also lovingly hold fast and insist that there is something afoot that transcends thinking from the position of subjectivity, from the position of my own limitedness and afflictions and incapacity. They do not abandon me to myself. They think better of me than I can often think. "You lose great purpose when you are distracted in idle chatter and amusement which are the source of much pointless suffering. Meditate on this" (Tsong-kha-pa, 2004, p. 187). When we meet, David and I never lingered much in bouts of idleness, right from the moment we met. And even when we don't meet much, I am still surrounding with an affection I have never earned.

So as to avoid too much mush, here, it was David who introduced me to Chogyam Trungpa's (2003, p. 236; see McCaffrey, 2015) idea of "idiot compassion," whereby the effort to honour the presence and life of one's students can turn into indiscriminate "confirmation":

> Trungpa's cautionary phrase . . . is not meant as an insult, but only as a corrective, to keep compassion in proportion, where it belongs with all our emotions, motives and actions in the phantasmagoria of human consciousness. Compassion is an event often wonderful when it manifest, but evanescent, complicated, and mercurial. Attempts to essentialize and idealize compassion risk losing sight of the event of compassion in favour of moral exhortation. (McCaffrey, 2015, p. 20)

This is why the bodhisattva of wisdom, Manjushri, wields a sword. The sword is ready to slice through foolishness and ignorance, but is equally adept at cutting off woozy Romanticizing about connectedness, relations, wholeness and compassion in favour of the tough work and long practice needed to be ready for the event of such things: "the sword of reasoning cuts *through* phenomena" (Tsong-kha-pa, 2002, p. 343). Note that this entails that the work of seeking wisdom does not work *around* or *above* phenomena, but *through* them. It doesn't turn away. It turns towards our living. In the face of one's teachers, sometimes it is I myself that needs cutting through.

So, this is why not just alertness but generosity, patience, perseverance, discipline, and wisdom are the cluster of the *paramitas*, the aspired-to perfections in Buddhist practice. David has said to me more than once, but never quite in these words, and always with great affection: "Practice those things that you can practice now. Do not use your own incapacity as a reason to repudiate what you cannot engage in" (Tsong-kha-pa, 2000, p. 49).

I hope this has been appropriately hesitant praise of one of my teachers, for he and I are both these clumsy bodies bumping our way along, laughing and full of grief, and taking refuge in each other.

"Remembering this, [I] weep" (Tsong-kha-pa, 2000, p. 83).

7

"It's All One Meditation" (1999)

> It is as if you people ask for, above all else, not only a genuine responsiveness from their elders but also a certain direct authenticity, a sense of that deep human resonance so easily suppressed under the smooth human-relations jargon teachers typically learn in college. Young people want to know if, under the cool and calm of efficient teaching and excellent time-on-task ratios, life itself has a chance, or whether the surface is all there is. And the best way to find out may be to provoke the teaching into showing himself or herself. (Smith, 1999a, p. 139)

I utilized this passage from David Smith's essay "Children and the Gods of War" in a recent course on the ethics of teaching. The attempt was to break through crusted notions of ethics-as-rules-and-regulations, and to invoke something of the notion of ethos as the characteristic sprit of a people, a place or a community. What ensued was painful for us all—an odd shock of recognition, that very little of our school experience (university and otherwise) involved any joy or any deep recognition of the ways of things. Children had devolved into either preciousness or monstrousness, and the disciplines of the world had devolved into "fun activities for the kids."

This passage became for these students, as it became and has remained for me since I first read it in 1988, a clarion of memory in our class, something each of us took to heart and remembered, recited and recalled as the

In Praise of Radiant Beings, pages 93–95

class wore on and often down under questions like "Why didn't anyone tell us?" "Why does it have to be like this?" and, perhaps, most painfully, "What in hell can we do now?" most certain was the fact that none of us could henceforth pretend that we had not read these words and that we had not somehow recognized images and histories and traditions and discourses in which our lives were deeply and irremediably implicated. But even in the midst of the wonderful suffering that this passage caused, it was also quite evident that we, here, in this class, belonged together under the mark of these words and could take some comfort here, some common fortitude and strength. We all had to not only live individually with having read and understood these words. We had to live with the fact that these others, too, were here with us. All the relations, our teachers, our childhood's, our schooling, our children, our elders, all called to account a Great Council of Beings gathered, huddled around fires lit over ages, listening to the tales that hold us here.

We, here, had a brief glimpse of what it might mean to say that pedagogy has to do with wisdom, communities of relations and small, meticulous obligations often hidden under the cool and calm. A deeper cool and deeper calm.

And we also recognized that passages such as this one will hold us because they proceed from a generousness and spaciousness that invites as it teachers. We all knew this passage was about us all and that it was (dare one say it these days?) *good work.*

Of course, we are all living under the newly fashionable education jargon of "community" that has already ruined these words before they even had a chance. The lamentation continues: jargon is rooted in an old Welsh term *iargoun,* which means "the warbling of birds." At least the warbling of birds is done with some tilting pleasure at the sun add the air-blue arch that holds David's and my life together, this broad Chinook sky and the prairie abyss and the wind, and oh, the cold that cracks your bones, Alberta.

This is the sort of incident I've come to expect from David Smith's work—painful fits of often bloody-minded healing, unavoidable because their bearing is always slightly unanticipated. It is never quite clear from where the calling might call and just what might be at stake in such calling.

It will become evident as you read these texts that there is a critical edge to this work, similar, on the surface, to critical theory. Unlike critical theory, however, these essays do not begin with the self-satisfied certainty of what the problem is and who has it. The critical edge here is the crisis of a spirit dancing on the edge of the world coupled with a certain deadly playfulness, deadly because that is precisely what is at stake here: whether life itself has a chance. Many of us understand this crisis and the ways in which our children's lives, my child's life, my own life and the demons in the trees and Coyote howls in the wind are becoming co-opted by consumptive panic endemic to our so-called postmodern era. As the fragments crack, the genuineness and spirit and address of David Smith's work are only understandable as hopelessly naiveté. Let us all be naïve, then. Let us all give up hope. There, in that place of hopelessness, when the eschatological hallucinations of a "better world" are given up, genuine love and compassion are possible. There, life itself has a chance out from under the vicious, well-meant glare of "improving our schools."

These essays slow the pace of attention and reveal, in odd ways, how the author has had to bear the agony of that slowing and the effort required to live in the belly of a paradox, as he puts it—live, in fact, in the belly and the breath, and retain some courage to continue, not in spite of the agonies but in their embrace; in a love of them. David has taught me, in part through his work, in part through his example, that we must somehow love those students who make this request, "Tell me exactly what it is you want in this assignment" (from the essay "On Being Critical About Language" included in this book of his), for they are bearing on our behalf the agonies of the world, showing us our own pains and foibles and fears, providing us all with openings and events that, if we read them generously and well, might lead us all to health, to sanity, beyond the breathless rush of school.

> If we speed up the work in the garden, you'll just have to spend that much more time sitting in the zendo, and your legs will hurt more. It's all one meditation. I would like to take this all the way back down to what it means to get inside your belly and cross your legs and sit—to sit down on the ground of your mind, of your original nature, your place, your people's history. Right Action, then, means sweeping the garden. (Snyder, 1989, p. 252)

My debt to David Smith's work remains and is the sort that doesn't demand repayment. It is his encouragement that has made the lilt of these words possible. Quite a feat, to hand a former asthmatic back his breath. If you read these pages slowly, space will clear, restlessness will become irrelevant and words will erupt out of your throat without warning: *makyo* nightmarish visions of the original nature that houses us all.

Acknowledgment

This chapter was originally published as the Foreword to David G. Smith's (1999), *Pedagon: Interdisciplinary essays in the human sciences, pedagogy and culture.* New York, NY: Peter Lang Publishing.

PREAMBLE 8

Self-Abnegation

The Delusions We Believe In

> We can be conscious but not aware. In fact we can be conscious and totally deluded. But the delusions that we believe in affect consciousness. So, what we are actually doing in Buddhist meditation is using wisdom (prajna) to inform consciousness in order to let go of the distortions or delusions that we experience. (Sumedho, 2010, p. 33)

> A thing does not present itself to the hermeneutical experience without an effort special to it, namely, that of "being negative toward itself." [We are often] force[d] to make interpretive conjectures and to take them back again. The self-cancellation of in the interpretation makes it possible for the thing itself to assert itself and allows an infinity of meaning to be represented within it in a finite way. (Gadamer, 1989, p. 465)

These passages provide compelling images of the self-abnegation that is at the heart of Buddhism, hermeneutics and ecological thinking. It is linked, by a circuitous route, to the slowly cultivated experience of opening up fields of relations around "the thing itself" because the thing itself is its field of relations and nothing besides that. That is, in the process of "informing consciousness in order to let go of... distortions or delusions," my

In Praise of Radiant Beings, pages 97–105

"self" breaks open into all its relations, and, in perfect parallel, the thing my "self" is considering also breaks open.

Interpretive conjectures are thus doubly self-cancelling. They are on behalf of uprooting and untangling hidden reifications of belief and other layers of taken-for-granted-ness that I have come to take for granted which, in turn, have hardened the object being interpreted and harden my relationship to it, thus giving rise to attachment, hostility and grief. Interpretation, therefore, doesn't just mean getting lots of information about a topic, but, more radically, "breaking open the *being* of the object" (Gadamer, 1989, p. 360), that is, breaking the delusional spell that layers and layers and layers of inherited and self-made reifications have wrought. It also involves breaking open the being of the one doing the interpreting, this "I myself."

Edmund Husserl (1970b, p. 52) called this layering process that covers over and hardens "sedimentation" which "close[s] off" (p. 52) our ability to experience the "implications" (p. 52) (co-arisings, one might say) inherent in the thing itself and inherent in my (co-arising) relationship to it. Such sedimentations are produced by fear, power, the simple weight of historical or personal circumstances, personal pathologies, institutional distortions, flexes of power, unquestioned cultural presumptions, gender, race, money, inherencies in the language that surrounds us and its images and ideas and grammars, upbringing, or simply being tired and having had enough and needing a break.

The good news is that none of this is permanent or fixed, despite how vividly we might *experience it* to be fixed. In Buddhist thought, clinging and attaching to a (delusional) idea of fixity and permanence is the deepest delusion we face and it underlies whatever sedimented, encrusted layers then affix themselves to it and on its presumption, almost like a grain of sand in an oyster. "I" am not a hardened containment unit (a "subjectivity"), and the topic I am studying is not a hardened containment unit (an "objectivity"). In the life-world, "it" is a living field and "I" am enlivened, transformed, shaping and being shaped through my encounters with these living fields. This mutuality or "interbeing" is at the heart of ecological insight.

In short, I can learn through study (and, as Tsong-kha-pa would be wont to add, through patience, perseverance, discipline, generosity and stillness, these being the other *paramitas* or "perfections" that studying is surrounded with and supported by). But this, too, requires self-cancellation. As suggested by Gadamer's reflections (1989, pp. 9–18) on the old humanist idea of *Bildung*, learning isn't just "amassing of verified knowledge" (p. xxi) by a subject who now "has" more and more information inside the barricades and bulwarks of its "self." The sort of self-abnegating study being proffered here is not ever-increasing self-acquisition but *self-formation. I become someone* because of what I surround myself with and dedicate myself to. And, as explored in Preamble 6, the ever-receding *telos* of such formation is not "definitive knowledge" (Gadamer, 1989, p. 355) but a slowly emergent and expanding "openness to experience" (p. 355) itself. I become, shall we say, experienced in and accustomed to this unending process of formation. It is not a "lack" that needs to be filled or hurriedly pursued, even though, as David Loy (1999) details, it is often (delusionally) experienced as such. Such hurried pursuit to overcome this sense of lack thus cascades into relentless consumerism in an attempt to eat up enough to feel full and sated—enough marks, enough research grants, enough publications, enough possessions, enough. Again, a root of ecological concern, the need for a more alert, not-panic-driven "concept of *enough*" (Berry, 1983, p. 79).

In Buddhist thought, in hermeneutics, and in ecological work, this situation is not experienced as a lack but a state of "self-transcendence" and movement—"breaking forth" (Gadamer, 1989, p. 458). This sounds high-handed but again, it is profoundly ordinary. Just consider the chapter that follows, where young children were ushered into the worlds of Impressionism, of Van Gogh and his brother Theo, of Sister Wendy's adorable and eager love of Monet and water lilies. It does something to you in the presence of such surroundings. It asks me to let go of my self and enter into the play of this space (see Gadamer, 1989, pp. 101–110).

Thus, arises a question of deep concern for teachers. What shall we surround our students with? That is, what topics shall we study? And how shall we study them? Am I able, as a teacher, to find my own way into the living fields surrounding place value in a mathematics classroom? Can I experience its en-fieldedness (Friesen & Jardine, 2009) and find ways to invite students therein?

What we surround ourselves with is a matter of vital concern. This is why, in the Chapter that follows, it was such an astounding idea to have very young children produce "self-portraits," but not by drawing pictures "of themselves," but by portraying the rooms they live in.

"Animals and their habitats." Hah!

Good Morning Everyone

> If one's sight is clear and if one stays on and works well, one's love gradually responds to the place as it really is, and one's visions gradually imagine possibilities that are really in it. Vision, possibility, work, and life—all have

> changed by mutual correction. Correct discipline, given enough time, gradually removes one's self from one's line of sight. (Berry, 1983, p. 70)

> We should have no illusion. Bureaucratized teaching and learning systems dominate the scene, but nevertheless it is everyone's task to find his free space. The task of our human life in general is to find free spaces and learn to move therein. One learns slowly how a large amount must be excluded in order to finally arrive at the point where one finds the truly open questions and therefore the possibilities that exist. We with the youth and they with us learn to discover the possibilities and thereby possible ways of shaping our lives. There is this chain of generations . . . who must learn to create with one another new solidarities. (Gadamer, 1986, p. 59)

When an interviewer specifically suggested to Hans-Georg Gadamer that his work in Truth and Method (1989), especially the long and tangled explication of "The Subjectivization of Aesthetics Through the Kantian Critique" (1989, pp. 42–81) is a defense against subjectivism through an affirmation, instead, of intersubjectivity, his response is quite visceral and immediate: "Oh, please spare me that completely misleading concept of intersubjectivity, of a subjectivism doubled! (Gadamer, 2001, p. 59).

In my courses on curriculum in the Faculty of Education's undergraduate program, I would sometimes begin by discussing what it is like to walk into a, say, Grade One classroom. It is bursting full of different lives, different languages, different cultures and faces and expectations and fears. It is bursting over-full with myriad background knowledge and lack of knowledge, background experiences and lack of experience, timidity regarding exploration and over accelerated venturers, those who can't sit still and those who won't move, afflictions and powers of every possible sort, families of every stripe and good news/bad news, some with not enough food that morning or sugared-buzz over-feedings, wounded little things, gleeful and joyous beings, abuse large and small, physical and emotional, bully-based and otherwise, and the shadows of economic pressures and penumbras of jobs won or lost that hang in the air, laughter, teasing, hormones, internet taunts and media-hysteria promises and celebrity-culture monstrosities, great settled beings who seem ancient and wise, and on and on. Add to this, of course, my own mid-week weary life as a teacher, with my own never-pristine and often unconscious or repressed or muzzled responses and attractions and repulsions from each and every one of these precious or feared arrivals, coupled with a great and honest and abstract desire to honor each child as a precious moment of dear sentience and love and possibility. Thus, too, arises my own job, my patience, my own life streams and woes and joy, my own schooling, even the smell of the place or the too-familiar cadences of sing-songy voices—all this roiling around in my head all the while.

"Good morning everyone."

By now, many undergraduate pre-service students in those curriculum classes are agape and full of yes and yes and yes and oh no! What are we supposed to do? Just tell me what to do in the face of all this. Please!

If we begin and remain with these (presumed to be) individual, subjective "perspectives," it is easy to become simply paralyzed by difference and differentiation. Subjectivity doubled, tripled, quadrupled, and with each one that arrives, it is never just "one more" (see Chapter 2). All the others become shifted and changed in differentiating cascades of response, which themselves cause cascades. Such proliferation becomes easily experienced as a threat, leading to mechanisms of response geared, understandably, to overcoming that threat. Tell me what to do and I'll do it!

Hence arrive old alternatives that are commonplace in the orbit of educational theory and practice. We can either simply and forcibly override that myriad by imposing a singular task on everyone irrespective of differences. Or, more commonly these days, we can presume that proliferation and attempt to accommodate it by subjecting the field of study we were about to enter to fragmentation and measured dispensation. The once-living and variegated field is broken apart and doled out requisite to each subjective requirement, each student's "needs." The classroom becomes like "the postmodern community of the shopping mall, a community devoid of communality, where people come together to mind their own business" (Dressman, 1993, p. 259).

Once we head down this path, there is no "environment" that surrounds us in its keep and provides refuge for us all. We each and everyone become "*solus ipse*" (Husserl, 1970, p. 89). Solidarities become competitions and pedagogy becomes, in the end, an act of war (Jardine, 2012a) in what some teachers euphemistically call "the trenches."

"Pulverize the Deep Falsehood"

> The "community" of the classroom... is not a collection of individuals tethered to each other psychologically. Rather, those tethers are mediated through the common worldly work that is done that allows us to experience each other "in place" rather than through the psychologistic utopianism of "individuality" and "uniqueness." (Jardine, Bastock, George, & Martin, 2008, p. 36)

> When I go out into the garden with my seven-year-old son, I don't send him off to a "developmentally appropriate garden." I take him to the same garden where I am going to work. Now, once we get there and get to the work

> that place needs, of course, each of us will work as each of us is able. We are not identical in ability, experience, strength, patience, and so on. But both of us will be working in the same place doing some part of the real work that the garden requires, part of the "continuity of attention and devotion" this place needs to remain as healthy and whole as possible, under the circumstances. (Jardine, Clifford & Friesen, 2003, pp. 111–112)

> The root of all problems is the ignorance that superimposes intrinsic existence. There is only one consciousness that can uproot it by apprehending things in a way that explicitly contradicts it. That consciousness is the wisdom that knows selflessness. (Tsong-kha-pa, 2002, p. 193)

In order to "pulverize the deep falsehood" (Tsong-kha-pa, 2002, p. 334) that headed us down this path to entrenchment, Tsong-kha-pa gives interesting and helpful advice. Even though "dependent-arising refutes the essential or intrinsic existence of persons and phenomena," he suggests that, "in order to stop inaccurate consciousness, you must first refute the object which that consciousness apprehends." (Tsong-kha-pa, 2002, p. 204, italics mine).

This "refutation" is, in effect, interpreting the object (the "topic," like Impressionism or Van Gogh or right-angled triangles or poetry, or any other mandated curriculum matter) by breaking open its (supposedly self-contained) being and thereby revealing its being in multifarious horizons of possibilities, of relations, of connections and arising. Thus, refutation, here, is not like "destroying a pot with a hammer," but rather "developing a certain knowledge that recognizes the nonexistent (i.e., not empty of self-existence; i.e., full, instead, of relations) *as* nonexistent" (Tsong-kha-pa, 2002, p. 204). As the thing "expand[s] outward" (2002, p. 63), so does my self expand in concert and so does the "room"—the array of possibilities of thinking, action, investigation, adoration, questioning—emergent from that thing for a wide array of different venturers into its ways.

In other words, take your students to a beautiful, rich, abundant place and *then* let them explore, because that place will help curb and shape and heal their self-contained urgencies. Their "uniqueness" can be worked *out* in such a rich field (see Chapter 12); my own exploration of Van Gogh and Gadamer's metaphysics of genius were read back to me differently because of the field in which I encountered these young children, their teacher, and their work, detailed in the following chapter. Starting with the object provides an easier path, because the troublesome yet joyous delight that can arise in feeling the world come alive can provide refuge for the more intimate insight that I, too, arise and perish. There is "lightness and buoyancy" (Tsong-kha-pa, 2002, p. 82) to this hitherto concealed experience.

I must add, however, that this places a certain burden on me as a teacher. I must, for myself, take on this difficult path of refutation. I myself must learn about this topic in and as its dependently arising surroundings. It is difficult but time spent worthwhile, to find a topic that is *itself* "differentiated" and that therefore has, *by its very abundant and dependently co-arising nature,* "room" for the teeming differences of students because *it is diverse.*

So, in the chapter that follows, when I read my own explorations of "the Vacant Throne" in Van Gogh's portrait of his room, this exploration is not simply "one more" added to an amassing "subjective variety of conceptions" (Gadamer, 1989, p. 118). Rather, it is "the [topic's] own possibilities of being that emerge as the [topic] explicates itself, as it were, in the variety of *its* aspects" (Gadamer, 1989, p. 118, italics mine). Simply put, my understanding and exploration is an understanding and exploration *of it,* and to the extent that that exploration was well done (to the extent that it can stand the measure of the *mensuratio ad rem*), it adds itself to the array of possibilities of the thing itself. All of our experiences of this thing become enriched by *her* work, or *his* writing. And each one of these helps me experience my own explorations as possible but not necessary. The topic is various.

Traversing this rich field thus can free me from self-enclosure and delusional confines of self-belief:

> We all have our obsessions, identities, peculiarities and so on; we carry them with us and identify with them. Now, it isn't a matter of dismissing or denying these, but of putting them into perspective. (Sumedho, 2010, p. 41)

In the presence of a powerful topic my peculiarity gets drawn out into the rich and relieving perspective of a field in which I can let my self loose of its self and its "personal" and "opinion-filled" confines. After all, "the way my personality has developed over the years causes me a lot of suffering" (Sumehdo, 2010, p. 4). Study can relieve me a bit. My long-standing love of Vincent Van Gogh's work got pulled out into the presence of Nathan's writing and his sense that the chill of that room painting in Arles portended Van Gogh's suicide. What was heretofore just my own love got honed and shaped and nurtured and roughed up, and frankly, humiliated by the surroundings of other possibilities. In other words, I'm not stuck with myself. Nathan's words, Jennifer's work, shall we say, freed me from my self. "I can still have viewpoints and opinions, but I don't trust them. That is not where my refuge is" (Sumedho 2010, p. 81). I don't have to give up what I know. I do, however, have to stop simply believing them, and holding on to them and buttressing them against the threat of other opinions. I have to give them over to the play of possibilities. I have to give up:

> Produced and producer, path and traveller, viewed and viewer, valid cognition and object of comprehension, etc.,—every thing should be understood not as existing essentially [in self-isolation] but only as existing in mutual dependence. (Tsong-kha-pa, 2002, p. 311)
>
> And so the great poet [like Nathan] does not express his or her self, he expresses all of our selves. And to express all of our selves you have to go beyond your own self. Like Dogen, the Zen master, said, "We study the self to forget the self. And when you forget the self, you become one with all things." (Snyder, 1980, p. 65)

This, then, "un-reifies" my "self" and, in parallel, "un-reifies" the topic we are exploring together and reveals "a 'selflessness of objects' and a 'selflessness of persons'" (Tsong-kha-pa, 2002, p. 213).

An Endnote

The description of a classroom venture in the following chapter thus feeds back in telling ways into the life of schools. What do we surround ourselves with? What surroundings are enforced around us? What do these surroundings say about us? How do these surroundings make us into something? What, for example, does the clutter around the classroom do to us? Or, the laminated alphabet letters above the white-board? Or the worksheets stuck on fridges and fluttering by at a panicky pace in some classrooms?

Mindlessly boring worksheets dependently co-arise with bored students, classrooms geared to management and a technical form of accountability; and this is perfectly parallel to how Nathan's chilling meditations on Van Gogh and his brother *also* dependently co-arises with a classroom full of long conversations on Impressionism, viewings of videos exploring Water Lilies and long bouts of talk and writing and looking deeply into lines and colors.

If I surround myself with junk, my life gets junked. With surroundings of anger, it gets angry. With surroundings of disposability and the reject of care and attention and devotion, I become disposable and unable to become practiced in careful attention (Jardine, 2015). Where the pedagogy of "guess what's in the teacher's head" governs, so arises "Tell me exactly what it is you want on this assignment" (Smith, 1999d, p. 111) or simply stubborn, understandable refusal borne of seeing through that guessing game but not being able to utter anything about it in the regimes of schooling.

The difference between all these scenarios is not on this level. All involve dependent co-arising. But some block and suppress our ability to *experience that circumstance of arising* and instead delude us with or simply subject us to promises of fixity and finality. So here's an audacious contention. The difference between these scenarios is that, with, for example, Jennifer Batycky's work in her classroom, not only can dependent co-arising be experienced and understood and cultivated. *Such experience and understanding and cultivation are necessary to the work being done.* In composing themselves around this luscious topic, students and teachers alike (and then me, meandering in and thinking about Van Gogh and his brother and listening to Nathan's story) feeling themselves composed by their own surroundings and by the surroundings-portraits of others working in that same field.

"Threads, interweaving and criss-crossing" (Wittgenstein, 1968, p. 33) is what this place is and what I become in entering into it and getting to work. Therefore, and of course, in order to produce a self-portrait, one might portrait one's room(iness).

8

Filling This Empty Chair

On Genius and Repose (2004)

David W. Jardine
Jennifer Batycky

"A Little Smokeless Pipe"

I [Jennifer] listened to many classes about hermeneutics, and after each class I seemed to be filled with the same feeling of confusion. It was not so much a confusion about what hermeneutics was, but more a perplexed feeling about how this style of inquiry was going to impact my life as a teacher. From what I initially gathered, in some sort of "magical" way, something remarkable from the life world of the classroom would simply present itself to me. It seemed that my role would be to take up this particular event and care for its message, so that the beauty of its daily-ness was gently uncovered and honored. Well, I certainly had no intention of holding my breath and waiting for the hand of the curriculum god to tap me on the shoulder, delivering a profound message! As a teacher, I felt so tangled up in the everyday-ness of the classroom, I wondered if I could ever step far enough out of the

In Praise of Radiant Beings, pages 107–121

situation to see and hear the possibilities that presented themselves daily. By the middle of October, I had resigned myself to the fact that everyone in my graduate course had received a special message from Mercury, except for me.

Wednesday, October 28th, 1998. My plan for the morning was to provide the children with an opportunity to apply their imagination and skills to a descriptive writing passage. Rather than simply "teaching" all about what descriptive writing entails, I decided to select an art reproduction and share my own writing about it. My intention was to draw upon our collective background experience with art and use that as a springboard to create beautiful writing. Since the beginning of the year, the walls of the classroom had been filled with reproductions of the works of van Gogh, Gauguin, Monet, Manet, Matisse and several others. Available, too, was a large pile of smaller, 8" x 10" reproductions that children could take to their work areas and ponder. Daily, we would sit in front of large reproductions and talk about them, how they made us feel, made us think, and we learned of the lives of these artists, their troubles and successes. As I read my own paragraph based on Van Gogh's painting of a bedroom, I could instantly sense a connection between myself and the children. I remember thinking "This is going to be a great lesson."

One of the first student books I picked up to read was Nathan's. He had written two pages on the image of Van Gogh's chair:

> The sad and lonely chair sits alone in a cold and empty room. The only warmth is a little smokeless pipe. So as the chair sits alone with still only a little warmth, the chair waits for something. But what is it? It still waits for the moment, that moment that the chair thinks will never come. The brick floor gives a chill in the air. The chair still sits by the door, waiting for the moment. But the door doesn't budge. Days pass, but everything is still. Still as a rock. So everything goes like this day after day after day. This goes on and nobody sits on the chair. Nobody even notices the chair and that's how it will stay.

When I read Nathan's passage, I felt a chill up my spine, knowing that the chair was waiting for van Gogh to return from the field in which he shot himself. During the weeks that followed, I shared Nathan's writing with colleagues both at my own school and in the system. I also shared it with friends and family members because I didn't want this event to simply be held under an awful educational gaze. Each time I shared his writing, I was met with a stunned look, followed by always well-meant comments which always seemed to dismiss this gift Nathan had given us:

"Nathan is so thoughtful. He always says the most amazing things."

"What grade did you say you teach?"

"You are so lucky. I could never do that with the children in my class. They just aren't capable."

"Nathan is really gifted. He really ought to be tested."

"Well, how are you going to extend this child's learning now? Perhaps he should have an opportunity to take his own writing and create his own picture."

How should I extend Nathan's learning? How absurd! The real question that Nathan's writing presented me with was about my own learning being extended. For days I carried his book and picture around with me; to my home, to meetings, around the school . . . just wondering what to do next. I found myself tempted to sit Nathan down and drill him about why he wrote what he did about Van Gogh's work and what it meant. Thank goodness I refrained. because, upon reflection, I realized that asking Nathan about his own work in this way was not going to give me the answer or the questions I was looking for.

In almost all of the responses to Nathan's writing no one could find a way to speak of *the work* he produced: what does this writing tell us about this painting and what we ourselves may have failed to see, to feel, to understand? About the loneliness and sadness and isolation and emptiness that van Gogh often hides under such colorful images? About our beliefs as teachers about children's ability to even express such things?

What also became troublesome were questions like these: would Nathan's writing have been this rich if he had no images to build from, to rely on, if we had not pursued and practiced, with the whole class, how to respond to such works with care and thoughtfulness, if we had not deeply explored the worlds that these painters evoked and how they offered us a new vision of our own world, if we had not listened to what each other said about the paintings we were looking at? Most responses to Nathan's work failed to respond to *his work*. The reason for this is that many people tried to start with Nathan himself. I realized that the only way that I could take care of Nathan's writing was to start with the world opened up by van Gogh's work, because *that* is what his writing is about.

By the way, when David [Jardine] came into the class later that week, I asked Nathan to read his work to him. Nathan had been reading passages from Van Gogh's letters to his brother, and we had watched portions of *Sister Wendy's Story of Painting*, a charming and moving video series on the history of art (http://www.tpt.org/BTW_folder/Sept/wendy.html).

They went out into a quiet spot in the hall, and after reading his work to David, Nathan said:

> "He's buried next to his brother, you know."

Empty Chairs

> Empty chairs had been a feature of van Gogh's thinking since childhood. The memories that crowd behind this single image are connected with deep mournfulness, with thoughts of the omnipresence of death.
>
> . . .
>
> His own chair, simple and none too comfortable, with his dearly loved pipe lying on it, stands for the artist himself. We may well be tempted to recall the pictorial tradition that provided van Gogh with his earliest artistic impressions. Dutch Calvinism sternly insisted on an iconographic ban that prohibited all images of the Holy Family except symbolic ones: the danger that the faithful might be distracted by the beauty of the human form had to be avoided at all costs. Thus Christ could be represented by a "vacant throne." (Walther & Metzger, 1997, p. 8).

Thus, too, van Gogh himself, not just his death but aspects of his living, can be represented by his room, by the place he has inhabited—the pipe, the chair, the modesty of the surroundings, the colors that speak of Arles (unlike, say, the dark muddiness of *The Potato Eaters* (1885), which places its inhabitants so differently, in hues and colors that seem to place them right into the ground out of which their meal has come.

Jennifer had her Grade One students doing "self-portraits" this same year as Nathan arrived, not by literally drawing pictures "of themselves," but by drawing pictures of their rooms, the spaces they live within. She also introduced me to a wonderful, disorienting book called *Room Behaviour* (1997) by Rob Kovitz. From the back cover:

> *Room Behaviour* is a book about rooms. Composed of texts and images from the most varied sources, including crime novels, decorating manuals anthropological studies, performance art, crime scene photos, literature and the Bible, Kovitz shapes the material . . . to create an original, fascinating and darkly funny rumination about the behaviour of rooms and the people they keep.

Those room portraits that the children did, like van Gogh's painting, were akin to portraits of "vacant thrones"—portraits of spaces that a non-portrayed "subject" (for lack of a better term) inhabits. But this is not quite correct—"the subject" *is* portrayed, but the portrait is of a particular *sort of subject.* These are not portraits of an isolated, autonomous, egocentric "I myself" that somehow sits enclosed at the center of any inhabitation, but of a "self" that issues up out of and leaves traces within an inhabitation, a "keep," up out of and in to a world of voices and relations and ancestries and kin, of colors and palettes and hues, images and tales, up out of places, memories and topographies and even up out of the most ordinary, everyday objects that we find ourselves surrounded by. The "self" that these "room-portraits" portray is, so to speak, an ecological (non-substantial, unable to exist by its self) "self," not an isolated "I."

So the empty "room portrait" somehow *is* "of" the self, but now treated as empty of a self-existence independent of its Earthly relations. This interpretive thread is, of course, *not at all* in line with the Dutch Calvinist idea of "the vacant throne." On the contrary, what we are pointing to here is a way of loving the world and its places and loving our own straggly emergence into being who we are.

These Grade One room portraits thus provide a simple critique of Cartesianism and its belief in the logical and ontological precedence of an abstract, empty, worldless "I am," in favor, instead, of an inhabitation that is the Earthly self's keep and an "I" that grows up out of its sojourns in the world.

This Grade One venture highlights the oddness of many curriculum guides which go through a social studies curriculum sequence like this: me, me and my family, maps of our classroom, our neighborhood, our city, our city past and present, the province etc. This sequence presumes that what is somehow most immediate in the life of the child is his- or her self and that curriculum should radiate, so to speak, "outwards" from there. This, of course, is totally unsupported both by developmental theory (see Piaget, 1952; Jardine, 2005) and by the common sense we develop by living around children and carefully listening to what they are saying to us about these matters. As Kieran Egan (1986, 1992) shows so well, the worlds of imagination and mythology and great stories of places and people far away are much more *immediate, compelling,* and *understandable* than is the abstraction "my self." Children are much more drawn to, capable within, and articulate about large, troublesome, ancient, venturous, living, imaginal "spaces" of Impressionist painting, the allure of old geometries or Pythagorean cults, the spell of trickster tales (e.g., Clifford, Friesen and Jardine, 2008; Lensmire, 2000), or the age-old troubles of time and its telling (Clifford & Friesen, 1993), than they are within the cramped and literal-minded enclosure of "myself."

"Myself" doesn't simply disappear in ventures into such alluring, difficult places, only its metaphysical (i.e., non-experiential, dis-embodied, uninhabiting, hallucinatory, ideational, logically consistent but ecologically insane [Bordo, 1988]) sense of enclosure. This "myself"is experienced as issuing up out of the course of the experiences, not that I *have* (*Erlebnisse* [see Gadamer, 1989, pp. 60–70]) but that I *undergo* (*Erfahrung* [see Gadamer, 1989, pp. 240–262]) in and through the world. This world in which I undergo or suffer experiences, is not just inhabited and formed and fashioned by myself and by and within by own(ed) experiences, but is always and already experienced, articulated, and inhabited. It has always and already been formed and fashioned by shared and contested inheritances, voices and ancestries, up out of which I must slowly and continually "find" myself becoming who I am. I am surrounded by a "multifariousness of voices" (Gadamer, 1989, p. 295)—and not just up out of the human inheritance but all Earthly calls and keeps.

Even these late autumn birds locate, form and fashion this worldly "I am" (Jardine 2000) in ways far "beyond my wanting and doing" [Gadamer, 1989, p. xxviii])—here, spotted by these Pine Grosbeaks "before I know it" and whether I have a "lived experience" of it or not (differently put, this is a way to distinguish between phenomenology and hermeneutics).

In just this way, this "world" of Impressionist paintings is *already long-since inhabited* before Jennifer, her Grade One class, or I arrive. Therefore, because this world is not simply "our experiences" or "our constructs," or "our meanings" or "our perspectives," entering this world requires some measure of giving ourselves over to *its* "wantings and doings"(Gadamer, 1989, p. xxviii)—*its* measure of what it wants of *us*. It helps form and fashion who we each become in venturing through it. That is to simply say, we *learn* from it. But now, learning does not just mean that there is a subjectivity who now has, as some interior possession, new information. Rather, it means that each one of us who ventures to this place becomes someone who, in different and multiple ways, has come to know her or his way around (*ex-peri*) this place–someone "experienced" in it. The experiences undergone are experiences *of the place* and not simply and only and obviously experiences somehow "of" the experiencer. Simply put, Nathan's words are *about* van Gogh and self-portraits and rooms and loneliness and dying. They are *of* Arles and Theo. They invoke the muddiness of *The Potato Eaters* (even if Nathan never *meant* to refer to it or to the Dutch Calvinists portrayed in it). When we take his words to be *about Nathan* (which, as teachers, we surely must do as part of our obligation to him), we have changed topics. We have, so to speak, "switched rooms" by now taking these words out of the worlds they invoke and re-placing them into Nathan's life and biography and psychology.

This frail, contingent, finite, emergent, dependent "self," then, slowly finds and forms itself in and through its inhabitations, through the "rooms" that are this self's keep. But here, the possessive case is still misleading because each individual self (whatever this exactly now means) does not simply possess its keeps but is also kept by them. The character (*Bildung* [see Gadamer, 1989, p. 9 and following) of this emerging self is dependent, at least in part, at least to some terrible extent, upon the company it keeps.

It is no accident, however, that we find such talk so odd and disturbing. We have inherited a great and variegated and sometimes contradictory faith in individuality, autonomy, freedom, independence, genius, creativity. We are suckers for talk of courage and heros, partly because we have grown up into the inhabitation of and under the auspices of the European Enlightenment and its faith in an off-stage, disembodied Reason. Immanuel Kant (1983, p. 41) named any sense of Earthly dependence a form of "immaturity":

> Enlightenment is man's emergence from his self-imposed immaturity. *Immaturity* is the inability to use one's understanding without guidance from another. This immaturity is *self-imposed* when its cause lies not in a lack of understanding, but in a lack of resolve and courage to use it without guidance from another. *Sapere Aude*!: "Have courage to use your own understanding!" —that is the motto of enlightenment.

We need only courage and resolve, to lead the way with a Reason conceived as not "of" the world but as the (Vacant?) seat of judgment before which the world can be forced to give witness:

> A light broke upon the students of nature. They learned that reason has insight only into that which it produces after a plan of its own, and that it must not allow itself to be kept, as it were, in nature's leading-strings, but must itself show the way with principles of judgment based on fixed laws, constraining nature to give answer to questions of reason's own determining. Reason ... must approach nature in order to be taught by it. It must not, however, do so in the character of a pupil who listens to everything the teacher chooses to say, but of an appointed judge who compels the witnesses to answer questions which he had himself formulated. While reason must seek in nature, not fictitiously ascribe to it, whatever has to be learnt, if learnt at all, only from nature, it must adopt as its guide, in so seeking, that which it has itself put into nature. (Kant, 1964, p. 20)

Reason is thus conceived as broad, empty "forms" of thinking which, when applied to things, form and fashion them and demand of them that they "shape up" (it is from this philosophical juncture that Jean Piaget developed his notion of "cognitive schemata" [see Jardine, 2005] hence, of course another kin of a "vacant throne [as] a symbol of [a] judgment and power" [Walther & Metzger, 1997, p. 8] that is "out of this world," un-kept in or by the frailties of our Earthly human countenance.

And, unless we miss this point, Kant does suggest that our immature sense of dependence is *self-imposed.*

What Is to Come

Consider, then, another take on something oddly both akin and radically different than "the vacant throne." Jacques Derrida is speaking to the question of the difficulty of his own writing and an image arrives:

> One does not always write with a desire to be understood—that there is a paradoxical desire not to be understood. It's not simple, but there is a certain "I hope that not everyone understands everything about this text," because if such a transparency of intelligibility were ensured it would destroy the text, it would show that the text has no future [*avenir*], that it does not overflow the present, that it is consumed immediately. Thus, there is the desire, which may appear a bit perverse, to write things that not everyone will be able to appropriate through immediate understanding. There is a demand in my writing for this excess . . . a sort of opening, play, indetermination be left, signifying hospitality for what is to come [*avenir*]. As the Bible puts it—the place left vacant for who is to come [*pour qui va venir*]. (Derrida & Ferraris 2001, pp. 30–31)

Here, the place left vacant with bread and wine at the Seder table, waiting for Elijah to arrive, does not bespeak someone who has *left* but someone who is *coming*. As with "the vacant throne," it represents someone who is not here, who is not a given, not present, but this absence is now not a once-present and now vacated Self which is elsewhere and still governing, like the risen Christ or some Cartesian "I am" or some Husserlian "transcendental subjectivity" which experiences itself as "above this world" (Husserl, 1970, p. 50). This empty chair now stands for *a future which has yet to come* (*avenir*). The futurity represented by the empty chair is not a given, not "frozen" (Smith, 2000; Loy, 1999), not "foreclosed" (Smith, 1999a) but "yet to be decided." What will become of me, what will become of this work I am producing—all this is still coming, is not yet settled, and no amount of hurry or anxiety or effort will outrun this eventuality.

This is what is "given": this empty chair.

In this light, the empty chair, like the Grade One room-portraits, portray an inhabitant who *has a future,* who is always yet-to-be-itself, yet to fully and finally arrive. So, even Nathan's lamentations over van Gogh's empty chair and the impending sense of loss and death it portends points to the fact that here we are—who would have thought?—over a century later and half a world away, experiencing van Gogh's suicide and the work-signs he left of his life, and the room portrait trace of his leaving. Van Gogh has died and has no future. But imaginally speaking, here we are, still living out the work he left. Not unlike Nathan himself, what van Gogh's work will turn out to be is still yet-to-be-decided and it is being decided anew right here, right now, in this Grade One classroom.

Just to complicate matters further, not just this "self" but these "keeps" are *themselves* not frozen or foreclosed or finished. They are not givens but are "open for the future" (Gadamer, 1989, p. 340). The places we venture with (or without) children in (and out of) school—spelling, reading, mathematics, poetry, art, biology, chemistry, philosophy, Dutch Calvinism, Impressionism, writing, hermeneutics, ecology and so on—are continuously becoming constituted and understood and inhabited differently. They are, so to speak, *living* places or spaces or rooms, (or, if you will, "living disciplines") that form part of our living Earthly inheritance, and as such—as *living,* (i.e., as susceptible to the future)—we "must accept the fact that future generations will understand differently" (Gadamer, 1989, p. 340). When Jennifer surrounded her classroom with prints of van Gogh, Monet, Matisse, Picasso, she was providing her class with a "roomy," generous topic/topography (see Gadamer, 1989, p. 32) whose full meaning is, in its very temporal, finite, contingent nature, still being decided. There is not yet any final word on this place of Impressionism and van Gogh, even though much has been said. Our only option, then, is finding ways to *get in on this conversation* and to speak in ways that *keeps the conversation open* to being taken up anew (Smith, 1999a). To paraphrase a phrase of Derrida's, this topic still has an empty chair at its table of contents. It is still "open" to question, to debate, to transformation, to being understood differently, becoming ignored or forgotten, or to perhaps even becoming despised again as van Gogh and his works once were (Derrida & Ferraris, 2001, p. 32).

The Metaphysics of Genius

The Austrian art historian Hans Sedlmayr gives the title, "The vacant throne" to the final chapter of his essay in cultural criticism, *The Loss of the Centre [Verlust der Mitte]*. Sedlmayr writes: "In the 19th century there was an

> altogether new type of suffering artist: the lonely, lost, despairing artist on the brink of insanity." Van Gogh's chairs constitute a metaphor of the crisis of the entire century. (Walther & Metzger, 1997, p. 9)

This line of argument is also found in Gadamer's (1989) concern over the image of the artist as a mad or tortured genius who has no place in the world and whose works thus became like "vacant thrones." Under such an image:

> Whenever one "comes upon" something that cannot be found through learning and methodical work alone—i.e., whenever there is *inventio* where something is due to inspiration and not methodical calculation—the important thing is *ingenium*, genius. (Gadamer, 1989, p. 54)

Under such a logic, we don't look to the works and what they have to say to us, but to the creator, the one who has generated this work, its "genius" and what the work has to say about this creator-genius ("Nathan is really gifted. He ought to be tested"). We look for the "origin of the work of art" (Heidegger, 1971) in a subjectivity, some great, off-stage "I am" that has uttered the work into existence, sometimes seemingly *ex nihilo.* In this light, van Gogh's paintings are *all* "vacant thrones" that point to the off-stage creative, gifted, genius from whom they have issued and who is, somehow, their "reason" for being.

One of the greatest and most troublesome gifts that Hans-Georg Gadamer's work *Truth and Method* (1989) offers us as educators, a gift in part inherited from his teacher Martin Heidegger, is a disruption of this discourse of "the genius." Much of the early part of this work is dedicated to unearthing how, through what he calls the "subjectivization of aesthetics" (Gadamer, 1989, pp. 42–81), any sort of human production (the *work* of an artist like van Gogh, or the *work* of a burgeoning author and art connoisseur such as Nathan) had become reduced to a sort of "subjective production" that is available only through the equally subjective reactions or responses of a viewer, reader, listener and so on. (This tendency is what Edmund Husserl identified in his *Logical Investigations* [1972] as "psychologism" and to which his phenomenology—which greatly influenced Gadamer's work—was a response). Nathan's description of van Gogh's work and van Gogh's work itself are both understood, under such a logic, as subjective creations which point, most immediately and fundamentally, *to the subjectivity who produced them.* Worldly works are therefore understood as "creations" which are comprehensible only insofar as we unearth or recreate the "creator" of the work (this was, according to Gadamer [1989, p. 187 and following] a central desire of Schleiermacher's [1768–1834] version of hermeneutics, where understanding the work of a creator-genius, in fact, understanding any historical inheritance, becomes a matter of "congeniality"—a matter, one might say, of "like-mindedness").

In Nathan's case, rather than approaching his work and the worlds it opens up, and thus encountering him becoming himself *in the midst of* and *in the keep of* and *in relation to* these worlds, we pursue a type of subjective, psychologistic attribution of talents, backgrounds, skills, proclivities, likes, dislikes, or gifts. We want to fill the empty chair by metaphysically positing a presentable, knowable, assessable, given, self-identical generator of the work from whom the work gets its original/originary authoritative/authorial (Jardine, 1992b) bestowal of meaning, its *mens auctoris*. Thus, under the metaphysics of genius, we call out to the author to save us from the task of interpreting the questions that the work itself places *us* under.

Likewise, our responses to this painting or these words have themselves become subjectivized. Just think of how epistemologically timid we have become. I might suggest that Nathan's description of van Gogh's work is wonderful, but, under the metaphysics of genius, all I am actually reporting about is myself—my responses, my thoughts, my perspectives, my opinions, my experiences. Under the metaphysics of genius, we are not drawn out of ourselves into a worldly meditation with each other about a world that is already full of a "multifariousness of voices." Rather—and not disingenuously meant and not exactly false either—we get a commonplace educational adage, "Nathan is so thoughtful." The next most commonplace adage is "you are a really experienced teacher who loves art. I could never do that." In this later case, the metaphysics of genius is attributed to the teacher instead of the child, thus keeping in place the inability to explore—or to see the worthwhileness or even, sometimes, the *possibility* of exploring—the work itself and the worlds it might portend.

Under the metaphysics of genius, to understand the work, then, is, to some extent, to *turn away from the work itself* towards its creator through a de-coding of the author's intent or meaning or desire or experience or background circumstances or "knowledge, skills and attitudes" (all versions of the *mens auctoris*). This, of course, recapitulates a much older metaphysic: that the world itself, in all its rich array, is understandable, venerable, worthy of our attention, only insofar as it is understood as a sign of God's creative beneficence. All things are only *ens creata*, and, under this gaze, becoming enamored of any worldly thing in and for itself or in terms of its mundane, Earthly inhabitations is a form of fallen-ness and a source of potential deceit, deception, seduction or betrayal. Hence, an old argument that the Church has long-since had with the advent of modern science: figuring out the worldly causes of worldly things is a vacuous and pretentious enterprise. Why? Because, in their deepest reality, all worldly things are "vacant thrones" pointing to the One great off-stage Creator (which becomes recapitulated in the Enlightenment's capitalization of Reason). And, to the extent that humanity is made in God's image, we, too, although in much more contingent and mundane ways, are both the crown of the *ens creata* and are ourselves creators of works *ingenia*—all of which, again, becomes recapitulated in the Enlightenment's vision of Reason.

Even though it appears that we have arrived in a place that is quite arcane, traces of this phenomenon are rampant in education. To understand this gift that Nathan has handed us requires handing it back to him. It's *his.* Doing anything else, under the metaphysics of genius, would simply involve imposing our own views on his, robbing him of his voice and replacing his *ingenium* with ours. But then here comes the constructivist horror hidden in the metaphysics of genius—"the old mythology of an intellect which glues and rigs together the world's matter with its own forms" (Heidegger, 1985, p. 70). This pernicious phenomenon is at work for many "qualitative researchers" who tie themselves in knots taking transcripts back to their "authors" for checks on what the words mean *to the author,* all in a valiant effort to not "impose" on the transcripts their own "forms." It is at work, therefore, in the desire of many "qualitative researchers' to report to us what their participants mean (somehow imagining themselves as the "representatives" or "stand ins" for their absent participants [another appearance of a "vacant throne" in a transcript that now the qualitative researcher attempts to fill?]). Under this same metaphysics of genius, researchers become perpetually caught in the epistemological dead-end: "I can only tell you what I thought the participant meant when I took their transcript back to them with *my* interpretation of what it means and heard them say this about what I said they said." Even the sad and impossible question that some will ask ("How many times should I take it back to my participants?") bespeaks the spell of the metaphysics of genius.

And it is clearly at work in the profound silence Jennifer encountered from those who read Nathan's words. All in all, we hide a deep desire for the author to come fill this chair that has been left empty before us.

We can't believe, perhaps, that this chair has been left empty *for* us.

"So True, So Fully Existing"

> Martin] Heidegger shows that the work of art [and, in his later work, Earthly things and even words themselves] [are] not merely the product of an ingenious creative process, but that [they can be] *works* that [have their] own

> brightness in [themselves]; [they are] there [*da*], "so true, so fully existing." (Gadamer, 1994, pp. 23–24)

> The chair waits for something
> The brick floor gives a chill in the air
> Days pass, but everything is still
> nobody sits on the chair
> Nobody even notices

These passages have been recited because returning to it helps dislodge a final feature of the metaphysics of genius by introducing a phenomenon that does not make an appearance under the metaphysics of genius: the worldly repose of things.

Having been through the twists and turns of this chapter, I now experience how both van Gogh's painting and Nathan's writing have each become much more fulsome and troublesome and provocative and substantial than they initially were. Each of them has become, so to speak, "stronger" and more robust than either would have been without the appearance of the other. This is a version of the "art of strengthening" that Gadamer (1989, p. 367) suggests defines a true conversation:

> [It] consists not in trying to discover the weakness of what is said, but in bringing out its real strength. It is not the art of arguing (which can make a strong case out of a weak one), but the art of thinking (which can strengthen by referring to the subject matter).

In fact, unexpectedly venturing into this world of Impressionist painting once again in this Grade One classroom, having been in this place many times before, facing Nathan's words and the reappearance of van Gogh and this cascade of empty chairs and vacant thrones and dreams of rooms and habitations, I'm struck again by how incommensurate to this Earthly place is my knowledge and experience of it (a first beginning of an ecological humiliation of "constructivism," wherein the limits of my own experience are experienced). In fact, the more I experience of this place, the more often I find my way around it, the more threads of referentiality and ancestry and dependence and kin that I can muster, the more incommensurate my knowledge and experience become.

Put the other way around, the more often I venture to this place, the more experiences I have of it, the better *it* gets.

This is, in fact, a rather ordinary thing: the more we learn and experience about a particular artist or composer, or about a painting or piece of music, the more often we return to a piece of wilderness in all its various seasons, the more we pay attention to the cycles of Pine Grosbeaks and their tethers to weather and sun, the more often we arc together circle-segment cross-hatches in the bisecting of angles the more deeply do we experience the fact that these things have lives of their own, "beyond my wanting and doing" (Gadamer, 1989, p. xxviii), beyond my "rigging and gluing" (Heidegger, 1985, p. 70).

Therefore, as my experience-of-this-place grows, I come to realize more and more deeply a profound ecological point: *this place is not just here for me.* It does not just "face this way," so to speak. It "stands-in-itself." It has its own "repose":

> The existing thing does not simply offer us a recognizable and familiar surface contour; it also has an inner depth of self-sufficiency that Heidegger calls "standing-in-itself." The complete unhiddenness of all beings, their total objectification (by means of a representation that conceives things in their perfect state [fully given, fully present, fully presented, finished]) would negate this standing-in-itself of beings and lead to a total leveling of them. A complete objectification of this kind would no longer represent beings that stand in their own being. Rather, it would represent nothing more than our opportunity for using beings, and what would be manifest would be the will that seizes upon and dominates things. [In the face of van Gogh's work, or Nathan's] we experience an absolute opposition to this will-to-control, not in the sense of a rigid resistance to the presumption of our will, which is bent on utilizing things, but in the sense of the superior and intrusive power of a being reposing in itself. (Gadamer, 1977, pp. 226–227)

There is an empty chair, not just facing here, inviting, welcoming, waiting, but also on this table's hither side.

This is where the notion of the metaphysics of genius really begins to hit home pedagogically. When Jennifer chose to surround her Grade One children with works of the Impressionists, she understood that this world, this space, this place, this "room" has its own repose and part of the work of the classroom adorned with these works became to introduce her students to their repose. This is the great and necessary pretense of an experienced teacher: even though these children may not at the outset experience the repose of this place, their teacher is experienced in this place. They have come to know their way around which means that they have experienced for themselves that this place stands-in-itself and has a repose that is worthy of children's (and teachers') attention. An odd and pedagogically familiar faith follows here: as a teacher, I know that, if the right work can be done *here,* with *these* students, within all the frailties of *this* classroom, *this* year, that repose just might come forward and show itself in all its myriadness and generosity and openness and undecidedness:

> All things show faces, the world not only a coded signature to be read for meaning, but a physiognomy to be faced. As expressive forms, things speak; they show the shape they are in. They announce themselves, bear witness to their presence: "Look, here we are." They regard us beyond how we may regard them, our perspectives, what we intend with them, and how we dispose of them. (Hillman, 2006a, p. 33)

This strikes another ecological blow to the metaphysics of genius and the confidences of constructivism: that things might regard us beyond how we may regard them. That even in those times in which we force the witness to give answer to questions of our own determining, we are being witnessed as well, beyond our own determination.

As the above cited passage from Gadamer suggests, this experience of repose is not simple, familiar and easily had. Repose is not a "surface feature" that is simply lying there, somehow out in the open and immediate and obvious. The appearance of the living repose of things *requires something of us.* An experience of repose has to be *cultivated.*

Ecologically, this is such a simple point. It takes no time, patience, effort, learning, work or love to simply use this place for our own ends or to experience this place only in light of our own "wanting and doing," (Gadamer, 1989, p. xxviii) our own ingenious "rigging and gluing" (Heidegger 1985, p. 70), our own effortful "seizing and dominating"(Gadamer, 1977, pp. 226–227). It does, however, take time and effort and work and love and patience and learning to come to experience this place in its repose. Experiencing this place in its repose—say, this place of Impressionist paintings—is experiencing that it stands there in ways that no amount of our experiencing, however ingenious, can fill.

PREAMBLE 9

Guarding Waterways

I ask, "What can I do to survive in the midst of the show?"
not, "How do I improve show business?"
—Ivan Illich (2001, p. 3)

"Guarding the sensory facilities,"
means protecting your mind against attachment and hostility.
—Tsong-Kha-Pa (2000, p. 101)

The very idea of guarding the eye, guarding one's senses from the things that surround us can seem quite antiquated, especially in these days of relentless hyper-stimulation in all directions and at all times. Prudence in such matters has lost most of Latin origins of *prudentia*: "intelligence" or "discretion," and perhaps especially lost is the sense of the "wisdom to see what is virtuous" (On-Line Etymological Dictionary). But there is a glimmer here, of something vaguely familiar:

> Until quite recently, the guard of the eyes was not look upon as a fad, nor written off as internalized repression. Our taste was trained to judge all

In Praise of Radiant Beings, pages 123–126

> forms of gazing on the other. Today, things have changed. The shameless gaze is in, but I am not speaking of leering. (Illich, 2001, p. 5)

The "*custodia oculorum,* the guarding of the eye" (Illich, 2005, p. 108) thus involves judgment regarding *how we gaze,* but also judgment regarding *what* I might surround myself with that would aid in such custody.

More plainly put, as mentioned in Preamble 8, what I surround myself with will make a difference to what becomes of me. To the extent that I surround myself with junk or have this forced upon me by circumstance, my life risks living up to this surround. To the extent that my environs are filled with disposable, cheap things that not only do not need any concerted or careful attention but in fact repel such advances in the name of convenience or immediate satisfaction, to that extent, my attentiveness becomes stunted, my carefulness unpracticed, my gaze weakened or unpracticed.

I become disposable. And the same goes for the students in a classroom. The dumber the books, the dumber tests, the dumber the students (and the teacher) must be to live and survive in such surroundings and the gaze such surroundings put us under.

All this, of course, is linked to the extent to which I am free to choose or at least shape my surroundings and guard attention, cultivate devotion and the calm needed for the sudden of aesthesis, breath:

> The word for perception or sensation in Greek was *aesthesis,* which means at root a breathing in or taking in of the world, the gasp, "aha," the "uh" of the breath in wonder, shock, amazement, and aesthetic response. (Hillman, 2006a, p. 36)

Things in the world can take our breath away, and composing ourselves in the presence of such things takes practice and it does something to you when you do this. You become composed. All this is linked to finding a refuge wherein such shaping and practice might, however momentarily, be cultivated, honored, adored. And it may be that I cannot carry these things back into the school where I work or the Faculty from which I've retired but which still haunts.

Tsong-kha-pa (2000, p. 64): "Cultivate love for those who have gathered." And those gathered—my true "colleagues"—might not, for now, be those across the school hallway. One would always hope for this proximity and it requires a patient "consciousness that must leave the door ajar" (Hillman, 1979, p. 154) for this possibility. But it also means, at the same time, protecting, guarding so that such consciousness might develop and not be tricked out into its own despoiling. Sometimes, I cannot manage remaining composed, not because of some property of the object or person or surroundings I encounter, but because of the nature of the specific afflictions that I carry and sometimes bury, sometimes "work on," sometimes even deny.

In other words, my patience is often limited and my avoidance of hostility and attachment is fragile and specific. I must resign myself to the fact that certain things tempt me more than others, certain ideas, emotions, places, objects, images, are more luring and distracting than others. "Distraction," for example, or "anger" repeatedly plague all sentient beings to varying degrees, but precisely how and when and whether these plagues *me* is specific, concrete, fading, getting worse, circumstantial, irrelevant, improving, proving to be too much or not enough, then relevant again unexpectedly, and so on. Such matters are common human concerns. What is of importance in our commiserations about it is not to occlude how this always comes home to roost with great specificity.

As a child, my asthmatic tendency needed protection from those things that cued it off. Over and over again, I'd venture down to the end of Green Street to sit by Lake Ontario and listen, and let my boy attention drift outwards over a large expanse—outbreath, in its way, where rough exasperation turns to aspiration, composure of a sort.

> Swimming, 1957, Lake Ontario, off the redbrick Legion Hall parking lot south of Water Street, just after the Aylmer Factory had burped out the leftover bilge of tomato canning, and how this hot-scented red-scummed flotation that made the water flapthick muffled and fly surface buzzy melded into the Polio Scares and the summers of no swimming at all. (Jardine, 2008b, pp. 176–177)

This is probably why the sound of water—the audible expression of *its* aspiration—had such an effect and such a long lingering.

> When we find ourselves in dangerous situations in which there are abundant stimulants for the afflictions, we should cultivate the antidotes to them with a proportionate intensity and we should stand up to them in a thousand ways. It is said that the best practitioners use as the path the very object that gives rise to the afflictions. Average practitioners apply the antidotes and hold their ground. Practitioners of a more basic capacity must abandon such objects and retreat. (Pelden, 2007, pp. 253–254)

> I must learn to love that I *am* best, average and basic, slip-slidy. This myriad of "ams," too, gathers around. To listen. I have birdcalls in me. And the skulls of our dogs killed by cougars are implanted near my spine, clipped on with hard cold metal spikes, forming part of my rib caging, sometime too closely enclosing labored pulls of breath. (Jardine, 2014, p. 34)

Sometimes, and sometimes quite unexpectedly, I must abandon and retreat into refuges that will help me compose myself all over again. I might *think* things are "fine," and then be found out and betrayed by an unexpected circumstance.

When the tendency to skitter calms down, when I calm, the thing I am meditating upon also calms down and is given the freedom to elaborate itself, like this following chapter from 2008, where water, well attended, translated itself into a small piece, partially in honor of Ted Aoki and his keening. This goes right back to Preamble 1 and those courses at the University of Victoria in British Columbia years and years ago. It reminds me, too, of how, years and years ago, I was sitting watching quails skitter by up on Mount Douglas in Victoria, BC, and, eventually, they turned their attention away from me.

Once I was there, they became there as well.

Left in peace, "things appear in their *Eigen-licht,* their own sparkle" (Illich, 2001a, p. 9). "A being reposing in itself" (Gadamer, 1977, p. 227) such that this "in itself" is the whole of its surroundings which surrounds my attention as well. (Is this also Martin Heidegger's invocation of *eigentlich,* of "authenticity"—being oneself and no other—in *Being and Time* [1962]?)

One gesture, one sound of water.

This reminds me, too, of Gary Snyder's (1989) contention that the stillness of Zen meditation is probably linked to the long-practiced ability of a hunter to still themselves for the kill, so that game will appear (see Latremouille, 2015, Jardine, 2015b).

And in this particular surround, I have basic capacity. I am become the blood-letting of that very cougar I cannot yet forgive.

Meanwhile another cat walked by as I put this book together. I had clean and clear forgotten Shirane's (1996, p. 51) thoughts, cited in the following chapter: "*sabi*: the sound of the water paradoxically deepens the sense of surrounding quiet." Forgotten altogether when, six years later, Jackie Seidel and I wrote "*Wabi Sabi* and the Pedagogical Countenance of Names" (Seidel & Jardine, 2014b). This says something about the persistence of threads of family resemblance. Hints, too, in the following chapter, of an occasion of *pratitya-samutpada,* of dependent co-arising, from the following Chapter:

> "To read required that the text be inhabited by and inhabiting of the breath of the one reading."

9

Translating Water (2008)

> Water is not only meant to reveal itself to the eye and the touch, but to speak and sing in seventeen different registers. Thus dream waters mumble and ebb and swell and roar and trickle and splash and stream and dally, and they wash you and can carry you away. They can rain from above and well up from the depths. (Illich, 1992, pp. 145–146)

All Translation Is Interpretation

All translation is interpretation.
—Hans-Georg Gadamer (1900–2002)

Furuike ya kawazu tobikomu izu no oto
An old pond: a frog jumps in—the sound of water.
—Matsuo Basho (1644–1694)

Matsuo Basho's (1644–1694) old haiku is lovingly attended to in Hiroaki Sato's book *One Hundred Frogs: From Renga to Haiku to English* (1983). Along with placing the delicate art of the word and its translation in a tangled nest of wonderful historical, philosophical, cultural, spiritual, aesthetic, linguistic, and ecological contexts, Sato gathers together "one

In Praise of Radiant Beings, pages 127–137

hundred frogs": dozens and dozens of suggested translations and takes on Basho's original work.

Already, the above citation (from Sato, 1983, p., 149) from Basho betrays the fact that the original Japanese text, which is itself already a translation of a deeply meditative, lived-experience, is herewith *transliterated.* Already, the betrayals of words and their ways are deep and abiding. I will leave it to others to delve this depth. All I have for pedagogical experience, here, is the weird work of teaching young children whose tongues are other-wise that, in English, you have to start at the left hand side of a word and move through it to the right in sounding it out. And this—"sounding it out"—needs to be done as a way of trying to work out a word you don't recognize "on sight," shall we say. As with, say, Japanese, "frog" is read by a reader "familiar" with this word, not as a string of soundable phonemes but as something recognized all at once, more like a picture seen in one glance and uttered in one sound, *frog.*

I must add, here, how fascinated a Grade 2 class was recently when we spoke together about the old, Early Medieval quarrels about "silent reading" (very common in contemporary elementary school classrooms) and "reading out-loud." It is lost to memory that the very idea of silent reading entered into European consciousness around the eleventh century (see Stock, 1983; Carruthers, 2003, 2005; Carruthers& Ziolkowski, 2002; Illich, 1992, 1993; Illich & Sanders, 1988), and has ancestries leading back to Augustine's idea of the "inner voice" or "inner word" (see Arthos, 2009).

In almost all cases, texts were 'til then *voiced* when read. The idea of "silent reading" made no sense, since, without the voice's mutterings, without transport on the breath, without the spirit performing the text, the text remained dead and useless and meaningless. To read required that the text be inhabited by and inhabiting of the breath of the one reading. This means becoming familiar with this habitat and its vestiges. We still recognize that some of us are better out-loud readers than others, and that to read silently something that one does not understand is one thing, but to try to read it aloud is truly strange and estranging. And all this is to say nothing yet about the differences, in elementary schools, between reading a story and telling a story.

Around the eleventh century, two co-incident movements of thought occurred with a common consequence. Once written texts became more widespread, it became more possible to imagine the voices of the ancients housed in texts outside of myself. As such, as the ancients moved outwards into the world beyond my breath and voice, my sense of "myself" moved inwards. "Myself" became increasingly more singular, purged, less haunted by the ghostly voices of others. Knowledge became "out there" as I became "in here," and European philosophy was ripe for the moves of Cartesianism that fulfills the purging (the "de-worlding," disincarnating) of the self with a clear and distinct but empty "I am."

As "myself" becomes more intimately "interior," "silent reading" starts to make more sense. Moreover, as the voice moved inwards and reading aloud became less and less predominant, texts began to have to be punctuated, chaptered, headlined, paginated, and spaces began to appear between words. All this work had to become written which was once done by the out-loud reading voice. Thus, began what Ivan Illich and Barry Sanders (1988) named "the alphabetization of the modern mind." Wonderfully, to name just these two for now, "silent reading" and "punctuation" in Grade Two are not simply language arts techniques to be mastered by children and bloodlessly inscribed as Curriculum Requirements. They are also lovely old stories about how things were once different about the voice, the breath, the sound of words, and the puncturing of calf-skins with inks.

Betrayal

There is an old Italian saying: "Traduttore, traditore [to translate is to betray]."

—Bethune, 2002)

The last part of Basho's (already translated and transliterated) text is what is of interest here. A great ecological and meditative confluence: the sound of water and its translation into words.

Translation—it "betrays" something, hands something over one to another, it gives something away and takes something back. And, hermeneutically understood, this is precisely the roots, too, of those traditions which are not only handed over to us and in whose "handing down" (Gadamer, 1989, p. 284) we are already inevitably involved, but to which, inversely, we have always already been handed over. Our very act of being human is already to be handed over, betrayed, visible and audible, presumed-upon, witnessed, not just witnessing, known, not just knowing. We don't begin as self-determining subjectivities but as already having been handed over to the ways of things (our language[s] and culture[s] and so on, all mixed and multifarious and, to the extent that we belong to them, often deathly silent and presumed). We are already betrayed by our belonging.

To *understand* this betrayal—to open them up to being other-wise—is the work of hermeneutics. To understand is to betray these betrayals, that is, to *interpret* them.

Kerplunk!

> What the expression expresses is not merely what is supposed to be expressed in it—what is meant by it—but primarily what is also expressed by the words without its being intended (i.e., what the expression, as it were, "betrays"). In this wider sense, the word "expression" refers to far more than linguistic expression; rather, it includes everything that we have to get behind, and that at the same time enables us to get behind it. Interpretation, therefore, does not refer to the sense intended, but to the sense that is hidden and has to be disclosed. The translator must preserve the character of his own language, the language into which he is translating, while still recognizing the value of the alien, even antagonistic character of [what is being translated]. (Gadamer, 1989, p. 336)

Back to Hiroaki Sato's book, consider the intimate relation between the translationary betrayals of words and this living, Earthly presence, in Basho's words, of "the sound of water." (Hamill & Kaji, 2000). Throughout Sato's collection, this last part of the *haiku* variously becomes voiced as "hark, water's music" (Bryan, in Sato, 1983, p. 152), "the splash" (Miyamori, in Sato, 1983, p. 152), "sleeping echoes awake" (Saito, in Sato, 1983, p. 153), "plop!" (Blyth, in Sato 1983, p. 154), "the water's noise" (Fraser, in Sato, 1983, p. 154), "WATERSPLASH" (Beilenson, in Sato, 1983, p. 155), "a deep resonance" (Yuasa, in Sato, 1983, p. 159), "a frog-leaps-in- splash . . . " (O'Donnol, in Sato, 1983, p. 159), "Kdang!" (Bond, in Sato, 1983, p. 160), "water-note" (Maeda, in Sato, 1983, p. 160), "with splash-splosh" (Ikeda, in Sato, 1983, p. 161).

There are dozens more that are offered. From Alan Ginsberg, from whose work we've come to expect a complex relation to such matters of poetry and sound and the Beat-East, we get (I'm tempted to say "of course"), "kerplunk" (Ginsberg, in Sato, 1983, p. 164):

> Ker—The first element in numerous onomatopoeic or echoic formations intended to imitate the sound or the effect of the fall of some heavy body, as *kerchunk, -flop, -plunk, -slam, -slap, -splash, -souse, -swash, -swosh, -thump, -whop,* etc. U.S. vulgar—1903, in *Outing* XLIII. 83/1 "The sound made by the water when the frog dives, we used to express when we were boys, by the word *'kerplunk'*." (Online Etymological Dictionary)

One could also consider trickle, slosh, plash, popple, ripple, burble, purl, gurgle, swash and murmur: various English soundings of "the play of water" (Gadamer, 1989, p. 332).

Surely, in this *haiku,* these final words also *mean something* (breaking the surface, interrupting the stillness, opening the depths, or perhaps the sudden crack of sound that announces enlightenment after the stillness of the pond is broken ["breaking open the *being* of the object" as Hans-Georg Gadamer (1989, p. 360) describes interpretation's betrayals]). But still there is (to coin a phrase) a "plop" in which the ear abides.

Remember with those boys in 1903 the great turbulent thunks of a flat stone tossed high and entering water perfectly straight at a great Pythagorean right-angle?

An air-capturing ga-goomp like a bullfroggy throating?

And how my using these words this way betrays a different world than Bryan's (Sato, 1983, p. 152) already cited neo-Victorian "Hark." What is betrayed in translating the sound of water into words is not just the sound of water but the sounding of the words themselves, portrayed, in this citation, with the sound-word "resonance":

> Every word breaks forth as if from a center and is related to a whole, through which alone it is a word. Every word causes the whole of the language to which it belongs to resonate. (Gadamer, 1989, p. 458)

It Will Startle You

> The French have a saying: "*Traduire, c'est trahir*—to translate is to betray." (Doublebirdie, 2005)
>
> The sound of water implies . . . the eye and the ear of a recluse attentive to the minute changes in nature and suggests a large meditative loneliness, sometimes referred to as *sabi*: the sound of the water paradoxically deepens the sense of surrounding quiet. (Shirane, 1996, p. 51)
>
> **Number**: 38848
>
> **Quotation**: "Meditation and water are wedded forever."
>
> **Attribution:** Herman Melville (1819–1891), U.S. author. Moby-Dick (1851), chapter 1, *The Writings of Herman Melville*, vol. 6, eds. Harrison Hayford, Hershel Parker, and G. Thomas Tanselle (1988).
>
> (http://www.bartleby.com/66/48/38848.html)

Out for a walk by the Elbow River and the various creeks that trickle into it. Remembering another of Basho's great invocations, this time to the pine tree:

> From the pine tree
> learn of the pine tree,
> And from the bamboo
> of the bamboo.
> (see the spectacular http://www.ahapoetry.com/haiku.htm)

And so too it is with the sound of water. Basho's Haiku-invocation is a chance to remember that Earth-places can be great teachers, that there is learning to be had in the terrible presence of things and their ways. There is perishing here in this walking meditation that hears, a great sense of *passing*:

> If there are such things as natural symbols, then sounds are surely the natural symbol of transience and the lostness of past time. They are essentially evanescent, an exact correlative of wistfulness and poignant regret, not to mention sentimentality. They seem to be nature's way of mourning. (Ree, 2000, pp. 23–24)

Again, a great mediaeval debate. To read out loud is to interpret, because casting written texts up into the voice is an act of incarnating, enspiriting and bringing to life what it is saying to us ("awakened into spoken language," as Gadamer [1989, 394] puts it). Reading a text out loud means that I (and not just the text's "author") am *saying* these words. Something happens when we read something aloud. The voice is asked to experience the truth of the words in uttering them, and that truth is carried on a voice full of perishing and mourning and lostness, even when, perhaps especially when the words sounded speak to a truth that will outlast the breath of that frail voice itself. The voice and its sounds "passes by" like texts do not. The voice and its breathing pass away into silence. The airs stop moving, even while the written text remains, now the corpse of the vanished breath.

Where water sounds, water breathes. Hearing the sound of water is hearing the breathing (aeration) of water:

> a frog-pond ploomp!
> makes it breathe.
> (Flygare, in Sato, 1983, p. 167)

To hear the breathing of water is to be one who breathes:

> Seeing the frailty of your life through seeing the breath is the meditation on the recollection of death. Just realizing this fact—that if the breath goes in but does not go out again, or goes out but does not come in again, your life is over—is enough to change the mind. It will startle you into being aware. (Chah, 2001, p. 44)

Soundwalk near the river's edge with a difficult task in mind, and as a form of meditative obedience, to hear or to heed such perishing—the "emptying out" of things beyond their feigned and timid self-containment, out into all their relations. Caught in the sounding bristles of water's tricks over rocks, listening to the auditory spaciousness of the place and how the soundplays of water play out a huge, sensuous, multifarious voicing. This sound of riverwater sounds the distance of that rock face on the far side and later, as the face slopes downwards and away, the sound sounds this movement of rock (which is at once a movement of an animal body past such rock movements. This is *one thing*, not two) and can be heard to belong properly to it. Listening to its shifts and flutters as we walk—shifts in how these sounds are spread out territorially, marked around this animal-body and its bi-aurality: lefts, rights, distances, closeness, aheads, behinds, echoes off of steep rock-shorelines. The sound is framed by distant read squirrel chits and chats whose scold is not about us. There's something up over there—bear? Other hikers? A hawk perhaps?

Riversound. Woodswater. Pinepitched. Mourning. That heart-breaking sound of an unseen Red-Tailed Hawk overhead downstream has already disappeared without a trace.

("An asthmatic squeal, *keeer-r-r* [slurring downwards]) (Peterson, 1980, p. 154), like scratching the underside of the sky's blue.

Sharpness of small fast bitty-trickles make breath rush a bit in a new wash of sounds. Listening to the breadth of this river's sounding is listening to a great three-dimensional space that surrounds this body. *This* body, here, now, full of aches, and now, in writing, remembered specifically in attempts to compose this waterwalk in the composures of writing.

But this is not quite yet a good betrayal of the sound of water. Consider: that these specific soundings, to be *just thus*, require *just these* rocks placed *just so*. These exact sounds require *exactly this* relation between gravels and shallows and high-pitched trickles. This is the sound, not just of these gravels, but of their having arrived here, with all the flooded stormwearing meticulousness that requires, with gravities and icecold rockbreakings and the shatters of falling cliffpieces. All of this is what this sound *is*.

This is its betrayal.

Further along, *these* exact sounds require *exactly this* placement of large rocks that can capture drumskins of air into deep, hollow-sounding adumbrations. And all of this requires all the ages of glaciers and plate shifts and spring run-offs and water-wearings and those cold ice Alberta winters and bear scramblings that, over a vast and patient time, placed just *that* pebble *there*. Consider: what am I *hearing* in the sound of water? It is an abstraction to think of sound waves and auditory canals alone (recall, however, that auditory canals are themselves partially swirls of water's sound-bearings). It is equally abstract to think that I am not hearing the ancestral ecological voices of this whole place, echoing just here, just now, in all its frail and passing particularity.

Shirane's *sabi*: a small, delicate water-sound like the lap at the water's edge can only sound in an acre of quiet. The smaller the sound, the larger the quiet must be. The smaller the sound, the larger the quiet becomes. *Hearing* the rock ancestries of this small sound "deepens the sense of surrounding quiet." It is the rocks-having-happened-to-fall-here sounding:

> Stillness and activity are actually the same thing. This short poem demonstrates that if there were no stillness to the old pond, there would be no sound as a frog jumps into the water. The activity exists as the same moment as the non-activity, they are the same thing. (http://openpoetry.com/BashoMatsuo)

It is ages sounding, just right here. It is all this handing-down that is betrayed. This trickle of water greened from the mineral-spring richness, *this* trickle betrays all things.

This is called "ecological awareness."

A Being Reposing in Itself

> License is not precisely betrayal, but another kind of faithfulness. But from the point of view of fidelity, understood as being bound to the literal text, it may well be that that other order of faithfulness, the one associated with freedom and license, can only be read as betrayal. (Butler, 2004, p. 82)

Every translation of the sound of water into words, as with every translation of the words for the sound of water into another tongue—every translation is a betrayal, an interpretation that breaks open the being of the object and makes it vulnerable to the otherwise ear and tongue and imagination.

However, as Judith Butler hints, this need not be understood only negatively, as if human language somehow necessarily distorts or despoils the immediacies of ecological experience (standing here, body-facing, sounding water all around). Every translation of the sound of water into written words is also capable of *betraying something* of the sound of water, that is, revealing something, making something *show* about the sound of water, as much as leaving the sound of water still unsaid. It is easy to imagine that the betrayal of words means simply that words fail and do badly by things (I've often wondered if this is what David Abram [1996] is suggesting, paradoxically given how beautiful a writer he is). I'm suggesting that in their very failure to capture and claim the thing altogether (in their failure to make the thing face this way and no other), they succeed in presenting the sound of water that, even though it is uttered in words, remains experienced, in these words, as *there,* "beyond my wanting and doing" [Gadamer, 1989, p. xxviii]), "standing there" (Heidegger's *Da*], reposing beyond the words themselves:

> The existing thing does not simply offer us a recognizable and familiar surface contour; it also has an inner depth of self-sufficiency that Heidegger calls "standing-in-itself." [Illich's *Eigen-licht*?] The complete unhiddenness of all beings, their total objectification (by means of a representation that conceives things in their perfect state [fully given, fully present, fully presented, fully written or spoken, finished]) would negate this standing-in-itself of beings and lead to a total leveling of them. A complete objectification of this kind would no longer represent beings that stand in their own being. Rather, it would represent nothing more than our opportunity for using beings, and what would be manifest would be the will that seizes upon and dominates things. In [hermeneutic experience] we experience an absolute opposition to this will-to-control, not in the sense of a rigid resistance to the presumption of our will, which is bent on utilizing things, but in the sense of the superior and intrusive power of a being reposing in itself. (Gadamer, 1977, pp. 226–227)

Cultivating this experience of the repose of things is what hermeneutics calls "the art of writing" (Gadamer, 1989, p. 390). In regard to the arguments regarding silent reading and reading out loud and speaking, Gadamer suggests that some writing that is well wrought "reads itself," (p. 390), writing which "draws readers into the course of thought," (p. 390), its "productive movement" (p. 390) in which the art of writing appears artless and disappears in favour of the appearance of the thing itself.

Moreover, every translation of the sound of the words for the sound of water into another tongue *betrays something* of the life of the words translated (in *both* tongues—"Hark," "kerplunk") and of the sound of water (it *shows* something about words and tongues and water's sounds and how each tongue sings such sounds out loud). Words are not *representations of things.* Words are not *stand-ins.* Words that bespeak the sound of water are meant to make it present, to show it off, to lead us to it and offer us up to its ways, not to stand in front of it and block our way. They are not substitutes but rather heralds of the arrival of the thing.

Words are another kind of faithfulness, a presentation of water's sound, a voice of the voicing thing.

In words, the thing appears. It is not just *referred to.*

Opening Ripples

Jane Reichhold, [see http://www.ahapoetry.com/haiku.htm], who fires off missives on *haiku* over the Internet claims that Basho's final phrase can be literally "water of sound" in Japanese: "The water of sound. Sound as water. Sound moving as water does. Sound rippling outward as water does when disturbed." She's suggesting that Basho's concluding phrase is an actual visual image—in water—of how sound moves. But I noticed—amazingly could feel—that the final Japanese words make an auditory equivalent of how waves of sound/water circle outward from their source fading as they go: *mizu-no-oto.* Do you hear those opening ripples in the repeated o's and in their duration? O's don't cut off like the p's in "plop!" They fade away. Like a *haiku* voiced out. (Bakken, 2003)

Floating in a Jar of Rain

There is an old Italian saying that equates the translator's craft with treason: *"Traduttore, traditore."* A French version, laced with misogyny, suggests that a translation's fidelity to the original is inversely proportional to its aesthetic value: "*Les traductions sont comme les femmes, ou belles ou fideles* ["Translations are like women, either beautiful or faithful/true."]. (Gurria-Quintana, 2006)

Even if translation is treason, it is a necessary form of treachery on which readers depend. (Gurria-Quintana, 2006)

Swallowing
Life rafts of pain pills—
with sips of chills
Basho's frog
floating in a jar of rain—
—Hortensia Anderson (2006, 2007)

Final Pedagogical Reflection

once upon a time ther was a rain drop and it gope on a bird then the sun trd into a watrvapr the radrop fad his bovrsrs and trnd into a fofe white cloud and then it trnd in too a havie plak kloub and then it trd in bake to the sam radrop and gropt on the sam bird.
—Name Eric

Below is a translation which opens this water-text out into a field of "conventionality" and allows its meaning to become visible and audible while, at the same time, betraying its frailty, this young boy and his ear for the soundings of words and their meaning—six years old at the time, writing at the computer—now slipped away into adulthood:

Once upon a time there was a raindrop.
And it dropped on a bird.
The sun turned into a water vapor.
The raindrop found his brothers
And turned into a fluffy white cloud.
And then it turned into a heavy black cloud.
And then it turned back into the same raindrop
And dropped on to the same bird.
—Eric Jardine

I cite it here to be read out loud. It is my chance to mourn anew the sound of water and its passing.

PREAMBLE 10

"Every Secret Loses Its Force"

> Despite the likely alien and awkward feel of the concepts involved, we might, when hearing a sutra, experience a quite innocent sense of wonder—a brief moment of almost childlike, delightful surprise, perhaps colored by a subtle tone of promise and potential. In line with the teachings set out in this book, we might say that just such a brief clearing within simple, unprepared wonder is what constitutes the awakening of faith in the Great Vehicle.
>
> —From the "Translators' Introduction" to Ornament of the Great Vehicle Sutras: Maitreya's Mahayanasutralamakara. (Doctor, 2014, p. vii)

As an undergraduate (in a dual degree of philosophy and religious studies, class of '72) and then as an MA student (in philosophy, class of '75; see Jardine 2016), I recall clear as day that the Mill's Library at McMaster University, Hamilton, Ontario, had a collection of editor Max Müller's Sacred Books of the East. This 50-volume behemoth was a set of English translations produced between 1879 and 1910 and published by Oxford University Press over that time period. It took up several shelves, and the books themselves, especially the earlier volumes, were slick and shiny leather-bound, a sort of dark brownish dried blood color that made the collection look like the hide of some great and exotic beast, slivers of which you could slide out and open.

In Praise of Radiant Beings, pages 139–143

Quite exotic and a slight and trembled taboo for a boy from Burlington, Ontario.

I only pretended to such a collection and mention it because its exotic cast fit with the ways that Buddhism was being interpreted in my philosophy and religious studies classes—Buddhism as a "denial of the will" is a very Schopenhauer-like (1963), Germanic understanding of letting go of the tendency to attach in neurotic ways to things that lure our attention. Sanskrit: Cetanā, something like the urging of the mind to move, to attach. And, of course, this latter rendering is a very pop-culture version of the former. The use of the term "neuroses" for things more "traditionally" translated in Buddhist literature as "afflictions" is one of the weird gifts to this lineage of Chogyam Trungpa (1988, 1990, 2006, 2013).

All translation is betrayal, as detailed in Chapter 9. But this means that all translation "reveals" or opens something; not simply that it blurs or distorts. Such, too, with my long and fraught and often rather silly and flirtatious love affair with Buddhism. Frankly, those M*ü*ller books were way beyond my ken. Boring, frankly. It was "secondary," more "popular" literature that caught my heart and eye.

In 1968, I was reading *The Book: On the Taboo Against Knowing Who You Are* by Alan Watts and other books such as this:

> It is a special kind of enlightenment to have this feeling that the usual, the way things normally are, is odd—uncanny and highly improbable. G.K. Chesteron once said that it is one thing to be amazed at a gorgon or a griffin, creatures which do not exist; but it is quite another and much higher thing to be amazed at a rhinoceros or a giraffe, creatures which do exist and look as if they don't. This feeling of universal oddity includes a basic and intense wondering about the sense of things. (Watts, 1970, pp. 3–4)
>
> . . .
>
> Is there, then, some kind of lowdown on this astounding scheme of things, something that never really gets out through the usual channels? There is. (pp. 4–5)

Much more my speed, more in the cadence I needed at the time, and much more the cadence of the just-post-late-60s times themselves. And it was the first paperback edition of Watts' Myth and Ritual in Christianity (1968) that arrived like a Christmas present, lighting up multi-coloured threads of family resemblance in the Mass that no one every spoke of—no one ever knew?—even in my days as an altar boy. You need no further proof than this from the Preface (p. 1):

> One of the special delights of my childhood was to go and see the cases of illuminated manuscripts in the British museum, and to walk, as every child can, right into their pages—losing myself in an enchanted world of gold, vermillion and cobalt arabesques, of palaces, gardens, landscapes and skies whose colours were indwelt with light as if their sun shone not above but in them [radiant beings!]. Most marvelous of all were the many manuscripts mysteriously entitled "Book of Hours"... scenes of times and seasons—ploughing in springtime, formal gardens bright in summer with heraldic roses, autumn harvesting, and logging in winter snow under clear, cold skies see through a filigree screen of black trees.
>
> ...
>
> I could see that these books were somehow connected with the wonderful recurrence of interesting seasons with strange names—Advent, Christmas, Epiphany, Lent, Easter, Whitsun, Trinity, Michaelmas—names which marked the rotation of the calendar and lent a kind of form and music to the simple succession of days.

Not that I remained especially rapt by my diluted Christian upbringing, but, reading this book, I was startled by the fact that, despite all that, even this had underlying it a sort of secret fabric that seemed, still seems, to be unnoticed and unspoken.

And I am astounded, looking back now in retrospect to those passages from *The Book*—there are hints of a line of thought that it is *even more vital and astounding* (the word "higher" makes me cringe a bit) to be amazed at the turn of an intensely familiar Pine Siskin. Where it becomes the lowdown and I become the oddity. There is even a hint, here, of the idea of "a hitherto concealed experience" (Gadamer, 1989, p. 100), "the existence of which is not even suspected" (Blankelder & Flecther, 2002, p. 9): "something that never gets through the regular channels." And this, of course, implies not just a different subjective state, but implies that there is a different world to be experienced that is not suspected, that is hitherto concealed. The world itself is different than one might ordinarily suspect in the day-to-day distractions and exhaustions of living. One way or another, these popular, often rather psychedelic readings of Buddhist-like thinking (e.g., Ram Dass 1971, and so on) cued off in me a desire to dig beyond the Sixties sense of this word. Hopefully my cringing now can be some sort of lesson. I must admit I'm in love with this secret history.

All of this is to say that there is no such a thing as innocence or perfection in such matters even when they are experienced innocently, naively but deeply felt. Language, and our individual and collective cultural inheritances, aspirations, expectations and the like, color, cloud, and sometimes illuminate, sometimes all in one sentence, one gesture, one word.

Thus, the truths lurking in Buddhist thought face anyone in any era or circumstance, practiced or unpracticed, with a double task whose two tines are not necessarily compatible. I must let what it says stand there and experience how this letting-stand wants to burn off, or shape, or cuddle and care for, or adamantly refuse some of the presumptions I carry, often concealed and unnoticed. I become caught in its light.

Inversely, I am not a Buddhist scholar intent on that lineage in and for itself. My work is in education, in classrooms, with teachers, about curriculum, about our hurried lives and the lusciousness of properly, patiently noticing Siskins that just might, just briefly, provide some refuge and relief. My task, therefore, is also to call threads of Buddhist thought to account for circumstances that it could not have envisaged, via ways of speaking and thinking that are rooted in the life of the circumstances I live in. I am no purist and I don't consider mixing hermeneutic, ecological consciousness and Buddhism together in service of education an act of multi-leveled contamination. Just like did Watts' book on myth and ritual, it made Christianity even harder to *believe* but easier to *adore* (see Chapter 18).

"All understanding is interpretation," as per Chapter 9. All that is needed in such interpretive betrayals is to remain ever wary of how easy it is to be lured into the well-intended pop-culture simplicities that, for example, introduce, with presumed good intentions, "mindfulness practices" into schools (see, e.g., Campbell, 2013, Olson, 2014, Saltzman, 2014 and countless others) and that are already mockingly being called in some quarters "McMindfulness." But if I can be even somewhat forgiven for Alan Watts and Ram Dass and Timothy Leary, surely I can gentle some understanding here, and hope that some light peaks through (for teachers and student alike in this new initiative) like it did for me back at the end of high school.

This persistent, irremediable danger of trivialization and loss of nourishment is described by Martin Heidegger (1962, p. 165) as the tendency towards "leveling down" in the day to day-ness of our lives—where "every secret loses its force" (p. 165) and something like an interest in Buddhism becomes an object of mockery or too *de rigueur* for words.

Facing this danger means going back, again and again, to bloodlines, to sources, to details, to names and dates and places, like any good scholar must do, all in an attempt to burn off "the naïve self-esteem of the present moment" (Gadamer, 1989, p. xxii). Here, and of course, is my own only-half-hidden history of pop-culture naiveties. I was 17 in 1967, and felt on to something secret, something sacred, hidden underneath false but well-meant smiles and false promises of a mind-numbing future. Forgive me if it still shows, but something of it should still show, despite its ignoble origins.

Included here, of course, is the great disappointment when this secret loses its force, the great disillusionment:

> The OED (9th ed.) defines disillusion as 'freedom from illusion; disenchantment', with illusion (< L. illudere, 'mock', < ludere, 'play') meaning variously, 'deception; delusion', 'misapprehension of the true state of affairs.' What is interesting in each of these definitions is the underlying virtue of disillusion; namely, freedom—from illusion, mistakenness, faulty perception. Moreover, the implication is that the freedom inspired by disillusion involves a restoration of the ludic quality of human life, the joy of true play. (Smith, 2014, p. 114)

Is something at play that never gets through the usual channels? There is. Something at play. German: Spiel: "Something is going on, (im Spiele ist), something is happening (sich abspielt)" (Gadamer, 1989, p. 104).

This early flirtation with Buddhism atrophied partly because it was illusory and this means, partly, that it was not really in play in my life. It was, dare I say, a popularly exotic embodiment of an alternative to the surface sheen of things. A still-illusory alternative to an illusion.

So, part of this proved correct, that there was this surface sheen of falsity, and the energies of parsing this "astounding scheme of things" hidden by this sheen, continued unabated. Philosophy, phenomenology, Edmund Husserl, Martin Heidegger, then Jean Piaget and Hans-Georg Gadamer, and so on. It was years before that secret love, that secreted secret, came slowly arcing back and started taking root. Real root, Latin *radice,* radical, not just something carefully studied, but something that changes breath and step. Something with disillusion at its heart, as its goal and practice.

I'm mentioning these vaguely embarrassing (and, dare I say, for me still slightly endearing) autobiographical things merely as a way to encourage anyone to just get started with what's in front of you, and remain alert. Differently put, find a source, a topic, a topography, a well-spring that attracts and holds your attention, and seek alertness in its presence. Don't believe it. Beware of leveling. Stay awake. Sit. Dig.

This is the circumstance we face, that every secret loses its force. Thus it was, when an invitation came to write a Foreword to a collection of essays that demonstrated, in myriad ways, precisely such loving wariness and tough scholarly work (Wang & Eppert 2008), I agreed without hesitation. To be even imagined standing in any line of work like this was and still is a surprise and an honor. It may be that every secret loses its force, but *that* insight—Shhh! with air expelling—can have great force and spark.

10

"The Sickness of the West" (2008)

Understanding is the expression of the affinity of the one who understands to the one whom he understands and to that which he understands.

—Hans-Georg Gadamer (1983, p. 48)

What is this affinity that seems to have developed over the past few decades between the interpretive disciplines in contemporary curriculum theory and, shall we say, the ways of the East? What is the affinity that has allured this wide array of teachers and scholars here, to this place, to this wonderful book you hold in your hands, coming, as they do, from East and West, to meet here, over East and West?

Each of these authors will give answer to this cluster of questions in their own way(s) in the chapters [of this book}. These answers, like these questions, are mighty and prophetic. As "globalism" raises its Hydra-like nest-of-heads, one thing is for sure. This moment, this juncture, feels monumental. East and West just might be on the verge of tearing themselves to pieces all over again, as we have witnessed so often in the course of human affairs. The tragic singular logic that underwrites the West and which

In Praise of Radiant Beings, pages 145–150

shapes and directs its relationships with others—"you are either for us or against us" being only the latest formulation—seems to be sadly inevitable.

Or, maybe, this time, a bit more of the real conversation that we need to have *between* us will have time to occur, to ripen, to heal, even just a bit, just for now. Maybe the conversation can go on. Maybe we can breathe a little while longer. And yet, maybe not. Either way, this book steps into a vital breach.

We(sterners) have had this dance before countless times. In the mid-nineteenth century, Arthur Schopenhauer gobbled up new German translations of Buddhist texts and found his own Kantian face: things "in themselves" are "will" and when things in themselves become tethered to our will, the result is a world of representation, a world that only exists in relation to our willing, a world, Schopenhauer suggests, of *illusion*:

> "The world is my representation": This is a truth valid with reference to every living and knowing being, although man alone can bring it into reflective, abstract consciousness. If he really does so, philosophical discernment has dawned on him. It then becomes clear and certain to him that he does not know a sun and an earth, but only an eye that sees a sun, a hand that feels an earth; that the world around him is there only as representation, in other words, only in reference to another thing, namely, that which represents, and this is himself. (1963, p. 63)

The only remedy to getting caught in this web of illusion was weirdly almost Buddhist: the will must be denied. Willing is the source of desire and desire is the source of illusory attachment (or, better, an attachment to illusions) and attachment is the source of suffering. This is, of course, only one step away from Wagner's *Der Ring Des Nibelungen* immolation scenes where willing is heroically broken and willful gods find their twilight. Even the musical motifs in this work suggest nature and desire as undulating, rising E-flat harmonics, and the power of Wotan's staff descending down the same tonal sequence with great, triumphal, patriarchal willfulness.

And, of course, we get, as happens in the for-or-against logic of the West, the exact inverse of this denial of the will. Friedrich Nietzsche (1975) calls such denials sheepish Christian meekness and proposes instead a triumphal *affirmation* of the will (compare this thread of Nietzsche's work with the current Triumphal Willfulness of the Christian Right and their Christian Soldiers). For Nietzsche, every proposition of truth hides a common theme: *whatever* is proposed as true, as basic, as originary, as real, that proposing is an attempt to affirm willful dominance. Any claim to hold "the truth" is a claim of the will to hold sway over things, over any "other" that might resist. Knowledge is understood and affirmed as domination. Thus, the "truth" hidden in each object affirmed to be true is not "in the object," but is precisely the will to power (over things, over others) itself.

Rather than denying such will, therefore, we should affirm it (we are told), because it is our true (Western) nature and we need only gobble up into our self-affirmation any who resist.

This, of course, is the logic of war. And I can't resist the end-game: The Triumph of the Will is an indirect, unintended outcome of a terribly recent East/West flirtation. So, anyone who thought that East-flirtations or Romantic Orientalism is adequate in these matters, or that there is only good news to be had is sorely mistaken. This book faces up to these facts and requires such facing and effacing of its readers.

Something in me still deeply believes the truths that this book opens before our eyes, that a conversation between East and West is a spot of perennial hope (and, of course, equally perennial suffering). But the teacher in me knows that, as Gadamer (that most beautiful of un-Eastern men), said, "every experience worthy of the name involves suffering" (1989, p. 356). Even in such suffering, when these conversations work, when the courage is there, a myriad of strong and generous voices emerge. That is what we find in this book—spots of hope borne of suffering. Strong, generous voices, each resisting, in their own way, the gobbling up of East by West or West by East. Let's remember, too, Derrida's caution, that even here, we still presume will, albeit "good will" (see Michelfelder & Palmer, 1989). But this is the good news. A real conversation entails that I am always ready to hesitate and cup my ear again, not just towards the voice of another, but again toward the ghosts howling in my own voice.

This text moves "in-between," in a spot of great fecundity, a locus of interpretation ("*The true locus of hermeneutics is this in-between* [Gadamer, 1989, 295), a locus, one might say, of pedagogy itself. Under the sway of the voices in texts like this one, how I get to think about classrooms and kids and teachers gets more vigorous and difficult. Curriculum topics lose their Protestant-Eurocentric isolation and loneliness and burst open and outwards into all their relations. When these conversations work, both East and West can understand their character, their power, and their foibles, in ways that each could have never experienced through simple self-reflection. When it fails—when each side deafens and fundamentalizes and literalizes—well, we get what we seem to have quite a lot of these days: a post-9/11 pedagogy, premised on paranoia, surveillance, incarceration, interrogation, schools called "Foundations for the Future," "No Child Left Behind" uttered as a however-well-meant threat, and so on.

Shh! We're in a wee bit of an entrenchment currently in North American culture and North American schools. This is one reason, among so many, why this book is so timely.

In the articulations of the ways of the East, many of us have found ways we might, if not cure, then at least care for the great illness of the Euro-Enlightenment project of (self-) consciousness and its consequent violence. This is why this book is so vital. It is an old pedagogical adage. We don't listen to others simply in order to understand *them.* We listen to others also in order to understand *ourselves,* because others can read our lives and our deafness and blindness back to us in ways that we cannot read them alone. This book's authors do not simply run with abandon to some exotic other, but use anotherness as a moment for a more generous and expansive self-understanding (Buddha names this the emptying of self, and St. Augustine says that, as we learn, the self becomes "roomier" [cited in Carruthers, 2005, p. 199]). We find our limits in each other and in those spots of liminality, well, there is sometimes a sharp intake of breath, and, as the Buddha and Gadamer said, there is likely pain to pay in the venture.

In a conversation with Gary Snyder, the price of not venturing is finally named, a price that flows easily from the citation above from Schopenhauer's *The World as Will and Representation*:

> **Geneson:** So when Sartre . . . goes to the tree, touches the tree trunk and says, "I feel in an absurd position. I cannot break through my skin to get in touch with this bark, which is outside me," the Japanese poet would say . . . ?
>
> **Snyder:** Sartre is confessing the sickness of the West. At least he is honest. The [poet] will say, "But there are ways to do it, my friend. It's no big deal." It's no big deal, especially if you get attuned to that possibility from early in life. (Snyder, 1980, p. 67)

It is good to see that right at the cusp of the confession of sickness, pedagogy-as-attunement is invoked and a path is almost laid out.

So, at this terrifying end of the idea of self-containedness let's do one more step that puts into sharper light the timeliness of this text and its wisdoms.

The affirmation of the constructs of a willful subjectivity are at the heart of contemporary pedagogy in the guise of constructivism and the profoundly colonial character of this epistemology has been recently documented (see Bowers, 2005, Jardine, 2006, Johnson, Fawcett & Jardine, 2006, Smith, 2006). As Western consciousness has so often portended, if we hold in hand the conditions of reasonableness, morality and civility, it is our duty, as Westerners, to impose such matters on the world, and to "construct" it in our own image without hesitation or apology, without *heed.*

A senior advisor to the [George W.] Bush administration affirmed the terrible truth we already know, that the sickness of the West is full bore: "We are an empire now, and when we act, we create our own reality. And while you're studying that reality—judiciously as you will—we'll act again, creating other new realities, which you can study, too, and that's how things will sort out" (cited in MacMillan, 2006, A19). We can hear the mockery of studying and the (sometimes subtle and schooled, often literal) death of others. Under the sway of Empire, what, after all, I there to study when another is only what I understand and allow them to be?

These days, who needs a book on East and West if we create our own reality of what the East can be? As George W. Bush has declared with great clarity, the United States already understands what the East can properly think about the West, and therefore it need not listen.

Sickness.

My own work, my writing, my teaching, my own life and breath, have been intimately shaped by the ways of the East and the ways that those ways have helped me understand my own Western raising better. The trouble is, I'm feeling a bit like Sartre lately, encased, enclosed, entrenched, far away from that jeweled heart. When you are living with war, things start to shut down, possibilities narrow, conversations cease. And in the ensuing silence, "untruth" (Smith, 2006) is perpetrated under what Alice Miller (1989) identified as a "black pedagogy": we are lied to, as the title of one of her books suggests, "for our own good." Untruth becomes truth because it is willed to be so.

Worse yet, perhaps, war makes those who might have a conversation more alike in their exaggerated unwillingness to listen to another, their inability to imagine or tolerate anything beyond the world they have constructed. This is not just a sickness of the West. It is the sickness of Fundamentalism and the deafness and fear and war-footing it feeds upon, supports, aggravates, and declares as necessary always and only because of *the other's* deafness. It is no coincidence, speaking of East and West these days, that *both* are meeting each other armed and dangerous, the meeting of Crusade and Jihad:

> War tends to make cultures alike whereas peace is that condition under which each culture flourishes in its own incomparable way. From this, it fol-

> lows that peace cannot be exported; it is inevitably corrupted by transfer, its attempted export means war. (Illich, 1992, p. 17)

This is one last reason, for now, why this book is so amazing and so timely and so true. "War, which makes cultures alike, is all too often used by historians as the framework or skeleton of their narratives" (Illich, 1992, p. 19) and the same may be said, too often, of curriculum, of pedagogy, of education. In this book, East and West have, instead, been "left in peace" (Illich, 1992, p. 16).

Thus, we have, here, in our hands, the possibility that a real conversation might begin again. It is this possibility, in all its myriad ways and dependent co-arisings, that is at the heart, and that defines the hope of pedagogy. Enjoy it. Savor it. And do not turn away from the suffering.

Acknowledgment

This text is the Foreword to Claudia Eppert & Hongyu Wang [Eds.] [2008]. *Cross-Cultural Studies in Curriculum: Eastern Thought, Educational Insights*).

PREAMBLE 11

"A Temporary Medicine"

> The Book that I would slip to my children would itself be slippery. It would slip them into a new domain, not of ideas alone but of experience and feeling. It would be a temporary medicine, not a diet. (Watts, 1970, p. 9)

> Emptiness is the antidote to all views,
> But if one clings to the concept of emptiness,
> Like a purgative turned into poison,
> It becomes ineffective.
> Like two sticks that when rubbed together
> Are consumed in the fire of their own making
> The antidote itself must disappear of its own accord.
>
> Namgyal (1871–1926) (2007, p. 16)

The following chapter is part of the Introduction to Pedagogy Left in Peace (Jardine, 2012). In it, I attempted to crystallize what can be called an iatrogenic loop. Glance back to Preamble and Chapter 10 where Friedrich Nietzsche's "will to power" is discussed, because this describes, in a way, the great delusion of iatrogenesis, that the grasping for permanence causes the feeling of resistance (and subsequent hardening and reification) and the feeling of resistance causes us to grip more and feel more resistance to that grasping. This provides a great analogue to Buddhist thoughts on grasping

In Praise of Radiant Beings, pages 151–153

for permanence, the resultant reifications that occur, the attachments that then come, and the regimes of hostility and war-footing that ensue.

Iatrogenesis was originally coined to indicate how certain medical actions could unwittingly cause precisely the disease that they were intended to cure. Ivan Illich (1976) broadened the applicability of this term to the ways in which a wide array of institutional responses to the sufferings and confusions of human life become counterproductive—schools can, in the name of knowledge, come to produce ignorance, hospitals produce superbugs, freeways produce congestion, cell phones produce an increasing sense of isolation, and so on. What occurs in such cases is that the antidote becomes complicit, wittingly or otherwise, in maintaining, in fact producing, the trouble it was intended to ameliorate (see Gilham, 2015, 2015a, Gilham & Jardine, in preparation). Cause and effect become oddly inverted. Remedy becomes a concealed cause. To the extent that this is not recognized, it inevitably leads to a pathology of acceleration and frantic pursuit and inevitable frustration: the remedy is pursued with ever increasing vigor, and any thought to the contrary—any attempt to interrupt this cycle—becomes increasingly profoundly suspect. One of the most pernicious moves in this cycle is, as we've explored already, that being caught in it becomes identified with "the real world" and daring to interrupt it becomes therefore easily marginalized as "not understanding how things really work."

We could even add, under, perhaps, the term "market iatrogenics," that some "remedies" are shaped in order precisely to *maintain* the illness they cure as a justification for their own continuance and therefore wittingly and deliberately hide their complicity in such maintenance.

"We should have no illusion" (Gadamer 1986, p. 56):

> In this light, I now offer this, from Kevin O'Leary. It is cited from the Canadian Broadcasting Company's series "Dragon's Den." O'Leary has more recently been seen on the American TV show "Shark Tank." He is affiliated with The Learning Company, currently owned by Houghton Mifflin Harcourt, one of North America's largest providers of various packaged educational products and "learn to read" series such as Carmen Sandiego and Reader Rabbit:
>
>> I'm all for children, but I want to make a buck. I am "Carmen Sandiego." I am "Reader Rabbit." People will do anything for their children to help them in math and reading scores. I made a fortune just servicing that market. I love the terror in a mother's heart when she sees her child fall behind in reading. I made a fortune from that. (O'Leary, 2012)
>
> —(Jardine, in press)

The sketch that follows is focused on an ontological delusion that hides like a secret wound underneath such things. It is a delusion about how things exist, their manner of being. It describes briefly how, under threat and panic and anxiety and regret ("terror"), we tend to entrench and pull back into the "tried and true" and we do the same with our surroundings. We demand to be surrounded with objects that can be controlled, predicated and manipulated (Jurgen Habermas' [1973] characterizations of the scientific enterprise). To be an object is to be isolated, separate, manageable, dispensable, and consumable without a further thought. Dependent co-arising, relatedness, interdependence, come to appear as the blurring of what is "in reality" clear and distinct (see Descartes, 1955). This delusion is itself iatrogenic because the threat that caused the hostility that caused the reification is concealed, forgotten, suppressed, and the dependently co-arising outcome of such a set of moves is set out as existing in the real world: separate, permanent, graspable objects.

11

An Ontological Delusion (2012)

As will become evident to readers, the scholarly, experiential, and practical refuge of my own work has long been an odd mixture and admittedly skewed reading of convivial links between hermeneutics, ecology and Buddhism. These three inheritances provide two interrelated sources of refuge for me and, indirectly, have given me a way to articulate and keep clear the sometimes downright miraculous classroom work I have witnessed and that has arisen right in the midst of and in spite of our real, common, and perennial suffering.

First of all, these three inheritances allow for a multifaceted identification of what can be described as an *ontological delusion*, a real, terrible and pervasive trap into which thinking, practice, and experience devolve. Much of what follows in this book will begin unwinding detailed, often ancient, threads of this powerful and false-promising trap.

Here, as an introduction and alert for readers, I will simply sketch this ontological delusion in skeletal form. I portray it here as sequential steps but in fact each of these steps dependently co-arises with the rest. Each

In Praise of Radiant Beings, pages 155–159

seemingly separate "step" illuminates what appears to come before and afterwards:

- We understandably "retract" from adventurous work and the risky venture of experiencing and understanding our convivial being in the world because of the woes we face that make us feel threatened and embattled. We revert to what is tried and true and relatively secured and securable (see Jardine, 1992b). Such retraction produces a sort of "hardened identity" (Huntington 2003, p. 266)—an exaggerated and often then trumpeted sense of an autonomous, self-secured and independently existing "I am" that is seemingly separate from any sense of or reliance on our worldly conviviality. The monstrous shape and size of these exaggerations and the loudness of this trumpeting are themselves ways to keep the threat at bay—feigned and marshaled monsters meant to be equal to the monstrosities we fear (see Jardine, 1994a).
- From this locale of threatened retreat, we then treat things in the world as if they are also full of potentially threatening, unsecured and suspect convivialities that must themselves be retracted and secured. On behalf of securing our surroundings in order to further secure our threatened "selves," the world becomes fragmented into separate, self-existing objects whose convivial relations to and dependencies upon each other have either been inquisitionally purged or reduced to those that can be put under securable, standardizable control and surveillance (akin David Smith's "conditions of mastery and explanation" [1999a, p. 139]). A commonplace of common sense, that one thing is different than another, gets hardened into what is, in the Western tradition stretching back at least to Aristotle, a logic of substance (here as inherited by Rene Descartes [1955, p. 255]): " a substance is that which requires nothing except itself in order to exist." We can sense here seeds of ecological disaster, as the world is put under the threat of methodical doubt that underwrites the advent of modern European science Also here are the nebulous origins of colonial issuances from a secured and univocal center as well as the first tethers between colonization and constructivist images of knowledge Here, too, the seeds of how the industrial model of efficiency and sequential assembly of separate parts boded for its holus bolus adoption into our images of education (see Friesen & Jardine, 2009; Callahan, 1964).
- We then get caught in a sort of forgetful ontological projection. What was in fact the often-understandable *outcome* of embattle-

ment and threat (e.g., Descartes' threat of methodical doubt that renders the world into mathematically secured and manageable objects; F.W. Taylor's desire for increased industrial efficiency that fragments things into sequentially assemble-able bits and pieces under regimes of surveillance, de-skilling and standardization) becomes understood as simply *the way the world exists*—or, as I've often heard it expressed by teachers as they pull back from suggestions of abundance and free space, "*this* is the real world." What were understandable retractions under threat become no longer experienceable as often suitable and warranted responses to troublesome causes and conditions. A sort of ontological amnesia sets in, a neurosis, where we can't remember what has been done to us, or that there might be any perpetrating causes and conditions at all. We become deluded into believing that hardened identities and a fragmented world that are the *outcomes* of threat are, instead, an *intractable ontological given*: things *are* retracted, separate, isolated, autonomous, and fragmented. I am a separate, autonomous, self-determining "I." Each of my students is a unique, autonomous and self-determining individual. These supposedly autonomous sites then become understood as the secured platforms from which constructivism and even social constructivism are launched. At the cultural level, they become the sites out of which multiculturalism is often unwittingly cobbled together through the bringing together of hardened ethnic "identities" and "differences." Thus, in one of our deepest delves into trying to overcome the singularities of race, gender, culture and the like is encoded a hidden "hardness" that blocks our access to the difficult, mixed, contested and lived convivialities that antedate such hardening.

- Against this deluded ontological background ("things are what they are independently of everything else"—what is called in Tibetan Buddhism the delusion of inherent self-existence), we get what Edmund Husserl (1970b, p. 48), the father of contemporary phenomenology, called a "surreptitious substitution," a sort of weird, suppressed *inversion*. What is in reality an in-the-end delusional outcome of threat (acting and thinking as if things are inherently self-existent) gets codified as more "basic" (see Jardine, Clifford & Friesen, 2003, 2008) and more "real" than that convivial, dependently co-arising life left in peace *from which* threat induced a retraction. Opening free spaces, experiencing the conviviality of the world and creating new solidarities with the young in the face of the mortality of the world—all this becomes understood, under this inversion, as secondary, post hoc, optional, a "frill," something we might get to once and if the hardened realities are dealt with. Convivial life—the "life world," to use the phenomenological term) becomes understood and treated as epiphenomenal. It and our experience in and of it become subjectivized and most assuredly *post hoc* to the separate and hardened "realities" of "the real world."

- This secured reality of separate selves and separate things, borne of this ontological delusion precipitated by threat, becomes linguistically, culturally, and institutionally encoded into the very structure of schooling itself and into the fragmentation of the living disciplines of the world's knowledge. Once thus codified, images of entering into the convivial life of knowledge and exploring its possibilities with the young seems to be pointing to something that no longer exists, perhaps never existed, some old Romantic, subjective, liberal, unaccountable dream. As is not unexpected, given how it dominates the scene, out of this ontological delusion is borne the belief that those who don't accept these "facts" are, well, *deluded.*
- In one final inversion, suggestions pointing to the exploration of free spaces with the young, intergenerationality, risk and venture, and creating solidarities aimed at "setting right anew," become experienced as not only misunderstanding of the "basic" and secured reality of things. The proposal of a pedagogy left in peace becomes understandable as precisely *the key source of threat to that security.* Peace becomes a threat.

So powerful and hidden is this ontological delusion it ends up feeding its own hiddenness under the guise of something like a conspiracy theory: anyone questioning it is clearly deluded. This, of course, is a sign of its dominance; that it is in a position to negatively characterize, name and marginalize any questioning of that dominance. In this way, many good hearted, well-meaning and thoughtful attempts to ameliorate the difficult circumstances that surround teachers and students in school, or to "reform" education or to instigate more inquiry based learning in the classroom (or whatever the new catch-phrase will be once these have worn out), get unwittingly enacted from a hidden-but-dominant site (a site that need not, because of its dominance, give an account of itself) that *has already been deeply encoded with the ontological seeds of their own inevitable failure.*

Differently put, until these hidden seeds of affliction are unearthed, attempts at imagining a pedagogy left in peace are often deployed from a site already constructed and construed under threat.

Hermeneutics, Buddhism and ecology, each in their own ways, can be brought to bear on this threat-retract-project mechanism and all three approach it at its ontological root: hermeneutics in its critique of substance and its avowal of a hermeneutic experience in which the convivial, interdependent "worlding" of things beyond the feigns of self-enclosed self-identity can be cultivated and studied; Buddhism in its understanding of how things are empty (Sanskrit: *shunya*) of self-existence (Sanskrit: *svabhava*) and are, instead, in their deepest reality, dependently co-arising (Sanskrit: *pratitya-samutpada*); and ecology's insistence that we are part of the Earth's fabric, its weaves, its texts and textures and that this can be experienced, understood, and we can learn to live with this reality out from under the delusions of unearthly independence and autonomy.

PREAMBLE 12

"Keep Radiantly Well"

> Only beauty can save the planet. Let me explain. Even the strongest combination of guilty feelings, economic reasoning and scientific evidence are not enough to turn the tide so that our planet's life may continue. Nevertheless—and here is where beauty comes in—if you love something, you want it to stay around and stay close, and keep radiantly well. And it is precisely beauty that makes you fall in love. [It] gives you the feeling that what is here is to be treasured and not misused or harmed, and certainly not to be regarded in terms of functional usefulness or economic return, for such is to look at the world as a slave or a whore. (Hillman, 2006b, p. 192)

I clearly recall a student teacher, years ago, that I was supervising in a high school chemistry class. This guy was a chemical engineer, and had the students, however briefly, in the palm of his hand. Also in his open palm, the Periodic Table gracefully held open for all to see. We all were leaning in to this gathering of light cast on us. As his lesson continued, the classroom teacher, seated beside me at the back of the room, interrupted on more than one occasion, brusquely marching to the front, saying "excuse me," taking the chalk and circling something on the board, and declaring, with a great desire to help, "Now *that's* on the test."

Here is the real reason that I've pursued this connection between education, Buddhism, ecology and hermeneutics. It has to do with the cultivation and protection of our affection for the life and beauty of the world and wanting to rescue it, shall we say, from its often-ugly demeanor. Not that this

In Praise of Radiant Beings, pages 161–166

ugly demeanor is less "real" than a more beautiful one, but that ugliness causes us to retract and clench and therefore hides this intimate dance under the always-false-promise illusions of reification—the panic clutches, say, of "the test" that "that" is on—that "that" now a securable chemistry fact that can be gripped and held until the test is over.

All this, of course, is at once an attempt to rescue myself from precisely the ugly demeanor that an ugly world demands of me, of us. Rescuing it and rescuing myself is one gesture, and my work has tended to begin with the object, that public face, curriculum, our course, and all the fields of knowledge entrusted to teachers and students in schools:

> Below the ecological crisis lies a deeper crisis of love, that our love has left the world; that the world is loveless results directly from the repression of beauty, its beauty and our sensitivity to beauty. For love to return to the world, beauty must first return, else we love the world only as a moral duty: clean it up, preserve its nature, and exploit it less. If love depends on beauty, then beauty comes first. Separated from beauty, love becomes a duty. Love thy neighbor becomes a moral obligation, almost a commandment, and [separated from beauty] the world's alluring face becomes a temptress [a siren-like distraction leading us off "the rutted path" of curriculum (Bransford, Brown & Cocking, 2000, p. 138)]. (Hillman, 2006d, p. 175)

I can't help adding here about my son coming home from early days in Grade 10 with his "Chem. 10" textbook and opening the inside front cover in front of me and saying in great wonder "Dad, have you *seen* this?"

Ah, yes, the Periodic Table, here, again and for the first time all at once, spread out, an open field, wonder-filled, difficult, venturous, demanding of careful attention and long devotion. Adorable. This didn't last very long for him in the confines of school, and I, too, had to return to the Periodic Table again and again, in my role as someone hired to "teach curriculum," and had to re-learn to fall in love with it all over again. This is, in part and again, the asthmatic me who needs lovely places of rest and openness from which to carefully win back my own stillness and affection. Sometimes, in schools, the sickness and breathlessness is all there is. It's heartbreaking. And although it is profoundly commonplace, such sickness is always only *possible. There is nothing necessary about it* despite the great heft and sway it seems to hold.

A Buddhist reminder is necessary here. Love, here, is not attachment and fixity, but neither is it a "vague licentiousness" (Smith, 1999a, p. 139) that drops the reins and lets kids run wild and lustful and literally self-involved in schools. This lovely learning involves suffering (*pathei mathos*), a certain dedication and willingness to stay put, enduring, undergoing,

-> Beautiful stories

because it means tossing off the terrible numbness that our culture has perfected on so many fronts, and allowing ourselves to experience our circumstances as they are: "this anesthesia [note, literally, no *aesthesis*, no feel for the beauty of things] is largely the modern human condition. And, it is supported and promoted by our economics, our entertainment, our modes of communication and transportation, and, of course our medications" (Hillman, 2006c, p. 144), to say nothing of our schools.

And let there be no doubt. It is far harder for me to love that chemistry classroom teacher's harsh suffering in the confines of schooling, but it, too, needs interpretation and not just reprimand. Tsk-tsking and blaming falsely names that teacher as the author of our current circumstances, and forgets that he, too, is living out a life in this world. This leads to little more than hostility, leading to retrenchment and reification, leading to deeper gravities and less and less love and compassion. It has led to senseless and repeated and always-heated arguments about "teaching methods" that always come to nothing more than their heat and subsequent retrenchments. I deeply regret in retrospect, but not until right now in writing this sentence, that I never knew and will never know whether that Chemistry teacher ever loved chemistry and how he may have been suffering the confines of schooling and just trying to do the right thing by his student-teacher, rescuing him from the temptress of the University and its lack of understanding of "the real world" of high schools, where you better just get on with it, get through it, get it over and done with.

The retraction from interpretation, from beauty, from ecological awareness of the surrounds and the kept-radiance of things, makes a terrible sense, of course, because it involves sometimes-unbearable sorrow about our lot, and can lead to terrible immobility. This sounds arcane, but I can't tell you how many teachers I've spoken to over 30 years who have said something like this: "I used to love Shakespeare [make whatever substitute you like at this point] until I started to teach."

But there is a trick, here, and a nick, a concealed inversion the unearthing of which provides a way to proceed.

Many teachers I've worked with are attempting to do beautiful work with children in an often-ugly world, one often *made ugly* through panic, defeat, fear, retraction, entrenchment, reification, and hostility (see Preamble and Chapter 11). If I pull away from such ugliness and leave it behind in order to "cure myself, "it becomes near-unbearable when I return to that desecrated world I left behind, even more unbearable, sometimes, now that I have become more alert to its suffering:

> By denying the reality of the *anima mundi* and its reflection within our personal soul, we take all suffering on ourselves, *mea culpa,* and remain oblivious to the suffering in the world soul—how tortured its structures, how it longs to return to a cosmology that gives first place to its beauty. (Hillman, 2006c, pp. 144–145)

Refuge, then, doesn't mean retreat or withdrawal (there are countless texts on Buddhist action in the world; Hanh, 1993, Macy & Johnstone ,2012 and countless others). The refuge, for me, is *curriculum work*—a way to work in the world, to work with the world and help it heal, opening up "free spaces" (Gadamer, 1986, p. 59) in what seems like a closed and finished world of the knowledge entrusted to teachers and students in schools. Breathing space.

The subtitle of Joanna Macy and Chris Johnstone's text provides the key, however: "how to face the mess we're in without going crazy." Facing the mess doesn't mean fixing it once and for all: "You don't just fix up a car to fix it, but to *restore* it" (Hillman, 2006e, p. 152, italics mine) but you cannot do this without knowing that such restoration will not last, will have to be done again, under different circumstances and inevitably. Restoration—"saving the planet," "improving schools"—is in the hands of the coming and going of the world, the rising of fear and exhaustion, and the settling of love and devotion, acts of beauty and acts of hostile retreat, all this, back and forth. This is what I've witnessed over many years, that beautiful work will rise up in a certain school, with particular teachers, and will then sometimes settle back into panic after a while, eroded by the woes of the world:

> To preserve the world against the mortality of its creators and inhabitants, it must be constantly set right anew. The problem is simply to educate in such a way that setting right remains actually possible, even though it can, of course, never be assured. (Arendt, 1969, p. 192)

It can never be assured, and *that* is the assurance of refuge. This is why "finitude" and "mortality" and "impermanence" are so much of the imaginal and practice terrain of Buddhism, hermeneutics and in the becoming-animal-ness of ecological insight. It is a refuge *in* the suffering of the world, not *from* it. It is why there is this difficult truth to face (one now-understandably not in my purview with Alan Watts in 1968), and one seen so often from those wanting to save the world or fix up schools: "moral suasion touches guilt, but not the deeper desire for loveliness and grace. Ethics without aesthetics will not hold us for long. We get earnest, driven, obstinate, and eventually ugly" (Hillman, 2006e, p. 152).

So here's the tricky inversion. James Hillman did a wonderful series of interviews with Michael Ventura in a book whose title explains much: *We've*

Had a Hundred Years of Psychotherapy and the World's Getting Worse (1992). That book traces out how our withdrawals into curing our inner ills can involve a retreat from the world, an abandoning of the world to ecological, economic, warring ravages based, not on affection but on panic, on market driven falsehoods and on the tempting of our afflictions into security regimes:

> **Hillman:** I'm outraged after having driven to my analyst on the freeway. The fucking trucks almost ran me off the road. I'm terrified, I'm in my little car, and I get to my therapist's and I'm shaking. My therapist says, "We've gotta talk about this." My thin skin and my frailty and vulnerability. We convert my fear into anxiety—an inner state. [We] don't work on what that outrage is telling you about potholes, about trucks, about Florida strawberries in Vermont in March, about burning oil, about energy politics, nuclear waste, that homeless woman over there with sores on her feet. (Hillman & Ventura, 1992, p. 12)

Subjectivization. Going "inwards" and curing myself of my woes over the world leaves the world behind and, in fact, *makes it worse* precisely through the withdrawal of my affection and concerted action:

> **Ventura:** you're not saying that we don't need introspection, an introspective guy like you?
>
> **Hillman:** Put this in italics so that nobody can just pass over it: *This is not to deny that you do need to go inside*—but we have to see what we're doing when we do that. By going inside we're maintaining the Cartesian view that the world out there is dead matter and the world inside is living. (Hillman & Ventura 1992, p. 12)

Here is where a sort of Buddhist topspin on this idea can help.

If we simply let go of that "Cartesian view" then going "out" into the world, say, of schooling and its dependent co-arisings is going out into the field-fabric *of my very self* that arose and still arises in the sway of schooling. Risking sounding too 1967 about this, "going out," properly done, *is* "going inside," because it is going inside of the fabric of which I am a fold. It is just like how caring for the watershed in the Foothills *is* caring for my self and loving the world, quite literally, as my self, not just loving the world *as well as* myself. Exploring the work of F. W. Taylor (see Chapter 13) and how the efficiency movement shaped and formed contemporary education *is* "going inside." It is self-exploration; understanding *it* in great detail *is* understanding my self insofar as that self arose, in part, in that ancestral field of the world. To re-cite:

> All understanding is selfunderstanding, but not in the sense of a preliminary selfpossession or of one finally and definitively achieved. For selfunderstanding only realizes itself in the understanding of a subject matter and does not have the character of a free selfrealization. The self that we are does not possess itself; one could say that it "happens." (Gadamer, 1977, p. 55)

Interpreting the world "out there" and tirelessly undoing its "sickness" and finding its beauty, its free spaces, is finding my self's freedom from the self that has become a frightened confine in the face of a sick world.

So, finally, this. There is pedagogy at work here in this work of working the world and wanting to keep it radiantly well:

> The more we study in this way, the more we are able to feel the pull of the fabrics of the world. And the more this happens, the more we are able to enter into that fabrication, that, in Latin, *textus.* Two things. We become agents in the stories we have inherited, tellers and re-tellers and, at the same time, we don't just fall into these stories but become conscious of them as stories. If we lose sight of this dependently co-arising fabric(action), we begin to believe that it is not a fabrication but "just the way things are" (reification—making into a permanent and intractable given, an object). "Mental tendencies congeal and we bind ourselves without a rope" (Loy, 2010, p. vii). The "outer" parallel with this "inner" tendency to congeal is called reification. Becoming uncongealed, therefore, is not just an issue of a sort of meditative inner life, but of unbinding the world as well and letting ourselves fall in love again with its ongoing flow of arising and falling. Parallel here is all the Buddhist talk of not "grasping" when we feel the vertigo of such movement, but settling, composing ourselves, and, for me, composing, writing this, not as a way of stopping this flow but of inviting readers into an experience of it and its ways. (Jardine, in press a)

There is a pedagogy, here: "sometimes it is necessary to reteach a thing its loveliness" (Kinnell, 2002, n.p.).

That is the connection between Buddhism and education.

12

"Sickness Is Now 'Out There'" (2012)

"Where We Think We Are"

I find today that patients are more sensitive than the worlds they live in. Rather than patients not being able to perceive and adapt "realistically," it is the reality of the world's phenomena that seems unable to adapt to the sensitivity of the patients. I am astounded by the life and beauty in the patients vis-à-vis the dead and ugly world they inhabit. The heightened awareness of subjective realities, that soul sophistication resulting from one hundred years of psychoanalysis, has become incommensurable with the retarded state of external reality, which moved during the same one hundred years towards brutal uniformity and degradation of quality.

...

Ecology movements, futurism, feminism, urbanism, protest and disarmament, personal individuation cannot alone save the world from the catastrophe inherent in our very idea of the world.

...

To place neurosis and psychopathology solely in personal reality is a delusional repression of what is actually, realistically, being experienced.

...

In Praise of Radiant Beings, pages 167–172

> Sickness is now "out there." (Hillman, 2006a, pp. 28, 47, 28, and 30)

In these passages from James Hillman's "*Anima Mundi*: Returning of Soul to The World," I believe there is a cluster of insights that are key to the well-being of education itself and which give clear voice to what seems, sometimes, to be a systemic blindness in our profession. If we leave "our very idea of world" fragmented, degraded, and brutalized, knowledge of that world becomes fragmented, degraded, and brutalized. If this happens, our understanding of the disciplines of knowledge themselves become fragmented, degraded, and brutalized. And thus the world *into which* we are educating new teachers and into which they, in turn, are educating their students, will be degraded, retarded, and brutal. In one last awful turn, if I become educated in such a world, I, too, must become degraded, retarded, and brutal in order to live and survive in such a world. Either that or I must retract and retreat into subjective realities more sensitive and beautiful than the world that surrounds me. In such sadly understandable retraction and retreat, the well-being of the world is abandoned, its degradation thus deepens which, in turn, deepens our cause for retreat.

I am reminded, in passing, of Wendell Berry's (1986, p. 51) disturbing reminder of this terrible intimacy between the world in which we nestle and what becomes of us in such nestling:

> It is impossible to divorce the question of what we do from the question of where we are—or, rather, where we think we are. That no sane creature befouls its own nest is accepted as generally true. What we conceive to be our nest, and where we think it is, are therefore questions of the greatest importance.

No matter how abundantly, rapidly, and twitterly "connected" are our inner lives, it is *where we think we are* that has become un-nestled. As the etymology of the word "nest" betrays, in the confines of schools, there is nowhere left in the world(s) of knowledge entrusted to teachers and students, to *sit down* together and nestle in the comfort of such world(s) and learn to inhabit them, care for them and become someone *worldly* in the process. In the dimwitted confines of one more boring mathematics worksheet-fragment, *the living world of mathematics itself* has fallen ill. It has become uninhabitable, inhospitable, uninviting.

First thesis, following Hillman: there is a catastrophe inherent in our very idea of the world and *this* is what needs our love and devotion and attention. This is where the root of our sickness is held and the way to our sanity lies. Even though we feel it intimately, sickness and its remedy are outside of our *selves.*

Sickness is now "out there." Inward meditations on our grief, melancholy, and insanity will no longer suffice.

Second thesis: our turns "inward" to beautiful subjective realities, understandable as a refuge from a befouled world, has had an unintended hand in perpetrating, perpetuating, codifying and confirming the reality of the very befouled world from which it has retreated.

"Restlessness Becomes Irrelevant"

> Meditation is working with our speed, our restlessness, our constant busyness. Meditation provides space or ground in which restlessness might function. Meditation practice is not a matter of trying to produce a hypnotic state of mind or create a sense of restfulness. Trying to achieve a restful state of mind reflects a mentality of poverty. Seeking a restful state of mind, one is on guard against restlessness. There is a constant state of paranoia and limitation. We feel we need to be on guard. This guarding process limits the scope of the mind by not accepting whatever comes. Instead, meditation should reflect a mentality of richness in the sense of using everything that occurs in the state of mind. Thus, if we provide enough room for restlessness so that it might function within the space, then the energy ceases to be restless because it can trust itself fundamentally. Meditation is giving a huge, luscious meadow to a restless cow. The cow might be restless for a while in its huge meadow, but at some stage, because there is so much space, the restlessness becomes irrelevant. (Trungpa, 2003, pp. 218–219)

David G. Smith showed me this passage from Chogyam Trungpa's *The Myth of Freedom and the Way of Meditation* (first published in 1998) years ago now, and it has served well ever since as abundantly full of images for pedagogy and its prospects, for what happens when it goes right and what happens when it goes wrong.

When it goes right, pedagogy is akin to a meditative practice which, *when practiced*, can come to provide enough imaginative and intellectually vigorous and compelling "room" for students and teachers alike. Pedagogy can provide huge and luscious meadows, where each seemingly isolated topic mandated by the curriculum becomes visible and available and knowable as part of a living *topica* (like the roots of the term topography, or topology, the logos of a "place" and its inscriptions; see Gadamer, 1989, p. 21) ripe for the cultivation of memory and character (see Gadamer, 1989, p. 21; Jardine, 2006; Jardine et al., 2008) and the ameliorating of restlessness. In a beautiful, diverse, and abundant field, restlessness can become adventurousness, love, affection, exploration, creation. When it goes right, we can begin to catch sight of those who have worked this field before our arrival:

ancestral bloodlines, ancestral workings of this field, traces of *works* handed down to us, each a "transformation into structure" (Gadamer, 1989, p. 110 ff.) of *Spiels* played out in this living field.

This, with all its gaps and occlusions and contestations, is our nest, and it no longer has:

> the character of an object that stands over and against us. We are no longer able to approach this like an object of knowledge, grasping, measuring and controlling. Rather than meeting us in our world, it is much more a world [a field] into which we ourselves are drawn. [It] possesses its own worldliness and, thus, the center of its own Being so long as it is not placed into the object-world of producing and marketing. The Being of this thing cannot be accessed by objectively measuring and estimating; rather, *the totality of a lived context has entered into and is present in the thing*. And we belong to it as well. Our orientation to it is always something like our orientation to an inheritance that this thing belongs to, be it from a stranger's life or from our own. (Gadamer, 1994, pp. 191–192, italics mine)

The restlessness that then might still arise has been invited outside of itself into worlds of relations that give it a place to work itself out.

When Things Go Wrong

> My theories of neurosis and categories of psychopathology must be radically extended if they are not to foster the very pathologies which my job is to ameliorate. (Hillman, 2006a, p. 28)

And, make no mistake, what might be won, here, in the practice of meditative interpretation, is also a deepening experience of the horrors that have been wrought and the sicknesses that have been produced "out there" in the narrowing hallways of some schools, some classrooms, some students' and teachers' lives. Chogyam Trungpa's words help sketch out what happens *when things go wrong*. The experience of abundance requires a form of practice and thinking that is not especially indigenous to schooling and its efficiency-driven (see Boyle, 2006, Callahan, 1964, Gatto, 2006, Kanigel, 2005, Friesen & Jardine, 2009 and especially Taylor, 1903, 1911), "anti-intellectual" (Callahan, 1964, p. 8), surveillance and management structures. Such talk of abundance too often ends up being experienced as nothing more than a threat to the efficiencies and surveillance regimes that many schools have worked so hard to establish. What might seem to count for understanding our circumstances starts to appear as fairy tales, as not understanding "the real world" of schools and their ways.

What very often happens in schools when students become restless and encounter difficulties with the work they face is that teachers (and sometimes assessors, testers, curriculum developers, and remediators) zoom in on that trouble, narrowing attention, making the "meadow," the "field of relations" available to that restless student less huge, luscious, rich and spacious (this defines, of course, precisely what can happen to a restless teacher in a school as well). As Trungpa notes, paranoia and limitation *increase* in response to restlessness. In a tragic but terribly understandable turn, restlessness begins to be blamed on the fact that the field is *too* big, *too* luscious, alluring and distracting. Abundance, lusciousness, variegation and multifariousness become transformed into threats set on breaching the narrowing security fences.

Abundance is thus replaced with scarcity and paucity, lusciousness with thin gruel, variegation and multifariousness with uniformity, all this on behalf of fixing the source of restlessness.

Inside of such narrows, the locale of restlessness, the reason we had to "clamp down" in the first place, becomes more and more clearly targeted: *It's the cow.* What can be witnessed here is "what [Enrique] Dussel (1995) called the 'gigantic *inversion*' [where] 'the innocent victim becomes culpable and the culpable victimizer becomes innocent'" (Smith, 2006, p. 76). And in a horrifyingly familiar fell swoop we glimpse a version of the logic of abuse: "She made me do it." "I warned her." "It is for her own good."

This abusiveness takes on great specificity in some classrooms. Tasks facing a restless student become stupider, more menial and demeaning, more degrading to be part of, less interesting, less alluring, and all of this *because of the student and their restlessness.* Thus, in the early twentieth century, schooling was ripe for the arrival of the efficiency movement as proposed by Fredrick Winslow Taylor (1903, 1911), whose images of industrial assembly took educational reform by storm (see Raymond Callahan's now-classic [1964] detailing of this [still ongoing] storm in *America, education and the cult of efficiency*; see Ayres, 1915, Boyle, 2006, Braverman, 1998, Cubberley, 1922, Dufour & Eaker, 1998, Gatto, 2006, Friesen & Jardine, 2009, Kanigel, 2005, Wrege & Greenwood ,1991). As with the worker on Taylor's assembly line (here cited from one of his lectures from June 4th 1906), ideally one is aiming for a situation in which "we do not ask for the initiative of our men. We do not want any initiative. All we want of them is to obey the orders we give them, do what we say, and do it quickly" (cited in Kanigel, 2005, p. 169). The worldly correlate to such obedience and, so to speak, "disinitiative," is to require of the worker the doing of an increasingly narrow and meager task, one that *does not require* initiative but obedience, not only to what is to be done but to precisely how, when and for how long it is to be done. "What [Taylor] really wanted working men to be [is] focused [to use the language of education, "task oriented"], uncomplicated and compliant" (Boyle, 2006); parallel to this, the world inhabited by the worker at the same time becomes degraded, retarded, ugly, and demeaning.

Thus, when this shadow falls over schools, even if initiative and interest might accidentally rear up in the midst of the endless lines of disconnected, meaningless, rote work, there is, so to speak, nowhere (no "where," no "field") in the world of such a classroom that might warrant or reward or embrace such rearing up. In fact, the opposite becomes true. A world of bits and pieces under managerial surveillance *rejects* and *rebukes* rearing up. Initiative becomes a *detriment* to efficiency. The rearing up of initiative and interest becomes subjectivized into a *property of the restless student* and not at all something called for by the work at hand. Such rearing only meets reprimand for its interrupting of the uniform movement of "the line." Or, alternatively, such rearing is coded as "gifted" (and then the gifted student gets bullied in order to help him or her get "back in line"), which is simply another way of ejecting interruption from the "normal" line of the "ordinary" classroom.

And so it continues like a wheel turning. The *more* trouble a student has, the *smaller* and *simpler* and *less interesting* the "bit" doled out to them.

And the more restless they become.

And the more our paranoia and need for limitedness increases.

In this catastrophic logic, *time itself changes* (see Chapter 13, Ross, 2004, Ross & Jardine, 2009). As things fragment, time accelerates because there is nothing to slow it down since not one of these isolated bits or pieces requires any prolonged attention. Thus, any ancestral tethers or memories or tales or field-relations are only invoked in classrooms as *means* of getting across the requisite bits and pieces. Moreover, the future constantly becomes experienced as larger, more looming, more high-stakes, increasingly imminent, *ever-sooner.*

We get, therefore, increasingly restless. To harken back to Chogyam Trungpa's words, in the process of such accelerating narrowing, restlessness does not become irrelevant. It becomes *paramount.*

Poor restless cow has a problem. And the sickness 'out there' remains regnant.

PREAMBLE 13

Hells

Understand "meditation" as it is explained in Dharmamitra's *Clear Words Commentary (Prasphuta-pada)*:

> "Meditating" is making the mind take on the state or condition of the object of meditation. (Tsong-kha-pa, 2000, p. 111)

This re-cited passage needs re-reading. It needs to be applied more broadly than I first realized. Not meditating upon and studying the object of meditation, but instead falling prey to the rushing of the world also is letting the mind take on the state or condition of the object of a *lack of meditation.* "The mind takes on the state or condition of the object" and if the object has become fragmented, sequenced, standardized, reified, entrenched, exhausting, bent on obedient assembly without thought or care, then I become fragmented, sequenced, standardized, and exhaustedly bent on such obedience and thoughtlessness. I rush.

In detailing the consequences of losing ourselves in the fray of things, become distracted, afflicted, overtaken, unalert, Tsong-kha-pa (2000,

In Praise of Radiant Beings, pages 173–178

p. 163ff.) carries on an old Tibetan tradition, of describing the countless hellish fates that await us if we falter. He cites Asanga (born in India, circa 300 CE) from his *Levels of Yogic Deeds,* where we read of Crushing Hell ("cutting, splitting, smashing"), Howling Hell ("incinerated by blazing fire"), Hot Hell ("deep frying them like fish"), "the Pit of Embers, the Swamp of Putrid Corpses or the Swamp of Excrement that Sinks Like a Corpse, the Path of Razors and Such, and the River with No Ford" (p. 165), 'Blistering Hell' (p. 166), 'the Chattering-teeth, Weeping and Moaning Hell' (p. 166) and on and on it goes, capped by an off-handed 'this is only a rough description'" (p. 164). Having seen schools and classrooms and school boards come and go in the drifts of things, and having worked at a University where self-studies and new rubrics and plans come and go under great heat and sorrow, I'm especially fascinated by the *Reviving Hell:*

> Living beings of the Reviving Hell assemble and hack each other with various weapons that appear one by one, until they swoon and fall to the ground. Then a voice form the sky commands "Revive!" and they rise up again, hack each other as before, and experience measureless suffering. (Tsong-kha-pa, 2000, p. 163)

This is certainly familiar providing we remain calm and think of it allegorically. We've all been hacked and have swooned, and commanded to revive. It is helpful, therefore, to read Tsong-kha-pa's hell meditations, not merely as a schoolboy's list of threats of punishment if you don't obey. However, it is equally important to remember, here, now, in the midst of all this happy glorification of Buddhism and the flowery ecologies that it is often linked to, that, like any other spiritual discipline in a "leveling" world, this obey-or-be-punished scenario is *precisely* how it is most frequently wielded in the day-to-day practice of Buddhism. But again, a caveat:

> If you are content just to listen and know all this intellectually, without making it a living experience, you will just become one of those obdurate and arrogant practitioners criticized by sublime beings and condemned by the wise. (Patrul, 1998, p. 71)

I take these hell-meditations as an imaginally guised phenomenology precisely of our living experience and lived circumstances, and an enticement to pay attention to these matters, these forms of suffering right in front of me, not in some future punishment realm. "There are countless beings living in those realms right now" (Patrul, 1998, p. 67). Look. The fly spin-buzzing on the October windowsill on its back, heading towards desiccation but only with new flies to arrive, again and again, reviving this scene, pulling on the dry skin on the back of my hands that now stands up a while, aged.

The crushed wasp against the clear glass. The smoke in the air from forest fires down south in northern Washington State that is making the wary dogs stay inside, a bit more strangely alert than usual. That ache in my leg that comes and goes like a portent some days. Being crushed, distracted, depressed, silenced, fooled, careless, deluded, over-exuberant, foolish, exhausted, over-heated, cutting, chilled and frightened. The daily grind, or that terribly delicious image some teacher use for working in schools: "The Trenches."

These hells are neither fact nor fiction. They are allegories to our actual circumstances and invocations, here, now, to turn towards our circumstances and decode our living:

> If you do not contemplate these things now, when you fall into a miserable realm, you will not find a refuge to protect you from these terrors even though you seek one. At that time, you will not have the intelligence to understand that which you should adopt and that which you should cast aside. (Tsong-kha-pa, 2000, p. 175)

This, again, is why Tsong-kha-pa (2004, p. 219) said that "you can't get anywhere without reading a yak's load of books." Study helps us not merely fall into our circumstances, but to decode them, unravel their spells, and unravel what has happened to us, often "over and above our wanting and doing" (Gadamer, 1989. p. xxviii). This is why a phenomenology of how these things are experienced is not enough, because our experience, even in its very intimacy and clarity, is already full of secrets, of concealed encodings. Teachers do, in fact, experience a terrible rush in schools, but that immediacy hides things that need unconcealment, and that unconcealment needs interpretation and study, not just a description of its surface immediacy. Sharing our stories about our experience of it is not enough. Ears need popping. And, of course, that rush is precisely designed (some days I'd say "deliberately") to marginalize, trivialize, and exhaust the effort of unconcealing. Those who profit from our exhaustion get only a temporary glean. They have their own hell to pay, as we all do.

In interpretive work, these things that have spellbound us lose some of their grip, *but only some of it.* Our hells don't simply disappear—rather, their seeming permanence becomes permeable. They become translucent: you can see through them and perhaps, then, outsmart them, side-step them, end-run them, or at least speak them out loud and find refuges of commiseration with others in similar spots. "The first Noble Truth is all about accepting or welcoming unsatisfactoriness or suffering (*dukkha*) rather than trying to resist it. You will notice then that its nature is to change and drop away (Sumedho, 2010, p. 37). I, then, can become a bit freed from the "hardened identity" (Huntington, 2003, p. 266) that simply living in and living out these circumstances produced in me. I can become slightly temporarily translucent. I say "temporarily" from experience. It seems to come and go.

A warning, however. The terrible burden of such study is that it can make us aware of the forces that have been driving us unseen and can also make us unbearably aware that sometimes, *there may not be much we can do:*

> Some wishes cannot succeed; some victories cannot be won; some loneliness is incorrigible. But there is relief and freedom in knowing what is real; these givens come to us out of the perennial reality of the world, like the terrain we live on. One does not care for this ground to make it a different place, or to make it perfect, but to make it inhabitable and to make it better. To flee from its realities is only to arrive at them unprepared. (Berry, 1983, p. 92)

The danger, of course, is to become transfixed by what such study reveals and paralyzed. That, too, is attachment, another hell to pay. Equally true is the fact that to simply flee towards "its realities" and get caught up in a battle with them tends to reify and harden both them and me, thus resulting, again, being unprepared to work with the arising and perishing of things, unable to remain in that spot "in between," neither fleeing or falling for. *"The true locus of hermeneutics is this in-between"* (Gadamer, 1989, p. 295). Easier said than done, of course.

Thus the great paradox of pulling ourselves out of our troubles only to turn back towards them:

> Reflection does not withdraw from the world. It steps back [from being "lost in the performance of acts" [Husserl, 1970, p. 55] to watch the forms of transcendence fly up like sparks from a fire; it slackens the intentional threads which attach us to the world and thus brings them to our notice. (Merleau-Ponty , 1964, p. xiii)

I can't resist adding here how this links in a circuitous thread with a Buddhist focus on suffering: "People are born into suffering as readily as sparks fly up from a fire" (Job 5:7).

So, hells. These should not be thought of as universal or literal or general or abstract. They, like everything else, are brought about by circumstances, causes and conditions (Sanskrit *pratitya-samutpada*—"dependent co-arising,"). We're back around, here, an idea that is parallel to that high-school discussion I've had so often about it being "the real world" (implying, of course, the otherworldliness of "the University"). I'm always wont to say that no, this is not "the real world." It is just how the world happens to have turned out thus far, and that arising can be understood, and untangled, and set right anew, to paraphrase Hannah Arendt.

So, too with "hells." The capture of what education is currently suffering is not a permanent state, nor is it a universal one. Its contemporary "hell" is dependently co-arising. Hell is thus defined as the circumstances that prevent our realization of what is happening to us, causing suffering, intentionally or not, resisting insight or relief, exhausting and distracting us, premised on reification, fragmentation and so on. A great swath of contemporary education, of schooling, has been caught in the sway of a movement initiated at the beginning of the twentieth century: the efficiency movement. This movement—which had proven itself effective in reorganizing industrial work (but which lead to alienation from that work, "de-skilling" [Braverman 1998], distraction, market manipulation of desire [Leach 1994], media distraction and social sorrows)—has insinuated itself into the very meat of education and far beyond that as well. What initially appeared as a way to revive the work of industrial production has now inculcated itself into our very experience of time and attention and knowledge; it has preyed on our animal panic, inducing it and then promising to relieve it, all in one swath. It has made us exhausted. Without study, we'll feel the rush of time running out and think that that is just the way things are. Of course, this hellish circumstance is not permanent or fixed. It is finding slippages in ecological movements, and both trivial and profound glances to Wisdom traditions and often-near-lost indigenous knowledges. But also, at this writing, Donald Trump is leading in the Iowa polls, and Kevin O'Leary (2012) is considering running to be the leader of the Canadian Conservative Party.

None of this is just the way things are. It just happened to turn out this way, and finding out how and why can be a small refuge in the midst of it. We'll still feel the rush of time, but our attachment to it just might be lessened, just might become sufferable, nameable. We might become more awake to our circumstances. More scholarly.

What follows, then, is an elaboration of the work and influence of F.W. Taylor's so-called "efficiency movement" and what affects it has, first on encoding a "sickness out there" of fragmentation, standardization and mind-numbing, deliberate disincentives, and, second, how our experience of time shifts in this shifting. This is no Ivory Tower exercise. It is autobiographical because it is peeling its way into one of the ancestral threads that has shaped my very being who I am whether I know it or not. "Texts are instructions for practice" (Tsong-kha-pa, 2000, p. 52) and this tightly woven fabric of efficiency must be carefully read as a key, among others, to my own well-being. Study as healing—and this wound is "in me" because it is in the world I inhabit. And, of course, vice-versa.

A warning, then. Demonization is itself a form of reification, of hardening. Hostility towards efficiency leaves it un-interpreted, a mere object of complaint. To interpret these historical circumstances that gave rise to efficiency is to free ourselves from it being "the way things are in the real world" and put us in the position of seeing that proceeding efficiently is still possible, still, perhaps, just what is needed in certain circumstances.

And one other wee warning: "The more intense the practice, the more intense the demons? (Patrul, 1998, p. 189)

13

"*Time Is Always Running Out*" (*2014*)

"A Slow Sort of Country!"

> Perhaps it is only when we focus our minds on our machines that time seems short. Time is always running out for machines. They shorten our work . . . by simplifying it and speeding it up, but our work perishes quickly. (Berry, 1983, p. 76)

It is beyond doubt that teachers and students alike experience this phenomenon of time always running out with great intimacy and regularity. Teachers and students alike have become accustomed to the mood, tempo and consequences, personal and pedagogical, of how attempts to try to keep up with this time that is always running out, seem, in the end and seemingly inevitably, to give us less and less time:

> "Well, in our country," said Alice, still panting a little, "you'd generally get to somewhere else—if you run very fast for a long time, as we've been doing."
>
> "A slow sort of country!" said the Queen. "Now, here, you see, it takes all the running you can do, to keep in the same place. If you want to get somewhere else, you must run at least twice as fast as that!" (Carroll, L., 1871, p. 16)

In Praise of Radiant Beings, pages 179–192

An old story, this. In some schools, this clockwork "machine time," like a demanding Red Queen, seems to render classroom experiences to its relentless demands, pressing itself in on what we do, how we think and imagine, even whether there is time to think much at all. There is almost too much to consider in this orbit—market-driven obsolescence ("our work perishes quickly"), flickering attention spans ("speeding it up") and how such spans then create a world ("simplifying it") that does not *require* much attention, thus aggravating this circle of consequence. Once this voracious and insatiable wheel starts turning, something else kicks in: as the Red Queen suggested, the only relief or fulfillment of this itch is to be found in, not in speed but in *acceleration.*

This suffering is real and palpable. It has become a familiar story—laments about time and its running—both inside and outside of schools, to the extent that talk of any other sense of time, of whiling time and the gathering that happens around good stories, good work, well sought inquiry, and thoughtfulness, seems, in the life of "real world" schools, simply fanciful, unreal almost:

> To be glib, [in this "real world"] little requires human application, so little cultivates it. Long alienated from abiding in inquiry as a form of life and way of being, a restless humanity defers to models, systems, operations, procedures, the ready-made strategic plan, and first and last to reified concepts, long impervious to deconstruction. (Ross, 2006, p. 111)

Deep and rich explorations of the abundance of the world—this experience of time now seems the wonderland. Countless teachers have told me this: they would love to do this, but they simply don't have time, they are always already late no matter what they do, no matter how they try.

This is the core of a sort of ontological delusion that sets in: this sense of relentless, perpetually running-out machine time has become so obsequious that it becomes experienced as if it is simply "the way things are." As I hear so often from so many teachers, including those who wish it otherwise, this is simply "the real world." This is where the real perniciousness lies, because once codified as simply "the real world," any attempts to interrupt this spell and suggest that there is a life to pedagogy out from under this ontological delusion are looked upon with great suspicion, accusations of not understanding what it is like, so goes the telling phrase, "in the trenches."

The trick here, of course, is to remember that this is *not* the real world in some intransigent, ontological sense. Rather, *it is how the world has turned out* and therefore, two things. First, there are causes and conditions that can be untangled that can help us understand something of how and why things turned out like this, thus loosening their grip on our imaginations and practice. Second, we can perhaps begin to shift the story being told to one that is more amenable to "abiding in inquiry as a form of life and way of being" (Ross, 2006, p. 111). This loosening and shifting re-telling is, of course, perennial and tough and full of heartache and therefore cannot be fully fulfilled here.

So, for now, a small offering: two short stories that might help start decoding this familiar story about time running out.

Story One: Empty Time and a Succession of Nows

> The designation "empty time" is how [Hans-Georg] Gadamer terms time conceived of as the constant, flowing succession of 'nows' coming from a future and receding into the past. This is time subjugated to quantitative measurement. It is 'empty' because measuring time requires a separation of the temporal units which measure from that which is measured; to separate time from its contents is to 'empty' it [Ross here references Gadamer, 1970, pp. 342–343]. It is in fact the utility function of measured time—time made available for use—that Gadamer says is at the root of this emptying. (Ross, 2006, p. 110)

Once we detach our understanding and experience of time from any substantive thing measured in time, time becomes pictured as an empty sequence or stretch. Like this, simple: "we've got two [empty] hours this morning with the kids." This empty time can now be "filled" or "used" as we see fit or as circumstances allow. Time thus emptied becomes imagined as something utile, something "useable." Also, and *because of* this imaginal shift, time becomes understood as something that can be "used up," something that can therefore "run out."

Pedagogy is therefore understood as occurring within specific measures of useable time, empty time. This is where the turn occurs: the work that can then be pursued under such auspices is *rendered measurable* by such empty, formal, and clockwork temporality. It is not simply that the things we have to do are molded into a tempo that is fast and efficient. Those very things themselves must, of a necessity borne of this empty time cast in a sequence of "nows," become fragmented into pieces that can fit the measure of empty time itself. What we have to do changes in order to shape itself to the useable-ness of empty time. Given the sequence march of empty time, then, only once things are fragmented into sequence-able bits and pieces can the things we do "fit" the ever-accelerating succession of "nows" that empty, measurable, machine-like time demands of things. To the extent that what we do *cannot* thus shape itself, to that extent, we have to eradicate such pursuits.

We don't have time.

Thus, time is not simply *subjugated to quantitative measurement.* Empty time now *subjugates* anything to which it is applied and marginalizes anything that cannot be thus subjugated. The thing now measured "in [empty] time" must itself, in its very substance, become the objective equivalent of a series of "nows"—separate, self-contained, isolatable fragments or pieces—that must be then assembled in sequenced, ordered, managed, and standardized in order to be adequately temporally measured and, especially, in order to be, as the saying goes "covered" in the allotted time. Thus, a hidden logic churns: as things fragment, time accelerates *because* there is nothing to slow it down since no one of these isolated bits or pieces *requires* any prolonged attention. Once detached from the thing that lives in time, empty time produces fragments that no longer *need* "continuity of [our] attention and devotion" (Berry, 1986, p 32). Worse yet, these fragments reject and cause to atrophy that very sense of devotion, making it seem, not surprisingly, like a "waste of time."

Empty time thus now rules the work being done. But it is important to re-emphasize what has happened here. This is not just a matter of demanding that the same work being done be done "faster" (this would be as mistaken as imagining that the "slow food movement" is suggesting cooking fast food slowly). Nor does empty time simply rule *how* the work is to be done. *The very nature of the work itself changes,* as does the relationship that one can strike up with the work. And, to reiterate a point noted above, work "covered" in used-up, empty time work becomes understood as more "basic" than the (now thought to be) luxuriousness of "abiding in inquiry." Worse yet, what might be attended to in a luxurious way—say a beautifully illustrated story like *Wabi Sabi* (Reibstein, 2008), or the wetland down the way from the school that we might visit and "study"—is understood to be "really" made up of pieces and in order to get to the whole of that story, we must have the pieces out of which it is made *beforehand.* We must, as goes the familiar phrase, start with "the basics."

What happens then is also all too familiar. This trumping of empty time is not just a matter of chronological deferral—"we'll get to that later if we have leftover time that hasn't been used up." *That which we might get to later* becomes not simply (possibly) "later," but becomes understood as a "frill" that is unnecessary to the "real world" reality of things. Such matters are leftovers. In the real world of schools and Provincial examinations and parents' demands for "accountability," getting to it "later" is not really an especially urgent manner "in the real world." After all, "first things first."

But here is a school reality that is hard to admit: those sorts of work that fit the clockwork, one-thing-after-the-other, always accelerating rush of empty time bully themselves to the front of the line and provide a way to not just marginalize but humiliate those who might suggest that there is thoughtfulness, rigorousness, authenticity and good work to be had out from under this running-out panic.

Story Two: Industrial Production and the Efficiency of Schooling

> The uniformity, standardization, and bureaucracy of the factory model soon became predominant characteristics of the school district. The key was to have the thinkers of the organization specify exactly what and how to teach at each grade level and then to provide strict supervision to ensure that teachers did as they were told. Decisions flowed from state boards of education down the ladder of the educational bureaucracy to local school boards, superintendents, and principals. Eventually, decisions would be directed to teachers who, like factory workers, were viewed as underlings responsible for carrying out the decisions of their bosses. Students were simply the raw material transported along the educational assembly line. They would be moved to a station where a teacher would "pour" in mathematics until the bell rang; then they would be moved to the next station where another teacher would "assemble" the nuts and bolts of English until the next bell rang, and so on. Those who completed this 13-year trek on the assembly line would emerge as finished products, ready to function efficiently in the industrial world. (Dufour & Eaker, 1998, n.p.)

> Most schooled tasks have been stripped of that character which would take a while. Taking a while over some phenomenon is very often not simply *unnecessary* but *impossible* because the school-matters at hand have been stripped of the very memorability and relatedness... that might require and sustain and reward such attention and devotion. From the point of view of efficiency and management, intellectual whiling in the leisures (*schola*) of school simply seems dense and unproductive. [Little in school tasks organized thus is] worth *while*. (Jardine, 2012h, p. 175)

At the beginning of the twentieth century, there was a profound shift in the way in which industrial production was imagined, organized, and carried out, and what was, at first, a brilliant shift, occurred, full of enthusiasm. F. W. Taylor (1856–1915), most explicitly in his still-published text *The Principles of Scientific Management* (1911), instituted what was later to be called "the efficiency movement" (Callahan, 1964). This movement arose out of

Taylor's observations on the shop floors of various industries on the East Coast of America (Bethlehem Steel, for example) and his development of what he called time and motion studies.

It had been that artisans and workers would gather around the work to be done in ways that we age old and linked to ancient guild and master/apprentice organizations and to the sometimes written, but often oral transmission of knowledge and craft, of hand laid over hand, of breath and bread shared over the immediacies of laboring. Taylor entered this fray as an observer, and conducted time and motion studies of such industrial production. Essentially, he measured every step of the work being done—who was doing what, what others were doing in the meantime, even literally how many steps and in what direction anyone would take to get materials, to work around other workers or wait for them, and so on. In effect, Taylor temporally ("time") and spatially ("motion") broke down any particular industrial task into its, shall we say, basic, component parts and laid out ways in which the organization, management and sequencing of that task could be more efficiently organized. He experimented in great and meticulous detail with the sequence of the work, the portioning of the work, the effects of placing accessible parts or tools here or there, with this first instead of that, of this worker doing these three things, or two, or perhaps having this one arduous task done by two workers, turning to the left to grab the next part to be assembled, or to the right, working and resting for these lengths, in this order or that, this amount of training done this way, that way, and on and on, tumbling these components all with an eye to the elimination of waste—wasted time, wasted materials, essentially, wasted money—and all this with an eye to increasing the efficiency and productivity of the work being done, decreasing the errors and glitches encountered, and increasing, thus, *efficiency*.

All of these studies were traced with stopwatch in hand, notebooks and measuring tape, leading to a new invention, flow-charts for the work being done. As was the atmosphere of the early twentieth century, this work of Taylor's was touted with the portentous term "*scientific* management" to contrast it with old, rule of thumb, practically based work—we need to keep our eye on this shift, because this is part of the movement of evacuating from front-line practices any knowledge or worth and placing in the hands of managers/administrators/principals the task of organizing work so that workers need not think, need not be "skilled" but only obedient to the system of work devised by management, thus making labor cheaper and thus increasing the efficiency of production as a whole (on the "deskilling" that comes from this movement, see Braverman, 1998).

Henry Ford's car assembly line provides us with an easily recognizable image of what was, in fact, a "culmination of a decades-long process" (Watts, 2006, p. 153) initiated by Taylor: each worker has placed in front of them an isolated, repeated task to be done with singular, standardized procedures and invariant materials (on Taylorism and Fordism, see Kanigel, 2005, p. 49):

> The basic procedure made management the absolute arbiters of when, at what speed, and in what fashion the work was performed. The assembly line's smooth, continuous flow, in the words of Horace Arnold, worked by "hurrying the slow men, holding the fast men back... and acting as an all-around adjuster and equalizer." It was the apotheosis of scientific management. (Watts, 2006, p. 154)

(I can't help but think, here, of the mathematics department in a local High School requiring all those teaching mathematics in Grade Ten to be on the same chapter at the same time over the course of the semester). Even though there is no evidence that Henry Ford actually read or was directly influenced by Taylor's work, "the Ford Motor Company was 'Taylorized without Taylor'" (Watts, 2006, p. 153):

> Factory managers struggled to break the hold of artisan craftsmen, with their traditions of stubborn independence, and fought to eradicate... "pre-modern" work culture, with its agricultural aversion to disciplined, time-oriented labor. They sought to construct a new model of labor more attuned to the demands of efficiency and mass production. (p. 153)

Note in passing here how the profound cleaving to a deep and well-understood sense of time that is indigenous to the ways of agriculture is simply swept aside in this statement, and how, therefore, the specific sort of "discipline" that comes with empty time casts agriculture as seemingly undisciplined, slack, stubborn—note, too, how "independence" becomes cast as a disparagement.

So, under the auspices of efficiency, all tethers of one specified task to any other tasks or to the object being assembled or any tether between this worker and other workers, or tethers to the ancient arts of craft and work, or tethers to any concern for the quality of what is being done or the purpose, or the even the locale of this bit of work in front of me to what is being built—all this has been systematically eradicated as detrimental to the efficiency of the work being done:

> "Every day, year in and year out, each man should ask himself over and over again, two questions," said Taylor in his standard lecture. "First, 'What is the

> name of the man I am now working for?' And having answered this definitely then 'What does this man want me to do, right now?' Not, 'What ought I to do in the interests of the company I am working for?' Not, 'What are the duties of the position I am filling? Not, 'What did I agree to do when I came here?' Not, 'What should I do for my own best interest?' but plainly and simply, 'What does this man want me to do right now?'" (cited in Boyle, 2006)

I should also not ask why we are doing this, what this is part of or leading to, what my role is in all of this. The task for industrial factory workers is simply to learn by rote and repetition the efficient accomplishment of this one, isolated task and then to either simply repeat that task or get on to the next, equally isolated task at hand.

The, shall we say, "pay-off" for doing monotonous and unfulfilling work is not found in the work, but in its resultant "consumer abundance" (Watts, 2006, p. 155). The ethic of work and its fulfilling pleasures is replaced with the ethic of consumption—the pleasure to be had, to be purchased, *after* the work is done:

> Work and play should not be mixed. "When we are at work we ought to be at work. When we are at play we ought to be at play," [Ford] wrote. "When the work is done, then the play can come, but not before." (Watts, 2006, p. 155)

The once-"playful" pleasures and engagement and fulfillment of good work are evacuated from the work itself (which becomes fragmented, routine and monotonous) and the higher wages then paid for obediently enduring such monotony can be exchanged, afterwards, for purchasable, enjoyable things. Engagement itself becomes a leftover caught in regimes of market-exchange, a great analogy to justifying and enduring the boredom of routinized High School classes in order to receive marks that can *then* be exchanged for future employment that *then* can be exchanged for one's chosen enjoyments. Note the great eschatological arc of empty time here, where the present is drained of its life with the promise of future fulfillment: some time in the future, time will no longer be empty but full.

As a result of F. W. Taylor's re-imagining of industrial production, industrial efficiency, production and profit increased dramatically. Moreover, this image of efficiency and its promise took over the public imagination and swept through all facets of then-contemporary life, from mayor's offices to hospitals to how housewives should organize their kitchens and their housework schedules and on and on (for more detail on these matters see see Taylor, 1903, 1911, Kanige, 2005, Dufour & Eaker, 1998, Callahan, 1964, Gatto, 2006, Wrege & Greenwood, 1991, Friesen & Jardine, 2009, to name but a few available sources). Dozens of articles in popular magazines and scholarly journals were written and poured over, along with recurrent declamatory newspaper articles about the inefficiencies of this or that facet of then-contemporary life. "What about efficiency?" became a polemical, even moral clarion call in all quarters of North American consciousness: "Taylor's thinking so permeates the soil of modern life we no longer realize it's there. It has become, as Edward Eyre Hunt, an aide to future President Herbert Hoover, could grandly declaim in 1924, 'part of our moral inheritance'" (Kanigel, 2005, p. 7).

In reference to Hans-Georg Gadamer's explorations of empty time that is always running out, Sheila Ross (2006, p. 118) suggests that "the dominance of this modality of thought... is arguably pathological." Just as a reminder, it is not that this way of thinking is pathological. It is its *dominance* that is at issue here, and how easily it has come to occlude, bully and marginalize other ways of experiencing work, time, engagement, learning, and so on. It has lost its sense of proportion and place due, in fact, to its being *premised on* the fragmentation of any territory it enters and considers. It thus cannot be expected to find its own limit. It is, thus, pathological in its sway.

Given the burgeoning numbers of immigrant children entering large East Coast American cities, and the equally burgeoning need for minimally educated workers in industry, schools had become overwhelmed early in the twentieth century, and the promise of more efficient schooling was irresistible: "educators needed little prompting" (Dufour & Eaker, 1998). Thus, we hear from Ellwood P. Cubberley, Dean of the School of Education at Stanford, from his book *Public School Administration*, originally published in 1916 [cited here from Callahan 1964, p. 97]):

> In time it will be possible for any school system to maintain a continuous survey of all of the different phases of its work, through tests made by its corps of efficiency experts, and to detect weak points in its work almost as soon as they appear. Every manufacturing establishment that turns out a standard product or series of products of any kind maintains a force of efficiency experts to study methods of procedures and to measure and test the output of its works. Such men... [also] train the workmen to produce a larger and a better output. Our schools are in a sense factories in which raw products (children) are to be shaped and fashioned into products to meet the various demands of life. The specifications for manufacturing come from the demands of twentieth-century civilization, and it is the business of the school to build its pupils according to the specifications laid down.

There is, of course, much, much more to this story of the re-capitulation of empty time sequences in the shape of industrial production and how these images found a great ally in a then-emerging theory of knowledge which imagined knowledge as built out of separate bits and pieces:

> As behaviorism grew in prominence during the period between the two world wars, the scientific management movement in education was being promoted by [Franklin] Bobbitt (1924), a curriculum specialist who, citing the need for efficiency and using the steel industry as his model, attempted to apply the techniques of business to the schools. In the name of efficiency, he gave paramount importance to the setting of acceptable performance standards and to their measurement. He formulated long and detailed lists of objectives which he felt would enable learners to prepare for life by mastering specific skills and subskills. (Tumposky, 1984, p. 296)

Part of the attractiveness of Taylor's industrial promise of efficiency thus dovetailed with the logic of fragmentation borne from a since-outdated version of the empirical sciences in the early twentieth century. The then-emerging Behavioral Sciences produced an image of knowledge as built up one "basic" bit at a time. Each separate fragment is itself and has only "revocable and provisional" (Gray, 1998, pp. 35–36) connections to anything else. "The basics," in education, became identified with those not-further-divisible "bits" out of which any knowledge was built, and "back to the basics" (see Jardine, Clifford & Friesen, 2008) comes to mean back to a version of knowledge-assembly right in line with Taylor's industrial assembly principles. Taylor's influence thus found broad affiliations when applied to education, and its influence filtered down into the very ways in which the topics covered in schools were imagined to exist: sequences of separate parts and therefore, through the grades, assignable parts of such assembly to be "covered" in each grade. It may be that classrooms prior to such infiltration were already cast this way, but Taylor's work, coupled with Behavioral Theory, gave this cast an air of modernity, of seriousness and scientific warrant that provide a way to trump any resistance to its influence.

A Few Closing Bits and Pieces

It is impossible to detail all this in the present context. Instead, then, just a few closing bits and pieces, trails that can be followed, half-forgotten stories that can be hunted out, filled out, and re-told:

- From Henry Ford's (2007, p. 14) autobiography: "eliminate the useless parts. This applies to everything—a shoe, a dress, a house, a piece of machinery, an airplane, a steamship." Following the inculcation of Taylorism into education, this applies to each and every minute spent in the classroom, each and every topic that is learned, how schools and school departments are organized, and how the work of students, teachers and administrators are apportioned. Eliminate useless parts as well as useless replications of time and motion and effort, where, in each case, "uselessness" is defined in advance as that which cannot be efficiently learned, efficiently tested, and accounted for. For example, heated conversations in a Grade Ten classroom about the exportation of democracy to other countries via pre-emptive, invasive actions are deemed "useless" in light of standardized assessment regimes that will be testing for students' ability to name four characteristics of democracy on upcoming Provincial Examinations. Those conversations become "a waste of time."

- The product thus efficiently and repeatedly produced becomes effectively identical every time. "Any customer can have a car painted any color that he wants so long as it is black" (Ford, 2007, p. 72). Because the desired product is thus standardized, a standardized assessment of the results of production can be developed and applied uniformly and without variation.
- Not only is the *product* standardized. Efficiency requires the "complete standardization of all details and methods. [It] is not only desirable but absolutely indispensable as a preliminary to specifying the time in which each operation shall be done, and then insisting that it shall be done within the time allowed" (Taylor, 1903). There is thus only "one best way" (Kanigel, 2005) for *what* is being done, *how* it is being done, *how long each step takes* to be done and the precise and undeviating *order* of such steps. Moreover, exactly *who* is responsible for *what* can also be specified with precisely the same standardization and uniformity. Anything that now deviates from this is considered an error in the system that needs eradication. Luckily, because of the standardization, the source of error is easy to find. For example, if we have a child who does not understand "place-value," we can specify precisely where "on the line" this understanding was to be "built," precisely where on the line one would have tested to ensure such building (or ensured that this line-step was repeated until such assurance was had) and so on.
- Of course, there may not be a defect "in the system." There may, rather, be a defect in, to use Elwood Cubberley's phrase, "the raw product"—the child may be "defective." And as those of us in education know full well, such possible "defects" have lead to

astoundingly complex regimes of alternate assembly lines for everything from "the retarded" to "laggards in our schools" (Ayres 1909), to children with special needs, to learning delays, slow children, Individual Program Plans (ready-made and individually designed assembly lines geared to the precise "raw product" deficits [see Gilham, 2015, 2015a]). Thus, even though, in *The Principles of Scientific Management* (1911, p. 2), Taylor insists "in the past the man has been first; in the future the system must be first," the school system leaves the fragmentation and sequencing of Taylorism in place and then simply starts, on behalf of the well-being of students and their diversity and difference, to multiply that system into sub-assembly lines, ejecting less abled students from the main assembly line, purportedly for their own good and to accommodate their special needs, but there is another reason, too. Such ejection is the most efficient way to maintain the efficiency of the main line of schooling.

- From a June 4th, 1906 lecture by F. W. Taylor (cited in Kanigel, 2005, p. 169): "In our scheme we do not ask for the initiative of our men. We do not want any initiative. All we want of them is to obey the orders we give them, do what we say, and do it quickly." Recall "little requires human application, so little cultivates it" (Ross, 2006, p. 111). Initiative and interest become cast as a *detriment to efficiency itself.* Both students and teachers learn this quickly and become complicit in this logic. The restless student becomes named as suffering from Oppositional Defiance Disorders in the same gesture that names the new enthusiastic teacher green and naive. And all that in a system now hysterically aroused over issues of bullying.
- Taylor's "declared purpose was to take all control from the hands of the workman (whom he regularly compared to oxen or horses) and place it in those of management" (Kanigel, 2005, p. 19). "What [Taylor] really wanted working men to be [is] focused, uncomplicated and compliant" (Boyle, 2006). Educational psychology then often unwittingly conspires with theories of normality and abnormality, deviance and resistance, theories of giftedness and slowness, in order to codify these purposes.
- Since effective schooling becomes linked with the obedient following of rules and following them the way anyone and everyone follows them, to be a student *and* to be a teacher means to be *completely and utterly replaceable.* This is part of the "scientific" character of "scientific management," one of the consequences

of how it operates. To the extent that who is learning and who is teaching makes a difference in the classroom, that teaching has become, as goes the term in a failed experiment, *contaminated.* Any innovative practices are thus marginalized as the gifts of a particular teacher, thus once again preventing the normalcy of efficient schooling that can be done by anyone from being interrupted by such examples.

- Given this link of contamination with inefficiency, consider that H. Martyn Hart, the Dean of St. John's Cathedral in Denver, from the September 1912 issue of the *Ladies' Home Journal* decried decreases in character, increases in divorce and crime, lack of self-control, illicit political machinations and attributed all of this to *inefficiency* in "the system of schooling" (Cited in Callahan, 1964, p. 52). Simply consider here how contemporary schools have become "hot spots" in this regard, where economic, social, cultural, political, and moral praise and blame swirl.
- What then happens is a sort of "ghost echo." This tangled story of efficiency and its insinuation into education is not just a story produced in closed system, but is dedicated to *producing* closure. Any attempt to interrupt this story can be cast aside without hesitation because that attempt can now only be speaking on behalf of *inefficiency.* After declaring that "the man" used to be first but now "the system" is first, Taylor goes on to write that "this in no sense implies that great men are not needed. On the contrary, the first object of any good system must be that of developing first-class men; and under systematic management the best man rises to the top more certainly and more rapidly than ever before" (Taylor, 1911, p. 2). Remember, though, that "greatness" and "first-class" here mean those who can maintain the system and its efficiencies. Taylor's purpose in the introduction of the suggestion box in such settings is to take suggestions that, over time, *eliminate the need for further suggestions*—this is the moment where the system becomes first, and "the man" is simply either fitting into it or ejected out of it (teachers and students alike). This is the same "closed circle" echo found in *The Fraser Institute's Annual Report Card on Alberta Schools*: "If teachers were following the provincial curriculum by definition they would be teaching to the test. If they're not teaching to the test, then they're not doing their job" (McGinnis, 2008, p. B5, citing the institute's Peter Cowley). Once this loop closes, the dominance of this form of thinking then projects upon any dissent the character of being

irresponsible, being "unaccountable." "Abiding in inquiry" looks like letting kids do whatever they want and to hell with the curriculum, let's just be free and arty and "creative."

- One last thing in this lengthening short story. Looping back to our considerations of time, and weaving this with our contemporary concerns in Canadian schools with the burgeoning multicultural face of our classrooms, consider this brief reminiscence from "William C. Klann, foreman of motor assembly at the Highland Park facility" (Watts, 2006, p. 142): "one [phrase] every foreman had to learn in English, German, Polish, and Italian [and now Hindi, Urdu, Arabic, Mandarin and others] was 'hurry up'" (cited in Watts, 2006, p. 154).
- Finally, schooling, *of all things*, becomes rife with anti-intellectualism (see Callahan, 1964, p. 8). Study becomes foolishness, slackness, suspect. Those suspected of thinking become conspiracy theorists or, even better, if you think, you just don't understand.

As I've witnessed in many schools, there is the unuttered belief inside this closed circle that if you let go for a minute of the narrowed and fenced regimes of management and control, quite literally, *all Hell will break lose.* That this hallucinatory vision of the threatening Hellishness portended by restlessness is, in some part and however unintentionally, *produced by* the very narrowing that has been set up to protect us from such a threat—this becomes too horrible to contemplate—that we may be causing our own exhaustion, distraction and grief and then blaming our children for it.

PREAMBLE 14

"Well, Lyle"

Do not explain the teachings without being requested to do so.
—Tsong-kha-pa, 2000, p. 65

There was a comic strip called Animal Crackers that had a panel that Gail (Jardine) and I cut out and saved years and years ago. This particular one had Lyle the Lion and one of his friends (can't remember which one) standing outside at night on a hill. As I remember it, Lyle looks up to the vast and starry heavens and cries out "What does it all mean?"

His companion says "Well, Lyle, first of all . . . "

Even though, as has become evident, Buddhism leaked early on into my written work, it kept an ecological and hermeneutic disguise in much of my teaching, and even those disguises were often suppressed or mediated in classes on Early Childhood and Elementary School Curriculum, practicum courses and practicum supervision in schools. Graduate courses in Interpretive Research Methods were comparatively straightforward.

In Praise of Radiant Beings, pages 193–197

Face-to-face, I felt far more measured in my work and far less qualified to even mention Buddhism at all, for fear, frankly, that someone might take that mention seriously enough to turn to me and expect things I could not give. I know what to do if a hermeneutic study gets in trouble. I can even explain parts of Martin Heidegger's later work, given enough air. I don't know what to do when breathing halts and the looming of emptiness threatens to drop the bottom out of someone's life, or gruesome visions come in meditation practice. I cited the following passage as a reason for the name of the vanity press I started, Makyo Press, where I self-published *Speaking with a Boneless Tongue* in 1992:

> Makyo, "mysterious vision" [is] a deep dream experience. Certain religious traditions place great importance on makyo. Visions and heavenly voices are seriously considered to be signs of enlightenment and salvation. These phenomena may be of general interest, for they reveal the rich potential of human experience, but they reveal little of the true nature of the one who experiences them. If you do experience it you can recognize that you are walking near your true home [but] no matter how interesting and encouraging makyo may be, they are self-limited. (Aitken, 1982, p. 46)

But I didn't know then and don't know much now about decoding such visions within the confines of Buddhist thinking. I tend, because of my hermeneutic background, to draw towards such visions and their studied interpretation as a means of gaining, for me, less risky proximity to that "true home."

The emphasis on study is not encouraged in the Zen tradition to the same extent or in the same way as it is in that of the Gelug tradition of Tsong-kha-pa, a main reason that the academic in me prefers the latter. A negative version of *makyo* might be regimes of efficiency (See Preamble and Chapter 13), and the purpose of studying this uprising is not to change it into something else, but *to change it into what it is*—not "the way things are" or some permanent, hardened "reality," but a possible way for us to act among myriad others. Beatific visions must undergo the same sort of dissolution, or, better "disillusion," to follow David G. Smith's tough insight (2014). Just like there is no such a (permanent, fixed, real-world) "thing" as efficiency, so, too, there is no such "thing" as "the individual child" or any other precious or feared reification. It, too, is a dependently co-arising, possible way to think through our circumstances.

This hermeneutic audacity should not be confused with me being a Buddhist practitioner (it comes and goes, here and there, now and then), let alone a Buddhist teacher. Some days I feel like I'm simply toying with it. I'm not even much of a Buddhist scholar except insofar as it can be raided for a relief from some of the joyless and morbid nonsense of educational theory and practice language, culture and often self-inflicted and unnecessary sorrows. The hermeneutic adage about "restoring life to its original difficulty" (Caputo, 1987, p. 2; see Jardine, 1992c) is an effort to see through these self-inflicted sorrows to the sorrowful suffering, enduring and undergoing that is our human lot. The joy of a vertiginous mathematical insight in a Grade Six classroom is precisely such an undergoing, simple as that. It portends that we must now endure the venture opened up in front of us, these living fields of dependent co-arising that surround this moment of insight. A path is set out through the middle of things, and, as a reminder:

> here is the great, seemingly paradoxical situation: "keeping ourselves open" and "keeping the world open" (Eliade, 1968, p. 139) are the same thing. (Jardine, Bastock George & Martin, 2008, p. 53)

Thus, my own self-imposed comeuppance has been couching this sense of always-too-grandiose "well, Lyle" sentiments regarding Buddhism into the particular earthiness of curriculum locales, spaces, topics, and territories. This couching is called for by hermeneutics (in its insistence on how application to arising cases curbs the audacity of rules, idealizations, conceptualizations and brings them to account in the face of the rough faces of the world), by ecological work (and its insistence on locales, places, topographies, and bodily intimacy) as well as by Buddhism's insistence that "it's all one meditation" (Snyder, 1989, p. 252) but that the manifestations of the active working of such attention are only had in doing "this and this" (Wallace, 1987, p. 111):

> Impartiality, love and compassion—without... taking up specific objects of meditation, but only using a general object from the outset, you will just seem to generate these attitudes. Then, when you try to apply them to specific individuals, you will not be able to actually generate these attitudes toward anyone. But once you have a transformative experience towards an individual in... practice... (Tsong-kha-pa, 2002, p. 44)

Once you learn to apply the opening-into-dependent-co-arising work of interpretation to, say, place value or multiplying by fractions, *then,* sidelong and just glanced out of the corner of your eye, you'll get a sense of what "emptiness" and "dependent co-arising" might mean, why these are not simply abstractions or floating, mystical puffery, of what exhilaration comes with such vertiginous openness and spaciousness regarding the most mundane of things, what radiance.

These last three terms sound bloody ridiculous by themselves with no referent to hold them in place and curb their woozy enthusiasms. They sound too much like what might come after "well, Lyle." This reminds me of the response I learned early on when graduate students would ask me about hermeneutics. My first response was always "What's your topic?" and as we continued to talk, how hermeneutics might get air under the wings of *this* working space was allowed to emerge *in place* and, shall we say, in the proper measure of the object that might call for interpretation—which just might, shall we say, request "explaining the teachings" under the warrant of the case at hand. The topic—this child's trouble with reading, this comment from a parent, this circle inscribed inside a square—is "the bridle set with sharp nails" (Tsong-kha-pa, 2000, p. 71) that pulls thinking back down to earthly composure and specificity. Otherwise, hermeneutics, too, sounds puffy and ridiculous, too much like ecological sentimentalities like "love the earth" and "save the planet."

Yuck.

So this stifling of the links between Buddhism and education lifted a bit as my career was ending. I had the great pleasure and privilege of co-teaching (with Jackie Seidel) two sets of four courses under the titles "Roots of Classroom Inquiry" (those roots being hermeneutics and ecology) and "Storytelling and the Ecological Heart of Curriculum." In these courses we read, among other things, David Loy's work and that of David G. Smith, Thich Nhat Hanh, Ajhan Chah, Maxine Greene, Joseph Campbell, Wendell Berry and many, many others over the course of two years. What resulted were a text that Jackie and I put together (2014)—the next chapter is its Introduction—as well as a forthcoming collection of writing by many of the teachers who took those ventures with us (Seidel & Jardine, in press).

What resulted, too, was a slight sense that I had been asked to explain some of the teachings just a bit, just a bit. Jackie and I even called our classes a refuge from the distraction and hurrying, and many classes were spent opening up space, studying, come to trust the rising sense of a "hitherto concealed experience" of school, of students, of teaching and learning. And, to the extent that Buddhism peeked above the parapets, the good news was, just like my classes on hermeneutics, what confronted this peek was 20–25 practicing teachers just arrived from the classroom that day, 4:30 p.m., tired, bringing food to share and the lived realities of their work that day, that week. As with everything we read, different threads of experience and thinking in Buddhism were answerable to specific suffering, specific joys, faces, names, children, anxieties, worries over roughshod administrative initiatives, moments of breakthrough and so on.

So what follows is the introduction to that book produced over those two miraculous years—with no hesitation that the etymology, here, roots down from Latin *mirus* "wonderful, astonishing, amazing" into "earlier *smeiros,* from PIE [Proto-Indo-European] *smei-* "to smile, laugh" (Cognates: Sanskri *smerah* "smiling," Greek *meidan* "to smile," Old Church Slavnoic *smejo* "to laugh" (OED). That book—*Ecological Pedagogy, Buddhist Pedagogy, Hermeneutic Pedagogy: Experiments in a Curriculum for Miracles* (Seidel & Jardine, 2014)—was the first appearance of the "title track" of the current collection.

14

Introduction: "We Are Here, We Are Here"

Jackie Seidel
David W. Jardine (2014)

Preamble

Call up to the creators; we are here, we are here.
—Innes, 2014, p. 102

We begin with this passage from a poem by Judson Innes because it contains a summoning, a calling, similar in tone to the way that Geshe Lhundub Sopa begins his enormous, multi-volume commentary on Tsong-kha-pa's *The great treatise on the stages of the path to enlightenment* (2000, 2002, 2004).

At the very beginning of the 1720 pages of three volumes published thus far Geshe Sopa (2004, p. 1) starts thus:

> So, here we are. Right now, you have a life that is precious and valuable.

In Praise of Radiant Beings, pages 199–203

So many teachers and students that we have worked with over many years have done beautiful work that calls out, over and over, "we are here, we are here." So many have suffered enormously in the confines of schooling and its bluntings, fears, and shams. It is in recognition of these teachers and these students—our teachers, our students—that we undertake this book.

Again from Geshe Sopa (2004, p. 15), in an early Prologue section entitled "A Pledge to Compose this Work": "now, why does an author have to make a promise to write? Someone can compose a text without making promise to do so. Here, this pledge has a special purpose: to publically proclaim, 'I will do this.'" Our pledge, one that slowly emerged as this text itself emerged, adds this: this beautiful work between students and teachers, inside and outside of the confines of schooling, *exists*, sometimes in silence and isolation, sometimes in enclaves of refuge and support. Not only, then, "I will do this," but also "this has been done," "this can be done." This is why we saw fit in some of our recent graduate classes to call these gatherings "refuges." This is why we ate together, talked and read and listened and fell silent together. Up against the too often pronounced exhaustion and desperation and despair of "this sort of thing is not possible in my school/with my sort of students/in this part of town/at this grade level/with this school administration/in this school board/in this subject area/with these parents/under these economic conditions," and so, on and on, we offer an old and pointed response of our late colleague, teacher and friend, Patricia Clifford: "if it actually exists, it *must* be possible."

So, then, here we are. We will do this.

"So, Here We Are"

The central motivating factor of this book is to elaborate beautiful classroom work that we have witnessed, over and over again, in every grade and every sort of school circumstance, over the past several years. To do this, we explore three interrelated roots of scholarly work that have a supportive and elaborative affinity to authentic and engaging classroom inquiry: ecological consciousness, Buddhist epistemologies, philosophies and practices, and interpretive inquiry or "hermeneutics." Although these three roots originate outside of and extend far beyond most educational literature, understanding them can be of immense practical importance to the conduct of rich, rigorous, practicable, sustainable and adventurous classroom work for students and teachers alike. They can help break the spell of educational discourse that has become moribund and stuck, and, worse, yet, dangerous.

Consider the words of David G. Smith (1999b, 135–136), one great teacher and refuge for us:

> "Education is suffering from narration-sickness," says Paulo Freire. It speaks out of a story which was once full of enthusiasm, but now shows itself incapable of a surprise ending. The nausea of narration-sickness comes from having heard enough, of hearing many variations on a theme but no new theme. A narrative which is sick may claim to speak for all, yet has no *aporia*, no possibility of meeting a stranger because the text is complete already. Such narratives may be passed as excellent by those who certify clarity and for whom ambiguity is a disease to be excoriated. But the literalism of such narratives (speeches, lectures, stories) inevitably produces a pedagogy which, while it passes as being "for the good of children," does not recognize the violence against children inherent in its own claim. Because without an acknowledgement and positive appreciation of the full polysemic possibility which can explode forth from within any occasion when adult and child genuinely meet together: a possibility which resides precisely in the difference of every child, every person, a difference about which one can presume nothing despite the massive research literature (e.g., about children) available to us, and despite the fact that our children come from us, are our flesh and blood. Without an appreciation of the radical mystery which confronts us in the face of every other person, our theorizing must inexorably become stuck, for then we are no longer available for that which comes to meet us from beyond ourselves, having determined in advance the conditions under which any new thing will be acceptable, and thereby foreclosing on the possibility of our own transformation. This radical difference of every child, every other person, renders our pedagogical narratives ambiguous but at the same time hopeful, because the immanent ambiguity held within them opens a space for genuine speaking, holding out the promise that something new can be said from out of the mists of the oracle of our own flesh.

These three disciplines of ecology, Buddhism and hermeneutics, each in their own way, knows something of this oracularity of the flesh, of the opening, in the concert between teacher and student, of "free spaces" (Gadamer, 1986, p. 59) in intimate pedagogical acts of "responding and summoning" (Gadamer, 1989, p. 458). Each allows insight into our frail human circumstance, and offers ways to embrace and cultivate the wisdom of such frailty without balk or panic or denial.

Each of these three disciplines has cultivated, in its own way, a dual insight. First, each has carefully detailed ways to decode something of our contemporary lot in education: the wide-spread dominance of models of industrial assembly as befitting teaching and learning, the fragmentation of the living fields of knowledge, and the consequent acceleration and proliferation of demands on the lives and attention of teachers and students alike. Each speaks of distraction, of the leveling of experience and insight commonplace to everyday life.

In addition to such critiques, all three offer concrete, practicable alternatives to this fix we have inherited. They offer vivid ways of understanding issues of identity and diversity; they provide images of stillness and a slowing of time and attention linked to the pursuit of wisdom; they elaborate a sense of lineage, ancestry, or intergenerationality and the difficult comforts to be found in such elaborations; they detail ideas of living fields full of relations of dependent co-arising that can be explored, cared for, and understood; they confront head-on ideas of finitude and impermanence that are inevitably linked to the generative and ongoing character of knowledge and its pursuit. All three, therefore, offer a *pedagogy* that both decodes our current circumstances and provides what we suggest is vivid, rigorous, practical and scholarly alternatives to those circumstances.

We have witnessed in numerous classrooms how these matters actually work themselves out in the day-to-day life of classrooms dedicated to rich, engaging, deliberate work, and our book will draw upon and detail many real-world examples of from our field work.

Hence our subtitle. Right in the midst of the often-debilitating contemporary circumstances of schools, we have witnessed the near-miraculous appearance of beautiful and engaging work across a wide array of classroom settings.

It has happened. Therefore, it must be possible.

"The Aviator"

The cover illustration is of a lovely painting by Alberta artist Connie Geerts (www.conniegeerts.com) entitled "The Aviator." In local lore, the Magpie is known as a smart thief. Connie's permission to use her work for our book summoned up the quiet demand of such a beautiful work—to remain with it, to look again and again, to become, slowly and surely, able to experience what is there and has been there all along. We're reminded of Hans-Georg Gadamer's (2007c, p. 131) recognition of the "joyous and frightening shock" that comes when the true message of a beautiful work starts to hit home: "You must change your life."

We have found something of this sense of aesthetic repose in the work we have done, over the past year, with a group of classroom teachers and administrators where examples of classroom work, or small and ordinary events, took on the character and repose needed to stop each of us in our tracks and tell us that the promises and presumptions that heretofore carrying us through the days and hours of school would no longer do. This is the great and pleasurable work of hermeneutics, of ecology, of Buddhism, that we must, over and over again, face ourselves and our limited afflictions and, with each other's grace and aid, we can find a sustainable and joyous refuge in an ever expanding sense of our "selves" as housed in a reality far beyond the meager panics we often are asked to take, in education, for "the real world."

For this wee little gift, we are most grateful, and the promise to write this book, now fulfilled, will hopefully provide a wee gift to those who read it and a wee sense of engaging readers, then, in an unspoken promise of their own with such reading.

After all, as a wise woman once insisted, don't tell me it's not possible. If it actually exists, it *must* be possible.

So, here we are.

Acknowledgment

This chapter is the Introduction to Jackie Seidel & David W. Jardine (2014) *Ecological Pedagogy, Buddhist Pedagogy, Hermeneutic Pedagogy: Experiments in a Curriculum for Miracles.*

PREAMBLE 15

"If You Are Frightened"

> Given our culture's fear of pain and the high value it sets on optimism, feelings of despair are repressed. Hidden like a secret sore, they breed a sense of isolation. But when one's pain for the world is redefined as compassion, it serves as a trigger or gateway to a more encompassing sense of identity. It is seen as part of the connective tissue that binds us to all beings. This self is experienced as inseparable from the web to life in which we are as intricately interconnected as cells in a larger body. (Macy, 1989, p. 204)

> It's like the water of a river. It naturally flows down the gradient; it never flows against it; that's its nature. If a person were to go and stand on a riverbank and, seeing the water flowing swiftly down its course, foolishly want it to flow back up the gradient, he would suffer. The Buddha told us to see the way things are and then let go of our clinging to them. Take this feeling of letting go as your refuge. (Chah, 1987, n.p.)

When Christopher Gilham, Graham McCaffrey and I undertook to pull together an edited collection called On the Pedagogy of Suffering (2015), our relations to such an audacious topic were quite varied. Graham McCaffrey's background is in nursing, and his work often involved facing the most dire moments of suffering. Christopher Gilham worked with troubled children in schools and was often called upon to visit classrooms and teachers and students at the worst of times.

In Praise of Radiant Beings, pages 205–211

My own relations to these matters of suffering are far more meager, for now. I began with the almost flirtatious interest in how, in classroom, when students become taken by the onrush of insight into a rich and abundant topic, they will lean inwards into the difficult work that arises. I think, for example, of going into a Grade One class years ago (Jennifer Batycky's class, in fact [see Chapter 8]), and the children were tracing out letters in their books after discussions about repetition and practice and the woes of that sore hot spot on your middle finger from gripping the pencil tightly. In a lull, I said to the class "Do you know why you are finding it hard to learn to write?"

Pause.

"It's because it's difficult to do."

There was, then, an odd sigh of collective relief around the class, as if a hidden, repressed encumbrance had been lifted and their suffering at the hands of this learning was confirmed to be not trivial or pathological, but worth the endurances it might take and, moreover, shared—not just suffered by all, but suffered somehow *together*. Difficult things require hard work and this is a difficult thing. There is little to be gained by adding on the terrible burden of believing it should not be so and having, then, to suffer anyway. They all leaned back into the task at hand, relieved a bit of the hidden demons in the dark, in particular, the monster of isolation and secret, private failing.

A public monster shuddered, too, one I've often helped student teachers and teachers in schools fight off with small gestures instead of grand ones. The large and unwieldy and sometimes paralyzing monster of "Literacy" in the early grades is suddenly dispersed into something accomplishable, immediate, simple, and our suffering over it becomes a bit joyous:

> If you are frightened, wondering whether there is a demon in a strange cave at night, your fear is not dispelled until you light a lamp and carefully investigate whether it is there. (Tsong-kha-pa, 2002, p. 334)

This is part of the remedy for "the terror in a mother's heart when she sees her child fall behind in reading" (O'Leary, 2012; see Preamble 11). I showed the Grade One students the callus I still have traces of on my left-hand middle finger from penmanship, and the ones on my fingertips from playing the guitar for years. Real things, simple things, commiserations aimed at allowing our small sufferings to be as real as they actually are, and thus allowing monstrosities to not build up in the dark. Differently put, attempts to avoid such day-to-day practices of real work as if they were always and everywhere simply errors to be corrected gives rise, one might say, to reified monstrosities that are produced by our efforts to avoid the real work of practice, of learning, of pathei mathos. Sometimes, of course, they are errors of a sort, or imposed morality plays that are nothing more than guised exercises of power and punishment. Alice Miller's work (see 1989) lays out in great detail such exercises. But we need, too, to give up the ghost that haunts, that, if we work hard enough, everything will be simple, straightforward and easily had. No. Some things are only "won by a certain labour" (Ross & Jardine, 2009).

The thing is, with these matters of Buddhism and ecology and hermeneutics, they, too, can become monstrously capitalized in romances of "interconnectedness" and the like. When Graham McCaffrey was doing a talk as part of his (successful) application for a position in the Faculty of Nursing at the University of Calgary, two audience members brought up the idea of "wholeness" as a form of relief to the strictures of medicalized thinking and action in their profession. Graham's answer regarding this summoning of "the whole," as I recall, was clear and clean: "You do realize that there is no such a thing, don't you?"

This is why I have titled an as-yet-unfinished paper "On Death and Dying and Other Joys of Literacy," because that Capitalized Monstrosity—Literacy! Pitched with a near-hysterical voice—must be killed off.

This monster isn't really there.

There is no such a thing.

What is there instead is difficult, repeated, surrounded acts of learning to read and write now brought back onto the path of love, beauty, care, and the long trails of beautiful books, tangled languages and grammars, and the tough, warm practice of sitting together with the young around tales to be told and re-told. Until we set our way along this rich, abundant, joyous, difficult path, monsters will defeat us because they will rise up to our rising up, and there will always be a new and improved plan to slay the monsters of our own making. Little imps (*kleshas*—see Chapter 17) puffed up, distended and distorted by our panicky responses to them. Cynthia Chambers, "Spelling and Other Illiteracies" (2012, p.188): "Divorced from knowledge and tradition and imagination, literacy becomes a technology instead of a practiced craft," and, as such, it becomes caught in the outdated-ness of Market Economics and O'Leary's lust for new terrors in a mother's heart. It becomes wielded in the hands of those whom David G. Smith named so well in a conversation years ago: techno-bullies.

This is so commonplace in education, a new theory, a great idea, all of which are bent on gripping the monster by the throat and making learning to read and write easy as pie. It is hard work, in classroom practices, to refuse such trivializations. The relinquishing of the power of refusal leads to precisely that sense of rootlessness and powerlessness and futility that makes one susceptible to becoming a relentless consumer who is unable to refuse. A passage worth reading again:

> People whose governing habit is the relinquishment of power, competence and responsibility, and whose characteristic suffering is the anxiety of futility, make excellent spenders. They are the ideal consumers. By inducing in them little panics of boredom, powerlessness, sexual failure, mortality, paranoia, they can be made to buy virtually anything that is "attractively packaged." (Berry, 1986, p. 24)

I cannot help but read this passage in relation to an old, now-even-more-lurid advertisement that haunted an educational magazine, "the [once-upon-a-time] latest thing," purchasable and consumable with, it seems, little cost, little agony and little real work:

> Dr. Terry Johnson will show you (quickly and easily) how to turn your classroom into a whole language showplace. You'll learn everything you need to know to profoundly increase your whole language teaching skills (And we'll even buy you lunch!). (Johnson, 1990, p. 32)

I can hear the tut-tutting over the mention of that old and antiquated bandwagon of "whole language" as if the latest wagon's promise of sobriety is the real news. "Don't do that. Do this and everything will be fine." As with Buddhism, hermeneutics and ecological thoughtfulness, what is called for, here, is a refusal of this sort of puerile promising, as if the suffering and endurances of our lives were simply errors, as if the work of practice and patience and learning and becoming someone in the process were all trivial and avoidable:

> What we call the modern world is not necessarily, and not often, the real world, and there is no virtue in being up-to-date in it. It is a false world, based upon economies and values and desires that are fantastical—a world in which millions of people have lost any idea of the materials, the disciplines, the restraints, and the work necessary to support human life, and have thus become dangerous to their own lives and to the possibility of life. The job now is to get back to that perennial and substantial world in which we really do live, in which the foundations of our life will be visible to us, and in which we can accept our responsibilities again within the conditions of necessity and mystery. (Berry, 1983, p. 13)

So, once again, we're back to that ontological delusion (see Chapter 12), of having our panic-reaction gripping onto things create reifications towards which one then becomes hostile. And, again, the more we grip, the greater the grip we are in:

> Like trying to grab cornstarch dissolved in water, the faster and harder and more desperately we try to seize these matters and cling to something hard and permanent, the more substantial they feel and the more is aggravated our desire to grip even tighter. (Jardine, 2012d, p. 219)

The result of this gripping (reifying) work is a "Titanic mind-set," (Bowers, 2008, p. 11), caught up in what Edward Said calls the "vocabulary of giantism and apocalypse [Literacy! Accountability! High-Stakes Testing! Falling Behind! A Parent's Right to Know!] each use of which is plainly designed not to edify but to inflame" (2001, p. 4):

> Ivan Illich almost playfully names the inflaming and exaggerating urge in these matters a sort of "apocalyptic randiness"—basically framed, "I have an even more horrible example to tell you! Let's imagine an even worse situation!" (Illich & Cayley, 1992, p. 127), spoken or written with a sort of energizing, arousing, inciting, conspiratorial glee coupled with a strange tinge of superiority, distain, and moral indignation. This, of course, is reminiscent of school staffroom conversations: "You think that kid is trouble? A couple of years ago, I had a kid in my class who. . . . " (Jardine, Naqvi, Jardine, & Zaidi, 2010, pp. 27–28)

But again, a caveat born of Graham McCaffrey's warnings about woozy and happy and hushed talk of "the whole":

> When speaking of apocalyptic randiness, Ivan Illich (& Cayley, 1992, p. 127) also warns of falling prey to its opposite, Romanticism, where, with equal exaggeration, simplification and thoughtlessness, one sees good news everywhere. (Jardine, Naqvi, Jardine, & Zaidi, 2010, pp. 35–36)

In the passage cited above where Tsong-kha-pa urges us to turn on the light, he admonishes those whose "position is something like saying, 'Hold the mind and do not allow it to move to the thought of a demon'" (2002, p. 334). In attempts to find refuge, some say one should not pay attention to the public outcry regarding, say, "Literacy" and all its attendant monstrosities. Instead, go "inside" and do what you feel is right and don't be moved by thought of the demon. This is not the path of the Gelug tradition of Buddhism. No. Don't replace thinking with heartfelt feeling and inner stillness alone. Instead, light up this ancestry of literacy, study it, think, become well versed in it, learn all you can about the place, learn about how panic ensues, how market-manipulated lies are forged, and undo them, thread by thread, "twisting fiber on fiber." Only then can you begin to give a non-monstrous answer to the panics that are wheeling around us all:

> **Bill Moyers:** What do you say to those people who say "Wendell, please tell me what I can do."
>
> **Wendell Berry:** Well, you've put me in the place I'm always winding up in. That is to say, well, we've acknowledged that the problems are big, now where's the big solution? When you ask the question "What is the big answer?" then you're implying that we can impose the answer. But that's the problem we're in to start with. We've tried to impose the answer. The answers will come, not from walking up to your farm and saying "This is what I want and this is what I expect from you." You walk up and you say, "What do you need?" And this can't be hurried. This is the dreadful position that young people are in and I think of them, and I say that the situation you're in now is going to call for a lot of patience, and to be patient in an emergency is a terrible trial. I say to young people, don't get into this if you think you're going to solve all the problems, even in your lifetime. The important thing to do is to learn all you can about where you are, to make common cause with that place, and then, resigning yourself, become patient enough to work with it over a long time. And then, what you do is increase the possibility that you'll make a good example. And what we're looking for in this is good examples. (Berry & Moyers, 2013)

So, we're right back to how an attention to stubborn particulars ameliorates suffering (see Preamble and Chapter 3), not by eliminating it, but by making it sufferable, because such attention is dis-gigantic, un-reifying (not just non-reifying—it also serves to untangle the reifications it encounters because it doesn't panic), intimate.

Scaling down the monsters is only possible when we accept the suffering of being alive as a key locale of practice, of study:

> An aesthetic response to particulars [see Preamble 18 for more on this aesthetic response] would radically slow us down. To notice each even would limit our appetite for events, and this very slowing down of consumption would affect inflations, hyper-growth, the manic defenses and expansionism of civilization. Perhaps events speed up in proportion to their not being appreciated; perhaps events grow to cataclysmic size and intensity in proportion to their not being noticed. Perhaps, as the senses become refined, there is a scaling down of giantism and titanism, those mythically perennial enemies—giants and titans—of culture. (Hillman, 2006a, p. 41)

But, but, I'd love to do this, but there's no time, but there's so much to do and so much curriculum to cover!

> **Bill Moyers:** Do we have time, given what [is happening]?
>
> **Wendell Berry:** We don't have a right to ask that question. We have to ask, "What's the right thing to do?" and go ahead and do it. And take no thought for the morrow. (Berry & Moyers, 2013, emphasis mine)

15

"Just This Once"

An Introduction to the Pedagogy of Suffering

David W. Jardine
Graham McCaffrey
Christopher Gilham

The *Descent Into the Womb Sutra* states:

> Even though you have been born a human with such limitless suffering, you still have the best of situations. It is difficult to attain this even in ten million eons. Even when a deity dies, the other deities say, "May you have a happy rebirth." By happy rebirth they mean a human rebirth.

Why would I waste this... good life? When I act as though it were insignificant, I am deceiving myself. What could be more foolish than this? Just this once I am free. (Tsong-kha-pa, 2000, p. 121)

Although we have sunk into the midst of cyclic existence
An ocean of suffering with neither bottom nor shore
We are not disenchanted; we are pleased and excited.
We boast of happiness. This seems insane. (p. 333)

In Praise of Radiant Beings, pages 213–216

> We ought to be like elephants in the noontime sun in summer, when they are tormented by heat and thirst and catch sight of a cool lake. They throw themselves into the water with the greatest pleasure and without a moment's hesitation. In just the same way, for the sake of ourselves and others, we should give ourselves joyfully to the practice. (Pelden, 2007, p. 255)

The cover illustration to *On the Pedagogy of Suffering* by Katy Orme was done in a wonderful Kindergarten classroom. Each year without fail, the teacher selects a particular artist or period of an artist's work, or has a local artist visit the classroom, and this becomes the locale of intense observation, appreciation, and emulation. The children imitate, practice, and talk with each other about the place they have found themselves in. In this particular case, we find ourselves in Pablo Picasso's *Blue Period.* If you are going to venture yourself to this time and place and palette, let alone in the company of very young children, you need to be, well, good, well-practiced. Discussions were had about Picasso's loss of a dear friend, about sadness, about colors and their emotional effects, about how the distortion or elongation of the face helps betray difficult things where words fail and images rise up. The children were gently pushed up against the limitations of the colors available to them and were encouraged to talk about how this hemmed them in and kept them focused and seemed to open up possibilities while at once constricting them. All in all, tough, wonderful work. It is a mild and lovely instance of coming to learn through letting oneself undergo the trials and tribulations of a venture beyond oneself and the locales of one's comfort, and to return from that venture changed. It is an instance of the difficult work of pedagogical judgment, where the suicide of Picasso's friend was held in abeyance—too much, it was decided, would overwhelm the venture altogether. That turning thus towards a measure of suffering and endurance and transformation can afford, paradoxically, a great pleasure, is the sweet spot of our considerations of the *pedagogy of suffering.*

Many of our colleagues have been quite adamant: "This seems insane." But then, as teachers (and, we are finding, beyond this to many of those in other professions, and to many in their most intimate lives), we recognize something of the urge to test oneself against the world, to cultivate and practice this tough measure again and again, even though one could just as easily not do so. "Why don't they just stop?" (Jardine, Clifford & Friesen, 2008a, p. 213). Because somehow, despite its lack of necessity and crass, "real world" utility, the gift of practice, of study, of *deliberately* suffering the consequences of coming to understand, lures and allures because, in its very lack of necessity, attending to suffering portends a lessening of suffering and an upwelling of generosity, love, compassion, and joy that emerges both because of and in spite of suffering itself:

> It is always and necessarily unnecessary. It is excessive (Schrift, 1997, p. 7). It is an abundance (Hyde, 1983, p. 22) that does not diminish but increases in the giving away. It is a form of love because, "as in love, our satisfaction sets us at ease because we know that somehow its use at once assures its plenty" (p. 22). (Jardine, Clifford & Friesen, 2008a, p. 211)

On the Pedagogy of Suffering: Hermeneutic and Buddhist Meditations aims to understand and articulate how and why suffering *can be* pedagogical in character and how it is often key to authentic and meaningful acts of teaching and learning. This is an ancient idea from the Greek tragedies of Aeschylus (c. 525 BCE)—*pathei mathos* or "learning through suffering." In our understandable rush to ameliorate suffering at every turn, and to consider every instance of it as an error to be avoided at all costs, we explore how the pedagogy that can come from suffering becomes obscured, and that something vital to a rich and vibrant pedagogy can become lost. This collection threads through education, nursing, psychiatry, ecology, and medicine, through scholarship and intimate breaths, and blends together affinities between hermeneutic conceptions of the cultivation of character and Buddhist meditations on suffering and its locale in our lives.

A key element in contemporary hermeneutic theory of experience is that there is something unavoidably difficult, and transformative in the act of becoming experienced in the ways of the world. This experience extends across the whole gamut of human life, from small, exhilarating interruptions of one's expectations (moments of inquiry, learning, engagement, investigation, questioning) to traumatic experiences of mortality, impermanence, and illness, to cultural and intercultural, personal and imaginal histories of grief, conflict and potential reconciliation. Hermeneutically understood, education is centered on a concept from the Humanist tradition: *Bildung*, a German term meaning "self-formation." It is a process of *becoming someone*, a process that is undergone, endured or "suffered" in the act of coming to know about oneself and the world.

Key elements of Buddhist thought and practice are insights into the suffering and impermanence of life, and the practices of mindfulness, compassion and right conduct that might make such suffering endurable. Buddhism also provides articulations of how the panicky retreat from such realities only increases suffering and its hold. Buddhism's understanding of suffering thus provides, in many of the chapters of our text, an elaboration of how suffering can be understood, endured, and utilized as a site for the cultivation of knowledge and wisdom.

We fully understand the fact that all of the professions represented in our text are fraught with both histories and contemporary instances of inflicting suffering, as Alice Miller (1989) horrifyingly put it, "for your own good." We understand how our venture must be met with caution and concern. We know, too, how the amelioration of unnecessary suffering is precisely the work of these disciplines. That is why we will proceed hermeneutically in these explorations, that is, by paying close attention to cases, events and episodes that open up the nature, limits, dangers and potentialities of a pedagogy of suffering. We are interested, therefore, in the contingent and difficult *practices* that emerge in our professions around this phenomenon and the comportment of caution and hesitancy that is necessary to such practices precisely *because of* the risk inherent in the phenomenon of suffering. It is through paying close attention to those instances of suffering as a *pedagogic* experience that we can propose ways of finding the optimal balance between the opposite dangers for practitioners of being overwhelmed by suffering, or of denying it through mechanical routines.

Acknowledgment

This chapter is the Introduction to David W. Jardine, Christopher Gilham, & Graham McCaffrey, G. [2015]. *On the Pedagogy of Suffering: Hermeneutic and Buddhist Meditations.*)

PREAMBLE 16

"The Unspoken Vow"

First

Don't let the next chapter fool you.

Don't let my ability to write miles beyond my ability to practice fool you.

During the death-throes of my career at the University of Calgary's Faculty of Education, unprovoked and suddenly, I went into my office at home and took a very solid oak desk chair up over my head and beat it to bits on the floor, slamming it down over and over and over and over again.

I spent many other evenings sitting and screaming and growling in anger and frustration. It could have been a lot worse had I not quit drinking in '03.

This work hurts sometimes, this pulling yourself up by the blood-roots, this dis-illusion. Often, I'm simply not up to it. It has flesh stuck to it, and nerve endings. Still and again, "what is interesting in each of [the] definitions [of disillusion] is the underlying virtue of disillusion, namely, *freedom*" (Smith, 2014, p. 114).

"To know things as they are is to free oneself from their tyranny" (Blankelder & Fletcher, 2002, p. 9). The problem, here and always, is what can

In Praise of Radiant Beings, pages 217–222

happen when my capacity to know gets out of sync with what needs to be known. Chairs break and I have to start all over again, shamed. And worse than this, there is a terrible sort of retroactive erasure of any previous pretence to any merit whatsoever. Not just a shame. A sham.

To repeat Kunzang Pelden's advice (2007, pp. 253–254), "[regarding] the very object that gives rise to the afflictions, practitioners of a more basic capacity must abandon such objects and retreat." Far too often I failed to do so and instead, in full-blown incapacity, turned and faced the objects that give rise to my own afflictions and lost myself in outrageous, unforgivable, humiliating acts. And I've put other dear souls through far more and far worse than they deserved. Receiving undeserved affection in return is a miraculous thing. I did much to test it.

So don't be fooled by the parts of this book that make the kinships between Buddhism and education and ecology seem like a nice walk in the woods. It is rough work, uprooting my self, trying to stay awake and alert, especially when what I write can sometimes cause me to expect more of myself than I have to give, and to fool others through overly expectant words:

> "Do not place your hopes on sheer determination" (Tsong-kha-pa, 2002, p. 62). Only repeated practice will help, full of citatiousness, study, and a deepening knowledge of the ancestral lineages that we have often unwittingly inherited, that need to get committed to memory or written out and savored and read to friends and neighbors. Hermeneutics, thus, involves a dedication to the careful, suspicious reading and re-reading, interpreting and re-interpreting the texts and textures of our individual and common lives and worlds. And then, in the middle of all that, hermeneutics demands that I take on the task of composing myself while composing something about this world, while writing a "hermeneutic study." "I compose this in order to condition my own mind" (Tsong-kha-pa, 2000, p. 111) and through such conditioning and composition, I always hope to provide some relief to the suffering and affliction that has spellbound me and my chosen profession. This is the unspoken vow. And this is a warning that knows no heed: once you catch sight of that water and its promise of relief, you might find that you can't turn back, that you can't undo the glimpse, that you've taken the vow without knowing it and that you're tethered to it even if you can't then fulfill what that vow demands. (Jardine, 2012h, p. 2)

So, when Gadamer (1986, p. 59), at age 86, reminds me "we should have no illusion. Bureaucratized teaching and learning systems dominate the scene, but nevertheless it is everyone's task to find his free space," this finding, this task, is endless and fragile. It involves *turning towards* the suffering of the world, the suffering of illusion and disillusion, the suffering of impermanence, frailty, finitude. It asks that I "take on a life of suffering . . . in order to help all living beings (Tsong-kha-pa, 2004, p. 29), that I take on a certain phenomenological dedication: to "remain in the realm in which beings dwell" (Tsong-kha-pa, 2004, p. 30). The good news, for me, is that there is no condition placed on precisely how well one takes up these tasks. I find it a little too much to say:

> At the instant destitute beings
> Bound in the prison of existence give rise to this spirit
> They are called "*sugatas'* children" (p. 33)

Being called a child of the Buddha, a child of someone awake, is overblown just enough to cascade back towards me and make me think of living up to such a lineage of being awake. There is something to be said, I guess, for trying to face in the right direction however much one then accomplishes along that path. This is certainly a pedagogical mood of teachers regarding even their most troubled students. It is why some forms of assessment that are measures of precisely how many path footfalls are "done" can be so disturbing to endure with a child we've come to love and whose heart *beats* against the walls of school.

But this vow also asks something more intimate of me, of you: "if you do not first consider your own suffering, you will not reach the key point of the practice" (Tsong-kha-pa, 2002, p. 44):

> As you continually experience . . . suffering . . . you must know how to bring it into the path. Otherwise . . . you either generate hostility [leading, as we've seen, to reification, attachment and, then, suffering, hostility, reification . . .] or you become discouraged. (Tsong-kha-pa, 2004, p. 172)

The perennial circumstance, then, is this. How do I "become open to the world that we are living in" (Trungpa, 2006, n.p.), but not simply "afflicted by openness" (Hillman, 1979, p. 33)? It may be that "perception of opportunities [*portas,* opening] requires a sensitivity given through one's own wounds. The weak place opens us to what is in the air" (p. 161) but the danger lurks of lack of practice and capacity, whereby "through wounds [one] may feed others, but may [oneself] be drained thereby" (p. 154):

> One of the penalties of an ecological education is that one lives alone in a world of wounds. [The ecologist] must be the doctor who sees the marks of death in a community that believes itself well and does not want to be told otherwise. (Leopold, 1993, p. 165)

Finding free space, "the possibilities that exist" (Gadamer, 1986, p. 59) means this: "One can only play with serious possibilities. Obviously this means that one may become so engrossed in them that they outplay and prevail over one" (Gadamer, 1989, p. 106). In this deadly serious work of coming to know our circumstances without illusion, I am not alone, even though the play can outplay the player and suffering can ensue from the very attempt to ameliorate it:

> Be careful. As a teacher in Tsong-kha-pa's lineage warns, watch out for that pretty face and that rushing cool lake allure: "the more intense the practice, the more intense the demons," this from Patrul Rinpoche (1808–1887) in his *The Words of my Perfect Teacher* (Patrul, 1998, p. 189). (Jardine, 2012h, p. 5)

Then I think of Thich Nhat Hanh's trembling voice and hands: "There are so many. There are so many" (David Suzuki Foundation, 2011).

Second

> You must accept [suffering] when [it] arise[s] because (1) if you do not do this, in addition to the basic suffering, you have the suffering of worry that is produced by your own thoughts, and then the suffering becomes very difficult for you to bear; (2) if you accept the suffering, you let the basic suffering be and do not stop it, but you never have the suffering of worry that creates discontentment when you focus on the basic suffering; and (3) since you are using a method to bring even basic sufferings into the path, you greatly lessen your suffering, so you can bear it. Therefore, it is very crucial that you generate the patience that accepts suffering. (Tsong-kha-pa, 2004, pp. 172–173)
>
> This idea of "let[ting] the basic suffering be" is an interestingly phenomenological move, similar to Martin Heidegger's (1962, p. 58) tortuous[ly translated] formulation: "'phenomenology' means . . . to let that which shows itself be seen from itself in the very way in which it shows itself from itself." He continues by asking "What is it that phenomenology is to 'let us see'?" (p. 59):
>
> > Manifestly, it is something that proximally and for the most part does *not* show itself at all: it is something that lies *hidden* . . . but at the same time it is something that belongs to what thus shows itself. That which remains *hidden* in an egregious sense, or which relapses and gets *covered up* again, or which shows itself only *'in disguise'*, is not just this entity or that, but rather the *Being* of entities. (p. 59)
>
> To the extent that hermeneutics proceeds to identify this Being of entities with impermanence, dependent co-arising, historicity, finitude, and the enduring of experience (*Erfahrung*, which is linked by Gadamer [1989, p. 356]

> to *pathei mathos*), this passage is rich and full and useful for our purposes. (Jardine, Gilham, & McCaffrey, 2015a, p. 100).

Third

An interesting aside, here. Tsong-kha-pa deals with a qualm raised regarding why the Buddha put the four Noble Truths in this order:

1. The truth of suffering
2. The truth of the origin of suffering
3. The truth of the cessation of suffering
4. The truth of the path towards such cessation.

"The true origins are the causes and true sufferings are their effects. Why, then, did the Bhagavan reverse that order, if the origins precede sufferings?" (Tsong-kha-pa, 2000, p. 269). The response given is both pedagogical and phenomenological. "This reversal is vital for practice" (p. 269) because it begins by *facing students with the immediacy of their own lot*, available first hand in their experience of the world, and *then* introducing the fact that this severely present "given" is, in fact, something that has arisen through causes and conditions. It is *not* immediate even though it is *experienced as immediate.* "Once you recognize suffering, if you want to be liberated from suffering, you must counteract it" (p. 269). Thus, arises an attraction to what is the truth of suffering's origin, and how might it cease or lessen, and what might be the path to such cessation.

> When the First Noble Truth states that all life is suffering, accepting this truth and learning to be patient with its endless reappearance in our lives and the lives of our students, clients, patients, etc., prevents the arising of a sort of "secondary suffering" that is based on worrying about [or fleeing from, or suppressing] this "primary" or "basic" suffering, becoming frantic in relationship to it, complicating it with overlays of anxiety, anger, or resentment, as well as overlays of well-meaning sympathies, optimism, promises of cures or schemes of facilitation in its weakest senses (attempts to "make things facile/easy" [as per the promises of efficiency, for example]). (Jardine, Gilham, & McCaffrey, 2015a, pp. 99–100)

This, of course, is why working in schools can be so tough, because, to paraphrase Aldo Leopold cited above, schools are often communities that believe themselves to be well often despite the vivid low-level anxieties that roam the best hallways. They don't want to be told otherwise, as if admitting the weird ecological fix we are in and taking on study as our responsibility would just make things worse. Trying to work through the repressions, denials, and constraints (personal, institutional and otherwise) that seem to circle schools is difficult to not be drawn into or pushed away from.

Fourth

Meanwhile, as my career gave up its ghosts, I've been surrounded by young teachers suffering in the confines of this hardened, reified "real world" and the howling silences and brazen confidences that come with it, seeking refuge, on occasion, in things I'd written, and me full of these wee secrets, hitherto concealed. But they wrote and wrote (see Seidel & Jardine, in press) and talked and talked, and are gathering still and again, bringing suffering back onto the path. How can I help but "cultivate love for those who have gathered" (Tsong-kha-pa, 2000, p. 64) because they have given me just exactly the unspoken support I've needed, to say simply this: don't let the next chapter fool you with its calm parsing of regret. It hides the hurts of this sort of work, the terrible composing, and the *decomposing* it requires. In other words, your hurt, like mine, is no error, but it is also "not a permanent state; it is a room with a door on the other wall" (Bly, n.d., p. 11). It is a hint of the way. It is open to interpretation.

The thing is, the joy that comes in our gathering is also not a permanent state. Both joy and grief are impermanent—*this*, taken altogether, is, strange to say, the "cool lake" of refuge (Pelden, 2007, p. 255). A bit of a paradox, literally, "beyond belief":

> This is the true vocation of life-long work; namely, to live freely yet without certainty, except the certainty that clinging to concepts beyond their functional ability to serve the human prospect well will result in ever-deepening forms of estrangement as the concepts fail to address the new realities that confront them. An ability to face the necessary disillusionment points paradoxically to the source of our hope. (Smith, 2014, p. 117)

So, forgive me if my words outrun my ability. Don't be fooled. I have very little sandalwood. But I do recognize its scent.

16

Thoughts on Thinking Through Regret and How Afflictions Can Be Teachers (2015)

Prelude

> [This "perfection," i.e., way of "going beyond" (Sanskrit *paramita*) being simply tangled in the knots of our living, 'interweaving and criss-crossing"] is called ethical discipline because it does not acquiesce in the afflictions, because it is coolness since it quells the fire of regret. It is characterized by... abstention. (Tsong-kha-pa, 2004, p. 144)

> Instead of being "... lost in the performance of acts" [Husserl, 1970, p. 55]... we should rather [practice] "abstention" [Husserl, 1970a, p. 19]. [This does] not mean that we turn our attention "away" from the world, but rather that our "attention" has been "freed" from the naiveté of *presupposing the world*, so that *that very world* (*and* the... belief in that world) may now be seen. "When I turn away from a naive exploration of the world... I do not turn my back on the world to retreat to an unworldly, and, therefore, uninteresting special field of theoretical study. On the contrary [this abstention] enables me to explore the world radically [Husserl, 1960. p. 141]." (Jardine, 1976, pp. 76, 80–81)

In Praise of Radiant Beings, pages 223–235

Afflictions Can Teach, With a Side-Glance to the Will to Power

Properly considered—without acquiescence—afflictions can *teach.* They *can,* but there is nothing necessary about this. I know from repeated experience that this is a terrible risk, maintaining proximity to an arising affliction without falling for it.

Recently, I have been writing about rising in the morning, 5:00 a.m., with the dogs and first light, one Robin already warbling, and feeling full of regret regarding my upcoming retirement and whether "it" was all "worth it," and so on. Of course, such awakenings are ripe for a whole series of possible uprisings if one does not "abstain": anger, mulling over past events, summoning up arguments pro and con, blaming, emotional turmoils, making grotesqueries of this or that person, self-admonishments for real or imagined past sins and complicities, bland and blame attempts at self-justification and moral superiority and aggrandizements, growling solo conversations with real and imagined foes, and so on.

Once initiated, getting dragged into this arising of regret tends towards increasing heat and acceleration—one thing summons another, one exaggerating or surprising uprising exaggerates the required response needed as its equal, and so on. I become, quickly and with great facility, lost in the performance of acts.

So, this line of thought and consideration: don't let this arising of regret draw you in (don't first "acquiesce") and *then* try to resolve or think through or meditate upon such matters from, shall we say, *inside* such acquiescence. This *feels like* "really being in touch" with the life of it, but it is not. It is, instead, becoming the *outcome* of it. Because, *having been drawn into this circle* has already changed the game that seems afoot. "I" (having risen to the bait of a feeling of "regret" and all the summoned imaginings that go with it) meet in a dual uprising with "it" (an "it" which now responds in exact and measured parallel to my own uprising). I become captivated with a sense of "attachment and hostility with regard to [it]" (Tsong-kha-pa, 2000, p. 210) and therefore (this is a great, suppressed truth) I unwittingly want to remain proximal to it in order to feel the "aliveness" of this uprising (its and mine both).

This makes worth re-citing Friedrich Nietzsche's (1975) understanding of the will to power and its desire to feel resistance to its will in order to feel alive, leading to his characterization of truth as the feeling and overcoming of resistance. It is something slightly new, this naming of our desire for this desire. Speaking of being lost in the performance of acts:

> It is the highest degrees of performance that awakens belief in the "truth," that is to say reality of the object. The feeling of strength, of struggle, of resistance convinces us that there is something that is here being resisted. (Nietzsche, 1975, p. 290)

On our way by, let's take this further down Nietzsche's treacherous trail: "The will to power can manifest itself only against resistances; therefore it *seeks that which resists it*" (p. 346). Once that resistance is found, I can then revel in the power felt in overcoming an uprising—" a desire to overwhelm, a forming, shaping and reshaping, until at length that which has been overwhelmed has entirely gone over into the power domain of the aggressor and has increased the same" (p. 346). This then increases the possibility that this sort of seeking out of resistance will itself increase. It's not just that "we are seduced by them" (Chodron, 2007, p. 76). "*We welcome them*" (p. 91, emphasis added) because they confirm the feeling of lively ego power and the reality of my self, even in an example like failure and regret.

A perfect circle of abuse. It is not an accident that Buddhists call the world and it's suffering a "wheel": *Samsara* turns and turns but only from the energy that comes from being lost in the performance of acts, only if we fall prey to what becomes "a habitual tug" (Chodron, 2007, p. 119).

"If we can catch the seduction at this subtle stage, it's much easier to nip in the bud" (Chodron, 2007, p. 223). That is to say, all of this occurs if and only if I am unable to catch my own complicity in this particular arising of regret. Right here, I can hear the echo of "blaming the victim." I must keep my eye on this as I proceed. This is my biggest temptation: that my becoming composed about my regret is somehow allowing "them" to get away with something. But what is undeniable, here, is that the longer I linger "in" this circle, the more monstrous it becomes and the less likely I am to be able to "nip it in the bud." It loves my attention and feeds on it.

Little boy feelings of injustice, unfairness, if onlys, and so on. The "grrrr" of an unbecoming animal trapped under threat. Purring over it won't help, because it is equally caught in its contentment. I'm innocent! I did a good job in my job! C'mon!

So, little boy, sit, take it easy. I know you've been summoned from old and forgotten years of older-brother teasing and subsequent asthmatic breathlessness. Let me try this one on your behalf. My affection for you can't be shown by joining you in the breathless arising of regret. That is not love. It is attachment and nostalgia. And attachment is based on having already reified what is in fact an impermanent arising: "Chandrakirti's *Clear Words* says: 'all afflictions and all faults arise from the reifying view of the perishing aggregates'" (Tsong-kha-pa, 2002, p. 120). From Chandrakirti's *Commentary on the Four Hundred Stanzas:*

> It is said that one becomes attached to things by the power of an afflictive misunderstanding, a consciousness that superimposes an essence on things. (cited in Tsong-kha-pa, 2002, p. 207)
>
> So, "hush, child." (Latremouille, 2014, p. 30)

Return.

It arises only if and precisely to the extent that "I" take the bait: "hostility [is] driven by a reifying apprehension of the characteristics of the causes of harm" (Tsong-kha-pa, 2000, p. 225) (Nietzsche's "awaken[ing] belief in the 'truth,' that is to say reality of the object"). Dual uprisings meet and I, this regretful one, need to resolve it, regret, unaware that this caught-up, intent-on-solving "I" is part of that which needs solving. It is not just that I take the bait. The bait of regret also summons the "me" it needs and desires as its companion, the lover who will fall for it and draw close and acquiesce and confirm, and therefore not interrupt its arising but rather adore such arising.

And, in vicious circularity, I become therefore that very "me" whose arising is thus "confirmed" through such acquiescence. I become full of regret in the midst of a reifying apprehension of my very, now-regretful, self, lost, but felt-found in the performance of reifying acts:

Neu-sur-ba said:

> You must repeatedly fend off whatever affliction arises its head. Further, you must see any affliction as an enemy and attack it as soon as it arises. Otherwise, if you acquiesce when it first appears, and then nurture it with improper thoughts, you will have no way to defeat it, and it will conquer you in the end.
>
> You must not allow them to linger, but must immediately disperse them as though they were drawings on water. Do not let them be like drawings on stone. (Tsong-kha-pa, 2000, pp. 347–348)

Stop again, breath (this Buddhist invocation harks back to my asthmatic inheritance). Both cause and effect, harmed and harmer (including all the blurring of which is which), grasp each other in a prehensile embrace, and, like cornstarch dissolved in water, the tighter and faster I grip, the more solid it seems and the more vigorous I feel by telling such a gripping tale. Prehensile: such gripping needs pulling towards and pushing away in equal measure, the terrible balance of *attachment.*

The point, then, is how to not step into this circle in the first place but yet still allow this affliction to arise so that it can teach, so that its knots might loosen and free.

Two Paramitas

We are dealing now with a modification which in a certain sense completely removes and renders powerless every doxic [believing] modality to which it is related [including "negation"]. It cancels nothing, it "performs" nothing. (Husserl, 1969, p. 306)

> The transcending of the world which takes place... does not lead outside of or away from the world to... some other world. (Fink, 1970, p. 99)

> Through the abstention which inhibits this whole hitherto unbroken way of life, a complete transformation of all life is attained a thoroughly new way of life. (Husserl, 1970b, p. 150)

All this is why Tsong-kha-pa insisted on coupling two *paramitas* (two aspired-to "perfections" in the ongoing practice of untangling attachment, e.g., to regret and its arising) together. It is not enough to just catch sight of this process happening and then quell oneself in the face of this arising. Mindfulness (the so-called "fifth *paramita*" [see Tsong-kha-pa, 2004, pp. 209–224; 2002, pp. 13–106, and countless others.]) is not enough. This is not only a matter of calming down and becoming still and not taking the bait... my mother's sometimes-hysterical response to her child's asthmatic wheezing: "Don't get excited!" A great in-joke for those who know me—not so funny, really, when it afflicts as tempers that have so often arisen, with anger, resentment, regret, learned from her, in part, and then stupidly passed on in ways I can't quite recall without even more regretful uprising... but then watch out for reifying apprehension... she, poor thing, caught as much as I was in the wheeze of all this... and her in a great dance with her mother and sister and long-gone father. We are all cascades even though each of us has the task—hell, the slimmest chance, given the weight of the world—of seeing through what is happening to us over and above our wanting and doing—not simply what has been done to me but how "me" has come to be done, and what might then be undone. "It is everyone's task to find... free space" (Gadamer 1986, p. 59) and to not simply pass along as fixed or "real" what is only an outcome of causes and conditions that can be seen through and untangled.

One must catch sight, quell, and then, having thus not acquiesced in the uprising, I must turn *toward* this thing that has arisen, think it through, and untangle these knots, all with an eye to its "real nature" as empty of self-existence (Sanskrit *shunya*), that is, impermanent, and dependently co-arising (Sanskrit *pratitya-samutpada*), fleeting:

> We need to take afflictions as the path. This is very important because if we are unable to take them as the path, no matter how good our practice may be, we will be overcome by the afflictions. (Thrangu, 2011, p. 182)
>
> If we do not look at the essence of the afflictions, they will grow strong and stronger. The remedy is not to reject, block or suppress the emotion—as scientists these days say, repressing your disturbing emotions will lead to illness in your body. This, however, does not mean that we should just follow our afflictions and go wherever they lead us. Instead, we need to look at the essence of the afflictions. (p. 190)

"The essence of the afflictions is naturally empty" (Thrangu, 2011, p. 183). This: there is no stubborn, self-existent "thing" *to which* I might acquiesce, therefore the seemingly self-existent "I myself" that rises to the bait becomes visible as itself "empty" of self-existence and full only of dependently co-arising, here, now, in falsely taking regret to be self-existent. A sort of inverse dance of Descartes' I think, therefore I am. There is no object to acquiesce to. Therefore, there really is no acquiescence. Therefore, the whole logic of "I acquiesce therefore I am" collapses. Therefore the *sum* (the "I am") cannot be affirmed as self-existent. This is another instance of "starting with the object" (see Preamble 12).

That is, all this is *interpretable.* It is not some "thing" to be simply suffered by falling into it, or avoided through withdrawing quiescence. Interpretive work is thus not just the spinning of connections, the searching out of ancestries and bloodlines. "Distinguishing the exact particulars of an object" (Tsong-kha-pa, 2002, p. 17) is a vital and irreplaceable *part* of interpretive work, because regret is not just any (empty of self-existence) thing, and how precisely it traces itself through my life is a task I must take on for myself. However, all this is done deliberately against the terribly difficult practice of "breaking open the *being* [Greek *ontos*] of the object" (Gadamer, 1989, p. 382, emphasis added) under analysis (e.g., regret, the causes of regret, and the regretful self caught in and arising from such regretting).

Likewise, regret cannot be properly untangled by well-intentioned attempts to balance the scales with "You don't need to regret this. You did a pretty good job, you know? Your work has been important in the lives of many people. You made a difference, you know?" as if *these* self-existent objects relieve me from thinking through *those.* Their well-meant happy faces are, in their own way, even more worrisome than regret because they are so beautiful and quite complexly *self*-affirming.

Believing either of these—regret or a job well done—is a great error and a cause of great suffering, because both are based on a false reification of causes and conditions.

This is why Tsong-kha-pa coupled this fifth *paramita* of mindful serenity and stillness in the face of the arising of the afflictions with the sixth *paramita,* insight or wisdom (Tsong-kha-pa, 2002, pp. 107–367, 2004, pp. 209–224, and countless other texts): "Wisdom thoroughly discerns *the ontological status of the object under analysis*" (Tsong-kha-pa, 2004, p. 211). Mere quiet quelling of uprisings is not enough. Otherwise, the afflictive arising (of regret in this case) is simply suppressed:

> Forceful and long-lasting certainty about the meaning of selflessness is sustained analysis with discerning wisdom [the so-called sixth *paramita*]. Without such insight into the real nature, no matter how long you cultivate serenity [the fifth *paramita*], you can only suppress manifest afflictions [like regret]; you cannot eradicate their seeds. As Kamalasila's second *Stages of Meditation* says:
>
> > Cultivating just serenity alone does not get rid of a practitioner's obscurations ["Don't get excited. Calm. Breathe slowly. Let the feeling of regret dissipate into stillness"]; it only suppresses the afflictions for a while. Unless you have the light of wisdom, you do not destroy dormant tendencies. For this reason the *Sutra Unraveling the Intended Meaning* says:
> >
> > > Meditative stabilization suppresses afflictions; wisdom destroys dormant tendencies.
> >
> > Also, the *King of Concentrations Sutra* (*Samadhi-raja-sutra*) says:
> >
> > > Although worldly persons cultivate concentration
> > > They do not destroy the notion of self
> > > Their afflictions return and disturb them.
> > > (Tsong-kha-pa, 2002, p. 22)

Stingingly, Kamalasila admonishes those who become caught in mindful serenity without the tough, relentless and ongoing work of study, insight, wisdom, "who derive a sense of sufficiency from mere concentration fall by virtue of their pride into an inflated sense of themselves" (cited in Tsong-kha-pa, 2002, p. 23).

This is why, frankly, I am so happy yet so concerned about the rise of mindfulness practices in schools (see, e.g., Campbell, 2013, Olson, 2014, Saltzman, 2014, and countless recent others). My fear is that such things are unwittingly (and dare I say that I more deeply fear that it is quite wittingly) ways to get kids to settle down so they can go back to doing stupid and demeaning things in classrooms, while at once derailing any "uprising" into nothing more than a personal problem that needs quelling, rather than see it as an intelligent and intelligible insight into their institutionalized circumstances. "Increasingly, teachers are using the principles of mindfulness to help make the classroom a calmer place and to improve learning" (Campbell, 2013, n.p.), thus perhaps masking classroom conditions and expectations that might just warrant restlessness and discontent, and leaving in place, too, what "learning" and "improvement" are understood to be. Mindfulness thus becomes understood instrumentally against the background of, and in the service of, maintaining the status quo of school life whereas, in fact, once rooted back into its long legacies and ancestries, it involves and leads to precisely the breaking of the spell(s) of everyday life, waking up to the delusions and false promises of one's circumstances and acting accordingly.

"Although there are many purposes for developing this concentration (the attention of serenity), the chief purpose is for the sake of developing the knowledge of insight [into the myriads of dependent co-arising and the emptiness of self-existence and permanence]" (Tsong-Kha-Pa, 2002, p. 94). This is why this hesitation is not at all about mindfulness and its cultivation (in schools and otherwise) because:

> If you do not first establish in your mind-stream the concentration of serenity... it is not possible for the actual knowledge of insight, which is focused on either the real nature or the diversity of phenomena, to arise. (p. 95)

The caution, the hesitation, is regarding what may be the "many purposes" of mindfulness practice in schools. I'll leave this for another time, as well as the question of what happens when mindfulness loses its "chief purpose" and might be taking on the purpose of precisely maintaining delusion by quelling the disturbances of the deluded. I often repeat that old grunt I heard so often in schools: "this is the real world." No. I just happened to turn out this way.

I dearly hope that such mindfulness practices might help relieve some suffering. But I'll also admit a certain secret delight in the uprising of such practices in schools because, if they actually succeed, "the actual knowledge of insight" into the circumstances of schooling might arise in students and teachers alike. Schools in their current configuration are not "the real world." They just happened to have turned out that way. They are *interpretable.* Possible, not necessary and fixed. Schools can become locales where studying our current circumstances can change their nature and purpose.

Side Scrawls

Possessed with the madness of afflictions and then, noticing this madness, becoming madder, self-propelled inside a loop that is closed. The purpose of what I write is precisely here: to "break open" these closed loops and then compose. Entering into these loops of complaint simply applies salt to the wounds of affliction. It is so attractive, this circle of complaint. There is a feeling of "life" in it, of surge and justification.

I fall in love

and in hostility

towards my own reflection.

June 8th, 2014

. . .

Regret. Surprised yesterday @ lunch answering S.R.'s question about retiring. And ever since . . . woke up this morning feeling regret. Very deep and bodily. Part of this is simply tiredness lately and the rainy weather. But what is this upwelling? It feels slightly foolish and regressive to pay too much attention to it because I know full well about kleshas [a Tibetan term for the uprising of tempting afflictions, often pictured as little 'imps' or 'demons' patiently waiting for the right moment of weakness or distraction to strike out and allure us]. That tough balance between being drawn into it for the sake of burning it off and being simply inflamed by that approach and deepening the error of it. Regret. Part of me feels robbed of something. Yet robbery is premised on possession. What is this? Part of me feels like I had a good job that was taken away from me. I was good at it, damn it. Stop. Wait. I have aged. The world has shifted. What did you expect? For Jesus to come? To be anointed and exalted? Stop. Go read [Ajahn Chah's (1987) "Our Real Home: A Talk to an Aging Lay Disciple Approaching Death."].

> "Coming to terms with its nature" [Chah, 1987, n.p.] as a way of resolving our relations to it, letting them be what they are.
>
> "This is a great truth that you've presently encountered." [Chah, 1987, n.p.]
>
> "The time is ripe." [Chah, 1987, n.p.]
>
> "It could be no other way." [Chah, 1987, n.p.]
>
> "The Buddha told us to put down everything that lacks a real abiding substance. If you put down everything, you will see the truth, if you don't you won't. That's the way it is and it's the same for all, so don't worry." [Chah, 1987, n.p.]
>
> "Don't disturb me. You're not my business anymore." [Chah, 1987, n.p.]

June 14th, 2014

. . .

Awoke with another layer of regret, then. Deeper. No, wait. Don't do this. This affirmation of depth is an outcome of this arising, not its "real nature." It isn't really deeper in some important, "deep" sense. It is just more like forgotten, out-grown stuff. There is no deep truth here finally out in the open. Remember that, because these are the dreams of a child, it is the child that is called upon to respond and it is that [childish] response that makes these matters seem real and repressed and the honest and most genuine really true finally admitted and out in the open reaction to my retirement. There is nothing really real about this. It is an ephemeral flitting past of old ventures and a horribly effective summoning of an old and unpracticed "me," precisely the sleepyhead most susceptible to this temptation.

Take it easy, kid. I'll deal with this.

So, the inverse, that these things are precisely not "deep" at all, but surface flutters that long for reification or response so that they can become "real" and therefore attract even more anxiety and attention. Kleshas. Tempters. Ok, so, this is really important, this sense of inversion. It is just a temptation with no inherent reality except insofar as I fall "into" its spell and become precisely that spellbound "I" it needs to maintain its sense of reality.

Fire just flickers.

And even flickers end

+ even endings fade.

+ even evening fading disappears.

There is no Siskin even though there it is.

Lovely. To ride up over these arisings. So that the arising of regret does not need concretization or historicizing or personalizing or autobiographical detailing. All these do is reify.

June 15th, 2014

. . .

Wasp caught
Between window and screen
Kept coming back
To the buzz of being captured.

This is why
The plastic surgery convergence of faces into one look
Is so compelling.
Narcissus.
The face shaped
By being so very seen to be being seen.

Once you blink
There is no deep here.
There is no depth
    to the reflection
    of moonlight on water.

This is how Basho's frog
    Saves us without
        Intending to.
        Kerplunk. (A Perfectly Froggy Word!)

It's like those lovely abandoned children
            " . . . they've broken
    their reflections in the lake with sticks" [Goyette, 1998, p. 11].

June 21st, 2014

A Mis-Remembered Pythonesque Coda

> Unwholesome mental formations are like a tangled ball of string. When we try to untangle it, we only wind it around ourselves until we cannot move. These mental formations are sometimes called afflictions *kleshas*. Sometimes they are called obscurations because they confuse us and make us lose our way. (Hanh, 1999, pp. 73–74)

> *Thich Nhat Hanh*: People who know what is happening but . . . cannot do anything, there are so many of them, there are so many of them, because they have despair in them. (David Suzuki Foundation, 2011).

Oh, the great opulence of having the time and space to think about such things, to feel sorrow and regret within such safe confines and over such a minor thing in the world. It is almost embarrassing to think that I have ever experienced any regret worth the asking in this easy life. Indulgence indeed. And it has, in fact, been a bit of a gift to have such a relatively small affliction to work on, to hone practice just a wee bit over something comparatively simple, in preparation, in part, for what is surely to come to all of us. We scholars must remember—I must remember—that our work is born of leisure (Latin *schola*) and therefore is always subject to a very important scrutiny, a very harsh and unforgiving form of accountability far beyond the wearying and silly measures of public panics and external funding and the mind-numbing narrows of many discussions of "teacher accountability":

> Why would I waste . . . such a good life? When I act as though it were insignificant, I am deceiving myself. What could be more foolish than this? Just this once I am free from continuously trekking the many narrow cliff-paths

> of leisure-less conditions, the miserable realms. If I waste this freedom and return to those conditions, it would be similar to losing my mind. (Tsong-kha-pa, 2000, pp. 121–122)

I can't do much for those in the world who despair ("there are so many, there are so many") but I can do this last small and silly thing.

There is a very old Monty Python™ routine that I can just barely remember and don't want to look up, because it has turned, in memory, into something I need more than accurate recall. It shows two desperate men meeting in the desert and one, asking the other for water, finds that neither has any. One then says to the other, Wait! We're being *filmed*! Perhaps the camera operator has water!

The scene then pulls out and pans to show the two crawling up to a third man with a camera who is clearly in precisely the same dire straits that they are in. This third man has no water either. But then the three look up and into the camera: Wait! *We're being filmed again*! So off the three proceed to a wider pan.

But wait . . . !

Perhaps the ever-so-well-named punch line of this ever-expanding scenario is that this gathering council of suffering beings ("there are so many"), at each moment of panning outwards to include the next witness, looks up and into the very camera that is my own gazing and laughing at this unfolding scene and its absurdity. Each appearance of a new (camera) operator once again saves me to be lost, again, in the performance of acts, and saved, however momentarily, from this insight into my own gazing, while at once casting me back into a once- again-hidden implication in this unfolding scene, that moment where they all look up at me, these suffering beings. "There are so many. There are so many." Why have I ever thought that it was someone else's job to fall under this gaze?

I laugh at the quirky continuance of this remembered skit, but also at a weird, unspoken sense of something *nearing*. This whole thing is oriented towards the whole great council of sentient being showing up on *my* gazing doorstep and gathering *me* into this council while at the same time keeping me out of simple absorption into its thrall, asking me about the relief of the suffering of all these beings ("there are so many"). My mother, my son, my wife and dear love, those colleagues and friends I've loved or injured or both, Tsong-kha-pa and Gadamer here, too, and the real and imagined faces I argue with in my self-aggrandizing regret, here, all, in this thrall of beings.

I find that no matter how I try, I can never be simply one of the beings picked up along the way, but am unavoidably the very one under whose gaze all of this unfurls.

There would at least be some comfort amidst that throng, yes?

To be just one more vexed and regretful being with a story to tell in hopes of being listened to and relieved by such listening?

"Oh sorrow" (Seidel, 2014, p. 112).

This is why that Monty Python scene, through all the dark deflections and distortions of remembering it all these decades later, is so very funny.

And now you, reading this, catch me, as a writer, gazing at you and nearing. And as you take on the burden of being the one now under this whole gaze (that now includes me as one of this council of beings), I myself am not at all thereby divested of this burden, this task.

"From it no one can be exempt" (Gadamer, 1989, p. 362).

Understanding it does not exempt me and does not have exemption as its goal.

So, regret. "To look back with distress or sorrowful longing; to grieve for on remembering. Old Norse *grata* 'to weep, groan'" (OnLine Etymological Dictionary [OED], 2014), but also, then, this:

"Old French *regreter*, 'to ask the help of.'" (OED) Ah!

Afflictions, perhaps especially this affliction, can teach if we can learn to ask for its help and remain alert enough to not simply weep and groan.

PREAMBLE 17

"A Halt in the Rush of Things"

> The familiar idea [is] that beauty arrests motion. For example: you draw in your breath and stop still. The quick intake of breath, this little gasp—*hshshs* as the Japanese draw between their teeth when they see something beautiful in a garden—this *ahhhh* reaction is the aesthetic response just as certain, inevitable, objective and ubiquitous, as a wincing in pain and moaning in pleasure. Moreover, this quick intake of breath is also the very root of the work aesthetics, *aisthesis* in Greek, meaning sense-perception. *Aisthesis* goes back to the Homeric *aiou* and *aisthou* which means both "I perceive" as well as "I gasp, struggle for breath," as in *aisthomai,* I breath in. does this not suggest that if beauty is to appear, we must be stopped still. (Hillman, 2006d, p. 183)

> Hearing "Like A Rolling Stone"—that was my first encounter. I heard the song and I felt so transformed by it. My mother, she pulled into a drugstore to pick up something and I felt so changed by the song that I thought, when she came out, she wouldn't recognize me. And I couldn't tell you why. (Hiatt, 2003)

I'm right at the beginning of listening my way through 18 CDs of Bob Dylan's Bootleg Series #12, *The Cutting Edge,* covering the period surrounding when Dylan recorded and released "Like a Rolling Stone." This covers, for me, between the ages of 14 to just past age 16. Alan Watts was still a year and a half away—a lifetime away, in a way. July 20, 1965, 14 days away from

In Praise of Radiant Beings, pages 237–244

turning 15, gasping for breath on hearing "Like a Rolling Stone," becoming unrecognizable. That's what the experience of beauty will do to you. I must add, too, that reading John Hiatt's account had the same effect on me, an "ahhh" of recognition. His words made me admit, retroactively, that *that* was the concealed experience all along, now finally said in words, and now framed here again to become recognizable anew.

I'm mentioning these trivial autobiographical bits precisely because this experience of being arrested and having time brought to a halt and gathered up is such an ordinary thing. Listening to "Like a Rolling Stone" for the first time is not what it used to be. It's better because it has grown into itself, and that self that it has grown into has revealed itself as impermanent, malleable, various, regretting, ecstatic. This is how and why it can still "hit," because it is not done with itself and not done with me. It is dependently co-arising (*pratitya-samutpada*), without a permanent or fixed "identity" (*svabhava*)—it is empty (*shunya*) as am I. This is why we can meet and re-meet: "a constantly self-renewing contemporaneousness" (Gadamer, 1977, p. 19). This is why it is possible to love it without attachment, because there "is" nothing to be attached *to*, and attachment would simply reify it and thereby shut down its recurring hit and correlatively shut down my susceptibility to such a hit (again, there, the retraction mechanism against real or perceived threat).

As it becomes hardened, I become hardened. For fear of the hit, there can arise a desire for "the end":

> Education becomes akin to a sometimes overt, but more often subtle, war on the very possibility of unanticipated "uprising." Free spaces and those who cultivate them become suspect. Natality becomes experienced as a perennial insurgent threat to security that must be planned for and secured against. Education becomes cast as akin to a counterinsurgent war on terror—a perpetual war (Postel & Drury, 2003), given the perpetuity of the world's mortality. After all, a war against our response ("terror") to the very existence of uprising is, of necessity, perpetual. It is also profoundly Thantic—a longing for the end of this roil, for finality, fixity and death, but I'll leave this thread loose for now and for others to follow. (Jardine, 2012b, p. 5).

This experience and its avoidance or marginalization, or our attraction to or retraction from it, are ordinary. Precisely because of the ordinariness of this weirdly-elongated-but-not-simply-passing-by experience of time and the experience of people, things, ideas, memories, gestures, topics, words, or places "in" such a whiling temporality, trying to talk of it is easily scuttled:

> Here it is difficult as it were to keep our heads up, to see that we must stick to the subjects of our every-day thinking, and not go astray and imagine that we have to describe extreme subtleties. We feel as if we had to repair a torn spider's web with our fingers. (Wittgenstein, 1968, p. 46)

> The aspects of things that are most important for us are hidden because of their simplicity and familiarity. And this means: we fail to be struck by what, once seen, is most striking and powerful. (p. 50)

So, you know, brace yourself for some stumbles through language even more steep than those already encountered. The grammar of this "hitherto concealed experience" (concealed, we might say, *by* ordinariness) pushes ordinary words, since ordinarily, this experience either "goes without saying" or does not appear at all, and when it does, it seems arcane, occult, mystical, subjective and simply personal, and the like:

> The most difficult learning is to come to know actually and to the very foundations what we already know. Such learning, with which we are here solely concerned, demands dwelling continually on what appears to be nearest to us. (Heidegger, 1977b, p. 252)

It is very difficult to learn to stop over "being stopped still" and to "dwell continually" in it, while over it, and then, perhaps, to speak, to write. The public realm seduces me away from this experience as not being part of "the real world." The private realm wants this experience to be impotently subjective and nothing more than "moist gastric intimacy" (Sartre, 1970, p. 4). A contention that binds together Buddhism, ecology and hermeneutics is this:

> [I] must first learn to exist in the nameless. In the same way [I] must recognize the seduction of the public realm as well as the impotence of the private. Before [I] speak, [I] must first let [myself] be claimed again by Being, [and] tak[e] the risk that under this claim [I] will seldom have much to say. (Heidegger, 1977a, p. 199)

This concealed experience contains an experience of time that is not empty (see Chapter 13) but full, that is neither subjective nor objective (since the former and the latter are themselves dependently co-arising: "subject and object precipitate out simultaneously" [Weinsheimer, 1987, p. 5] and then *appear* separate and opposed to one another, raising endless epistemological questions of how to get them back together) but rather exists outside this complicit pairing and the wounds that each of these suffer—a worldless, private subjectivity, and a dead and fragmented world:

> Not only is fragmentation a disease, but the diseases of the disconnected parts are similar or analogous to one another. Thus, they memorialize their lost unity, their relation persisting in their disconnection. Any severance produces two wounds [two faces of suffering, one might say] that are, among other things, the record of how the severed parts once fitted together. (Berry, 1986, pp. 110–111)

Again, this experience of being arrested by the arrival of the world is neither inside of me nor outside of me:

> The hermeneutical experience is not that something is outside and desires admission. Rather, we are possessed by something and precisely by means of it we are opened up for the new, the different, the true. (Gadamer, 1977, p. 9)

This experience shatters my attempt to use this "me" as a reliable locator because, when it works, "she wouldn't recognize me." It is transformative.

It is, I have found, characteristic of what occurs in classrooms when the work deepens and becomes stilled over something wonderful and those involved are slowed and transformed in myriad ways into its presence (what Sheila Ross [2006, p. 111] calls "abiding in inquiry"). It is characteristic, I have found, in what happens, right here, when I'm trying to compose this Preamble and sideways-searching books for the right pages numbers, recalling passages long-since read and vaguely remembered, being lured by examples real and imagined and scrunching over what to include, what to abandon and the like (see Jardine, 2013, 2014a).

It is characteristic of the pacing back and forth with yet-to-be-split wood for next spring's splitting and feeling the bite of the Alberta November air, and the fact that it takes so long to be actually doing this without chattering to myself about fantasy ghosts and elsewhere.

"It's not so simple to do what you're doing" (Espe-Brown, in Dorrie 2007), but when it starts to gather, something halts. This halting experience of being "claimed" has two aspects.

The first aspect is that "we have a halt in the middle of the rush" (Gadamer, 1977, p. 15)—a familiar experience of being stopped in my tracks (by a word, a gesture, a sniff of Pine, an upwelling grief or nebulous worry, a child's comment, a newly downloaded jpeg of an old Jackson Pollock painting, before he became "himself," that is terrifyingly familiar—"Going West" almost a combination of the palette of Van Gogh's *The Potato Eaters* (see Chapter 18) and Thomas Hart Benton? Or, the imminence of that news flash that Turkey has shot down a Russian jet—how the imagination stretches forward into a future that doesn't really exist and which you, reading this, now know better that I am able. I am stopped in my tracks and brought into the questioning summons of the thing or person or idea or gesture that I have encountered, and this in such a way that that very "I" seems at stake.

So this first aspect of halt itself has two interrelated characteristics:

1. There is, as James Hillman noted, an inevitable and ubiquitous character to this experience of being halted. It is commonplace in an elusive way. Its commonplace-ness is elusive because it is also commonplace to ignore, marginalize, subjectivize or otherwise trivialize this experience. When a teacher tells a tale of a student's trouble in the staffroom and we all laugh, that breath-halting points to something more than it's being just a funny anecdote. It *hits* me, and that hit manifests as a repeated hee-haw of inhalation and exhalation, along with the grin-baring of teeth. Threat, sort of, because something hits, but the breath ensues almost as a form of composition, of composing myself. Following along this line, when Gadamer speaks of being struck, of words "breaking forth," and when Buddhism speaks of learning to still the breath over such moments, this points to how such arrivals are no mere anecdote or staff-room story. Something *true* is trying to break through in this hit. *Aletheia* (see Preamble Three). There is, here an experience of *energeia*, "aliveness" (see Palmer, 2007, Ross, 2006, pp. 107–108; see also Chapter 20), of, to paraphrase Martin Heidegger (1968), the experience of being summoned up, of something *calling for thinking*, something whose locale of summons is "beyond my wanting and doing" (Gadamer, 1989, p. xxviii), beyond, therefore, my ego-subjectivity, something, however that, when it arrives, becomes my self's venture beyond its (self-enclosed, hardened) self. *Something* stops *me*. Gadamer (1989, p. 458) uses the phrase "responding and summoning" in this regard because in this whiling, we can call out and we can be called out into its path. It doesn't just hit. It *draws* (Gadamer, 2007b, p. 198).
2. The second fold of this is that, with practice, I can learn to become more susceptible to such halting. I can become more ready to be taken off guard, halted. This is simple: I've listened to Duke Ellington enough to be more vulnerable than I used to be in hearing his music. I'm more able to let this listening "expand to its full analogous breadth of illuminative meaning" (Norris-Clarke, 1976, p. 72), to be caught up in its illuminativeness *because* of concerted and repeated practice. Become more practiced in such things means that I can become more able to experience these arrivals and calm down over them and both compose myself and experience the fullness of this arriving composition. I can become better,

> over time, at interpreting these matters, not just being bowled over by them and brought to a vibrant standstill. I can "attempt to make [myself] ready for this claim" (Heidegger, 1977a, p. 199). In other words, teaching and learning are possible. And the danger then always is that such practice will become too studious and will fall in love with itself and thereby block precisely that which it is practicing to release (precisely the always-present danger of iatrogenesis. See Preamble 13).

Hence the second aspect of this experience of time's halt is that it is not just an immediate, momentary, and fleeting thing (although this is, for the most part, how it is treated, as simply an eruption or subjective upwelling). From Chapter Thirteen:

> The sort of experience that is won, here, is only won by a certain labor (see Ross & Jardine, 2009). "Understanding *begins* when something addresses us" (Gadamer, 1989, p. 299, emphasis added), but it only *begins* there. This pedagogical experience of abundance is thus a practical matter *that must be practiced* in order for this experience to take root and grow. It must be cultivated, protected, shared, returned to, loved.

Such moments can be cared for, not in order to get some momentary hit to last forever, but in order to gather up that moment and make its avail available in words: "[Writing is] a tool, a net or trap to catch and present; a sharp edge; a medicine or a little awl that unties knots" (Snyder, 1979, p. 29)

Studying, then, is possible, but it is tough and repeated work. It is possible to become active and searching in this moment of halting, "to follow the movement of showing" (Heidegger, 1972, p. 2) and, in that following, gather together the threads of its dependent co-arising. In other words it is possible to make this arrival the locale of studying its ways and means, its shapes and forms. This is why, in *Truth and Method* (1989, p. 110 ff.), Gadamer follows the section on being drawn into the play of the world —"the movement no word is supposed to be able to say," with an austere sounding prospect of "Transformation into Structure." We can compose ourselves and, to whit, compose something of this beautiful thing that helps us remain open to its ways and expansive of that remaining (note a whiff of temporality here). We can gather, we can tend, we can cultivate, we can strive to be careful, prudent, proportional, patient, we can emulate ancestral cultivations, and study them, too, as part of our remaining calm and focused on this arriving energy. The result, here, is not immobility but an intense, ever-gathering stillness, not precisely me being the active actor, but me being gathering into the gathering that I have encountered. As per

Tsong-kha-pa's (2000, p. 111) citing of Shantideva "I compose this in order to condition my own mind," we can add, "I am composed *by* this and *it* conditions *me*."

Less esoterically put, when you finally break through in your understanding of the Pythagorean theorem, or when you suddenly come upon Picasso's *Guernica* in a New York museum, the "I" that is trying to compose itself loses itself and, in re-gaining its composure, it is no longer some self-enclosed "me" that is regained, but a self that is now dependently co-arising differently because of what it has encountered. Now compare this with the discussion of "room behavior" in Chapter 8. And recall that if I am surrounded by terrible sorrows with the children in my classroom, I will become an arising in commensurateness with such things, depending on how or whether or to what extent I am able to rise to such occasions and not simply fall frantic over them (see Molnar, 2014, Seidel, 2014, 2014a, Gilham, 2015, and many others).

Thus, one important caveat in all this giddiness, that this whiling inevitably reveals something of the pedagogy of suffering and a link to more difficult truths in Buddhist meditative practices. It reveals how the desecration and passing of places and sentient beings is a difficult but trustworthy and constant companion of ecological insight, and why finitude and *pathei mathos* ("learning through suffering") are constant penumbrae in hermeneutic work. After all, with "Like a Rolling Stone" comes the knowledge that I have aged 50 years since then, and all that follows from that knowledge.

Becoming, through practice, more and more susceptible to the halts of the world is a form of susceptibility to the truths of impermanence. This is why hermeneutic erudition should never be allowed to encrust hermeneutic experience itself. This is why Hermes is a trickster always bent on re-opening the wound, the passage, the movement, the *energeia*. Hence the slap that comes if meditation becomes sleepy and self-satisfied.

So, then, how do you do this sort of abiding in inquiry in the classroom? I dread, at this point, saying "Well, Lyle, first of all," because, though I've witnessed beautiful work countless times in real schools with real teachers and students under real circumstances, I have also witnessed far too many imported school-improvement initiates that, however well intended, feel empty and echo-y, where the words all seem to be right, but the sails don't quite billow. And I've vainly and foolishly tried initiating a few such ventures myself. So instead, I'm simply going to end with a passage from David Loy's brilliant book *Lack and Transcendence: The Problem of Death and Life in Psychotherapy, Existentialism and Buddhism* (1999, p. 49) where cites part of one of Rainer Maria Rilke's *Duino Elegies*:

> If no one else, the dying
> must notice how unreal, how full of pretense,
> is all that we accomplish here, where nothing
> is allowed to be itself
> we take the very young
> child and force it around, so that it sees
> Objects—not the Open, which is so deep in animals' faces. Free from death.

"There is nothing mystical about this" (Loy, 1999, p. 47). It is profoundly ordinary. That's why it's such tough work.

17

"Time Is a Bringer of Gifts" (2015)

> Time is a bringer of gifts. These gifts may be welcomed and cared for. To some extent they may be expected. They cannot in the usual sense be made. Only in the short term of industrial accounting can they be thought simply earnable. Over the real length of human time, to be earned they must be deserved. (Berry 1983, p. 77)

It is vital, as we turn back towards a richer experience of time—what H. G. Gadamer calls "full-filled" time in contrast to "empty time"—that we don't unwittingly drag with us entrails of the stories we are attempting to leave behind. An all-too-common critique of and resistance to the empty rush of Taylorism in schools is to *leave the bits and pieces in place* and *leave in place the underlying assumption of empty time,* and simply *de-standardize the assembly.* In what amounts to nothing more than an inversion of Taylor's (1911, p. 2) "in the past the man has been first; in the future the system must be first," each individual student is put "first" in a fragmented and scattershot world, each making what they will of the bits and pieces. We end up with assembly lines democratized, now plural and diverse and differentiated, minus surveillance and uniformity. This, of course, ends up simply multiplying the rush into a sort of post-modern proliferation and scattering, leading, seemingly inevitably, to reactionary backlashes and new invocations of "back to

In Praise of Radiant Beings, pages 245–253

the basics" as a tried and true remedy and fail-safe means to accountability. Thus, we seem stuck with old, worn-out options, between the closures and foreclosures of "the system" or wild, scattershot, undisciplined and un-disciplining, un-formative chaos:

"Time Is a Bringer of Gifts" (2015)

> The Gadamerian dystopia is not unlike others. In his version, to be glib, little requires human application, so little cultivates it. Long alienated from abiding in inquiry as a form of life and way of being, a restless humanity defers to models, systems, operations, procedures, the ready-made strategic plan, and first and last to reified concepts, long impervious to deconstruction. (Ross, 2006, p. 111)

As already cited in Chapter 3, this inversion ends with an:

> ideal-type channel-hopping viewer who flips through different images at such speed that she/he is unable to chain the signifiers together into a meaningful narrative, he/she merely enjoys the multiphrenic intensities and sensations of the surface of the images. (Usher & Edwards, 1994, p. 11)

We lose sight of the fact that these feared images of wild, scattershot, undisciplined chaos are, in part, precisely a *product of* precisely the system that deems "all Hell breaking loose" as the only alternative to its machinations. The most tragic end, here, is that, because of this misplaced inversion, we end up unpracticed and scattered and therefore, unwittingly or otherwise, deferring to or victimized by impervious, un-addressable, reified systems and rubrics as the only safe refuge from our now-unpracticed-ness. Why suffer learning anything, after all, when you can just look it up if you want to, and why would you want to if you always can.

"Nobody understood why I should be grieving" (Jardine, 2015).

The trouble is, for the gifts that full-filled time can bring to be deserved *requires something* of those anticipating such gifts. We need to *do* something and *stop* doing something, and it takes time to learn how. The worthwhile time of abiding in inquiry and coming to experience the gifts that can then arrive requires long, difficult, repeated, *practice*, and this requirement cannot be bypassed with Taylor-like false promises. All the promises of quick solutions simply induce inevitable failure, this, in part, because of the profound power that the industrial model of empty time still holds over our imagination. "Abiding in inquiry" is therefore susceptible to becoming one more bandwagon *precisely because the ubiquity of empty time renders it thus,* demanding that it be quick and easy and efficiently implemented in a sure-fire way because, after all, "time is always running out" and we need a quick fix.

As with music or painting, or reading, or writing, or getting good at listening to others tell of their worries over a child's reading, or becoming deft, as a teacher, at taking care of these responses and gathering them in to our collective care and attention, these matters take tough and repeated practice to get good at. They take study and thoughtful, rigorous, scholarly work, and the seeking out those who have been in these territories before. They take imitation and emulation and complex conversations held in the refuge of others dedicated to such work.

So arises a paradox that we cannot avoid. Our ability to welcome and care for the gifts that may come from abiding in inquiry must be cultivated "over time," and this ability must, of necessity, be cultivated over precisely the *sort* of time it presumes to cultivate. Unlike the immediate-yet-empty promises of procedurally driven Taylorism ("just do this and it will work"), full-filled time is not available as a procedure to simply be obediently and mindlessly followed instead of the empty time of efficiency. It is available as a mindful practice that takes precisely full-filled time in a field of practice to cultivate that practice and reveal its yield. Full-filled time is thus embedded in the fullness of the very topics being investigated and is therefore only available to be experienced and practiced through our involvement in traversing those very territories and seeking out the fullness of them. Its yields are only "won by a certain labor" (Ross & Jardine, 2009) proper to those (unfragmented, not pre-sequenced, dependently co-arising) fields. It therefore requires engagement in those topics and the time and attention and devotion *they* demand of *us*. More drastically put, "I am willing to endure the shame of falling short as the price of admission." (Berry & Moyers, 2013).

So, part of this practice involves precisely what is at the heart of the profession of education as a whole: *study*. This is difficult, detailed (albeit, in its own way, pleasurable and, so to speak, "fulfilling") work, but that is not a sign of an error in efficiency but of the worthwhileness of the object under consideration and the project of labor undertaken. Good work takes time because good things are complex and demanding of us and our attention and devotion.

Abiding in inquiry exists in the strangest sense of temporality. Full-filled time is the time *of* the work being done, the time belonging to the fullness of that work and its rich territoriality. It is migratory and returning, like gathering flocks. Or, perhaps like those Golden Eagles greeted, praised, and lovingly counted and re-counted in the mountains to the West of Calgary each year, year after year. Each new count gathers up where we were "before" and adds itself to the story already underway, as do those volunteering for the count and those they tell of what they have done. The territories of traverse, the arcs of seasons and links between weather and food sources, the maps drawn and re-drawn, the missives sent north and south along the migratory routes through emails and websites full of images, counts, concerns, advice—all this happens, not precisely "at" the same ("now") time of some empty "present" but rather "in" the same, shall we say, *presence.*

This is not a matter of one isolated piece of information (first before and then) after another, but of a gathering into a while of time. That work done "before" becomes part of the present, because the "present," in the life of such work, is no longer simply a "now." "Being present" has a different meaning:

> The concept of tarrying temporality [full-filled time] allows us to see how 'the present' posited as this (impossible) dimensional entity [a "now], has been abstracted from 'the present' as *that which is fully here for us,* as a matter about which we have, so to speak, presence of mind. This is the distinction between empty and filled time that Gadamer's [1970] title ["Concerning empty and ful-filled time"] alludes to. (Ross 2006, p. 110)

When such work goes well, we lose a sense of the dominance of the empty measure of clockwork time and fall into the time of the story, of the work itself, of "that which is fully here for us." Even if the Eagles are "late," this is not the lateness of industrial assembly, but a lateness that sits in a long, migratory gather of time and a longer gather of tracing these migrations over the years. Even if the migrating Eagles are "late" in passing overhead, this lateness finds its measure and its significance only in the wider arcs of "that which is fully here for us" in such a worthwhile study—seasonality, these birds, this place and its routes for migratory passages, and the gatherings of memory and knowledge and experience such a place induces and protects.

Thus, key to "abiding in inquiry" is working in the *presence* of a topic and working to bring that topic to presence—just rushing past it leaves it "hitherto concealed." It thus involves *the gatherings and the re-gatherings,* where what we've found, where we are "now," and "what is to be done next" are gathered together into the presence of "that which is [emergently] fully here for us"—the topic being investigated. These gatherings cultivate precisely this deep dependent co-arising key to worthwhile work: the sort of presence of mind that that which is fully present requires if it is to be thus present and if we are to have presence of mind about it. There is a phenomenologically undeniable sense in which each gesture of the study and exploration of a topic happens within "the same" full-filled time of "that which is fully here for us"—"presence (of mind)" not simply "the present [now]":

> One is absorbed in it. It is more like a tarrying that waits and preserves in such a way that the [work being meditated upon, the performance being watched, the topic being studied, the birds being observed or heard, the friendship that grows] is allowed to come forth [Heidegger and Gadamer sometimes use the phrase "comes to presence"]. To tarry is not to lose time. Being in the mode of tarrying is like an intensive back-and-forth. One "is completely there in it." It is not like running through a stretch of space until the finish line. It is like a growing fascination that hangs on and even hangs on through temporary disruptions [when I return to considering Pythagoras, the having-gathered remains to a certain degree, right where I left it] because the harmony with the whole grows [*Gebilde*] and demands our agreement. We know this with special clarity in listening to music. (Gadamer, 2007b, p. 211)

Such coming to presence is thus linked to forms of practice, but it is not fully adequate to think of this practice as occurring over a long string of "nows" but as itself recurring, remaining, somehow, in the same temporal locale of emerging presence.

Pushed one step further, this sense of full-filled time requires that we understand the topics entrusted to teachers and students in school as constituted, not by lifeless fragments and bits and pieces, but by living disciplines, live inheritances and fabrics into which our lives are already woven. This sense of aliveness (*lebensweltlich*) is thus key to resisting the rush of empty time: in inquiry we are dealing with "entit[ies] that exist only by always being something different. [They are] . . . temporal in a radical sense. [They have their] being only in becoming and return" (Gadamer, 1989, p. 123). The topics we explore with students—pronouncing words perhaps, or "democracy" and its exportation to the Middle East and further East, or the curves of highway off-ramps and their mathematics, or the political spins of statistics, or the fragility of the Weaselhead marshlands in Calgary, and on and on—are therefore no longer properly understood as simply fixed and finishing objects to be assembled or delivered, but are, rather living and often deeply contested "inheritances" that have been handed to us and to which we have be handed. They are living, ongoing gatherings into whose life of gathering we must enter into in order to come to understand them, in order for each of us to "gather" something of these gatherings. They are stories into whose tellings we must step and add ourselves. They are time-beings (Ozeki, 2013, Dōgen, 2007). To understand, then, is to "further" (Gadamer, 1989, p. xiv) the gathering—"only in the multifariousness of such voices does it exist" (p. 284). This requires that, in order to come to understand what is going on with a particular topic under investigation in the classroom ("Something is going on, [*im Spiele ist*], something is happening [*sich abspielt*]" [Gadamer, 1989, p. 104]) I myself enter into this "ordering and shaping" (Gadamer, 1989, p. 107), because *that* is what any living topic *is*: an ongoing, still-gathering ordering and shaping, not just a fixed and already finalized order and shape. Even the seemingly finished formulae of, say, quadratic equations, are always appearing and re-appearing in the life of the life world, demonstrating and re-demonstrating the character and limits of their applicability and usefulness.

Abiding in inquiry thus requires practice, requires engagement. Temporally put, "to be present means to *participate*" (Gadamer, 1989, p. 124). Full-filled time thus links coming to know a living field of work and its gatherings to the transformation of the one coming to know into someone who "know[s] one's way around" (Gadamer, 1989, p. 260): "this means that one knows one's way around *in it*" (p. 260), in the gatherings of and in the dependently co-arising gathering presence of mind regarding, a living field of work.

There is a sense, here, that time, in such gatherings, "slows down." But this isn't quite right. This isn't simply a slowing of the clock:

> It is not merely one's "taking time" to linger over something, as in the slackening or slowing down to contemplate. [This full-filled] temporality... is not a function of lackadaisical, meandering contemplation, least of all passive in any way, but is a function of the fullness and *intensity* of attention and engrossment. (Ross, 2006, p. 109)

We become enthralled and "enveloped in a time that does not pass" (Ross, 2006 p. 106), a time described by Hans-Georg Gadamer with the German term *Verweilen*—translatable as "tarrying" or "whiling" or "gathering":

> In this tarrying the contrast with the merely pragmatic realms of understand becomes clear. The *Weile* [the 'while' in *Verweilen*, tarrying] has this very special temporal structure—a structure of being moved, which one nevertheless cannot describe merely as duration. In it we tarry. (Gadamer, pp. 76–77)

This possibility of, shall we say, "absorption" and being moved and addressed and, shall we say, summoned or beckoned by the work itself, is phenomenologically familiar. When the work undertaken is worthwhile, the inquiry, the topic, the images, the ideas, the story:

> truly takes hold of us. [I]t is not an object that stands opposite us which we look at in hope of seeing through it to an intended conceptual meaning. Just the reverse. The work is an *Ereignis*—an event that 'appropriates us' into itself. It jolts us, it knocks us over, and sets up a world of its own, into which we are drawn, as it were. (Gadamer, 2001, p. 71)

This link between worthwhile work and the while of its full-filled time has a wonderful, pedagogically rich, double movement: the thing we tarry or while over, as well as our ability to experience it "... becomes ever richer and more diverse. The *volume* increases infinitely—and for this reason we learn from [it] how to tarry" (Gadamer 2001, pp. 76–77). In inquiry, the topic becomes richer and we who gather around it and while over it become more and more able, through participation and practice, to experience that richness and diversity. As the topic becomes richer and more diverse, we, as St. Augustine put it, become "roomier" (cited in Carruthers, 2005, p. 199).

There are important pedagogical hints in all this.

First, it is not just that good stories and good work ask us to linger over them and return and gather. Such things *teach us how to tarry*, to "while" by requiring this of us. "The 'self' is *forgotten* in the experience of tarrying" (Ross, 2006, p. 112) as we become absorbed in the while of the work. This is why I've left these heated signifiers—"good stories," "good work"—undefined, because they gain their signification and significance only through the concerted concern for and dedication to the question of what it is that is *worth* whiling over, worthwhile. "Who is to say what is worthwhile?" cannot be genuinely asked from a cynical distance by a self that is full of self-consciousness and who always wants to be first and who refuses the risk, refuses to let themselves enter the fray. The isolated and bereft, post-modern, cynical, self appears, now, as nothing more than a bullying, self-obsessed spoilsport who has fallen hook, line and sinker for the story of fragmentation and cool, safe, self-congratulatory distance and alienation.

Second, good work in the classroom becomes akin to an object gathering mass that, as it gathers, starts increasing its "draw" of attention. Its "gravity" increases as our knowledge and experience of it increases, which thereby draws our attention even more strongly. This, in fact, is a familiar experience. The more I while over something, the more it attracts my attention: "having become more experienced about some thing through whiling our time away over it has a strange result: *what is experienced* 'increases in being' (Gadamer 1989, p. 40)" (Jardine 2012h, p. 190). The more often those Golden Eagles are noted, the stronger the draw of that noteworthiness, and until I myself enter into that sway, that noteworthiness is not yet "present." It must be cultivated to be experienced. It does not lie there openly and anonymously available. That is, its coming to presence asks something of me. Unconcealedness cannot be deferred to someone else who can then simply show me the outcomes of their efforts.

This is why Gadamer (1989, pp. 122–123) parallels this whiling time to a sort of "festive" time, where, over time and through cyclical returning, something like a "tradition" is set up and why he suggests that "belonging" in this arc of telling and re-telling is a condition of the story's draw (p. 262) ("a sense of 'nativeness,' of belonging to the place [Snyder, 1980, p. 86]). We find this in classrooms where a time for storytelling—or any other experience considered by those gathering to be worth while—has been carved off and protected and reliably repeated. This is far from being simply the setting up of a classroom "routine" that is done simply for the sake of familiarity and predictability:

> [The world] compels over and over, and the better one knows it, the *more* compelling it is. There comes a moment when something is *there*, something one should not forget and cannot forget. This is not a matter of mastering an area of study. (Gadamer, 2007e, p. 115)

Thus, getting to return to something worthwhile has its own attraction that then teaches us about the worth of this kind of returning. The tough work is to be drawn into that compelling and *not* reifying what then arrives but rather making it more compelling and drawing others into this experience of dependent co-arising and gathering. This is what is *there*, something that beckons attention and continuance. Good, worthwhile work creates a desire for good, worthwhile work and impatience with trivial things that are not only not worthwhile but that ravage and atrophy and betray our keenness for worthwhile things. As Chris Dawson (1998, p. xxvi) notes in his "Translator's Introduction" to Hans-Georg Gadamer's *Praise of Theory*, this links to the hermeneutic interest in old Greek ideas of "the beautiful": "any beautiful thing has a radiant elegance about it which . . . points beyond itself and drives us to look for further elegant unities in other things." Again, then, whiling over a good story teaches something more than the tale being told. It "attracts the longing of love to it. [It] disposes people in its favor immediately" (Gadamer, 1989, p. 481) and it disposes us to seek out and surround ourselves with such things. It disposes us to clear out the junk we have surrounded ourselves with and the junking of our lives that such junk induces. It teaches us—teachers and student alike—something about the worth of whiling and what it requires of us and what happens when we strive to surround ourselves and fill our lives with things worthy of, quite literally, spending our lives on.

Worthwhile things are thus secretly honoring of our sense of our own finitude. This is the "hitherto concealed experience" of this *there.* Pursuing "good work" involves becoming more and more aware of the frail fabric of things, of the vulnerability of knowledge and scholarship itself in this rushing, often degrading, trivializing world and of the knife-edge limits of learning that is, as living, always and inevitably up against the edge of impermanence. Up against this edge, that abiding in inquiry *happens at all* in the real world of real schools is downright miraculous, and this makes it all the more beautiful and all the more honorable to be part of. The mindfulness of inquiry often requires bloody-mindedness and refusing to expend ourselves in the ever-accelerating rush of empty time that is deliberately designed to never be satisfied and to produce in us a cynicism about any viable alternative:

> Gadamer's uniquely concrete account of the temporality of tarrying facilitates . . . a view of [human] continuity that is profoundly participatory. It gives the deadening abstraction of cultural alienation a specific meaning: participation is, so to speak, only a thought away. This corrects the view that the existence of the cultural artifact obviates or delays indefinitely any need to inquiry into human continuity oneself, as though the cultural artifact performed this custodial service for us by itself. It becomes possible to see how identifying human historical continuity, not *with* the hermeneutical event [of tarrying and gathering *for oneself* and *with others also gathered*], but *as* 'elsewhere' [already in the book, already known nor remembered by others, easily accessible if I want to on-line at a moment's notice, already "amassed verified knowledge" (Gadamer, 1989, p. xxi), so why should I bother myself with learning it or tarrying over it?], merely lends itself to a self-understanding as helplessly alienated. The richness of the time of tarrying . . . provides a resource for revising our terms of engagement with the question of, say, the tragedy of our post-modern 'condition' by offering a way past the prognosis that this condition cannot be corrected. (Ross, 2006, p. 113)

It can be corrected, this "condition." Study. Adore. Sit. Stay.

PREAMBLE 18

"This is a Degenerate Time"

It'll Do

> It started the day after the attacks on the twin towers, with the discovery of a flight manual in Arabic and a copy of the Koran in a car hired by Mohammed Atta and abandoned at Boston airport. In the immediate shocked aftermath of the attacks, these findings were somehow reassuring: American intelligence was on the case; the perpetrators were no longer faceless. In less than a week came another find, two blocks away from the Twin Towers, in the shape of Atta's passport. Yet, we were still in the infancy of coincidence. (Karpf, 2002)

They happened to find a Syrian passport beside one of the men killed the day after the Paris bombings on November 13th, 2015. Carrying your passport to a shooting seems strange and finding a passport seems profoundly coincidental. Oh, and he happened to claim to be a refugee. Evidence wrapped in [false] flags. Terrible times. And right when we might start imagining monstrous Western Intelligence-Agency culpabilities in this case, "Thomas de Maiziere, the German interior minister, suggested on Tuesday that the passport found at the bombing scene might be a 'false trail' placed deliberately by the Islamic State attackers to turn public opinion against

In Praise of Radiant Beings, pages 255–259

Syrian refugees" (New York Times, 2015). Then again, that story of a false trail could have been planted in order to turn public opinion against the Islamic State's attempt to turn public opinion against the Syrian refugees.

False trails of trails. My own work has been deliberately timid in these matters, and I give thanks to scholars such as David G. Smith (2006, 2008, 2014) not only for his relentlessness in this regard, but for his ability to maintain himself in the face of these frays. Also, I must add, his ability to turn, shall we say, "eastward," having been down this trails is astounding and is a constant reminder, for me, of what is at stake in this work. Again, one's teacher stands as an example of how a life might be lived, not that a student must or can take on that life, but that a student must realize that he or she, too, is living a life and shaping a path.

I can't manage the full brunt of these trails except in small, meagre doses like the following chapter. On the face of it, there seems to be little connection between the following chapter and the proffered topic of this collection, but these things are often quite buried. Two things.

First, look in the chapter that follows. There is mention of Ferguson, Missouri and Michael Brown, names nearly lost to memory, events that were so fulsome at the time and that are fading, unevenly, of course, depending on your proximity to these matters, depending on your race or geography or precisely which distractions are swirling around. Dependently co-arising, of course.

But there is another lesson, here. "Wherever you are is a place to practice" (Tsong-kha-pa, 2004, p. 191).

A Russian jet shot down by Turkish missiles? New enough for you? It will seem ancient and probably already forgotten by the time you read this. There is a terrible and irresolvable mix, here, of holding on to things too long, and letting them go too soon, of having my holding-on entrench them into hostile objects that I love because of how much time I've invested, or of having letting go and turning away end up as mere cowardice, of placing too much faith in my power to decode our circumstances through the tight sheen of their appearance, or giving way to cynicism and exhaustion and depression:

> "If what you suggest is true, then everything changes." Indeed, the question "What is it that changes?" now becomes highly relevant. Possible changes can for the most part be cast in the language of loss and include loss of belief and trust in government, loss of belief in the value of democratic participation, loss of belief in my own tradition as the bearer of "civilization," loss of belief in the power of dialogue and compromise as a basis of civil society, loss of belief in openness and transparency in public policy. (Smith, 2014, p. 113)

There is a terrible mix, here, of too much and too little, both at the same time. What is portended, over and over again, is a loss of belief, and losing belief can seem like nothing more than giving up in the face of the world and turning away. "Can we console ourselves with that?" (Husserl, 1970b, p. 7).

This, here, is a lesson of Buddhist thought as well as one regarding hermeneutics—of abstaining from the energetics of believing and then turning *towards* the object that was once so believed, looking for trails underneath the reified surface produced of that belief. Loss of belief ("disillusion" [Smith, 2014]) lets the *lude* of the world "rise up like sparks from a fire" (Merleau-Ponty, 1964, p. xiii).

As with Buddhist practice, so too with hermeneutic work. Each of us must make our way to the extent that each of us is able, in the face of this arising and opening of trails, false or otherwise. And, as I've mentioned before (see Preamble 16), despite its timidity, my work, my writing, often runs far ahead of my self:

> A hermeneutic secret, then, that my failure to measure up to the work I do is a sign of why *its* success is not *mine*, a sign of how the child must outrun its forbearers if it is to have a quickened life of its own and how, paradoxically, again, my success in such matters is found in precisely this failure. This is part of the careful suffering at the heart of teaching, that students get up and walk away, just like my own child has done, and how this necessarily leaves me haunted by his death even though he is alive and kicking. Even in walking away, these young things then walk amidst songlines. Thus, caring, in hermeneutics, for the well-being of these lines is my only comfort. It is how the suffering of such matters might just be Noble. *Might* be—that "might" is why compassion is always necessary and why sorrow (German, *Sorge*, translated in the work of Martin Heidegger [1962] as "care") always necessarily ensues upon the joy of quickening. This is why the hermeneutic affection for quickening must learn to be about love and not attachment, about compassion, not rescue. Again, all of this roiling work only makes insight *possible*, not *necessary*. (Jardine, 2015c, p. 112)

This reminds me of a tough moment a few years back when I looked at Tsong-kha-pa's work, and Gadamer's, and realized something quite obvious: not everything is addressed therein, not every foe is sought and detangled, not every sorrow relieved. It could have been different. But it'll do.

"Lionizing Nostalgia and Progress at the Same Time"

"This is a degenerate time" (Tsong-kha-pa, 2000, p. 74). That was written in around 1400 CE in Tibet. Almost every text in this Buddhist lineage, whatever the century, country or circumstances describes, along with Patrul Rinpoche (1808–1887), "these degenerate times" (Patrul, 1998, p. 91). "We are in an age of decadence" (p. 190). And then Pabongka Rincpoche (1878–1941) says "we call the present time 'a degenerate period,' but we have never had a better opportunity than now" (Pabongka, 2006, p. 535); and again "these degenerate times can be most beneficial" (2006, p. 550) because we are faced with circumstances that call for practice, clarification, patience, perseverance, generosity and the like:

> It is difficult to generate the spirit of enlightenment...in these terrible times [there it is again—"these times"]. You generate the spirit of enlightenment *through seeing the difficulty required to develop it.* (Tsong-kha-pa, 2004, p. 22, italics mine)

And then this: "you should assume the present time to be these 'degenerate times'" (Pabongka, 2006, p. 243). I'm wondering, then, whether a certain level of insight into the doings of the world inevitably ends up with us sensing the particularly degenerate troubles occurring "now," not because of some objective measure of our current circumstances or of relative degenerativity, but because it is *these* troubles, now, that are of particular urgency, immediacy and concern.

In response to some of these musings, part of an unpublished email from Graham McCaffrey (see Chapter 15; see also McCaffrey, 2015, p. 21):

> Some thoughts going back to... the "degenerate age" and causes and conditions. Alongside the idea of the "degenerate age" [are both the] implying a golden age from which we are receding, [and a] counterpart of progress towards a better future. A feature of our contemporary condition is that in our culture we manage the feat of lionizing nostalgia and progress at the same time. Caught between an idealized past and [an idealized] future, suffering (in that First Noble Truth, existential-fact way) is always in the present.

In education, in that slim space between idealized "traditional methods" and idealized "new and improved pedagogical theories or kits or packages or sure-fire remedies lies an always present "terror in a mother's heart" (O'Leary, 2012), a terror produced and manipulated and maintained precisely by idealized visions of the past or future as well as monstrous visions of what we are currently up against once the present is evacuated into and seen from the belief-perspectives a Golden Past and/or a Golden Future.

What makes the present age degenerate is what has always made whatever "present" degenerate: the reifying forces of *believing* that react to threat by making us hold our breath, grasp tightly and seek the shelter of us-against-them/it, and then ask us to believe that this reified and hardened state is just "the way things are" and not a sensible response to our embattled circumstances. A sensible response to our embattled circumstances can be studied and understood and untangled, and this until the insight arrives that it is possible, this circumstance, not necessary. It is impermanent as is our attention to it. It can be studied and we can become composed in its presence.

Thinking Becomes Unthinkable

> As has happened post-9/11 in some quarters in North America, paying even scant attention to these complex histories of coexistence becomes vaguely suspect. Trying to act on the belief (inside or outside of schools) that the matters at hand need more intellectual subtlety than purged and clarified exaggerations-under-threat allow, starts to appear as an act of betrayal or sedition. Suggesting that there is more complexity to the story than the abstractions and idealizations allow is to be branded a conspiracy theorist. Wanting to know something more than the simplistic, threat-induced clarities about this "us" and "them" becomes egregious. *Knowledge and its pursuit become experienced as a threat to security.* Under threat, thinking becomes *unthinkable.* (Jardine, Naqvi, Jardine, & Zaidi, 2010, p. 32)

There is no innocent language on hand for pulling out of this vortex, and this is one of the tough lessons of hermeneutic work, that no matter where we turn for an uncontaminated refuge, our words will echo back to us in ways we didn't mean:

> In every lexicon, tolerance signifies the limits on what foreign, erroneous, objectionable or dangerous element can be allowed to cohabit with the host without destroying the host—whether the entity at issue is truth, structural soundness, health, community, or an organism. The very invocation of tolerance . . . indicates that something contaminating or dangerous is at hand. Tolerance appears, then, as a mode of incorporating and regulating the presence of the threatening Other within. (Brown, 2006, p. 27)

All life is suffering. So, as often cited in this text, when every word breaks forth as if from a center, this doesn't simply portend good news in what we then find swirling around it in veiled and open penumbras. Every word must be suffered if it is to be truly understood.

Happy Xmas, then. I'll do what I can.

18

An Ode To Xmas Present (2015)

Please don't let me fear anything I cannot explain.
I can't believe I'll never believe in anything again.
—Costello, 1991

To begin, consider David Pope's (2015) cartoon published at 7:09 a.m., January 7, 2015. Here: https://twitter.com/davpope/status/552844593046097920/photo/1. A slightly pudgy, balding man lying in a pool of blood, his pencil, bent glasses and a piece of paper with a sketch on it beside him. Standing over him, a hooded figure with an AK47, still smoking, saying:

"He drew first."

It is always rather disturbing to discover that something that I have felt or believed or been resigned to or took to be true is a fabrication that has no necessity to it at all. There is a terrible vertigo that comes in finding that believing it to be permanent or beyond question or fixed is just the outcome of causes and conditions that have fallen from memory and view.

In Praise of Radiant Beings, pages 261–264

Such occluding amnesia is, it seems, a perennial part of the human condition. It makes my intimate and heartfelt experiences *seem* immediate and obvious and "simply the way things are." A life of semblance has its own comforts, of course. Such "moon-sickness" (Gadamer, 1989, p. 25) makes it hard to see straight after recent events, and not let the inherited-and-forgotten immediacies of media flurries turn to white outs and skidding off the road. Nice Canadian metaphors, eh? There is nothing necessary about freedom of speech just as there is nothing necessary about real or feigned religious effrontery. Such things only persist in the persistence of one or another kind of "attention and devotion" (Berry, 1986, p. 33). Even studious claims of "false flag operations" (Barrett, 2015) are fabrications of fabrications. I mention this last thread following on conversations with a friend where we spoke of what happens when every single event in the world becomes full of a monotonously same hiddenness. When I got to this point in writing, I knew that if I looked, there would be false flag commentaries. Of course. It's simply the way things are. It's like Santa Claus, who is always just out of view and because you've never seen him that proves that he exists. The CIA as the new monotheism behind every event, and all-new arguments from design take center stage in off stage suspicions.

Yet, please, I plead, don't get me wrong. It is my lovely friend lying there in that cartoon, and our love itself lying bled out with glasses bent and askew.

When vertigo strikes, possibilities become endless and the bleeding cannot be stopped.

Hans-Georg Gadamer (1989, p. xxii) nailed something of this phenomenon with great precision and a wicked sting: "the naive self-esteem of the present moment." To find that the world is nothing but Santa Clauses all the way down, and to feel again and again that terrible ear popping of growing up that came with finding out the truths about this taken-to-be-saint, and the whole worlds of experience that had to be left behind in such finding—such is the lot of interpretation. Once glimpsed, nothing can stop this cascading collapse, not even the ground on which that body slumps.

But it is essential that this be properly counterbalanced, because the naive self-esteem of the present moment is only *initially* replaced with a vague humiliation at having been so sleepy and at the hot bile that comes up the esophagus. This pivot point is profoundly important, because if one gets stuck there, what can follow is a life of cynicism, paranoia, and complaint and the life goal of breaking everyone else's bubble in an act of skillful woe. There is, right at this pivot, a "hitherto concealed experience" (Gadamer, 1989, p. 100)—a way of engaging this vertigo world of dependent arising—whose bristling radiance far outshines what was lost in the shifting. In fact, I'd venture that what is gained is an understanding that there is, in fact, something "true" of the thunder and lightning of reindeer, and the saintliness of the gift, and the Northern Hemispheric brainstem draw of passing the stopping of the sun's sinking and feeling its *tropos,* its "turning," that goes far beyond the surface story. There is something true in the arrival of the child that outruns every attempt to give it a proper name. Even your eye's ability to dance over these words belies fundamentalism of any sort, whether Christian, Islamic or hidden or overt American ops in the name of freedom and terror. Fuck that. And this isn't either for or against Christianity, Islam or America. It is against false and delusional *believing* that turns the agony of our living into a hardened enemy and turns our believing into something whose hardening we don't have to face. It functions like a hidden wound, festering precisely because of its unutterable hiddenness. Unutterable because of liberal openness to "difference" and "diversity." Self-cancelling, because we must be open to that which despises openness, tolerant of that which is intolerant. And no, not just "Islam" at its worst (or Christianity at its historical nadir—I'll leave it to you to decide when that might have been). The CIA, too, protecting market-economics at all costs under the guise of protecting "democracy" at all costs. Droning hits of civilians. Beheadings. Tea Parties? Take your pick.

Robert Bly said it somewhere: if you want to survive this world, study. But not the bland study of piling one piece after another of "amassed verified knowledge" (Gadamer, 1989, p. xxi) on top of a pile whose weight simply weighs us down and confirms our cynicism and gives us grey gravity. No. The studying that provides some relief to the weight of the world is studying one's living itself, studying that very movement of vertigo that comes in the collapsing of the world and the arrival of the child. We build it up to let it go. The goal is not gravity but lightness, even in the face of a fellow writer killed for writing, killed for the very giggled child-heralding that is writing's goal, pushed up against the senilities, seriousness, and naive self-esteem of the present circumstances. Trickster poof and prod and dance, pivoting on that sidewalk even in the moment of being shot, of falling.

Like this: to herald that a child is born is something that will take a lifetime and more to fully understand. Because that child will awaken in our loving arms and see Ferguson, Missouri, hear of Michael Brown, see cartoonists being offensive and being shot for it, see claims of hidden hands at work in the world, and evidence upon evidence of muttered common breaths co-inspiring ("Hush, a child is born, I hear"), and look us in the eye and say "*what?*" What *is* this? What the *hell* is going on? That, I'm afraid to say (because saying so lays out a "terrible trial" [Berry & Moyers, 2013] of being patient in an erupting emergency that follows in the wake of such giving), is the magi's gift no matter how or whether we answer these questions.

And I get it, this contradiction between the eruption of the child and the call to grow up and give up the naivety of believing.

Freedom of speech is a fabrication the protection of which is a decision, not a God-given or God-forbidden right. Decide.

Guess what God, the CIA, the faculty I'm leaving, the flags, false or otherwise, the scurrying, the distraction, the fear mongered and felt? Guess what, Xmas? Guess what, Gadamer or fat Buddha squat? I don't *believe* in any of you.

Instead, I write. *That* is how I love you all.

Je suis Charlie, but guess what? I don't *believe* that either.

Happy Xmas, then.

PREAMBLE **19**

"The Sleep of Reason Brings Forth Monsters"

Non Sum Qualis Eram

> Christopher Hitchens: Michael Krasny interviewed me the other day in San Francisco, the home of the American Buddhists, said had I followed the genocide trials in Cambodia, and I said no, I'd been busy and I hadn't been. Civil society has recovered in Cambodia to the extent that it looks like the Khmer Rouge criminals are going to be tried for genocide. The Buddhist party in Cambodia doesn't want it. It says, "Why do this? All those people who were killed had committed sins in previous lives." This is a mental surrender. And a moral one, too, this kind of contemplative nonsense. "Turn off the mind and you'll have bliss" has ghastly consequences. "The sleep of reason brings forth monsters." That's Buddhism—the resort everyone goes to when they've exhausted monotheism. I'm not so sure that if you change your climate from East to West that you escape human irrationality. Seems to me that it follows you wherever you go as long as you're willing to surrender your mind. (Nightjarflying, 2011)

There are many videos on YouTube where, during debates about his then-recent *God is Not Great: How Religion Poisons Everything* (2008), Hitchens

In Praise of Radiant Beings, pages 265–270

speaks about how Zen meditation practices were used to train Kamikaze pilots in the Second World War. He cites and recommends Brian Daizen Victoria's *Zen at War* (2006), and details this and other qualms. This made Hitchens suggest to a person who had raised a question (in a specific video I can no longer find) something to the effect "You've got to keep your eye on those guys, too."

In the sometimes-woozy Faculty of Education graduate research atmosphere of early love affairs with "qualitative research," and mind-numbing invocations of feelings and stories and yogic practices and oneness, Hitchens has been a reliable companion, a good reminder.

Buddhism can be as dumb and mind numbing as any other human practice. Mindlessly spinning prayer wheels in order to be an obedient boy or a good girl is, well, as mindless as me being an altar boy in the Anglican Church in order to avoid the dreaded Sunday school.

So, I offer these in light of Hitchens' reference to the surrender of the mind and the monsters that ensue:

> You must experience . . . suffering until the force of your karma is exhausted. (Tsong-kha-pa, 2000, p. 164)
>
> Know that the sole cause of . . . [your] suffering is your physical, verbal, and mental wrongdoing. (p. 169)
>
> If you have not accumulated the karma that is the cause for an experience of happiness or suffering, you will in no way experience the happiness or suffering that is its effect. (p. 214)

These are very easy to find and are relatively toned down compared to many other texts in this Buddhist lineage.

The trick, here, for me, is a pedagogical one. Sometimes the greatest gift a student can give his or her teacher is to rescue them from themselves, and say "no" to some of the entrails that encrust our teachers' stories and that have become too hard and hardened to crack. Reading and rereading Tsong-kha-pa has led to overflowing margin notes around these ideas—trying to take it on and take it seriously and think through whether my resistance to these ideas needs eroding or whether it needs to be read allegorically, or tossing it aside and X-ing out passages altogether in disgust.

In the end, I'm with Hitchens on this one, almost, but then, a story.

I frequented a school which, for nearly a decade, became a lovely place to visit, to place and supervise student-teachers, and to spend days working with teachers and students and to soak up events, language, cadences and circumstances that informed my own research and writing:

> I recall, ages ago now, having a brief talk with the Grade One teacher at [that school] about what I'd learned about monsters: from the Latin *monere,* to heed, to warn, to teach. Her immediate response was to ask me to come into the class and talk about this with the children. We had a lovely time talking about monsters and how they appear in books they had been reading, in dreams and in movies and in life. Strong, big scary, green, gigantic, my sister, run! I then wrote down this Latin term, and we talked and speculated a bit about why monsters appear, whom they appear to and when. What is it that they are trying to do, to say? Not *just* to frighten, but also to get our attention, to show, to *teach*—at which point the sweet laughs started as they looked at their teacher, the monster. I urged the children to write down the Latin term in their notebooks and let their parents know that they are learning Latin at school. We all laughed, but they did take note. And then, unannounced and unexpectedly, five years later, a familiar face, a then-Grade Five student from the school stopped me in the hall hugging a then-new copy of some Harry Potter book:
>
> "You're the monsters guy, right? I want to show you something." *This* is the sort of work [I] had the pleasure to be a small part of. (Jardine, 2011, p. 34)

Stick with me here. I took a group of student teachers to this school early on in their undergraduate degrees. All of them already visited practicum placements in other elementary schools around town. When we visited this *monere*-school, every one of them said something to the effect that these children aren't like the children in *their* school.

This is where an old standby came out in our next University practicum class together. It's a lovely thought by Lewis Hyde, from his wonderfully named book *The Gift: On The Erotic Nature of Property*: "The way we treat a thing can sometimes change its nature" (Hyde, 1983, p. iii).

Now, to the extent that the nature of a thing is not fixed but dependently co-arising, here's where our discussion went, and why it's relevant to a preamble about a chapter featuring reflections on Christopher Hitchens. No, those children are not different than the ones in your school, and they're not the same either. They have been relatively consistently *treated a certain way* over the course of their K–6 education, and their nature has become dependently co-arising with that treatment. Simple. It is difficult to not reify. "They're not like the kids in my school" *conceals* the causes and conditions of this difference. How were they treated to end up like this? Of course, how children are treated in schools cannot override every other cause and condition but can only admix with them—matters socio-economic, cultural, familial, being in a home surrounding of affection or stress and violence, and on and on. But schools can be refuges: *this* is what happens here whatever other circumstances and sufferings we each bring with us. And, as we all know as teachers, this "this" will be sorely tested and sometimes fail or falter. Refuge is no simply or easy matter, nor is it forged once and for all. That *monere*-school has since drifted, only for that good work to find other roots and sources and manifestations (see Seidel & Jardine, in press).

"Karma that you experience here and now is the effect of actions which ripen in the very lifetime in which you do the actions" (Tsong-kha-pa, 2000, p. 241)—but also ripening here is your surroundings and those you are surrounded with, because, as dependently co-arising, this is what I *am.* In short, no student *deserves* a bad teacher because of their past deeds. That turns karma into nothing more that comeuppance, into retribution and pay back. However, if a student *does* get a bad teacher, *that treatment can change their nature as much as might a good teacher.*

As for the Cambodian Buddhist party, and all their metaphysical architectures of retributive karma and passive acceptance, well, not interested, because, frankly, the proposed actions of a civil society calling the Khmer Rouge to account for genocidal actions are *themselves* dependently co-arising, karmic actions that are aimed at making our actions accountable to our dependent co-arising. The Cambodian Buddhist party simply sounds like the Westboro Baptist Church picketing the funerals of army personnel because the government allows gays in the military with "God Hates Fags" signs. It's just stupid and mean and frightened and institutionalized, as are old Church indulgences or inquisitions, or the lives of Danish cartoonists and Parisian ones, and on and on and on.

It may be that how I walk into a classroom will make possible, perhaps even summon, the arising of students of a certain sort, and how students walk into a classroom having been treated terribly over years of schooling will try to summon a teacher of a certain sort. But none of us is locked in to an inevitable fate. There is "free space" and the wisdom and contemplation needed to burn off the encrustations we've inherited, is always on hand, always *possible.* It is no accident, this list of *paramitas*: generousity, patience, discipline, perseverance, stillness, and wisdom. And it is also always possible for the inherited conditions of the students in a particular class to rise up and overwhelm my own capacities. Of course.

I guess this makes clear again why my relationship to Buddhism has been so flickering, picking and choosing, and, to admit it, how much of my understanding of and attraction to Buddhism is borne from the "privilege of youth" (Gadamer, 1986, p. 56) where it first started. That's why it is good to have people like Christopher Hitchens around.

Thus, this book has never been about *believing in* Buddhism and swallowing it whole. "All of the scriptures are instructions for practice" (Tsong-kha-pa, 2000, p. 52), but watch out, scriptures! Practice is a relentlessly questioning student who will not let go and will ask, again and again, that the worth of precepts be demonstrated. Here. Now. In this circumstance. After all, if everything is dependently co-arising, if everything is impermanent and open to the arrival of circumstances, the scriptures, too, are open to vigorous and well-intended and meticulous interpretation. This is why the Tibetan demand of *blang dor*—the meticulous, day-to-day work of "'engage-abandon,' i.e., engage in what is to be practiced and give up what is to be abandoned" (Richards, 2006, p. 731) is, for me, a trump card with no fixed and unquestionable "foundation" (scriptures included, dogma included, beliefs included). This Cambodian Buddhist Party's thinking must be abandoned, that is, it must be eroded, interpreted, untangled, let go of, on behalf of relieving Buddhism of its calcified, ungenerous, impatient, childish, and moribund origins. Civil trials can be treated as an attempt to clear away the reifications and regimes of reified power that lead to genocidal actions (premised on the us-and-them logic of enclosed identity) in the first place.

In the above-cited video, Christopher Hitchens effortlessly summons up *El sueño de la razón produce monstruos*, the name of an etching by Francisco Goya circa 1787. And don't worry. I'd never heard of it either. I found it on-line because I wanted to be able to remember it fully myself. This is part of good practice. I'm just now looking again at that date, when Immanuel Kant's *Critique of Pure Reason* (1964) was first published. The sleep of reason brings forth monsters, and hiding away from such monsters or falling for them altogether, won't do. Either of these ways does not demonstrate, does not *teach.* "Your fear is not dispelled until you light a lamp and carefully investigate whether it is there" (Tsong-kha-pa, 2002, p. 334).

As Hitchens shows in the following chapter, his ability to summon Horace and Ernest Dowson to give voice to his gaunt and failing demeanour summons thoughtful and sturdy companionship and solidarity: *non sum qualis eram.* Even though I remain, at this writing, hale, it's good to know there are these companions around, too, for what is to come. I am not as I was, is what I am.

The Linger Itself

Again, as per Preamble and Chapter 18 regarding Buddhism (or hermeneutics, for that matter), don't believe it and simply *follow* it. It is a practice whose fruits require relentless scrutiny because it is, in the lineage of

Tsong-kha-pa, precisely a practice of relentless scrutiny and not simply a matter of "mental surrender." Reading Victoria's text, then, is not a practice of giving up on Buddhism, but letting go, with study and careful scrutiny, of "the privilege of youth" (Gadamer, 1986, p. 59) that can lead to believing it, that can lead to grasping it, that can lead to reification, that can lead to protecting it from real or perceived threat, that can lead to hostility, that leads to . . . well, we've been around these turns before. I'm not a Buddhist. I just find it useful in burning off skins of this encrusting life and finding little joys.

This is why I've included the following brief reflection on Christopher Hitchens in this collection. Having not heard of him until after his death (the same thing happened to me with David Foster Wallace), I watched countless video interviews of him in the throes of illness and they were sometimes a revelation because of the downright delicious acuity with which he could express his circumstances and in answer to an innocent question:

> *Christopher Hitchens:* How am I feeling? I'm on a slight sort of plateau at the moment. I'm the prisoner of chemotherapy, so everything depends on putting poison directly into my veins. So sometimes if I don't feel terrible, I think, "Damn, it's not working." You want to feel you're being poisoned because you want to feel that the enemy within is also feeling bad and feeling like giving up. So today I feel reasonably fit and secretly worried that I'd be better off feeling much worse. (Hitchens & Taylor, 2011)

In the following chapter, the moment of Hitchens' hesitation over an unfinished thought is a glimpse of trying to keep the world open and keep myself open to it. So the following reflection arises out of me being a writer and what it is like to stick with an ephemeral and lingering experience and betray but not betray it (see Chapter 9) with words: me "trying to write so that the *linger itself* will be a bit legible."

19

A Failed Attempt to Finish a Thought Left in Mid-Air by Christopher Hitchens (2015)

Banish all dismay, extinguish every sorrow.
If I'm lost or I'm forgiven, the birds will still be singing.
—Costello, 1993

It is an odd thing when something you read or hear actually *haunts* you and bids remembering, repeated thought and writing, especially when that thing is precisely about being haunted, in a certain way, about hesitating and staying one's actions. It is odd to have an idea, an image, an off-hand comment or a hunch stay with you despite its refusal to cede its secrets.

This is part of the practice of writing. Learning to let stay. It is an urgent patience, a weird joy.

The late Christopher Hitchens is well known enough for me to not pause for long over his work except to say that his adamant critiques of religion (Hitchens, 2008) and other forms of totalitarianism were complemented by the work of Richard Dawkins (2006) and Hitchens received, quite near his death, *The Richard Dawkins Award* at the 2011 *Texas Free*

In Praise of Radiant Beings, pages 271–275

Thought Convention, one of Hitchens' final public appearances. From that appearance:

> *Christopher Hitchens*: Some of you know, I suppose you all know now, that the words of one of my favorite poets Ernest Dowson are quite often with me. Dowson stole them actually from the Roman poet Horace: *Non sum qualis eram,* "I am not as I was."
>
> . . .
>
> In the meantime, we have the same job we've always had. There are no final solutions. There is no absolute truth. There is no supreme leader. There is no totalitarian solution that says "If you would just give up your freedom of inquiry, if you would simply abandon your critical faculties, a world of idiotic bliss can be yours." You will certainly lose the faculties, and you may not know as a result, that idiotic bliss is even more idiotic than it looks. But we have to begin by repudiating *all* such claims. Grand Rabbis, Chief Ayatollahs, infallible Popes, the peddlers of surrogate and mutant quasi-political religion and worship—the dear leader, the great leader, we have no need of any of this. And looking at them, and their record, and the pathos of their supporters, I realize that it is they who are the grand imposters, and my own imposture this evening was mild by comparison. (Godless UK, 2013)

The reason I mention the connection to Richard Dawkins in particular is because of what I find to be a still-amazing YouTube video clip of Hitchens and Douglas James Wilson (ObjectiveBob, 2010). Reverend Wilson is the pastor at Christ Church in Moscow, Idaho, and has had many intense and easily accessible public debates and talking-head news encounters with Hitchens. This clip is the final moments of a 2009 documentary *Collision: Christopher Hitchens vs. Douglas Wilson* (Documentaryondemand, 2013).

Wilson and Hitchens appear to be in the back seat of a car and Hitchens mentions how those (like himself) arguing against the Divine design of things still take seriously the hairsbreadth of (what he understands to be) happenstance of "the Goldilocks effect," of the Earth being *just right* in its relation to the Sun and its sustenance: "you have to spend time thinking about it, working on it. It's not a trivial [thing]" (ObjectiveBob, 2010).

Hitchens refers to having had a particular conversation with Richard Dawkins. Then this:

> *Christopher Hitchens*: . . . and then at one point. I think this is not on camera, I said, if I could convert every one in the world—not convert, if I could convince—to be a non-believer, and I'd really done brilliantly, and there's only one left. One more and then it would be done. There'd be no more religion in the world. No more deism, theism. [Pause]. I wouldn't do it. [Pause]. And Dawkins said, "What do you *mean* you wouldn't do it?" I said, "I don't quite

> know why I wouldn't do it." And it's not just because there'd be nothing left to argue and no one left to argue with. Not just *that.* Though it *would* be that. Somehow, if I could drive it out of the world, I wouldn't. And the incredulity with which he [Dawkins] looked at me stays with me still. I've got to say. (ObjectiveBob, 2010)

As with Dawkins' look of incredulity, this clip now stays with me.

Thoughts first about the aesthetic "punch" that we often feel when we read or hear something:

> The word for perception or sensation in Greek was *aesthesis,* which means at root a breathing in or taking in of the world, the gasp, "aha," the "uh" of the breath in wonder, shock, amazement, and aesthetic response. (Hillman, 2006a, p. 36)

Tersely put, this is the reason for all those drudgery pages in Hans-Georg Gadamer's *Truth and Method* (1989, pp. 42–100) and his attempts to rescue this phenomenon of aesthetic address (p. 299) from its tragic subjectivization and marginalization in our understanding of the experience of truth. This video hits me still, and when I quickly re-created Hitchens' words for my son over the holidays just passed, all he said was "Yep."

Me too. I wouldn't do it. And "it would not deserve the interest [I] take in it if it did not have something to teach [me] that [I] could not know by [my]sel[f]" (Gadamer, 1989, p. xxxv).

But at first (and still), I just *suspected* this might be so, and Hitchens did, too, in a way. He himself remembered and retold this story and told it, as you can see in the video, with the sly grin of suspecting there's something to it. A kind of Coyote grin, a bit self-satisfied, a bit expectant, a bit joyous. Were it just a subjective incident with no loft or pitch to it beyond "moist gastric intimacy" (Sartre, 1970, p. 4), re-telling it seems very odd; sheer self-indulgence and entertainment. On the face of it at least, this isn't that.

Why do we re-tell? Trying, perhaps, to work it out or, better, to see if something works out if you work it a bit: "Something awakens our interest" (Gadamer, 2001, p. 50). "Something is going on, (*im Spiele ist*), something is happening (*sich abspielt*)" (Gadamer, 1989, p. 104). A clue, then, to Gadamer's (1989, p. 101 ff.) deep interest in (what is at) play (*Spiel*) (and, I guess, in my interest in that Hitchens video). *Something is going on.*

I suspect.

So then the risk you run as a writer: *maybe not,* but only staying put will prove the case for good or ill. Then there is that sort-of hoarder/gatherer/rummager thing that writers do—me, with this clip, saving it, transcribing it, wanting to remember it, telling people about it. There is something here that I need to keep with me, something of the way this idea hangs in the air, somehow, and then, too, of what this hesitation means. Lord knows I've tried: Compassion? Sympathy? Extinction? Like saving a rare bird? Knowing that if no one now *believes* these religious texts they quote, if no one adores these images and ideas, then something is perhaps irretrievably lost? Loss of "the other" as a loss of oneself? Levinas and the horror of facing the last face? Pity? That it would say something too much, too unbearable of me should I proceed? What about the second-last believer?

Bluntly put, yuck to all this.

And hence the irony, that many drafts of writing have been deleted and these deletions seem to have simply increased the glowing attraction of this clip. "[It] compels over and over, and the better one knows it, the *more* compelling it is. This is not a matter of mastering an area of study" (Gadamer, 2007e, p. 115).

This is why, as a writer, I have repeatedly found that it is not just a matter of paying patient attention to the world—to little happenings-by like this clip—but doing so *as if* I will be answerable *in writing* to such things as arrive in (and, I must say, in part *because of*) such patient attending. *That* prospect—of being answerable in writing—intensifies attention in a most delicious way.

And then comes the odd hermeneutic fidelity of trying to not betray this hovering linger of words and images and appeal and grins, but trying to keep it safe, trying to let it stand in itself, in its own repose. And then that impossible task, of trying to write so that *the linger itself* will be a bit legible in what I then write. The task of hermeneutic writing is to not fall for the falsehood that this lingering is an error that writing might fix. It is, rather, a truth that unfixes writing, makes it loft and swerve and exaggerate unpinned. This, of course, is why hermeneutic research is always prone to the writer's indulgences. The aim of writing is not giving myself free rein (Latin *indulgere*) but giving *this* free rein by finding what of *this* can be eked out in words: "I wouldn't do it."

"What do you mean you wouldn't do it?" *I don't know what I mean.* Maybe that just attests to the deeply buried hermeneutic assertion, that its work is not about what people or texts or things or signs *mean*, but about what might happen if they were true. "It is only when the attempt to accept what is said as true fails that we try to "understand" the text... as another's opinion" (Gadamer, 1989, p. 294).

"A text is not understood as a mere expression of life but is taken seriously in its claim to truth" (p. 297).

In remembering, repeating and caring for this chance little clip, it serves as a sort of sentinel waiting for an arrival that would bespeak its good sense. It is as if this tale itself provides a way to remain alert to the day-to-day events that come and go, *as if it is waiting for its own reprieve*, waiting to be called for, waiting to be recognized by some kin of the world—the off-hand event or bit of reading or news story or gesture of a child in a Grade One class, that will summon it, finally, to be what it is. I'm waiting for it to lift off my shoulders in a flight of its own, this sorrow.

Told and retold in almost ritual repetitions, worrying over bones or the great and ancient monastic murmuring of texts out loud and under the breath, seeking the truth of what it repeats, seeks its redemption in words. Monkish practices of scholarship.

Telling and re-telling are attempts to let it find its freedom from my own obsessive remembering of it within the confines of a life whose imposture is both too great and too small by itself to think this through.

Writing this aims to free me from it and to free it from me.

"The aim of interpretation, it could be said, is not just another interpretation but human freedom" (Smith, 1999c, p. 29).

To face these fleeting things and try to entail them with the right attention, the right affection, with a devotion that is not about deepening the attachments of believing (the first steps towards totalitarian solutions [see Jardine, 2015]) but the wonder that just might turn attachment into love.

The staying of Hitchens' words in the face the last person to be convinced is the same stay as the pleasure over not quite knowing why.

However, I don't quite know why.

PREAMBLE **20**

"These Things Are Fantastic"

One: "There Will Never Be a Time"

> **Berry:** A lot of my writing has been, when it hasn't been in defense of precious things, has been a giving of thanks for precious things.
>
> **Moyers:** What are the precious things that you think are in danger right now?
>
> **Berry:** It is might hard right now to think of anything that is precious that isn't in danger. But maybe that's an advantage. The poet William Butler Yeats said somewhere "Things reveal themselves passing away." And it may be that the danger that we have inflicted on every precious thing reveals the preciousness of it and shows us our duty. (Berry & Moyers, 2013)

This final chapter, along with an invitation from the editors of this series, is, in fact, where the impetus for this retrospective collection began. And this passage from William Bulter Yeats, "Things reveal themselves passing away," (Yeats, 2010, p. 297) bespeaks how this whole arc of work is, in part, a sort of soft and coddled lamentation. I say coddled because there is no shadow of a doubt that I've been able to live a life of leisure and

In Praise of Radiant Beings, pages 277–287

opportunity in relative opulence, safety, indulgence, and lovely affection. Still, it is odd to note that this is a lament, in part, for my own passing that has swirled nearby of late. But again, I'm coddled, because I'm hale, for now.

But this nearing flight has showed me my duty, to consider this passing before it overwhelms and frightens me too much, or before sorrow or pain outrun my ability to compose myself.

Practice now, here and here, over this and this, while I have a bit of a chance, a nick in time. Practice over smaller passings so that I can become familiar with passing itself, befriending it a wee bit. But again, in mundane ways, with student teacher in a Grade Five classroom, full of worried mulling over lunch hour regarding multiplying by fractions and feeling at a dead end as to what to say.

"They don't get it."

I drew him back to talking as elaborately as possible about what you are actually doing when you multiply, say, 6 times 5. Back on more familiar ground, but still, stumble, because this ground has not been cultivated of late and is so very familiar that its arising is concealed. It has become reified, hardened into a burp-like utterance of "30" that so quickly rears up that sitting and thinking becomes like chipping cement.

Slowly. "You have six five times."

"Yes. Okay, so, six times one-half?" Cement. Chip. Chip.

"You don't even have it once!" and the rush of cool air inside this stuffy classroom is palpable. "You only have it half a time!" Whew, yes, and slowly the restlessness becomes irrelevant as the field becomes richer and more abundant, but, of course, it is always ready to rear at a moment's notice.

"Geshe Drom-don-ba asked Jen-nga, 'Are you mindful that you have a human life endowed with leisure and opportunity?'" (Tsong-kha-pa, 2000, p. 121). Well, yes and no. Woven in here is this retrospective feeling of having started too late, having been too timid, waited too long, fallen prey too easily and too often to too many distractions and temptations. And this is mixed with the strange feeling that whatever meagre insights I've gleaned are now clearly and undeniably parcelled up in inevitably failing flesh.

They always were.

"There will never be a time your life span does not diminish" (Tsong-kha-pa, 2000, p. 152), so relax, everything's not going to be okay. Hah. Because at the very same time, multiplying by fractions gets more and more undiminished.

Where have I been and what so urgent has been burning up this time? Actually facing this is what makes any of this insightful at all, however small and fleet. I feel, finally, on the verge of revealing myself passing away and facing whether anything precious might linger. But then this:

> [Nagarjuna's] *Friendly Letter* says:
>
> > Life is more impermanent than a water bubble
> > Batter by the winds of many perils.
> > Thus, that you can inhale after exhaling,
> > Or awaken from sleep—these things are fantastic.
>
> (Tsong-kha-pa, 2000, p. 156)

These things are fantastic, these fractions and numbers, this hard-won pronunciation, in the text chapter, of the name of a book by a Grade One child, where our small sufferings over them toughen our ability to carry on.

Right here, "where it seems impossible that one life even matters" (Wallace, 1987, p. 111), is the locale of practice. It is not a grand venture, this.

"As practitioners carry on their journey, they are preparing the road. Practitioners are not only journeyers, but they are also road builders" (Trungpa, 2013, p. 56–57). That is why this idea of a "hitherto concealed experience" has gained a certain urgency as my time passes, because the path it lays out must rip its way out of my flesh and leave it behind. "[Conceiving] the impermanent to be permanent is the avenue of much injury. You will continue to think that you will remain in this life" (Tsong-kha-pa, 2000, p. 145), and that thought of continuance and the fear of the open (of that rush of cool air) causes retraction and hunkering down into a rule that can be simply fixed in memory and applied without thinking, and we end up with the spaciousness of *schola* replaced with something that "causes much injury." It is why, repeatedly, when I would begin on-campus curriculum classes by writing "mathematics" on the board, I would turn back to the class to find tears. The capitalized Mathematics must be killed off, this monster beckoning the (actually false, actually delusional) relief of the fixed rules of its monstrous governance that ask only for submission and offer only punishment, caught in "the lonely school room, where on the sometimes tearful wicked say over undone sums" (Thomas, 1967, p. 13; see Jardine with Friesen, 1997). Teaching (*monere*) as punishment.

To experience *this* insight—hitherto concealed by cement of our own mixed, feeling real because of our feeling that we might not inhale if we dare exhale—as a relief is where the work lies. In breaking out into the open, the rules, of course, don't disappear. They reappear back in place, in proper proportion to this living field, wherein recourse to them becomes simply possible, occasionally useful, and so on. This is why I always encourage students to write, to publish, because leaving behind trace-lines of this work gives others a weird sort of example and permission. It builds a path out in the open, in public, in view. It builds a *Sangha* of sorts, a gathering of like-mindedness which provides its own sort of refuge.

Two: "Down in the Weeds"

There is a wonderful video conversation between Canadian environmentalist David Suzuki, James Hoggan, the Chair of the David Suzuki Foundation, and Vietnamese monk Thich Nhat Hanh (David Suzuki Foundation, 2011). They are discussing how, as the YouTube video title suggest, how to not let despair take over in our considerations and actions regarding the environment:

> **James Hoggan:** When the public is misinformed, and doesn't think that a problem is a problem, then it is very difficult for leaders to lead. David, I know that you speak out all the time about this.
>
> **David Suzuki:** We have the vote, and we can vote on the basis of these needs. The problem is that a lot of us aren't voting in Canada, but also that the discussion in Canada is down in the weeds. We're not having that discussion at that high level, and down in the weeds is where you get all kinds of confusion and the opportunity for mischief on the part of, often, the corporate sector.

My affection for David Suzuki is boundless, but, too, my frustration with his frustration and panic is important for me to name.

I often find that the energetics of his concern over "The Environment" (this capitalization is intentional) have the same shape as the energetics of those panicking over wanting to keep the engines of the market place in place. Both are based on the belief that if we do the right things, everything will be saved:

> As if swept away by the current of a river you will be immersed in a strong hostility toward what prevented you or what you fear might prevent you from having these objects of attachment. (Tsong-kha-pa, 2000, p. 145)

I watch and re-watch this video from down in the weeds, waiting for Thich Nhat Hanh's soft, urgent reply:

Thich Nhat Hanh: We have to accept that this civilization can be destroyed, not by something outside, but by ourselves. In fact, many civilizations have been destroyed in the past. So it's very important, our mental formations, our minds. I think if we allow despair to take over, we have no strength left over in order to do anything at all. And that is why we should do anything at all to prevent despair from happening, including mediation. So when we meditate on civilizations that have been destroyed in the past, and if we accept, we can have peace and become a better worker for the environment. Because people who know what is happening but allow it to happen and cannot do anything—there's so many of them so many, so many of them, because they have despair in them and they try only to survive. If we can help them to sort out the inside, help them to have hope, to have peace in themselves, then suddenly they have the strength to come back to themselves.

Ah, meant as an exhalation of insight and grief and relief all at once. *Of course our civilization will not last.* All the work I've done in schools with teachers and students has drifted. It has fallen apart here, only to arise anew there, coming, going. It is not just mischief on the part of those in power (although it's sometimes surely that), but in the nature of human effort, that we do what we can to lift confusion and name the mischief, but these efforts cannot "Save The Environment" any more than they can "Improve Schools." "There [are] no such thing[s]," Graham McCaffrey reminds me (see Preamble 15) and when we reify their existence and act in accord with the outcome of that reification, despair, exhaustion, and defeat are inevitable. We can only, here, now, in the weeds, momentarily clear the air and clear our minds, adore this little event in a classroom and give it the care, attention and devotion it needs, encourage others to do so, too, and love them for doing so. We can also stand by as an example of what is possible but never necessary.

Coming back to myself, I'm reminded of the adage from environmentalism, to think globally and act locally. No. The really tough work is to *think locally* and not let one's concern for "The Whole" give rise to monstrosities of our own making that deflect attention away from what is to be done, towards an in-fact-imaginary, monstrous, blare-trumpeted What Is To Be Done. That child's tough work of pronouncing words in the next chapter can be thought about deeply and entered into as a living field *only* once and if the monster of "Literacy" is killed. Don't disparage the weeds. There is great, perhaps greater mischief "at that high level":

> **David Suzuki:** So, in accepting the reality that this could very well end disastrously does not mean that one retreats to become passive. One can remain active, but with that acceptance. (David Suzuki Foundation, 2011)

I'm going to push this. Only when we accept the reality that this *will* end disastrously and then, perhaps, will rise up again—"everything around us teaches impermanence" (Tsong-kha-pa, 2000, p. 151)—is that acceptance fulfilled and effective work possible. Otherwise, we are gradually paralyzed by our own false hope.

Three: Generation Stage Meditation

> In this game nobody is above and before all the others; everybody is at the centre, is "it" in this game. Thus it is always his turn to be interpreting. (Gadamer, 1977, p. 32)

Tsong-kha-pa's grand, three volume work, *The Great Treatise on the Stages of the Path to Enlightenment* (2000, 2002, 2004) name lays out a pattern of meditations and courses of study that are both a reiteration of and reiterated upon a sequence of *paramitas*, aspired to "perfections" that draw out a path to be taken. They are to be read as practices to be taken up, not knowledge to be amassed. This path involves cultivating that acceptance mentioned by Thich Nhat Hanh, as well as cultivating the ability to stay put with one's attention and dig down into arising phenomena, parsing out their relations, breaking up the reifications you encounter out into all their relations.

That acceptance and the work of interpretation that follows is, as the next chapter details, an ontological matter of accepting that, in the language of hermeneutics, the Being of myself, of others, and of objects and topics and terrains and civilizations and ideas and images, is that of impermanence, of an emptiness of a solid, isolated, self-existence, of "substance" no matter how conceived.

But that acceptance is also, shall we say, an ontic practice, of taking this ontological insight in hand when considering, for example, "silent reading" in schools, or perusing the Periodic Table. These particular objects of consideration are empty of self-existence and *therefore* are dependently co-arising and therefore those cascading and abundant threads of dependent co-arising can be known, and in knowing them, the emptiness of the self-existence of *this* become intimately experience-able, knowable, learnable, teachable. In fact, what might seem like a terribly arcane insight becomes, shall we say, profoundly mundane. Things are full of relations. This is the great act of application in hermeneutic work:

> Tsong-kha-pa does say, earlier in the text, that "those who have developed the... spirit of enlightenment and [thus] aspire [to it], although they lack its application, still 'shine'" (2004, p. 16). I think, with student teachers for example, who sometimes desperately ask where to begin, of how *taking on the spirit of interpretability* is the key (Tsong-kha-pa calls this "aspiration"). It means, simply put, proceeding in light of an understanding of the interpretability of the world, seeking those dependent co-arisings that surround things, and resisting the logic of substance (Gadamer, 1989, p. 242) and the temptations of reification (Tsong-kha-pa, 2002, p. 120), both of which aim to suppress the uprisings of the world and seek false permanencies in this, the deeply human land of shadow. Even if you have not often practiced the application of such a spirit and have not therefore, built up the composures of practice, still, it is in this spirit that one proceeds in the repeated practice of application. Again, however, the repeated practice of application is essential: "if you have only an intellectual understanding of this spirit, then you likewise have only an intellectual understanding of what it means to be a... practitioner" (p. 17). It is always this child's life, that parent's woes, this client's nightmare, that patient's desire to let go in the face of impending death that is key. Interpretation always requires doing the work again in the face of the task we face. (Jardine, 2013, pp. 2–3)

It is the great conundrum of pedagogy itself, a great danger that this very book I'm compiling is subject to:

> It is an extremely important point. If you train in [what is being discussed here about interrelatedness and so on] without distinguishing and taking up specific objects... but only using a general object from the outset, you will just seem to generate these attitudes. Then, when you try to apply them to specific individuals, you will not be able to actually generate these attitudes toward anyone [or any thing]. But once you have a transformative experience towards an individual in your... practice... you may then gradually increase the number of individuals you visualize within your meditation. (Tsong-kha-pa, 2004, p. 35)

This is why, with student-teachers, we can go through the exercise of multiplying by fractions, but then, they are asked to "teach a lesson on commas" and they are faced, at first, with precisely the same kind of hard, unyielding, cement wall. The unraveling of threads has to be done all over again. This is why it is good to hear that:

> The more you practice these things, the more accustomed your mind will be- come to them, and the easier it will be to practice what you had initially found difficult to learn. (Tsong-kha-pa, 2000, pp. 185–186)

With all this, we're right back to some of those early explorations of analogical language discussed in Preamble and Chapter 1:

> To understand the analogical term, therefore, is not a matter of it "condensing, unifying" (Hillman, 1983, p. 51). We must allow it, rather, "to expand to its full analogous breadth of illuminative meaning" (Norris-Clarke, 1976, p. 72). Only in such breadth do all the lines and threads of sustenance come forth. In this way, the profound and essential disorientation begins: the full, "whole" [careful!] meaning of the analogical term . . . *is* its full breadth of interweaving meanings and interrelationships. The doors . . . are therefore *not shut* [think of that open field around that restless cow] Moreover, "whenever [such an analogical term] tries to become too precise, it contracts to become identical with just one of its modes and loses its analogical function" (Norris-Clarke, 1976, pp. 69–70) [think here, then, about the hostilities that arise when such contractions occur, how this becomes a state of war, or a war over how to teach the multiplication of fractions, or learning to read, and so on]. (Jardine, 1992, pp. 303–304)

W. Norris-Clarke (1976, p. 67) actually provides a wonderful image of what understanding, say, the efforts of pronunciation might mean under such auspices. It doesn't mean definitively naming what is self-identical at the centre of all the cases that arise and under which all cases then "fall," but rather "running up and down the known range of cases to which it applies, by actually calling up the spectrum of *different* exemplifications, and then *catching the point*." I'll have more to say on this image below.

So the six *paramitas* detailed by Tsong-kha-pa are directed in a double way, towards the insight into emptiness and impermanence and towards the studious (Tsong-kha-pa, 2000, p. 61) focussing of attention on the "stubborn particulars of grace" (Wallace, 1987). Generosity (Tsong-kha-pa, 2004, pp. 113–142), ethical discipline (pp. 143–150), patience (pp. 151–180), perseverance (pp. 181–208), meditative stillness or serenity (2002, pp. 13–106) and wisdom (pp. 107–350) are all considered in great detail here and in other texts that predate (e.g., Atisha [b. India 982] 1997, Shantideva [b India 8th century CE] 2006) or follow in this lineage (Patrul [b. Tibet 1808] 1998, Pelden [b. Tibet 1862] 2007, Pelzang [b. Tibet 1879] 2004, Pabongka [b. Tibet 1878] 2006, Sopa [b Tibet 1923] 2004, 2005, 2008, Yangsi [b. Nepal 1968] 2003, Dorje [b Tibet 1904] 2011, to name a scant few).

There are two other forms of meditative practice—commonly called the "generation or creation stage" and the "completion stage"—that are commented on by Tsong-kha-pa (2005) and others (Dorje, 2011, Kongtrul, 2002, and the collection by Lingpa, Patrul & Mahapandita, 2006, and many more). It is the first of these, also called the development stage, that provided me with not only an extension of these six *paramita* steps, but a crystallization that helped me understand this invocation of Gadamer's of a "hitherto concealed experience that transcends thinking from the position of subjectivity."

My hesitancy in all this must be put foursquare and plainly. I'm in over my head, here, and understand why Hermes appears as a thief. I won't even begin to talk of what is called, in this text, the Completion Stage, because it is, frankly, beyond me. But there is something of this Generation Stage that rings back into my work in schools and highlights something of the glow that comes from scholarship and careful attention to particulars. It is about cultivating, as Thich Nhat Hanh put it, the "strength to come back to myself." It is about, in effect, a way to meditate upon not only myself but things in the world in a way that invokes the experience of "running up and down the known range of cases," of experiencing the ecopedagogical surrounded-ness of things in a vivid, practical way—empty of self-existence and therefore abundantly, radiantly full of relations in a way that can be immediately *experienced.*

"The technique has the power to purify from within the mind the mundane presence of the conventional world" (Tsong-kha-pa, 2005, p. 125). What is this mundane presence? It is the common way in which we experience things and selves as separate entities, each bounded within itself and only striking up "relations" subsequent to this ontological self-existence (see the discussion in the following chapter regarding Edmund Husserl's "Ur-Doxa"—a founding belief that underlies everyday life).

What does this technique effect in us regarding this common presumption? The ability to experience ourselves and things in the world in a way already encountered countless times in this collection: "Within each dust mote is vast abundance" (Hongzhi, 1991, p. 14).

However, the way this technique is described is troublesome but I believe, worthy of seeing through. First, a reciting of two passages by Keiji Nishitani cited above way back in Chapter 1:

> All things in the world are linked together, one way or the other. Not a single thing comes into being without some relationship to every other thing. (Nishitani, 1982, p. 149)
>
> The center is everywhere. (p. 146).

And then this from Hans-Georg-Gadamer:

> *Everything* points to some other thing. ["everything is dependent on something else, and because that in turn is dependent, it is not autonomous" (Tsong-kha-pa 2004, p. 162]. Nothing comes forward just in the one meaning that is offered to us. Only because the universal relatedness of being is

> concealed from the human eye does it need to be discovered. (Gadamer, 2007c, p. 131)

So, generation stage meditation can be understood as a practice directed towards this discovery. It involves picturing myself, as well as picturing every entity I encounter (even that small event, in the next chapter, of a young child working to sound out some words), *as a deity sitting in the middle of a mandala.*

Okay, stop. It is very hard work to get over the rather occult-sounding gloss here, and it must be broken open. The very idea of picturing yourself (or anything else, for that matter) as a deity sitting in the middle of a mandala seems to hysterically distend and Capitalize precisely "the position of Subjectivity," now deigned an impenetrable, imperturbable god of some sort.

However, in this context, "deity" invokes, not, as per Western conceptions of divinity, some solid permanence in the middle of things or in the sky overlooking things. In Tibetan thought, to reiterate, "*everything* around us teaches impermanence" (Tsong-kha-pa, 2000, p. 151, emphasis added):

> These radiant beings, their bodies shining with light, their voices clear and soft, their minds limpid and free of stain, were as firm and stable as diamond yet they all passed, and even their teachings have gradually disappeared. (Dorje, 2011, p. 75).

> The protectors of the world—Brahma, Ishvara, Vishnu, Indra,—fill the world with great beams of light and are brighter than a thousand suns. Their majesty and merit are renowned through all the heavens and the earth. They are the lords of all worlds—subterranean, earthly, and heavenly,—adorned with the greatest fortune. And yet for them too the time will come to die. (pp. 75–76)

So this invocation of picturing deities is picturing radiance rather than eternal and/or elevated permanence. And this picturing of radiance is picturing how this or that particular idea, image, event, occurrence, gesture, word, and thought, properly treated, "lights up" its patterned surroundings. So "deity," there, should be thought of more like a Greek icon, something to be seen through, not to be looked at with a gaze that would solidify and reify it.

> Upon one particle there are buddhas as numerous as the
> Particles of those world, and
> All are seated in the midst of their children. (Tsong-kha-pa, 2000, p. 95)

Look, there, how pedagogy is hinted at, sitting in the midst of our children. And, then, the twist: *everything* has Buddha-nature, and Buddha-nature means, not fixed divinity in some particular personage, but the experience of radiant surroundedness that is the nature of all things. That is what the "sitting in the middle of a mandala" is meant to invoke—surrounded by our children, surrounded by our ancestors and relations, human and more-than-human, sentient and non-sentient, because even this snowfall today, November 2, 2015, has occluded that lingering smell of forest decay from a long and drawn out and dry Fall season, which itself summons the turning of the sun downwards, the last tomatoes in only last week from the greenhouse, the great bear ambled by weeks ago. Fields of relations, summoning me to sit in its midst and study how my self empties out into it and passes away into its light, its lightness.

Even that scent of decay *is* its surroundings if we treat it properly, according to its (not) being what it is(n't). That scent, properly experienced for what it *is*, is radiant. It *is* its full illuminative breadth. It is a great *topic* for a classroom; that smell. A wonderfully gross path for a Grade Five class, I'd say, in which the passing of solstice arrives, the turnings of Tropics, how fields are prepared for the fallow, right here, in Alberta, how we prepare ourselves to go "indoors" as the light lessens this far north. A Great Assembly of Beings, this.

I suggest that this exercise of picturing yourself and the things you encounter as a deity sitting in the middle of a mandala, confirms a most commonplace, but often concealed, experience: look at this stack of blocks piled in the preschool block center, the proportions, the balancing. Look. My only caution is this: you don't need to *believe* this, because the machinations of believing are not needed. It is a game, a practice, of experiencing the game we're part of. Back, then, to Alan Watts, it seems, and picturing a God that "*plays* the world from the inside" (1970, p. 16), but *only* if this helps me remember that there is no such a Thing.

Four: "This Means You!"

One last little note in ending. After all these years of studying reading and writing, all these visits to school classrooms, reading books to young children—after all that, this smallest of events of pronunciation, arrives, bursting full, with my name on it and shedding light all over me:

> The intimacy with which [this event] . . . touches us is at the same time, in enigmatic fashion, a shattering and demolishing of the familiar. It is not only the impact of a 'this means you!' ['Das bist du!'] that is disclosed in a joyous and frightening shock. It also says to us: "You must change your life!" (Gadamer, 2007c, p. 131)

It has changed my life even though I don't believe a word of it.

20

In Praise of Radiant Beings (2014)

A Preambling Couplet

"To hold that the world is eternal" the Buddha declared, "... is the jungle of theorizing, the wilderness of theorizing, the tangle of theorizing, the bondage and the shackles of theorizing, attended by illness, distress, perturbation, and fever." It is important to assimilate this passage in its entirety. It points to a reality that transcends ordinary thought but is nevertheless still knowable. To say that it is possible to know something that is beyond thought carries the important, indeed astonishing implication, that *there is in the mind a dimension that in the vast majority of living beings is wholly concealed, the existence of which is not even suspected.* (Blankelder & Fletcher, 2002, p. 9, emphasis added)

We will have to hold firmly to the standpoint of finiteness. [This] does not mean that [the human subjectivity] is radically temporal, so that it can no longer be considered as everlasting or eternal but is understandable only in relation to its own time and future. If this were its meaning, it would not be a critique and an overcoming of subjectivism, but an "existentialist" radicalization of it. The ... question involved here ... is directed precisely at this subjectivism itself. The latter is driven to its furthest point only in order to question it. In disclosing time as the ground hidden from [subjective] self-understanding

In Praise of Radiant Beings, pages 289–306

> it...opens itself *to a hitherto concealed experience that transcends thinking from the position of subjectivity.* (Gadamer, 1989, pp. 99–100, emphasis added).

"Even There"

> *Kai enthautha,* "even here," at the stove, in that ordinary place where every thing and every condition, each deed and thought is intimate and commonplace, "even there" *einai theous,* "the gods themselves are present." (Heidegger, 1977a, p. 234)

Spending time in schools where good work is being done has become increasing hard for me to bear, not because of something negative (this, of course, has often taken its own toll) but because of something profoundly positive and nearly unutterable. There is a practice at the heart of hermeneutic work (a practice shared in various and varying ways with ecological awareness and threads of Buddhist philosophy and practice) that results, mostly gradually, but sometimes suddenly and without warning, in the ability to intimately and immediately experience the dependently co-arising (Sanskrit: *pratitya-samutpada*) reality of things, ideas, word, selves, gestures, actions.

With deliberate practice, this ability, "hitherto concealed" by distraction and grasping at straws, builds, and as it builds, so too the build of the world and its ways (Dharma) flutters open and its interdependencies become more and more experienceable (a process parallel to Hans-Georg Gadamer's work [1989, pp. 9–18] on the old German idea of *Bildung,* where "becoming experienced" leads to an *increasing* susceptibility and vulnerability in one's ability to experience of the fabrics and textures of the world) more and more *loveable* "despite all my revulsions over its ugliness and injustice, and my bitterness over defeat at its hands" (Hillman, 2006f, p. 128).

"Even here," "not even suspected," the very tiniest and most meager of things, with experience and practice, can come to be experienced in beautiful repose.

Ah! Wabi Sabi

What is of concern here in this chapter is something extremely simple, but it is a simplicity in which is concealed something miraculous which, when it appears, is often treated too casually, laughed off in ways that do not recognize the deep aesthetic truth that comes when the breath halts and the body leans over laughter.

Consider: When a young child tips forward into a word and finds herself struggling to sound it out, humming and murmuring over its sonority and the ancient, specific, detailed links lurking there with the look of its letters, its words, its spaces, tossing it around her tongue and breath, tripping unknowingly over all those old mongrel roots of English, all inbred and tangled together and pushing and pulling of attention this way and that, perhaps not yet sensing the haunting presence of such forgotten ancestors and ancestries that are ripe and ready to be known even though we can get along quite famously in sheer ignorance of their life and lives. This simple act of pronunciation is at once the most ordinary of classroom events and a great, roiling thing, a great nexus full of the "silence of a world turning" (Domanski, 2002, p. 245).

And then suddenly, yes!

Pronounced.

This word and *that* sit ready to be carried up out of the dust of written letters and outwards on the voice, held up on great pillars of breath, enspirited ("*aesthesis*, which means at root a breathing in . . . of the world, the gasp, 'aha,' the uh' of the breath in wonder . . . and aesthetic response" [Hillman, 2006a, p. 36] and at once conspiratorial (Illich, 1998) because here I am, sit squat beside her in breathless anticipation of utterance.

"All writing is a kind of alienated speech, and its signs need to be transformed back into speech. This transformation is the real hermeneutical task" (Gadamer, 1989, p. 393).

Ah!

So *this* is what those words speak. *Wabi Sabi* (Reibstein & Young, 2008), that wandering cat off to find what her name means through the scrolling pages of this picture book. That young child's finger now pointing to the great, collaged images on the page, and then back to the cover, her hand rubbing its rough smoothness, and then, with the sound and the sight of this name now lodged in memory, safe for now in their keep, the story then continues to unfold, her smiling and pointing, me nodding in agreement, after all that tough and fruitful work along this book's path. And this young child's eye has ripened in its ability to scan the clusters of scrolling text for this cat's name's next appearance.

I have seen this so many times, such small events that have never happened before, here, now. "So that . . . sitting there, listening like that, becomes part of the story too," (Wallace, 1987, p. 47), me, a reader, having learned to read, having read countlessly about reading and its varying courses of ancient emergence, having been in hundreds of classrooms and felt this halt of breath over and over and over again, the life-breath of sounding out, as if the whole of the language itself depends for its very continuance, its very life, on this next moment's precarious venture. Again, and again, "where it seems impossible that one life even matters" (Wallace, 1987, p. 111), a small, simple, innocuous event that could easily be deemed perfectly trivial in the grand scheme of things becomes experienced as sitting in the center of worlds of relations, a residence, a "housing" (*ecos*). Right there in the very ordinariness and mundaneness of this event ("right now... *this*" [Wallace, 1987, p. 111]) we become huddled near the living origin of language itself, the very moment of its (oddly old-yet-brand-new, all at once) emergence, sustenance and survival. In this way, as a teacher, and in this smallest of examples, I get to be present as the world of language is being "set right anew" (Arendt, 1969, p. 197), right before my eyes and ears, revived, saved from its mortal lot just in the nick of time.

This sort of experience has become, for me, a simply *miraculous* thing to be around, something almost unbearable in its countenance. What is most deeply experienced here is the lovely, hearty frailness of these strange human ventures of reading, of speaking, of voice and utterance, and how the ancients in all human traditions have gathered around such ventures, most often unheralded and forgotten, and in myriad ways. They, too, are right "even here" in this act of breath, this pronunciation, holding their breath and ours in anticipation.

Hermeneutics and threads of the Gelug tradition of Tibetan Buddhism provide, in very different guises and for similar but still different motives, ways to articulate this kind of conspiratorial and deeply pedagogical experience of the world. Both detail how this way of experiencing the world can be cultivated through long and difficult practice ("one must learn how" [Gadamer, 2007b, p. 217]). They also share something of an *ontological theory* that attests to the reality of these experiences of dependent co-arising.

Both bespeak a "wisdom [which] thoroughly discerns *the ontological status of the object under analysis*" (Tsong-kha-pa, 2004, p. 211). The tough work of these scholarly traditions and practices helps keep at bay the commonplace trivializing of these experiences. The interlacing kinships between Gadamerian hermeneutics and the Gelug lineage of Tibetan Buddhism provide ways to elaborate what has become, for me, an elusive yet familiar experience in the haunts of schools, ways to remain with and true to these experiences.

"Protodoxa (Urdoxa)"

> To realize the full import of dependent-arising, namely that all phenomena are empty of inherent existence, is an extremely forceful experience that reorients one in the very depths of one's being. (Lobsang, 2006, p. 51)
>
> By virtue of repeated practice, you become free of your dysfunctional tendencies, undergoing a fundamental transformation. (Tsong-kha-pa, 2002, p. 36).
>
> Indeed, this true mode must include . . . a conversion of the standpoint of Reason. (Nishitani, 1982, p. 117)
>
> Perhaps it will become manifest that the total phenomenological attitude [is] destined in essence to effect, at first, a complete personal transformation, comparable in the beginning to a religious conversion. (Husserl, 1970b, p. 137).
>
> An *inner transformation.* (Husserl, 1970b, p. 100)

One element of Hans-Georg Gadamer's philosophical hermeneutics is an *ontological insight* into how things, ideas, images, and selves *exist,* their manner of Being. This insight is in lineage back through the work of Martin Heidegger and is rooted in the work of their teacher, Edmund Husserl, the "father" of contemporary phenomenology.

This ontological insight involves a *critique of substance*—an age-old idea that runs back through the work of Descartes (1955, p. 255) in the 1600s and is rooted in Aristotelian ontology: "a substance is that which requires nothing except itself in order to exist." Under such an auspice, any thing, image, idea, concept, object, or self *is what it is independently of anything else. To be* something real is *to be* separate, substantive, and independent, a "permanent, unitary and autonomous entit[y]" (Yangsi, 2003, p. 241), something thus "inherently self-existing" (Tsong-kha-pa, 2002, p. 120). To understand anything in the world (like that young child's efforts at pronouncing that new name found in a new book) is to separate it off from everything else. We must adopt a "reifying view" (Tsong-kha-pa, 2002, p. 120) regarding the ontological status of the thing being experienced: whatever this thing is, *it is what it is,* and it is not something else. Simple. We may not know *what* it is, *why* it is thus or *how it came to be* thus, but we know, with this reifying view, *that* it is what it is. So if we have no specific knowledge of it at all and it is simply some unknown "X," we *do* know that, whatever this "X" turns out to be, "X = X."

To use the language of Edmund Husserl's phenomenology (1969, p. 106), we may have doubts about this thing but, despite all this trepidation, "the 'it' remains ever in the sense of a general thesis, a world that has its being 'out there.'" Husserl (p. 169) called this the "general thesis of the natural attitude." It is, as he suggested, not simply one belief among others, but *the* founding belief of the commonplace way in which, "in everyday life our minds apprehend [things] as existing" (Yangsi, 2003, p. 200). Husserl (1969, p. 300) named this "the *primary belief* (*Urglaube*) or *Protodoxa* (*Urdoxa*)" of the natural attitude. Note, however, that *in* the natural attitude, this Urdoxa is understood to be precisely *not* "a belief" but simply "the way things are." It is assumed and projected as an ontological "given" against which our everyday experience of the world is to be understood. This is the odd breakthrough of Husserlian phenomenology, unearthing this Urdoxa as a thesis *of* the natural attitude that does not appear *as* a thesis *in* our ordinary experience of the world. This thesis thus describes the founding yet concealed and unquestioned prejudice of everyday life.

Within this (as Buddhism would have it, false or delusional) *belief*, "the essence of truth is identity" (Heidegger, 1978, p. 39), and the formal consort of this presumption of identity is the mathematical and formal logic principle of identity (X = X). This thus links up the possibility of *understanding* the substance/reality of things with logico-mathematically based, natural-scientific methodologies, concepts and categories. Since the thing itself is what it is (X = X), *knowledge of that thing* must itself have precisely such clarity and distinctness borne of one thing separated off from another.

"Break Open the Being of the Object"

> Because this causes living beings to be confused in their view of the actual state of things, it is a delusion; ignorance mistakenly superimposes upon things an essence that they do not have. It is constituted so as to block perception of their nature. It is a concealer. (Tsong-kha-pa, 2002, p. 208)

The hermeneutic critique of the dominance of natural-scientific methodologies sits squarely here, on a critique of the idea of substance—this concealed Urdoxic belief in separate and inherent self-existence (Sanskrit *svabhava*) as a formulation for how things exist. Gadamer (1989, p. 242) states this directly: "the concept of substance is . . . inadequate for historical being and knowledge. [There is a] radical challenge to thought implicit in this inadequacy." Understood hermeneutically, interpretation and questioning are therefore not just a matter of "making connections" between two inherently separate things (we are not dealing here with the *epistemology* of constructivism, where a subject puts separate things together and thus "produces" connections). Rather, interpretation and questioning have an *ontological* force: they "break open the [falsely presumed to be self-existent and substantive] *being* of the object" (Gadamer, 1989, p. 362), making visible, experiencable and understandable the ontological inherence of one thing in the very being of another.

In Buddhism, this phenomenon of "cosmic interpenetration" (Loy, 1993, p. 481) is described in conjunction with another equally important ontological insight: emptiness (Sanskrit *shunya*). This insight is named and/or translated in various ways: things, ideas, images, selves, are considered to be "empty of self-existence (*svabhavasunya*)" (Tsong-kha-pa, 2000, p. 24), "empty of having an inherent self-nature" (Tsong-kha-pa 2005, p. 183), having an "absence of self-nature" (Tsong-kha-pa, 2000, p. 20), possessing "not even an atom of... true existence" (Tsong-kha-pa, 2004, p. 215):

> The true mode of being of a thing as it is in itself, is selfness, for its self cannot be a self-identity in the sense of a substance. Indeed, this true mode must include a complete negation of such self-identity. (Nishitani, 1982, p. 117)

However, this "negation of self-identity [X = X]" does not lead to something null and void. "Empty of inherent existence" (Tsong-kha-pa, 2006, p. 33) is meant to point towards *how* things *do* exist—not as separate self-identical substances that need nothing except themselves to exist, but as, rather, "dependently co-arising" (Sanskrit: *pratitya-samutpada*): "the only way phenomena do exist is as interdependently related" (Lobsang, 2006, p. 51). Emptiness of substantive self-existence thus is identical to the fullness of dependently arising interrelatedness that defines things, words, objects, and selves. Things *are* thus—in the very being of every seemingly separate thing are nestled *worlds of relations* and our ordinary experience of this as simply a meager act of pronunciation leaves such worlds concealed. This is what is meant by the breaking open of the (falsely presumed to be self-enclosed) being of the object and thus releasing insight into the instead dependently co-arising being of the object. "Dependent-arising is the meaning of emptiness" (Tsong-kha-pa, 2002, p. 133). Emptiness (of separate self-existence) thus means fullness (of dependently arising existence).

"Every Word Breaks Forth"

There is a passage I have always loved in Hans-Georg Gadamer's *Truth and Method* (1989, p. 458) where he portrays something of the experience that follows from this gathering sense of "break[ing] open the being of the object":

> Every word [has an] inner dimension of multiplication: every word breaks forth as if from a center and is related to a whole, through which alone it

> is a word. Every word causes the whole of the language to which it belongs to resonate and the whole world-view that underlies it to appear. Thus every word, as the event of a moment, carries with it the unsaid, to which it is related by responding and summoning.

This "*as if* from a center" is vitally important.

As if, because "*the center is everywhere.* Each and every thing ["every word"] becomes the center of all things and, in that sense, becomes an absolute center. This is the absolute uniqueness of things, their reality" (Nishitani, 1982, p. 146). "We should apply this [as if] to *every* phenomenon. Every phenomenon... is empty of having an inherent self-nature that exists from its own side" (Tsong-kha-pa, 2005, p. 182). So that at "the periphery" of experiencing that young child's slow and agonizing work of pronunciation resides, for example, the phenomenon of names and how we are called by them, how they "summon and respond," or the appearance of spaces between words into written English in the eleventh century (see Carruthers, 2003, Illich, 1993, Illich & Sanders, 1988, Stock, 1983). There, too, is the example of a colleague (see Jardine & Naqvi, 2008) telling me of her daughter learning to read the Koran out loud, and how she often did this well-honed pronunciation without understanding what many of the words mean. I queried this and found that *uttering the very sound of the words themselves* was understood to be a mirroring of the very sound of God speaking to the prophet, so the very sonority itself was blessed and precious, independently of the meaning and message of the text. Yes, oral recitation, a commonplace of Canadian elementary school classrooms. Reading aloud, "even there." God uttering the world into existence over the face of the deep. And that silent reading didn't even enter European until around the eleventh century and, in doing so, propagated a new understanding of ourselves and our "interiority" and individuality/privacy (see Illich, 1993, Illich & Sanders, 1998). And there, too, is the full cascade of cultures and tongues that have found their ways here into this classroom, and how each has suffered in their own way the great modern hegemony of the English tongue (even, of course, the native English speakers), even here, in efforts to pronounce this Japanese transliteration of a deeply culturally embedded Japanese name for a Japanese cat in this child's new book.

So that slow breath of pronunciation is thus experienced, not as an isolated object of consideration, but as existing in a broad and generous "residence" of possibilities, lineages, intergenerational bloodlines, and the like. Hermeneutically understood, every however-common event of language *is* a dependently co-arising, living inheritance, and therefore the contingent, localized, frail and fragile *taking up of that inheritance*—this girl's efforts, here, now—is (however small a) part of its being what it is. As is my own inhaled breath, here, in this classroom, witnessing all over again the arrival of this old, familiar, tough-minded companion: pronunciation.

This *seems* paradoxical, that the center is everywhere and that, therefore, "none is the fundamental entity" (Hanh, 1986, p. 70) while, at the same time, any thing can be experience *as* ("if") the center of all things. This is only a "contradiction" against the presumed backdrop of the logic of substance. Nishitani Keiji (1982, p. 149) elaborates:

> To say that *a thing is not itself* means that, while continuing to be itself, it is in the home-ground of everything else. Figuratively speaking, its roots reach across into the ground of all other things and help to hold them up and keep them standing. It serves as a constitutive element of their being. *That a thing is itself* means that all other things, while continuing to be themselves, are in the home-ground of that thing. This way that everything has being on the home-ground of everything else, without ceasing to be on its own home-ground, means that the being of each thing is held up, kept standing, and made to be what it is by means of the being of all other things; or, put the other way around, that each being holds up the being of every other thing, keeps it standing and makes it what it is.

Our considerations can thus then shift to one of these constitutively surrounding things that constitute the peripheries of pronunciation. Such shifts would then make her efforts of pronunciation now peripheral to, but still constitutive of this new "as if" center of our attention. *As if,* because anything "at the center" *is* "itself" because it *is* the field of it's residing.

Thus Gadamer's "*as if* from a center," because in looking "into" that center and focusing in with great care on that child's pronunciation, enjoying, praising, encouraging, waiting, laughing, demonstrating, we don't experience it like some sort of some hard-shelled "core." In looking in to that center, we are cast "outwards" into worlds of relations. We are drawn "into" this child's efforts and find that in being drawn into that center, it:

> draws us entirely outside of ourselves. Rather than meeting us in our world, it is much more a world into which we ourselves are drawn. *[T]he totality of a lived context has entered into and is present in the thing.* And we belong to it as well." (Gadamer, 1994, pp. 191–192, my emphasis)

This is why, in nearing such events in a classroom, my own life as a teacher *necessarily* involves learning, because in properly taking up pronunciation as a teacher, I take up, inevitably, the implication of *my own being* in this phenomenon *and* my dependently co-arising responsibility for the well-being of this girl and this inheritance and our myriad places in this great residence.

This is why I am drawn to such events in the classroom, "responding" to this "summons," because, hermeneutically understood, I, too, am already "present in the thing." In interpretive work, then, we come to "recognize *[our]selves* in the mess of th[is] world" (Hillman, 1983, p. 49, emphasis added), by recognizing ourselves, not as some self-existent entity, but rather *as* the mess of the world. I myself, as with this young girl, as with her breath and mine—each of these is experienced as glancing through the reflected facets of the world, each being itself by being such glancing with no substance left over:

> A metaphor for such cosmic interpenetration and lack of self-presence is found in the Avatamsaka Sutra of Mahayana Buddhism: Indra's Net.
>
> > Far away in the heavenly abode of the great god Indra, there is a wonderful net that has been hung by some cunning artificer in such a manner that it stretches out infinitely in all directions. In accordance with the extravagant tastes of deities, the artificer has hung a single glittering jewel in each "eye" of the net, and since the net itself is infinite in all dimensions, the jewels are infinite in number. There hang the jewels, glittering like stars of the first magnitude, a wonderful sight to behold. If we now arbitrarily select one of these jewels for inspection and look closely at it, we will discover that in its polished surface there are reflected all the other jewels in the net, infinite in number. Not only that, but each of the jewels reflected in this one jewel is also reflecting all the other jewels, so that there is an infinite reflecting process occurring. (Loy, 1993, p. 481)

This not only means that we "are always open onto the horizons of others but also, more important, because [we] are *always already everywhere inhabited* by the Other in the context of the fully real." (Smith, 2006, p. xxiv). Oddly put, experiencing that young girl's efforts at pronunciation requires my experiencing that, in my fullest reality as dependently co-arising, *I am*, my very self, a dependently co-arising inhabitant of this very residence.

I am inhabited by her halting breath over that odd name. It is my very life being played out, here, in watching her paw that book's cover and loving its allure, just as surely as my life is played out in the grief I sometimes find in schools. Coming to understand, then, is "more a passion than an action" (Gadamer, 1989, p. 366), more an act of compassion for the suffering and impermanence that defines our deeply shared, often deeply concealed lot.

This is my own column of aging breath being summoned up in this event of pronunciation. In breaking open the being of the object, *my own being "myself" is broken open* and experienced as caught up and constitutively implicated in the very fabric of the object I meditate upon or study or happen upon in some local classroom. This great sentiment is so eloquently expressed by Rick Fields (cited in Ingram, 1990, p. xiv):

> My heart is broken,
> open.

This is why it is getting so tough to visit schools sometimes. That child's pronunciation venture is heartbreaking. And when it is ignored or trivialized in the day to day rush of things, as if *it* is trivial, we miss the fact that the rush is trivializing. "The way we treat a thing can sometimes change its nature" (Hyde, 1983, p. iii).

Therefore, in "[heart]breaking open the being" of this child's efforts at the pronunciation of a name, "we are not attempting to get rid of [it], only of the idea of [it] as self-existent" (Lobsang, 2006, p. 49). "Those objects that appear... do not stop appearing, but the concepts [e.g., "substance," or other reifications] that take them as having any true existence subside" (Patrul, 1998, p. 252). We still remain concerned after understanding pronunciation in the specificities of its appearance, here, with this child and this book and this name and all the oddities of its translations and transliterations. But, at the same time, "the object" of our consideration must also include "the emptiness of this [particular phenomenon], not just [the phenomenon]" (Yangsi, 2003, p. 433).

To use the language of Martin Heidegger (1962), our concern is not merely "ontic" ("What is this thing, pronunciation, and what are the threads of its dependent co-arising?") but "ontological" (our "ontic," interpretive concern for this particular entity is only authentically pursuable against the background of its *being* dependently co-arising). From Longchenpa (1308–1363):

> Knowledge is as infinite as the stars in the sky;
> There is no end to all the subjects one could study
> It is better to grasp straight away their very essence—
> The unchanging fortress of the dharmakaya. (cited in Patrul, 1998, p. 261)

("**Dharmakaya**—*chos sku,* lit. Dharma Body. The emptiness aspect of Buddhahood" [a glossary entry to Patrul, 1998, p. 410]). Thus, "studying subjects" like pronunciation must be done against the ontological "backdrop" of a knowledge of emptiness (a knowledge, that is, that pronunciation is *interpretable*) and these two ways of proceeding support and cultivate each other. Careful attention to the great detail, specificity and particularity of *this* appearance of pronunciation ("distinguishing the exact particulars of an object" (Tsong-kha-pa, 2002, p. 17) is possible *because* pronunciation is treated, interpretively, as empty of self-existence, as breaking forth *as if* from a center. And likewise, in interpreting pronunciation, we can get a glimpse of, an experience of, emptiness.

"Accordingly there is the examination and analysis of *both* the real nature [emptiness—the 'ontological status of the object under analysis' [Tsong-kha-pa, 2004, p. 21] and the [ontic] diversity of phenomena" (Tsong-kha-pa, 2002, p. 17). Properly understood, between these "there is compatibility and a lack of contradiction" (Tsong-kha-pa, 2004, p. 215). (This helps unravel a bit why Martin Heidegger always insisted that the Being of beings is not a being *and* he insisted that Being is always the Being of a being—I'll leave the tempt of this tangle for others to undo at their leisure).

"It Draws You Into Its Path"

> When [it] takes hold of us, it is not an object that stands opposite us which we look at in hope of seeing through it to an intended conceptual meaning. Just the reverse. The work [e.g., of pronunciation] is an *Ereignis*—an event that 'appropriates us' into itself. It jolts us, it knocks us over, and sets up a world of its own, into which we are drawn, as it were. (Gadamer, 2001, p. 71)

There is, of course, a danger here. The hermeneutic experience of the breaking open of the being of the object involves "the way you apprehend the object. By making the object extensive [you] expand your mind" (Tsong-kha-pa, 2002, p. 63). As "it" becomes more extensive we become, as St. Augustine put it, "roomier" (cited in Carruthers, 2005, p. 199). My "self" expands as my apprehension of the dependent co-arising of the world—the "residence" of my self—expands: "making the object of meditation extensive so as to expand your mind" (Tsong-kha-pa, 2002, p. 63).

And as the object "breaks forth," "it draws you into its path" (Gadamer, 2007b, p, 198).

Hence arises the danger that many new to hermeneutics (and Buddhist meditative practices) often experience: *Everything* seems connected, *everything* is rampantly full, *everything* starts to beckon and summon. It expands and I expand and get caught up in an onrush that seems impossible to stop. This is sometimes named the "monkey mind" in Buddhist practice (and this breaching an ironic humiliation in the *Wabi Sabi* book, where Monkey is the teacher).

> The more you practice these things, the more accustomed your mind will become to them, and the easier it will be to practice what you had initially

> found difficult to learn. You will have visions of the Buddha day and night. (Tsong-kha-pa, 2000, pp. 185–186)
>
> One arises from formal meditation and goes about daily activities, seeing the manifestations of the world and living beings as mandala deities. This is the Samadhi that transforms the world and its living brings into a most extraordinary vision. *All* experiences ["even here"] are taken as manifestations of great ecstasy. (Tsong-kha-pa, 2005, p. 125, emphasis added)

Everything is connected to *everything*. And hence a common complaint for some students of hermeneutics: "How do I get it to stop?" or "*Now* what?"

This outward expansiveness can easily lead to a ravaging exhaustion of attention, a sort of cascading, post-modern "connectionism": "you [can easily become] like the leading edge of water running downhill—you go anywhere you are led, taking anything said to be true, wanting to cry when you see others crying, wanting to laugh when you see others laugh" (Tsong-kha-pa, 2004, p. 222). It is easy to become swamped by possibilities and simply outrun. This is why Gadamer (1989, p. 106) talks about how it is that the dependent co-arising of play of things (e.g., what is expandingly experienced as "at play" in that breath of pronunciation) can "outplay the players." In the face of that simple event in an elementary school classroom, in the face of that lovely book and its allure, one can become simply burdened by unseemly and unending cloys of "relatedness" which can weigh down attention and make me simply give up in overwhelmed frustration. Tsong-kha-pa (2002, p. 62 ff.) thus warns against the extremes of "laxity [which simply gives up, spent in the face of the rush] and excitement [which simply pursues the rush ever faster and with accelerating distraction]."

A key task of hermeneutics as a practice (as well as a task in Buddhist practice) is thus the practice of *composure* in the face of this ecstatic experience of breaking forth. Tsong-kha-pa insists that the insight into emptiness that comes from pursuing wisdom be coupled with the practice of meditation, of one-pointed stillness and composure. He uses the term "equanimity" (2002, p. 68) to describe a process of "relaxing the effort, but not sacrificing the intensity of the way you apprehend the object" (p. 68). What is called for, then, is facing the delusions of inherent self-existence and *interpreting* them, that is, breaking open these delusions so that the realities of dependent co-arising can be experienced and understood. But this must be taken on at the same time as *not* simply becoming caught up in mere pursuit of the ensuing cascades. "I compose this in order to condition my own mind" (Tsong-kha-pa, 2000, p. 111).

Moreover, I read these compositions of Gadamer and Tsong-kha-pa in the very same pursuit of conditioning my own mind. "Texts are instructions for [the] practice" (Tsong-kha-pa, 2000, p. 52) of precisely paying more proper attention to that girl's way through the sounds of words.

It is notable, then, that we are right back to the issue of proper pronunciation and of learning to read, and, right here, in the face of this ordinary classroom event, this is, of course, exactly where we should be. Admittedly, it is difficult to read many scholarly texts this way, as instructions for practice, and this, too, takes practice, just *exactly* as does learning to "read" that singular moment in the classroom as "breaking forth," that is, as an exuberant "event of appearing [*Vollzug*]." About such moments, we ask:

> [how does] it begin, end, how long [does] it last[?]; how [does] it remain in one's mind, and in the end how [does] it fade away, and yet somehow remain with us and [be] able to surface again[?]. (Gadamer, 2007b, p. 217)

And this faces us with the dilemma: what should I do now? What should I say or write or show or save? What should be highlighted and what forgotten? This takes time, but a certain kind of time that is itself meditatively proper to such composition:

> Certainly one can call this process a "while" [*Weilen*], but this is something that nobody measures and that one does not find to be either boring or merely entertaining. The name I have for the way in which this event happens is "reading." With reading one does not imagine... that one can already do it. In reality, one must learn how.... Now the word *Lesen* ["read," a German kin to the English word "lesson"—I think, for example, of an old commonplace in Anglican church services, of saying "today's lesson is taken from Matthew," meaning both literally "a reading from Matthew" but also *reading* that reading for its "lesson"] carries within it a helpful multiplicity of harmonic words, such as gathering together [*Zusammenlesen*], picking up [*Auflesen*], picking out [*Auslesen*], or to sort out [*verlesen*]. All of these are associated with "harvest" (*Lese*), that is to say, the harvest of grapes, which persist in the harvest. The word *Lesen* also refers to something that begins with spelling out words, if one learns to write and read, and again we find numerous echo words. One can start to read a book [*anlesen*] or finish up reading it [*auslesen*], one can read further in it [*weiterlesen*], or just check into it [*nachlesen*], or one can read it aloud [*vorlesen*]. All of these point towards the harvest that is gathered in and from which one takes nourishment. (Gadamer, 2007b, pp. 217–218)

Harvest, gathering, nourishment. Lovely words to describe the yield that comes from the suffering undergone in learning to read. To pronounce.

This is why Gadamer follows his lovely exploration of the phenomenon of the play(s) of the world (1989, pp. 101–110)—like being drawn into what is "at play" in that girl's work with *Wabi Sabi*—with an imposingly titled section, "Transformation into Structure" (pp. 110–120). "Transformation into structure" is about creating, in the midst of the cascading and alluring play of the world that is experienced once it is broken open, a "play," a "work" or a "composition" which draws us into "what is at play" and makes possible a certain composure in the face of this insight. "Composition" thus "captures" something of the insight of breaking forth and, with practice ("one does not imagine... that one can already do it. In reality, one must learn how" [Gadamer, 2007b, p. 217]) a work can be shaped that can offer to others the possibility of engaging this insight. This is identical to the everyday work of a classroom that gathers students together to create beautiful things that will show others how their work is laced up in the dependent co-arising work of the world. In taking on the difficult work of composing such events of appearing, one offers an invitation into such arising worlds. They are thus things that allow me, invite me, into a "hitherto concealed experience that transcends thinking from the position of subjectivity" (Gadamer, 1989, p. 100), an experience of my own dependent co-arising in the face of such arisings.

This act of, shall we say, mutual composure, then, is not just a matter of achieving stillness in the face of the fray, but of cultivating a deep and well-studied knowledge of the topic of one's meditations and all the rich lineages and ancestries of thought that have handed this topic over to us and us over to it. It involves realizing that "you can't get anywhere without [also] reading a yak's load of books" (Tsong-kha-pa, 2004, p. 219). This study is a study *on behalf of* the practice of composure in the midst of every life. It is a matter of not simply slavishly following the heavy scholarly weigh of "tradition" but of, odd to say, having "delighted those who have come before" (Dorje, 2011, p. 16) as a way to thus oneself experience delight in this new arising. This is why Gadamer (see Grondin, 2003, p. 333) expressed soft and generous disappointment when he found certain works given in his honor at his 100th birthday celebration not very *lebensweltlich* (not very "life-worldly"). This accounts, also, for why, as a hermeneutic philosopher, I feel such an affinity to the Gelug stream of Buddhism that emphasizes the equanimity between study and practice. "Wisdom and the study that it causes are indispensable for proper practice" (Tsong-kha-pa, 2004, p. 220).

"Do not make study and practice into separate things" (Tsong-kha-pa, 2004, p. 221).

"Against fixity" hermeneutic work, strangely akin to Buddhist thought, "makes the object and all its possibilities fluid" (Gadamer, 1989, p. 367). Therefore, the purpose of a "hermeneutic study"—the purpose of composure, of composition—is to create something that will draw others into this hermeneutic experience of fluidity—*into* an experience of the dependent co-arising of the world and *out of* the delusions of substance and the grasping-at-permanence syndrome that is its root. And all this has as its aim not simply philosophical erudition and the like. The aim of such meditations and work is the cultivation of the intimacy and immediacy of the experience of everyday life, here, as this next child draws breath over a text, here, where reading aloud and learning to pronounce can too often be treated as simply ordinary and commonplace. Not only is "wherever you are... a place of practice" (Tsong-kha-pa, 2004, p. 191). Tsong-kha-pa also insists (and this is a feature that distinguishes the Gelug tradition from other Buddhist lineages and makes its affinity to hermeneutic ripe), the purpose and object of scholarly study is *precisely* the deepening of practice itself. After all, "why would you determine one thing by means of study and reflection, and then, when you go to practice, practice something else?" (2000, p. 52). And this is why Gadamer insists that hermeneutics, with all is philosophical erudition and study, is "a practical philosophy" (2007a) with both theoretical and practical tasks (2007d). All those complex philosophical and historical twists and turns that typify his work are meant, in the end, to make us more susceptible to the beautiful abundance of things as we walk around in the world. "Even here," in this ordinary place.

"Present in the Thing"

> [In learning to experience events in this way], we experience an absolute opposition to [our] will-to-control ["the syndrome of grasping at a self-nature" (Tsong-kha-pa 2005, p. 182)], not in the sense of a rigid resistance to the presumption of our will which is bent on utilizing things, but in the sense of [having come upon] the superior and intrusive power of a being reposing in itself. (Gadamer, 1977, 226–227)

All those complex lines of dependent co-arising that break forth from this event of pronunciation are experienced as being "present in the thing" (Gadamer, 1994, p. 192). This is not exactly a matter of attention "narrowing" back in on some separate thing, but rather of attention *intensifying* and this wee event becoming, one might say, "luminous," radiantly full of all its relations. This is akin to accounts of what is called "generation stage meditation" in the Gelug tradition of Buddhism:

> You develop the ability to see yourself as a... deity and your environment as the mandala or... abode of the deity. This is called *pure perception*: you perceive all objects of the physical senses and the mind the same way a meditational deity experiences them [as if sitting at the center of an open field of dependent co-arising, a mandala-like "residence"]. The opposite of this

> mode of perception is *impure perception*. This is ordinary appearance: seeing yourself as ordinary, seeing the world where you live as ordinary ["each deed and thought...intimate and commonplace"], and experiencing...objects...as ordinary ["familiar"]. This impure appearance is the main target to be removed by...practice. (Sopa, 2004, p. 30)

Tsong-kha-pa elaborates (2005, p. 182) that what is sought is the ability to see every phenomenon as such a radiant deity:

> We should apply this to *every* phenomenon. Every phenomenon... is empty of having an inherent self-nature that exists from its own side. One should understand exactly how strong the presence of the syndrome of grasping at a self-nature [X = X] is. On the basis of [applying this to every phenomenon] one transforms the...world and its inhabitants [from being experienced as separate, controllable, graspable substances] into the supporting and the supported mandala (i.e., residence and deities).

Picturing every phenomenon as a deity sitting in the middle of a mandala entails coming to experience every phenomenon as thus a *radiant being*, illuminatingly full of all its relations precisely by being empty of self-existence, a being in whose presence light is cast upon me, illuminating my own culpabilities. Such picturing, which arises as an often-agonizing of sustained practice:

> It is not merely one's "taking time" to linger over something, as in the slackening or slowing down to contemplate. [It is] not a function of lackadaisical, meandering contemplation, least of all passive in any way, but is a function of the fullness and *intensity* of attention and engrossment. (Ross, 2006, p. 109)

In cultivating this "hermeneutic experience," those radiating lines of dependently co-arising venture can be sensed shimmering all around "every phenomenon," akin to a "halo" of illumination. Jigme Lingpa (1729–1798): "concentration is to experience as deities all the appearances to which one clings" (cited in Patrul, 1998, p. 254), that is, as a footnote to this passage clarifies, "to meditate on appearances as deities. . . means as pure wisdom manifestations [pure manifestations of an emptiness of substantive self-existence] with no concrete reality" (Patrul,1998, p. 389, fnt. 166). With repeated and intense practice, even an ordinary appearance like the breath of pronunciation, shall we say, "glows."

That is, this girl's pronunciation is *beautiful* and, through practice, my own life can become more open and illuminated in its presence:

> That which manifests itself [in this way] attracts the longing of love to it. The beautiful disposes people in its favor immediately. The beautiful... has its own radiance. For "beauty alone has this quality: that it is what is most radiant (*ekphanestaton*) and lovely" [*Phaedrus*, 250 d 7]. (Gadamer, 1989, p. 481)

That "every phenomenon" (Tsong-kha-pa, 2005, p. 182) ("every word") hides this lesson is the great and difficult pedagogical affinity between hermeneutics and this old lineage of Buddhist thought and practice. *This* is "hermeneutic experience," that "the more... the work opens itself, the more luminous becomes [its] uniqueness" (Heidegger, 1971, pp. 65–66), just this, just here, just now, this lovely, simple, beautiful thing, right in the midst of all this frail and fraught suffering and endurance.

And so we look at each other, and the story continues, and she giggles as she sees the name again.

Post-Ambulatory Couplet

> Knowledge is not a projection in the sense of a plan, the extrapolation of the aims of the will, an ordering of things according to the wishes, prejudices, or promptings of the powerful; rather, it remains something adapted to the object, a *mensuratio ad rem*. Yet this thing is not a *factum brutum* [something "inherently existing "] but itself ultimately has the same mode of being as Dasein [human being]. [*Both* are dependently co-arising]. The important thing, however, is to understand this oft-repeated statement correctly. It does not mean simply that there is a "homogeneity" between the knower and the known. The coordination of all knowing activity with what is known is not based on *the fact that* they have the same mode of being but draws it significance from the *particular nature* of the mode of being that is common to them. It consists in the fact that neither the knower nor the known is [substantively] "present-at-hand." (Gadamer, 1989, p. 261)

> Because the ultimate mode of the existence of enlightened [radiant] beings and ordinary sentient beings is the same [even "enlightened beings" are dependently co-arising], we have the potential to be recipients of their divine activity. (Yangsi, 2003, p 133)

References

Abram, D. (1996). *The spell of the sensuous: Language in a more-than-human world.* New York, NY: Pantheon Books.

Abram, D., & Jardine, D. (2000). All knowledge is carnal knowledge: A conversation. *Canadian Journal of Environmental Education.* (5), 167–177.

Aitken, R. (1982). *Taking the Path of Zen.* San Francisco, CA: North Point Press.

Anderson, H. (2006). Teabags. On-line at: http://mothertongued.com/hortensia/teabags.htm. No longer accessible. Last accessed June 2007. See next citation for further information.

Anderson, H. (2007). *The plenitude of emptiness: A collection of the Asian poetic form known as haibun.* Available on-line at http://hortensiaanderson.blogspot.com

Aoki, T. (2005). *Curriculum in a new key: The collected works of Ted. T. Aoki.* Mahwah, NJ: Lawrence Erlbaum Associates.

Arendt, H. (1969). *Between Past and Future.* London, UK: Penguin Books.

Arthos, J. (2009). *The Inner Word in Gadamer's Hermeneutics.* Notre Dame, IN: Notre Dame University Press.

Atisha (1997). *Lamp for the Path to Enlightenment.* Ithaca, NY: Snow Lion Publications.

Ayres, L. (1909). *A measuring scale for ability in spelling.* Available on line at: donpotter.net.

Bakken, D. (2003). Ink that echoes. *The marquee.* Available on-line at: http://www.bisbeemarquee.com/www/2003/1116/c07.php. Accessed August 21, 2007.

Barrett, K. (2015). Planted ID card exposes Paris false flag. *PressTV.* January 10, 2015. On-line: http://www.presstv.ir/Detail/2015/01/10/392426/Planted-ID-card-exposes-Paris-false-flag

Berman, M. (1983). *The reenchantment of the world.* New York, NY: Bantam Books.

Berry, W. (1983). *Standing by words.* San Francisco, CA: North Point Press.

In Praise of Radiant Beings, pages 307–327

Berry, W. (1986). *The unsettling of America.* San Francisco, CA: Sierra Book Club.

Berry, W. (1989, March). The profit in work's pleasure. *Harper's Magazine,* (pp. 19–24).

Berry, W., & Moyers, B. (2013). Writer and farmer Wendell Berry on hope, direct action, and the "resettling" of the American countryside. Posted October 11, 2013 on-line in *Yes Magazine.* Accessed at: http://www.yesmagazine.org/planet/mad-farmer-wendell-berry-gets-madder-in-defense- of-earth.

Bethune, R. (2002). To translate is to betray? *ArtTimesJournal.* Available on-line at: http://www.arttimesjournal.com/theater/totranslate.htm. Accessed August 18, 2007.

Blankelder, H., & Fletcher W. (2002). Translator's Introduction to Chandrakirti (2002). *Introduction to the Middle Way: Chandrakirti's Madhyamakavatara with Commentary by Jamgon Mipham* (pp. 1–53). Boston MA: Shambala.

Bly, R. (n.d.). *When a hair turns to gold.* St. Paul MI: Ally Press.

Bobbitt, F. (1918). *The curriculum.* Boston, MA: Houghton Mifflin.

Bobbitt, F. (1924). *How to make a curriculum.* Boston, MA: Houghton Mifflin.

Bordo, S. (1988). *The flight to objectivity.* Albany, NY: State University of New York Press.

Bowers, C. A. (2005). *The false promises of constructivist theories of learning: A global and ecological critique.* New York, NY: Peter Lang Publishers.

Bowers, C. A. (2008). Transitions: Educational Reforms that Promote Ecological Intelligence or the Assumptions Underlying Modernity? University of Oregon Libraries. Retrieved March 10th, 2012 from https://scholarsbank.uoregon.edu/xmlui/handle/1794/3067

Boyle, D. (2006). The man who made us all work like this.... *BBC History Magazine,* June 2003. Accessed August 5, 2009 at: http://www.david-boyle.co.uk/history/frederickwinslowtaylor.html

Bransford, J., Brown, A., & Cocking, R. (2000). *How people learn.* Washington, DC: National Academies Press.

Braverman, H. (1998). *Labor and monopoly capital: The degradation of work in the twentieth century.* New York, NY: Monthly Review Press.

Brown, W. (2006). *Regulating aversion: Tolerance in the age of identity and empire.* Princeton, NJ: Princeton University Press.

Butler, J. (2004, Spring). Betrayal's felicity. *Diacritics. 34*(1), 82–87.

Callahan, R. (1964). *America, education and the cult of efficiency.* Chicago, IL: University of Chicago Press.

Campbell. A. (2013). Breathe in, breathe out a way to conquer students' stress. *The Globe and Mail,* Friday March 01, 2013. Retrieved online at: http://www.theglobeandmail.com/news/national/education/breathe-in-breathe-out-a-way-to-conquer-students-stress/article9156091/

Caputo, J. (1987). *Radical Hermeneutics: Repetition, deconstruction and the Hermeneutic project.* Bloomington: Indiana University Press.

Caputo, J. (1993) *Against ethics: Contributions to a poetics of obligation with constant reference to deconstruction.* Bloomington, IN: Indiana State University Press.

Carroll, L. (PD. Originally published 1871). *Through the looking-glass and what Alice found there.* Designed and published by PDFreeBooks.org. Full text accessed on-line August 9th 2012 from www.google.ca/books

Carruthers, M. (2003). *The craft of thought: Meditation, rhetoric, and the making of images, 400–1200.* Cambridge, England: Cambridge University Press.

Carruthers, M. (2005). *The book of memory: A study of memory in medieval culture.* Cambridge, England: Cambridge University Press.

Carruthers, M., & Ziolkowski, J. (2002). *The Medieval craft of memory: An anthology of texts and pictures.* Philadelphia, PA: University of Pennsylvania Press.

Chah, A. (n.d.). *Everything is teaching us.* Victoria AU: The Sangha. Bodhivana Monastery. Available for free download at: http://forestsanghapublications.org/viewAuthor.php?id=1

Chah, A. (2001). *Being Dharma: The essence of the Buddha's teachings.* Boston MA: Shambala Press.

Chah, A. (1987). Our real home: A talk to an aging lay disciple approaching death. *Access to Insight.* Accessed on line December 24th, 2010 at: http://www.accesstoinsight.org/lib/thai/chah/bl111.html.

Chah, A. (2001). *Being Dharma: The essence of the Buddha's teachings.* Boston, MA: Shambala Press.

Chah, A. (2005). *Food for the heart.* Sommerville MA: Wisdom Publications.

Chambers, C. (2012). Spelling and other illiteracies. In C. M. Chambers, E. Hasebe-Ludt, C. Leggo, & A. Sinner (Eds.), *A heart of wisdom: Life writing as empathetic inquiry* (pp. 183–189). New York, NY: Peter Lang.

Chodron, P. (2007). *No time to lose: A timely guide to the way of the Bodhisattva.* Boston MA: Shambhala.

Friesen, P., & Friesen, S. (1993). A curious plan: Managing on the twelfth. *Harvard Educational Review, 63*(3), 339–358.

Clifford, P., & Friesen, S. (1994) Choosing to be healers. *JCT Conference on Curriculum Theory and Classroom Practice.* Banff, Alberta, October.

Clifford, P., & Friesen, S. (2008). The transgressive energy of mythic wives and wilful children: Old stories for new times. In D. Jardine, P. Clifford, & S. Friesen (Eds.), *Back to the basics of teaching and learning: "Thinking the world together"* (pp. 79–90). New York, NY: Routledge.

Clifford, P., Friesen, S., & Jardine, D. (2008). "Whatever happens to him happens to us": Reading coyote reading the world. In D. Jardine, P. Clifford, & S. Friesen (Eds.), *Back to the basics of teaching and learning: "Thinking the world together"* (pp. 67–78). New York, NY: Routledge.

Colbert, S. (w. Fr. Thomas Roscia) (2015). *Stephen Colbert—Witness.* Accessed on-line at: https://www.youtube.com/watch?v=lF5tudIqN7w.

Costello, E. (1991). Couldn't call it unexpected No. 4. From E. Costello *Mighty Like a Rose.* First issue on Warner Brothers Records, #26575

Costello, E. (1993). The birds will still be singing. From E. Costello, *The Juliet Letters.* Warner Brothers CD #45180. Lyrics by E. Costello, copyright Plangent Visions Music Inc.

Cubberley, E.P. (1922). *A brief history of education: A history of the practice and progress and organization of education.* Boston, MA: Houghton Mifflin Co.

David Suzuki Foundation. (2011). *Do not let despair take over.* [YouTube video recording]. Retrieved from https://www.youtube.com/watch?v=RWqB4-em308

Dawkins, R. (2006). *The God delusion.* Boston, MA: Houghton Mifflin.

Dawson, C. (1998). Translator's introduction to H.G. Gadamer (1998). *Praise of theory: Speeches and essays* (pp. xv–Derby, M. (2015). *Towards a critical eco-hermeneutic approach to education: Place, being, relation.* New York, NY: Peter Lang Publishing.

Derrida, J., & Ferraris, M. (2001). *A taste for the secret.* Cambridge, England: Polity Press.

Descartes, R. (1955). *Descartes selections.* New York, NY: Charles Scribner's Sons.

Doctor, T. H. (2014). Translators' introduction to *Ornament of the Great Vehicle Sutras: Maitreya's Mahayanasutralamakara* (pp. vii–xvi). Boston, MA: Snow Lion.

Documentaryondemand (2013, April 20). *Colisao: Ateu X Pastor* [Video file]. (This is a subtitled version of *Collision: Christopher Hitchens, vs. Douglas Wilson.* LEVEL4 Studio, Phoenix AZ. Director: Darren Doane, October 27, 2009, ASIN: B002M3SHTO). Retrieved from https://www.youtube.com/watch?v=_JWySEcocc8

Dōgen. (2007). *Shobogenzo: The treasure house of the eye of the true teaching.* H Nearman, trans. Mount Shasta, CA: Shasta Abbey Press.

Doll, W. (1993). Curriculum possibilities in a "post"-future. *Journal of Curriculum and Supervision, 8*(4), 277–292.

Domanski, D. (2002). The wisdom of falling. An interview with S. D. Johnson. In T. Bowling (Ed.), *Where the words come from: Canadian Poets in conversation* (pp. 244–55). Roberts Creek, BC: Nightwood Press.

Domanski, D. (2013). *Bite down little whisper.* London, ON: Brick Books.

Dorje. L. (2011). *A torch lighting the way to freedom.* Boston, MA: Shambala.

Dorrie, D. (2007). *How to cook your life, with Zen Chef Edward Espe Brown.* DVD. Studio: Lions Gate. Release date: May 6, 2008.

Doublebirdie (2005). Three of six: A globetrotting American talks current events, pop culture, and theology. Available online at: http://threeofsix.blogspot.com/2005/07/to-translate-is-to-betray.html. Accessed August 8, 2007.

Dressman, M. (1993). Lionizing lone wolves: The cultural romantics of literacy workshops. *Curriculum inquiry,* 23(3), pp. 239–263.

DuFour, R., & Eaker, R. (1998). A New Model: The Professional Learning Community. Professional Learning Communities at Work: Best Practices for Enhancing Student Achievement. From *A New Model: The Professional Learning Community.* The Eisenhower National Clearinghouse for Mathematics and Science Education (ENC). Accessed on line at: http://www.myeport.com/published/t/uc/tucson73/collection/1/4/upload.doc

Dussel, E. (1995). *The invention of the Americas: Eclipse of the "other" and the myth of modernity.* New York, NY: Continuum Books.

Egan, K. (1986). *Teaching as story telling: An alternative approach to teaching and curriculum in elementary schools.* London, ON: Althouse Press

Egan, K. (1992). The roles of schools: The place of education. *Teacher's College Record, 93*(4), 641–645.

Eliade, M. (1968). *Myth and reality.* New York, NY: Harper and Row.

Eliade, M. (1975). *The quest: History and meaning in religion.* Chicago, IL: University of Chicago Press.

Elkind, D. (1967). Introduction to Piaget, J. (1967). *Six psychological studies.* (pp. v–xviii). New York, NY: Vintage Books.

Ford, H. (2007). *My life and work.* New York, NY: Cosimo Books.

Forman, R. K. C. (1989, October). Paramārtha and modern constructivists on mysticism: Epistemological monomorphism versus duomorphism. *Philosophy East and West, 39*(4), 393–418.

Fox, M. (1983). *Original blessing,* Santa Fe, NM: Bear and Company.

Friesen, S., Clifford, P., & Jardine, D. (2008). Meditations on classroom community and the intergenerational character of mathematical truth. In D. Jardine, P. Clifford, & S. Friesen (Eds.), *Back to the basics of teaching and learning: "Thinking the world together"* (pp. 117–130). New York, NY: Routledge.

Friesen, S., & Jardine, D. (2009). On field(ing) knowledge. In S. Goodchild & B. Sriraman (Eds.), *Relatively and philosophically e[a]rnest: Festschrifte in honour of Paul Ernest's 65th birthday. The Montana Mathematics Enthusiast: Monograph Series in Mathematics Education* (pp. 149–175). Charlotte, NC: Information Age Publishing.

Friesen, S., Jardine, D., & Gladstone, B. (2010). The first thunderclap of spring: An invitation into Aboriginal ways of knowing and the creative possibilities of digital technologies. In C. Craig & L. F. Deretchin (Ed.), *Teacher education yearbook XVIII: cultivating curious and creative minds: The role of teachers and teacher educators* (pp. 179–199). Landham, MD: Scarecrow Education.

Fink, E. (1970). The phenomenological philosophy of Edmund Husserl and contemporary criticism. In R. O. Elveton (Ed.), *The phenomenology of Husserl* (pp. 73–148). Chicago, IL: Quadrangle Books.

Fink, E. (1995). *Sixth Cartesian meditation: The idea of a transcendental theory of method.* Bloomington, IN: Indiana University Press.

Fukyama, F. (2006). *The end of history and the last man.* New York, NY: Free Press.

Gadamer, H. G. (1970, Winter). Concerning empty and ful-filled time. *Southern Journal of Philosophy,* 341–353.

Gadamer, Hans-Georg (1977). *Philosophical hermeneutics.* Berkeley, CA: University of California Press.

Gadamer, H. G. (1983). *Reason in the age of science.* Cambridge, MA: MIT Press.

Gadamer, H. G. (1984). The Hermeneutics of Suspicion. *Man and World, 17,* 313–323.

Gadamer, H. G. (1986). The idea of the university—Yesterday, today, tomorrow. In D. Misgeld & G. Nicholson (Eds. & trans.), *Hans-Georg Gadamer on Education, Poetry, and History: Applied Hermeneutics* (pp. 47–62). Albany, NY: SUNY Press.

Gadamer, H. G. (1989). *Truth and method.* New York, NY: Continuum Press.

Gadamer, H. G. (1994). *Heidegger's ways.* Boston, MA: MIT Press.

Gadamer, H. G. (2001). *Gadamer in conversation: Reflections and commentary.* R. Palmer, (Ed. and trans.), New Haven, CT: Yale University Press.

Gadamer, H. G. (2007). *The Gadamer reader: A Bouquet of the later writings.* In R. E. Palmer (Ed.), Evanston, IL: Northwestern University Press.

Gadamer, H. G. (2007a). Hermeneutics as practical philosophy. In R. E. Palmer (Ed.), *The Gadamer reader: A bouquet of the later writings* (pp. 227–245). Evanston, IL: Northwestern University Press.

Gadamer, H. G. (2007b). The artwork in word and image: "So True, So full of Being!" In H. G. Gadamer (2007). *The Gadamer reader: A bouquet of the later writings.* (pp. 195–224). R. E. Palmer (Ed.), Evanston, IL: Northwestern University Press.

Gadamer, H. G. (2007c). Aesthetics and hermeneutics. In R. E. Palmer (Ed.), *The Gadamer reader: A bouquet of the later writings* (pp. 124–131). Evanston, IL: Northwestern University Press.

Gadamer, H. G. (2007d). Hermeneutics as a theoretical and practical task. In R. E. Palmer (Ed.), *The Gadamer reader: A Bouquet of the later writings* (pp. 246–265). Evanston, IL: Northwestern University Press.

Gadamer, H. G. (2007e). From word to concept: The task of Hermeneutics as philosophy. In R. E. Palmer (Ed.), *The Gadamer reader: A bouquet of the later writings* (pp. 109–120). Evanston, IL: Northwestern University Press.

Gadamer, H. G., (2007f). A look back over the collected works and their effective history. In R. E. Palmer (Ed.), *The Gadamer reader: A bouquet of the later writings* (pp. 409–428)). Evanston, IL: Northwestern University Press.

Gandhi. (1982). Produced and directed by Richard Attenborough. Screenplay by John Briley, 188 min., 1982, Columbia Pictures.

Gatto, J. (2006). The national press attack on academic schooling. On-line at: http://www.rit.edu/~cma8660/mirror/www.johntaylorgatto.com/chapters/9d.htm.

Gick, M., & Holyoak, K. (1983). Schema induction and analogical transfer. *Psychology, 15,* 1–2.

Gilham, C. (2015). From the "science of disease" to the "understanding of those who suffer": The cultivation of an interpretive understanding of "behavior problems" in children. In D. Jardine, C. Gilham, & G. McCaffrey (Eds.), *On the pedagogy of suffering: Hermeneutic and Buddhist meditations* (pp. 29–26). New York, NY: Peter Lang Publishers.

Gilham, C. (2015a). Suffering "Like this": Interpretation and the pedagogical disruption of the dual system of Education. In D. Jardine, C. Gilham, & G. McCaffrey (Eds.), *On the pedagogy of suffering: Hermeneutic and Buddhist meditations* (pp. 213–226). New York, NY: Peter Lang Publishers.

Gilham, C. & Jardine, D. (in preparation). The poetics of pedagogical iatrogenesis.

Glieck, J. (1987). *Chaos: The making of a new science.* New York, NY: Penguin Books.

Godless UK (2013, June 30). *Christopher Hitchens—Last Public Appearance—Dawkins Award [Video File Dated October 8th 2011].* Retrieved from: https://www.youtube.com/watch?v=ud973COUVYs.

Goyette, S. (1998). *The true names of birds.* London, ON: Brick Books.

Gray, J. (1998). *False dawn: The delusions of global capitalism.* London, England: Granta Books.

Grondin, J. (2003). *Hans-Georg Gadamer: A biography.* New Haven, CT: Yale University Press.

Gurria-Quintana, A. (2006). *FT.com [Financial Times], Arts and Weekend, Books.* Available on-line at http://www.ft.com/cms/s/a6787988-5f43-11db-a011 0000779e2340.html. Published October 20 2006 16:47. Accessed June 2007.

Habermas, Jurgen (1972). *Knowledge and human interests.* Boston, MA: Beacon Books.

Hanh, T.N. (1993). *Love in action: Writings on nonviolent social change* San Francisco, CA: Parallax Press.

Hanh, T. N. (1986). *The miracle of mindfulness.* Berkeley, CA: Parallax Press.

Hanh, T. N. (1988). *The sun* in *my heart.* Berkeley, CA: Parallax Press.

Hanh, T. N. (1995). *The long road turns to joy: A guide to walking meditation.* Berkeley, CA: Parallax Press.

Hanh, T. N. (1999). *The heart of the Buddha's teaching.* New York, NY: Crown Publishing Group.

Hanh, T. N. (2003). *Interbeing: Commentaries on the Tiep Hien Precepts.* New Dehli, India: Full Circle Publishing.

Hanh, T. N. (n.d.). The Daily Vow. *Turn the Wheel* (website). On-line: http://www.math.cornell.edu/~goldberg/buddha.html

Hamill, S., & Kaji, A. (2000). *The sound of water: Haiku by Basho, Buson, Issa, & other poets.* Boston, MA: Shambhala.

Heidegger, M. (1962). *Being and time.* New York, NY: Harper and Row.

Heidegger, M. (1968). *What is Called Thinking?* New York, NY: Harper and Row.

Heidegger, M. (1971). The origin of the work of art. In M. Heidegger (Ed.), *Poetry language, thought* (pp. 15–88). New York, NY: Harper and Row Publishers.

Heidegger, M. (1971a). A dialogue on language between a Japanese and an inquirer. In M. Heidegger (Ed.), *On the way to language* (pp. 1–12). New York, NY: Harper and Row.

Heidegger, M. (1972). *On time and being.* New York, NY: Harper & Row Publishers.

Heidegger, M. (1977). The age of the world-picture. In *The question concerning technology* (pp. 115–154). New York, NY: Harper & Row.

Heidegger, M. (1977a). Letter on humanism. In M. Heidegger (Ed.), *Basic writings* (pp. 189–242). New York, NY: Harper and Row.

Heidegger, M. (1977b). Modern science, metaphysics and mathematics. In M. Heidegger (Eds.), *Basic writings.* (pp. 243–282). New York, NY: Harper and Row.

Heidegger, M. (1978). *The metaphysical foundations of logic.* Bloomington, IN: Indiana University Press.

Heidegger, M. (1985). *History of the concept of time.* Bloomington, IN: Indiana University Press.

Heidegger, M. (1987). Overcoming metaphysics. In *The End of Philosophy.* New York, NY: Harper and Row.

Hiatt, J. (2003). How Bob Dylan changed my life. *Harp Magazine Online: Harp Guides.* Retrieved May 2, 2009, from www.harpmagazine.com/reviews/cd_reviews/detail.cfm?article _id=1206

Hillman, J. (1979). *Puer papers.* Dallas, TX: Spring Publications.

Hillman, J. (1982) *Anima Mundi: Returning the soul to the world.* Putnam, CT: Spring Publications. Vol. 40, p. 1–37.

Hillman, J. (1983). *Healing fiction.* Barrytown, PA: Station Hill Press.

Hillman, J. (2006). *City and soul.* Putnam, CT: Spring Publications.

Hillman, J. (2006a). Anima Mundi: Returning the soul to the world. In J. Hillman (Ed.), *City and soul* (pp. 27–49). Putnam, CT: Spring Publications, Inc.

Hillman, J. (2006b). Segregation of beauty. In J. Hillman (Ed.), *City and soul* (pp. 187–193). Putnam, CT: Spring Publications.

Hillman, J. (2006c). Aesthetic response as political action. In J. Hillman (Ed), *City and Soul* (pp. 142–145). Putnam, CT: Spring Publications.

Hillman, J. (2006d). The Repression of Beauty. In J. Hillman (Ed.), *City and Soul* (pp. 172–186). Putnam, CT: Spring Publications.

Hillman, J. (2006e). Aesthetics and politics. In J. Hillman (Ed.), *City and Soul* (pp. 146–154). Putnam, CT: Spring Publications.

Hillman, J. (2006f). Loving the world anyway. In J. Hillman (Ed.), *City and Soul* (pp. 128–132). Putnam, CT: Spring Publications.

Hillman, J., & Ventura, M. (1992). *We've had a hundred years of psychotherapy—and the world's getting worse.* New York, NY: HarperOne.

Hillman, J. (2013). Notes on opportunism. In J. Hillman (Ed.), *Senex and Puer* (pp. 99–109). Putnam, CT: Spring Publications.

Hitchens, C. (2008). *God is not great: How religion poisons everything.* New York, NY: Emblem Editions.

Hitchens, C., & Taylor, L. (2011). *Christopher Hitchens—In confidence: Interview with Laurie Taylor.* On-line at: https://www.youtube.com/watch?v =NozRjiFL6Z4

Hongzhi, Z. (1991). *Cultiviating the empty field: The silent illumination of Zen Master Hongzhi.* T. D. Leighton & Wu, Y. trans. San Francisco, CA: North Point Press.

Huntington, S. (2003). T*he clash of civilizations and the remaking of world order.* New York, NY: Simon and Schuster Paperbacks.

Husserl, E. (1969). *Ideas towards a pure phenomenology*. London, England: Routledge and Kegan Paul.

Husserl, E. (1970). *Cartesian meditations*. The Hague, Netherlands: Martinus Nijhoff.

Husserl, E. (1970a). *The idea of phenomenology*. The Hague, Netherlands: Martinus Nijhoff.

Husserl, E. (1970b). *The crisis of European science and transcendental phenomenology*. Evanston, IL: Northwestern University Press.

Husserl, E. (1972). *Logical investigations*. New York, NY: Routledge and Kegan Paul.

Hyde, L. (1983). *The gift: Imagination and the erotic life of property*. New York, NY: Vintage Books.

Illich, I. (1976). *Medical nemesis: The expropriation of health*. New York, NY: Pantheon Books.

Illich, I. (1992). *In the mirror of the past: Lectures and addresses 1978–1990*. New York, NY: Marion Boyars.

Illich, I. (1993). *In the vineyard of the text: A commentary on Hugh's Didascalicon*. Chicago, IL: University of Chicago Press.

Illich, I. (1998). The cultivation of conspiracy. Accessed November 1, 2012 at: www.davidtinapple.com/illich.

Illich, I. (2001). Guarding the eye in the age of show. Accessed on-line August 31, 2011 at: http://www.davidtinapple.com/illich/.

Illich, I. (2001a). The Scoptic past and the ethics of the gaze. Accessed on-line August 31, 2011 at: http://www.davidtinapple.com/illich/.

Illich, I. (2005). *The Rivers North of the future*. Toronto, ON: House of Anansi Press.

Illich, I. & Cayley, D. (1992). *Ivan Illich in conversation*. Toronto, ON: House of Anansi Press.

Illich, I., & Sanders, B. (1988). *ABC: The alphabetization of the popular mind*. Berkley, CA: North Point Press.

Ingram, C. (1990). *In the footsteps of Gandhi: Conversations with spiritual social activists*. Berkeley, CA: Parallax Press.

Innes, J. (2014). A pocket full of darkness. In J. Seidel & D. Jardine (Eds.), *Ecological pedagogy, Buddhist pedagogy, hermeneutic pedagogy: Experiments in a curriculum for miracles* (p. 102). New York, NY: Peter Lang Publishers.

Jardine, D. (1976). The question of phenomenological immanence. Unpublished Master's Thesis. Retrieved on-line at: www.digitalcommons.mcmaster.ca/opendissertations/4567

Jardine, D. (1984). The Piagetian picture of the world. *Phenomenology + Pedagogy, 2*(3), 229–234.

Jardine, D. (1987). Reflection and self-understanding in Piagetian theory: A phenomenological critique. *Journal of Educational Thought, 21*(1), 10–19.

Jardine, D. (1988). "There are children all around us." *Journal of Educational Thought, 22*(2A), 178–186.

Jardine, D. (1990). On the humility of mathematical language. *Educational Theory,* 40, 181–191.

Jardine, D. (1991). On the integrity of things: Ecopedagogical reflections on the integrated curriculum. *Transescence: The Journal on Emerging Adolescent Education,* G. Vars, guest editor, *19*(1), 33–37.

Jardine, D. (1992). *Speaking with a boneless tongue.* Bragg Creek AB: Makyo Press. On line: https://www.academia.edu/7927867/Speaking_with_a_Boneless_Tongue.

Jardine, D. (1992a). Immanuel Kant, Jean Piaget and the rage for order: Hints of the colonial spirit in pedagogy. *Educational Philosophy and Theory, 23*(1), 28–43.

Jardine, D. (1992b). Naming children authors. *Readings in Canadian Literacy, 10*(4), 53–61.

Jardine, D. (1992c). Reflections on hermeneutics, education and ambiguity: Hermeneutics as a restoring of life to its original difficulty. In W. Pinar, & W. Reynolds (Eds.), *Understanding curriculum as phenomenological and deconstructed text.* New York, NY: Teacher's College Press.

Jardine, D. (1993). Ecopedagogical reflections on the integrated curriculum, scientific literacy, and the deep ecologies of science education. *Alberta Science Education Journal, 27*(1), 50–56.

Jardine, D. (1994). The ecologies of mathematics and the rhythms of the Earth. In P. Ernest, (Ed.), *Mathematics, philosophy and education: An international perspective, studies in mathematics education* (pp. 109–123). Volume 3. London, England: The Falmer Press.

Jardine, D. (1994a) Student-teaching, interpretation and the monstrous child. *Journal of Philosophy of Education, 28*(1), 17–24.

Jardine, D. (1994b). "Littered with literacy": An ecopedagogical reflection on whole language, pedocentrism and the necessity of refusal. *Journal of Curriculum Studies, 26*(5), 509–524.

Jardine, D. (1994c). Student-teaching, interpretation and the monstrous child. *British Journal of Philosophy of Education, 28*(1), 17–24.

Jardine, D. (1995). On the integrity of things: Ecopedagogical reflections on the integrated curriculum. In G. Vars (Ed.), *Current conceptions of core curriculum: Alternative designs for integrative programs.* Kent OH: National Association for Core Curriculum, 33–38.

Jardine, D. (2000). *"Under the Tough Old Stars": Ecopedagogical Essays.* Brandon, VT: Psychology Press / Holistic Education Press.

Jardine, D. (2000a). "Even there, the gods themselves are present." In D. Jardine (Ed.), *"Under the Tough Old Stars": Ecopedagogical Essays* (pp. 105–114). Brandon, VT: Psychology Press/Holistic Education Press.

Jardine, D. (2000b). Reflections on hermeneutics, education and ambiguity: Hermeneutics as a restoring of life to its original difficulty. In D. Jardine (Ed.), *Under the Tough Old Stars": Ecopedagogical Essays* (pp. 115–132). Brandon, VT: Psychology Press / Holistic Education Press.

Jardine, D. (2004). "A single truth alone": Some cultural currents from up north. Part of *Current Currents,* Presented by P. Bruce Urhmacher, Cassandra Trousas & C. Moroye (379–386). *The International Journal of Leadership in Education,* 7(4), October–December 2004, 382–386.

Jardine, D. (2005). *Piaget and education: A primer.* New York, NY: Peter Lang Publishing.

Jardine, D. (2005a). Cutting nature's leading strings: A cautionary tale about constructivism. *Canadian Journal of Environmental Education, 10,* 38–51.

Jardine, D. (2006). "Youth need images for their imaginations and for the formation of their memories." *Journal of Curriculum Theorizing, 22*(3), 3–12.

Jardine, D. (2006a). Unable to return to the gods that made them. In D. Jardine, S. Friesen, & P. Clifford (Eds.), *Curriculum in abundance.* (pp. 267–278). Mahwah, NJ: Lawrence Erlbaum and Associates.

Jardine, D. (2008). "'I Am' hath sent me": Arguments with myself and others on the subject of certain suspected allegories regarding democracy and education. In J. Wallin (Ed.), *Democratizing educational experience: Envisioning, embodying, enacting* (pp. 110–129). Troy, NY: Educator's International Press.

Jardine, D. (2008a). "Because it shows us the way at night: On Animism, writing, and the re-animation of Piagetian theory (pp. 105–166). In D. Jardine, P. Clifford, & S. Friesen (Eds.), *Back to the basics of teaching and learning: "Thinking the World Together"* (2nd ed., pp. 105–116). New York, NY: Routledge.

Jardine, D. (2008b). American dippers and Alberta winter strawberries. In D. Jardine, P. Clifford, & S. Friesen (Eds.), *Back to the basics of teaching and learning: "Thinking the World Together"* (2nd ed., pp. 175–180). New York, NY: Routledge.

Jardine, D. (2010). Ecopedagogy. In C. Kridel (Ed.), *Sage encyclopedia of curriculum studies* (pp. 312–313). New York, NY: Sage Publications.

Jardine, D. (2011). Inquiry in black and white. An appreciation. *One World in Dialogue. 1*(1), 33–36.

Jardine, D. (2012). "The memories of childhood have no order and no end": Pedagogical reflections on the occasion of the release, on October 9th 2009, of the re-mastered version of The Beatles' *Sergeant Pepper's Lonely Hearts Club Bandã. Journal of Applied Hermeneutics.* Online: http://136.159.25.71/jah/index.php/jah/article/view/7/pdf.

Jardine, D. (2012a). *Pedagogy left in peace: On the cultivation of free spaces in teaching and learning.* New York, NY: Bloomsbury Publishing.

Jardine, D. (2012b). Introduction: "Left in peace." In D. W. Jardine (2012a). *Pedagogy Left in Peace: On the cultivation of free spaces in teaching and learning* (pp. 1–22). New York, NY: Bloomsbury Publishing.

Jardine, D. (2012c). "Sickness is now 'out there'." In D. W. Jardine (2012a). *Pedagogy left in peace: On the cultivation of free spaces in teaching and learning* (pp. 73–90). New York, NY: Bloomsbury Publishing.

Jardine, D. (2012d). "Take the feeling of letting go as your refuge." In D. W. Jardine (2012a). *Pedagogy left in peace: On the cultivation of free spaces in teaching and learning* (pp. 217–230). New York, NY: Bloomsbury Publishing.

Jardine, D. (2012e). "A hitherto concealed experience that transcends thinking from the position of subjectivity." In D. W. Jardine (2012a). *Pedagogy left in peace: On the cultivation of free spaces in teaching and learning* (pp. 91–132). New York, NY: Bloomsbury Publishing.

Jardine, D. (2012f). "The savage childhood of the human race." In D. W. Jardine (2012a). *Pedagogy left in peace: On the cultivation of free spaces in teaching and learning* (pp. 55–72). New York, NY: Bloomsbury Publishing.

Jardine, D. (2012g). "Figures in hell." In D. W. Jardine (2012a). *Pedagogy left in peace: On the cultivation of free spaces in teaching and learning* (pp. 133–144). New York, NY: Bloomsbury Publishing.

Jardine, D. (2012h). On the while of things. In D. W. Jardine (2012a) *Pedagogy left in peace: On the cultivation of free spaces in teaching and learning* (pp. 173–192). New York, NY: Bloomsbury Publishing.

Jardine, D. (2012i). The Descartes lecture. *Journal of Applied Hermeneutics.* Online: http://jah.synergiesprairies.ca/jah/index.php/jah/article/view/27

Jardine, D. (2013). Guest editorial: Morning thoughts on application. *Journal of Applied Hermeneutics.* Online: http://jah.synergiesprairies.ca/jah/index.php/jah/article/view/52.

Jardine, D. (2014). On the Spring-Squall Arrival of a Pine Siskin (*Carduelis Pinus*). In J. Seidel & D. Jardine (2014). *Ecological pedagogy, Buddhist pedagogy, hermeneutic pedagogy: Experiments in a curriculum for miracles* (pp. 27–39). New York, NY: Peter Lang Publishers.

Jardine, D. (2014a). Guest Editorial: This is why we read. This is why we write. *Journal of Applied Hermeneutics.* Online: http://jah.journalhosting.ucalgary.ca/jah/index.php/jah/article/view/64/pdf.

Jardine, D. (2014b). Some introductory words for two little earth-cousins. *Journal of Applied Hermeneutics.* Online: http://jah.journalhosting.ucalgary.ca/jah/index.php/jah/article/view/61.

Jardine, D. (2015). "Nobody understood why I should be grieving." In D. Jardine, C. Gilham, & G. McCaffrey (Eds.), *On the pedagogy of suffering: Hermeneutic and Buddhist meditations* (pp. 157–166). New York, NY: Peter Lang Publishers.

Jardine, D. (2015a). Introduction: How to love black snow. Introduction to M. Derby (2015). *Towards a critical eco-hermeneutic approach to education: Place, being, relation* (pp. xv–xxiii). New York, NY: Peter Lang Publishing.

Jardine, D. (2015b). In appreciation of modern hunting traditions and a grouse's life unwasted. *One World in Dialogue, 3*(2), 7–8.

Jardine, D. (2015c). Quickening, patience, suffering. In D. Jardine, C. Gilham, & G. McCaffrey (Eds.), *On the pedagogy of suffering: Hermeneutic and Buddhist meditations* (pp. 101–122). New York, NY: Peter Lang Publishers.

Jardine, D. (2015d). "You're very clever young man." In D. Jardine, C. Gilham, & G. McCaffrey (Eds.). *On the pedagogy of suffering: Hermeneutic and Buddhist meditations* (pp. 7–18). New York, NY: Peter Lang Publishers.

Jardine, D. (2016). "There will not always be teachers like this": For G. B. M. *Journal of Applied Hermeneutics* http://jah.journalhosting.ucalgary.ca/jah/index.php/jah/article/view/110/pdf

Jardine, D. (in press). "I love the terror in a mother's heart." Forthcoming in J. Seidel & D. Jardine (in press). *The ecological heart of teaching: Radical tales of refuge and renewal for classrooms and communities.* New York, NY: Peter Lang Publishers.

Jardine, D. (in press a). Becoming Uncongealed. Forthcoming in J. Seidel & D. Jardine (in press). *The ecological heart of teaching: Radical tales of refuge and renewal for classrooms and communities.* New York, NY: Peter Lang

Jardine, D., Bastock, M., George, J., & Martin, J. (2008). Cleaving with affection: On grain elevators and the cultivation of memory. In D. Jardine, P. Clifford, & S. Friesen, (Eds.), *Back to the basics of teaching and learning: "Thinking the World Together"* (pp. 31–57). New York, NY: Routledge.

Jardine, D., Clifford, P., & Friesen, S. (Eds). (2003). *Back to the basics of teaching and learning: "Thinking the World Together."* (1st ed.) New York, NY: Routledge.

Jardine, D., Clifford, P., & Friesen, S. (2006). *Curriculum in abundance.* Mahwah NJ: Lawrence Erlbaum and Associates.

Jardine, D., Clifford, P., & Friesen, S. (Eds.). (2008). *Back to the basics of teaching and learning: "Thinking the World Together"* (2nd ed.) New York, NY: Routledge.

Jardine, D., Clifford, P., & Friesen, S. (2008a). Scenes from Calypso's Cave: On Globalization and The Pedagogical Prospects of the Gift. In D. Jardine, P. Clifford, & S. Friesen (Eds), (2008). *Back to the basics of teaching and learning: "Thinking the World Together"* (pp. 211–222). New York, NY: Routledge

Jardine, D., with Friesen, S. (1997). A play on the wickedness of undone sums, including a brief mytho- phenomenology of "x" and some speculations on the effects of its peculiar absence in elementary mathematics education. *Philosophy of Mathematics Education Journal 10.* Online: http://www.ex.ac.uk/~PErnest/pome10.

Jardine, D., Gilham, C., & McCaffrey, G. (2015). *On the pedagogy of suffering: Hermeneutic and Buddhist meditations.* New York, NY: Peter Lang Publishers.

Jardine, D., Gilham, C. & McCaffrey, G. (2015a). Fragment three: Bringing suffering into the path. In D. Jardine, C. Gilham, & G. McCaffrey, (Eds.), *On the pedagogy of suffering: Hermeneutic and Buddhist meditations* (pp. 99–100). New York, NY: Peter Lang Publishers.

Jardine, D., Graham, T., Clifford, P., & Friesen, S. (2006). In his own hand: Interpretation and the effacing of the scribe. In D. Jardine, S. Friesen, & P. Clifford (Eds.), *Curriculum in abundance* (pp. 247–264). Mahwah, NJ: Lawrence Erlbaum and Associates

Jardine, D., LaGrange, A., & Everest, B. (1998). "In these shoes is the silent call of the earth": Meditations on curriculum integration, conceptual violence and the ecologies of community and place. *Canadian Journal of Education, 23*(2), 121–130.

Jardine, D., & Morgan, G. (1987). Analogy as a model for the development of representational abilities in children. *Educational Theory, 37*(3) 209–218.

Jardine, D., & Morgan, G. (1987a). Analogical thinking in young children and the use of logico-mathematical knowledge as a paradigm in Jean Piaget's genetic epistemology. *Quarterly Newsletter of the Laboratory of Comparative Human Cognition, 9*(4), 95–101.

Jardine, D., & Naqvi, R. (2008). Learning not to speak in tongues: Thoughts on the librarian of Basra. *Canadian Journal of Education, 31*(3), 639–666.

Jardine, D., Naqvi, R., Jardine, E., & Zaidi, A. (2010). "A zone of deep shadow": Pedagogical and familial reflections on "The clash of civilizations." *Interchange: A Quarterly Review of Education, 41*(3), 209–232.

Johnson, T. (1990) Announcing . . . These Dynamite Workshops To Help You on the Road to Becoming a Whole Language Pro (Advertisement). *Reading Today, 8*(1), # 32.

Johnson, B., Fawcett, L., & Jardine, D., (2006). Further thoughts on cutting nature's leading strings: A conversation. In D. Jardine, S. Friesen, & P. Clifford (Eds.), *Curriculum in abundance.* (pp. 139–148). Mahwah, NJ: Lawrence Erlbaum and Associates.

Kanigel, R. (2005). *The one best way: Fredrick Winslow Taylor and the enigma of efficiency.* Cambridge, MT: The MIT Press.

Kant, I., (1964). *Critique of pure reason.* London, England: MacMillan.

Kant, I. (1983). *What is enlightenment? In Perpetual peace and other essays.* Indianapolis, IN: Hackett Pub. Co.

Karpf, A. (2002). Uncle Sam's Lucky Finds. The Guardian. Online: http://www.theguardian.com/world/2002/mar/19/september11.iraq

Kermode, F. (1979). *The genesis of secrecy: On the interpretation of narrative.* Cambridge, MA: Harvard University Press.

Kinnell, G. (2002). *Saint Francis and the sow.* Retrieved on October 30, 2014 from http://www.poetryfoundation.org/poem/171395.

Kongtrul, J. (2002). *Creation and completion.* Boston, MA: Wisdom Publications.

Kovitz, R. (1997). *Room behaviour.* Toronto, Canada: Insomniac Press

Latremouille, J. (2014). *Feasting on Whispers: Life Writing Towards a Pedagogy of Kinship.* Unpublished Master's Thesis, Werklund School of Education, University of Calgary.

Latremouille, J. (2015). A modern hunting tradition. *One World in Dialogue,* 3(2), 9–11.

Leach, W. (1994). *Land of desire: Merchants, power, and the rise of a new American culture.* New York, NY: Vintage Books.

Le Guin, U. (1987). *Buffalo gals and other animal presences.* Santa Barbara, CA: Capra Press.

Le Guin, U. (1989). Women/wildness. In J. Plant (Ed.), *Healing the wounds.* Toronto: Between the Lines Press.

Lensmire, T. (2000). *Powerful writing, responsible teaching (Critical Issues in Curriculum).* New York, NY: Teacher's College Press

Leopold, A. (1993). *Round river.* New York, NY: Oxford University Press.

Liddell, M. (in press). Thoughts on being neither finished nor unfinished. In J. Seidel & D. Jardine (in press). *The ecological heart of teaching: Radical tales of refuge and renewal for classrooms and communities.* New York, NY: Peter Lang Publishers.

Lingpa, J., Patrul, R., & Mahapandita, G. (2006). *Deity, Mantra and Wisdom: Development Stage Meditation.* Ithaca, NY: Snow Lion Publications.

Lobsang, G. (2006). Commentary to Tsong-kha-pa (2006). *The harmony of emptiness and dependent-arising.* New Delhi, India: Library of Tibetan Works and Archives.

Loy, D. (1993). Indra's postmodern net. *Philosophy east and west, 48*(3), 481–510.

Loy, D. (1998). The religion of the market. In H. Corad & D Maguire (Eds.), *Visions of a New Earth: Religious perspectives on population, consumption and ecology* (pp. 15–18). Albany, NY: SUNY Press.

Loy, D. (1999). *Lack and transcendence: The problem of death and life in psychotherapy, existentialism, and Buddhism.* New York, NY: Prometheus Books.

Loy, D. (2010). *The world is made of stories.* Boston, MA: Wisdom Publications.

MacMillan, M. (2006). What would Kissinger do? In *The Globe and Mail* (Toronto, Ontario), Saturday, February 2, 2006, A12.

MacPherson, C. B. (2010). *The political theory of possessive individualism.* Oxford, England: Oxford University Press.

Macy, J. (1989). Awakening the ecological self. In J. Plant (Ed.), *Healing the wounds: The promise of ecofeminism.* Toronto, Canada: Between the Lines.

Macy. J., & Johnstone, C. (2012). *Active hope: How to face the mess we're in without going crazy.* Novato, CA: New World Library.

Marra, M. (n.d.) A Dialogue on Language between a Japanese and an Inquirer Kuki Shūzō's Version. Online: https://nirc.nanzan-u.ac.jp/nfile/2070

McCaffrey, G. (2015). Idiot compassion. In D. Jardine, C. Gilham, & G. McCaffrey (Eds.), *On the pedagogy of suffering: Hermeneutic and Buddhist meditations* (pp. 19–28). New York, NY: Peter Lang Publishers.

McGinnis, S. (2008). Province urged to scrap high-stakes tests. *Calgary Herald,* September 8, 2008, p. B5.

McMurtry, J. (2002). *Value wars: The global market versus the life economy.* London, England: Pluto Press.

Merleau-Ponty, M. (1964). *The phenomenology of perception.* London, England: Routledge

Meschonnic, H. (1988). Rhyme and life. *Critical Inquiry, 15* (Autumn 1988).

Michelfelder, D., & Palmer, R. E. (1989). *Dialogue and deconstruction: The Gadamer-Derrida encounter.* Albany, NY: State University of New York Press.

Miller, A. (1989). *For your own good: Hidden cruelty in child-rearing and the roots of violence.* Toronto, Canada: Collins.

Molnar, C. (2014, Autumn). Life and mortality: A teacher's awakening. *In education, 20*(4), 90–10.

Molnar, C. (2014a). Cut the carrot. Part of J. Seidel, D. Jardine, D. Bailey, H. Gray, M. Hector, J. Innes, C. Jones, T. Kowalchuk, N. Mal, J. Meredith, C. Molnar, P. Rilstone, T. Savill, K. Sirup, L. Tait, L. Taylor & D. Vaast. Echolocations. In J. Seidel & D. Jardine (Eds.), *Ecological pedagogy, Buddhist pedagogy, hermeneutic pedagogy: Experiments in a curriculum for miracles* (pp. 91–110). New York, NY: Peter Lang Publishing.

Moules, N. J. (2015). Editorial: Aletheia—Remembering and enlivening. *Journal of Applied Hermeneutics.* Online: http://jah.journalhosting.ucalgary.ca/jah/index.php/jah/article/view/89

Moules, N. J., Jardine, D., McCaffrey, G., & Brown, C. (2015). "Isn't all oncology hermeneutic?" In D. Jardine, C. Gilham, & G. McCaffrey (2015). *On the pedagogy of suffering: Hermeneutic and Buddhist meditations* (pp. 173–182). New York, NY: Peter Lang Publishers

Namgyal, G. P (2007). *The great medicine that conquers clinging to the notion of reality.* With a commentary by Shechen Rabjam. Boston, MA: Shambala.

Nietzsche, F. (1975). *The will to power.* New York, NY: Random House.

New York Times (2015). Syrian Passport by Stadium Stolen or Fake, A.F.P. Reports. *New York Times On Line,* 3:01 PM ET, November 17, 2015. Online: http://www.nytimes.com/live/paris-attacks-live-updates/syrian-passport-reportedly-was-stolen-or-fake/

Newsom, J. (2006). Emily. From Joanna Newsom (2006). *Ys.* Drag Records.

Nightjarflying (2011, December 12). Hitchens '07: God is Not Great. Christopher Hitchens in conversation with Tim Rutten, Monday, June 4, 2007. Online: https://www.youtube.com/watch?v=bFXVR8W5Ngw&feature=youtu.be&t=24m12s

Nishitani, K. (1982). *Religion and nothingness.* Berkeley, CA: University of California Press.

Norris-Clarke, W. (1976). Analogy and the meaningfulness of language about God: A reply to Kai Nielsen. *The Thomist, 40,* 176–198.

ObjectiveBob (2010, July 5). *Christopher Hitchens makes a shocking confession* [Video file]. Retrieved from https://www.youtube.com/watch?v=E9TMwfkDwIY.

O'Leary, K. (2012). *Dragon's Den.* Produced by the Canadian Broadcasting Company. Series 6, Episode 19, first aired March 14, 2012. Accessed online at: www.cbc.ca/dragonsden/pitches/ukloo

Olson, K. (2014). *The invisible classroom: Relationships, neuroscience & mindfulness in school.* Toronto, ON: W.W. Norton & Co.

On-Line Etymological Dictionary (OED). http://www.etymonline.com/

Ozeki, R. (2013). *A tale for the time being.* New York, NY: The Penguin Group.

Pabongka (2006). *Liberation in the palm of your hand.* Boston, MA: Wisdom Publications.

Palmer, P. (1989). *To know as we are known: Education as a spiritual discipline.* New York, NY: Harper Collins.

Palmer, R. (2007). Introduction (pp. 192–194) to H. G. Gadamer. (2007b). The artwork in word and image: "So True, So full of Being!" In H.-G. Gadamer (2007). *The Gadamer reader: A Bouquet of the later writings* (pp. 195–224). R. E. Palmer (Ed.). Evanston, IL: Northwestern University Press.

Patrul R. (1998). *The words of my perfect teacher.* Boston, MA: Shambala Press.

Pelden, K. (2007). *The nectar of Manjushri's speech.* Boston, MA: Shambala Books.

Pelzang, K. (2004). *A guide to The Words of my Perfect Teacher.* Boston, MA: Shambala.

Peterson, R. T. (1980). *A field guide to the birds east of the Rockies* (4th ed). Boston, MA: Houghton Mifflin Company.

Piaget, J. (1952). *Origins of intelligence in children.* New York, NY: International Universities Press.

Piaget, J. 1971. *The construction of reality in the child.* New York, NY: Ballantine Books.

Pinar, W. (2006). Foreword: The lure that pulls flowerheads to face the sun. In D. Jardine, S. Friesen, & P. Clifford (Eds.), *Curriculum in abundance* (pp. ix–xxi). Mahwah, NJ: Lawrence Erlbaum and Associates.

Pope, D. (2015). "Can't sleep tonight..." Posted on twitter, January 7, 2015. On-line: https://twitter.com/davpope/status/552844593046097920/photo/1

Postel, D., & Drury, S. (2003). Noble lies and perpetual war: Leo Strauss, the Neo-Cons, and Iraq. Danny Postel interviews Shadia Drury. *Information clearing house.* October 2003. Retrieved October 1, 2007 from http://www.informationclearinghouse.info/ article5010.htm.

Ram Dass (1971). *Be here now.* Taos NM: Lama Foundation.

Ree, J. (2000). *I see a voice.* London, England: Flamingo.

Reibstein, M. (2008). *Wabi Sabi.* Young, E. (Illus.). New York, NY: Little, Brown and Company.

Richards, M. (2006). Translator's Footnotes to Pabongkha (2006). *Liberation in the palm of your hand.* (pp. 730–737). Boston, MA: Wisdom Publications.

Ross, D. (1999). *The gift of kinds [the good in abundance]: An ethic of earth.* Albany, NY: SUNY Press.

Ross, S. (2006). The temporality of tarrying in Gadamer. *Theory, Culture, & Society, 23*(1), 101–123.

Ross, S. M., & Jardine, D. (2009). Won by a certain labour: A conversation on the while of things. *Journal of the American Association for the Advancement of Curriculum Studies.* Accessed July 21, 2009 at: http://www.uwstout.edu/soe/jaaacs/Vol5/Ross_Jardine.htm

Said, E. (2001). The clash of ignorance. *The nation.* October 22, 2001. Accessed online October 22, 2006 at: http://www.thenation.com/doc/20011022/said

Saltzman, A. (2014). *A still quiet place: A mindfulness program for teaching children and adolescents to ease stress and difficult emotions.* New York, NY: New Harbinger Publications.

Sartre, J. P. (1970). Intentionality: A fundamental idea in Husserl's phenomenology. *Journal for the British Society for Phenomenology, 1*(2), 3–5.

Sato, H. (1983). *One hundred frogs: From Renga to Haiku to English.* New York, NY: Weatherhill.

Schopenhauer, A. (1963). *The world as will and representation.* 2 vols. New York, NY: Dover Books.

Schrift, A. (Ed.). (1997). *The logic of the gift: Toward an ethic of generosity.* New York, NY: Routledge.

Seidel, J. (2014). Hymn to the North Atlantic right whale. In J. Seidel & D. Jardine (Eds.), *Ecological pedagogy, Buddhist pedagogy, hermeneutic pedagogy: Experiments in a curriculum for miracles* (pp. 11–12). New York, NY: Peter Lang Publishers.

Seidel, J. (2014a). A curriculum for miracles. In J. Seidel & D. Jardine (Ed.), *Ecological pedagogy, Buddhist pedagogy, hermeneutic pedagogy: Experiments in a curriculum for miracles* (pp. 7–14). New York, NY: Peter Lang.

Seidel, J., & Jardine, D. (2014). *Ecological pedagogy, Buddhist pedagogy, hermeneutic pedagogy: Experiments in a curriculum for miracles.* New York, NY: Peter Lang Publishers.

Seidel, J., & Jardine, D. (2014a). Introduction: "We are here, we are here." In J. Seidel & D. Jardine (Eds.). *Ecological pedagogy, Buddhist pedagogy, hermeneutic pedagogy: Experiments in a curriculum for miracles* (pp. 1–6). New York, NY: Peter Lang Publishers.

Seidel, J., & Jardine, D. (2014b). *Wabi Sabi* and the pedagogical countenance of names. In J. Seidel & D. Jardine (Eds.), *Ecological pedagogy, Buddhist pedagogy, hermeneutic pedagogy: Experiments in a curriculum for miracles* (pp. 15–26). New York, NY: Peter Lang Publishers.

Seidel, J., & Jardine, D. (in press). *The ecological heart of teaching: Radical tales of refuge and renewal for classrooms and communities.* New York, NY: Peter Lang Publishers

Seidel, J., & Jardine D. (in press a). "The path and the goal." Forthcoming in J. Seidel & D. Jardine (in press). *The ecological heart of teaching: Radical tales of refuge and renewal for classrooms and communities.* New York, NY: Peter Lang Publishers.

Sekida, K. (1976). *Zen training: Methods and philosophy.* New York, NY: Weatherhill.

Shantideva (2006). *The way of the Bodhisattva.* Boston, MA: Shambala.

Shepard, P. (1996). *The others: How animals made us human.* Washington, DC: Island Press.

Shirane, H. (1996). *Traces of dreams: Landscape, cultural memory and the poetry of Basho.* Stanford, CT: Stanford University Press

Smith, D. G. (1999). *Pedagon: Interdisciplinary essays in the human sciences, pedagogy and culture* (pp. 137–142). New York, NY: Peter Lang Publishing.

Smith, D. G. (1999a). Children and the Gods of War. In D. G. Smith (Ed.), *Pedagon: Interdisciplinary essays in the human sciences, pedagogy and culture* (pp. 137–142). New York, NY: Peter Lang Publishing.

Smith, D. G. (1999b). Brighter than a thousand suns: Facing pedagogy in the nuclear shadow. In D. G. Smith (Ed.), *Pedagon: Interdisciplinary essays in the human sciences, pedagogy and culture* (pp. 127–136). New York, NY: Peter Lang Publishing.

Smith, D. G. (1999c). The hermeneutic imagination and the pedagogic text. In D. G. Smith (Ed.), *Pedagon: Interdisciplinary essays in the human sciences, pedagogy and culture* (pp. 27–44). New York, NY: Peter Lang Publishing.

Smith, D. G. (1999d). On being critical about language: The critical theory tradition and implications for language education. In D. G. Smith (Ed.). *Pedagon: Interdisciplinary essays in the human sciences, pedagogy and culture* (pp. 111–118). New York, NY: Peter Lang Publishing

Smith, D. (2000). The specific challenges of globalization for teaching and vice versa. In *Alberta Journal of Educational Research, 46*(1), 7–26.

Smith, D. G. (2006). *Trying to Teach in a Season of Great Untruth.* Rotterdam, NL: Sense Publications.

Smith, D.G. (2008, March). From Leo Strauss to collapse theory: Considering the Neoconservative attack on modernity and the work of education. *Critical Studies in Education, 49*(1), 33–48.

Smith, D. G. (2014). *Teaching as the practice of wisdom.* New York, NY: Continuum Books.

Snyder, G. (1974). *Turtle Island.* New York, NY: New Directions Books.

Snyder G. (1977). *The old ways.* New York, NY: New Directions Books.

Snyder, G. (1979). Poetry, community and climax. *Field, 20* (Spring 1979).

Snyder, G. (1980). *The real work.* New York, NY: New Directions Books.

Snyder, G. (1989). The original mind of Gary Snyder, June 1977. In *Meetings with Remarkable Men and Women.* Brookline, MA: East/West Health Books.

Snyder, G. (1990). *The practice of the wild.* New York, NY: North Point Press.

Sonam, R. (1997). Translator's and editors introduction to Atisha (1997). *Lamp for the Path to Enlightenment* (pp. 7–21). Ithaca, NY: Snow Lion Publications.

Sopa, L. (2004). *Steps on the path to enlightenment: A commentary on Tsongskhapa's Lamrim Chenmo. Volume 1: The foundational practices.* Boston, MA: Wisdom Books.

Sopa, L. (2005). *Steps on the path to enlightenment: A commentary on Tsongskhapa's Lamrim Chenmo. Volume 2: Karma* Boston, MA: Wisdom Books.

Sopa, L. (2008). *Steps on the path to enlightenment: A commentary on Tsongskhapa's Lamrim Chenmo. Volume 3: The way of the Bodhisattva.* Boston, MA: Wisdom Books.

Sopa, L. (2016). *Steps on the path to enlightenment: A commentary on Tsongskhapa's Lamrim Chenmo. Volume 4: Samatha.* Boston, MA: Wisdom Books.

Stock, B. (1983). *The implications of literacy: Written language and models of interpretation in the eleventh and twelfth centuries.* Princeton, NJ: Princeton University Press.

Sumedho, A. (2010). *Don't take your life personally.* Totnes, Devon, England: Buddhist Publishing Group.

Taylor, F. W. (1903) *Shop Management [Excerpts].* Accessed on line August 14, 2010 at: http://www.marxists.org/reference/subject/economics/taylor/shop management/abstract.htm

Taylor, F. W. (1911). *Scientific management, comprising shop management, the principles of scientific management and testimony before the special house committee.* New York, NY: Harper & Row.

Thomas, D. (1967). Reminiscences of childhood. In *Quite early one morning* (pp. 4–14). London, England: Aldine Press.

Thrangu, K. (2011). *Vivid awareness: The mind instructions of Khenpo Gangshar.* Boston, MA: Shambala.

Trungpa. C. (1988). *The myth of freedom and the way of meditation.* Boston, MA: Shambala Press.

Trungpa, C. (1990). *Cutting through spiritual materialism.* San Francisco, CA: Shambala Press.

Trungpa. C. (2003). The myth of freedom and the way of meditation. In C. Trungpa (Ed.), *The collected works of Chogyam Trungpa, Volume three.* Boston, MA: Shambala Press.

Trungpa, C. (2006). The Bodhisattva. *Lion's Roar: Buddhist Wisdom for Our Time.* November 1, 2006. Accessed online at: http://www.lionsroar.com/the-bodhisattva/

Trungpa, C. (2013). *The path of individual liberation.* Boston, MA: Shambala.

Tsong-Kha-Pa (2000). *The great treatise on the stages of the path to enlightenment (Lam rim chen mo).* Vol. 1. Ithaca, NY: Snow Lion Publications.

Tsong-Kha-Pa (2002). *The great treatise on the stages of the path to enlightenment (Lam rim chen mo).* Vol. 3. Ithaca, NY: Snow Lion Publications.

Tsong-Kha-Pa (2004). *The great treatise on the stages of the path to enlightenment (Lam rim chen mo).* Vol. 2. Ithaca, NY: Snow Lion Publications.

Tsong-Kha-Pa (2005). *The Six Yogas of Naropa.* Ithaca, NY: Snow Lion Publications.

Tsong-kha-pa (2006). *The harmony of emptiness and dependent-arising.* New Delhi, India: Library of Tibetan Works and Archives.

Tumposky, N. R. (1984, June). Behavioral objectives, the cult of efficiency, and foreign language learning: Are they compatible? *TESOL Quarterly, 18*(2), 295–310.

Turner, V. (1987). Betwixt and between: The liminal period in rites of passage. In L. Mahdi, S. Foster, & M. Little (Eds.), *Betwixt and between: Patterns of masculine and feminine initiation* (pp. 3–22). LaSalle, IL: Open Court.

Tyler, R. W. (1949). *Basic principles of curriculum and instruction.* Chicago, IL: The University of Chicago Press.

Usher, R., & Edwards, R. (1994). *Postmodernism and education.* London, England: Routledge.

Victoria, B. D. (2006). *Zen at war.* Lanham, MD: Rowman & Littlefield Publisher.

Wang, H., & Eppert, C. (2008). *Cross-cultural studies in curriculum: Eastern thought, educational insights.* Mahwah, NJ: Lawrence Erlbaum Associates.

Wallace, B. (1987). *The stubborn particulars of grace.* Toronto, Canada: McClelland and Stewart.

Walther, I., & Metzger, R. (1997). *Vincent van Gogh: The complete paintings.* New York, NY: Taschen.

Watts, A. (1970). *The book: On the taboo against knowing who you are.* New York, NY: Collier Books.

Watts, A. (1968). *Myth and Ritual in Christianity.* Boston, MA: Beacon Press.

Watts, S. (2006). *The peoples' tycoon: Henry Ford and the American Century.* New York, NY: Vintage Books.

Weinsheimer, J. (1987). *Gadamer's hermeneutics.* New Haven, CT: Yale University Press.

Williams, W. C. (1991). Spring and all (1923). In *The collected poems of William Carlos Williams.* Volume 1: 1909–1939. New York, NY: New Directions Books.

Wittgenstein, L. (1968). *Philosophical investigations.* Cambridge, England: Basil Blackwell.

Wrege, C. D., & Greenwood, R. (1991). *Frederick W. Taylor: The father of scientific management: Myth and reality.* New York, NY: Irwin Professional Publishing. Currently out of print. The text of *Chapter 9* is available on-line at: www.johntaylorgatto.com/chapters/9d.hFtm

Yangsi R. (2003). *Practicing the path.* Boston, MA: Wisdom Publications.

Yeats, W. B. (2010). *The collected works of W.B. Yeats Vol. III: Autobiographies.* New York, NY: Simon & Schuster.

Yolen, J. (1998). *Here there be dragons.* London, England: Sandpiper Books.

Yolen, J., & Cooney, B. (1995). *Letting Swift River go.* Boston, MA: Little, Brown Books for Young Readers.

Index

A

In Praise of Radiant Beings, pages 329–346

C

D

E

F

I

J

K

L

M

N

Q

R

S

U

V

W